IMPERIAL POLITICS AND SYMBOLICS IN ANCIENT JAPAN

IMPERIAL POLITICS

AND SYMBOLICS IN

ANCIENT JAPAN

The Tenmu Dynasty, 650–800

Herman Ooms

University of Hawai'i Press | Honolulu

14 13 12 11 10 09   6 5 4 3 2 1

Library of Congress Cataloging-in-Publication Data
Ooms, Herman.
Imperial politics and symbolics in ancient Japan : the
Tenmu dynasty, 650–800 / Herman Ooms.
    p. cm.
Includes bibliographical references and index.
ISBN 978-0-8248-3235-3 (hardcover : alk. paper)
    1. Japan — History — 645 – 794.   2. Tenmu, Emperor
of Japan, 631? – 686.   3. Religion and state — Japan —
History — To 1500.   I. Title.
DS855.O67   2008
952'.01 — dc22   2008012829

This book has been assisted by grants from the
following organizations:

JAPANFOUNDATION

and the University of California, Los Angeles, Paul I. and
Hisako Terasaki Center for Japanese Studies.

The poetry reproduced in this text is from Edwin Cranston, *A Waka Anthology. Volume One: The Gem-Glistening
Cup*, poem 495, page 281; and poem 998, page 531. Copy-
right © 1993 by the Board of Trustees of the Leland Stanford Jr. University

University of Hawai'i Press books are printed on acid-
free paper and meet the guidelines for permanence and
durability of the Council on Library Resources.

Designed by April Leidig-Higgins

Printed by The Maple-Vail Book Manufacturing Group

For Renata and Jonathan,
the sun and moon of my sky

L'État est sacré, l'Église est pouvoir.

Gilbert Dagron, *Empereur et prêtre*

CONTENTS

ILLUSTRATIONS

Figures

Tables

Plates

ACKNOWLEDGMENTS

Friends, scholars, and institutions contributed enormously to this book. I gratefully acknowledge the many debts I incurred during the nine years it took me to complete it. Without this support, I would still be writing.

Foremost, I would like to thank my friend Christine Schoppe, whose long-standing interest in matters Daoist came as a welcome surprise when I discovered how central this tradition was to my research. Her perceptive critiques of early drafts helped me to sharpen my analysis of key issues, and many of her insights and suggestions are woven into the book. David Bialock and Torquil Duthie, who I discovered late in this journey had been working on some of the same material, generously offered to read the final manuscript. Their meticulous comments have contributed significantly to the accuracy of information presented in these pages. Also very helpful in this respect were the two anonymous readers for the University of Hawai'i Press. In preparing the manuscript for publication, I have benefited greatly from the cheerful assistance of Patricia Crosby, executive editor at the press. I am grateful to all of these people for sharing their expertise with me. Their contributions have made this a better book.

A number of my colleagues at UCLA as well as several scholars at other universities in Southern California responded readily to my queries. By supplementing my knowledge in different fields, these local experts made me feel that Los Angeles was just the right place to undertake this research project. At UCLA, John Duncan introduced me to early Korean history, Lothar von Falkenhausen and Richard von Glahn gave me tips on Daoism and Chinese antiquity, William Bodiford was always eager to fine-tune my notions about Buddhism, and Torquil Duthie to set me straight on readings of Manyōshū poems. Allan Grapard let me tap his vast knowledge of Shinto, and it was Lori Meeks who answered with a "probably" my question regarding the nun empress Shōtoku: Did she receive the full tonsure (and thus have her head shaved)? If so, it made one wonder how her enemies could have cast a spell on her by stealing some of her hair and stuffing it into a skull! I also benefited from discussions with David Lurie and Michael Como during their visits to UCLA. Special mention must be made of Neil Kiley, under whom I began my graduate work at the University of Chicago. My return to the subject of ancient Japan will be gratifying to him since forty years ago he urged me to explore this fascinating period of Japanese history. It is advice well taken, even if a bit late.

In Japan, Professors Ishigami Ei'ichi, Mizubayashi Takeshi, and Shin-kawa Tokio spared neither time nor patience introducing me to the latest scholarship in the field, while Professor Sonoda Minoru and Baba Hajime, researcher at the National Research Institute for Cultural Properties of Nara, helped secure permission to use the exquisite color plates that grace this book. Oka Kiyoshi deserves a special word of thanks for coming to my rescue when I lost my way in the digital forest as do Reza Tavassoli and my son Jonathan, both of whom contributed their time and technological know-how to helping me get the maps and figures into proper shape.

Over the years, I benefited greatly from collegial discussions and scholarly exchange when I presented my research in more formal contexts. I am grateful for these opportunities, created by invitations from the University of Southern California in Los Angeles, the University of British Columbia at Vancouver, the Institut National des Langues et Civilizations Orientales in Paris, and a unique conference on monsters in Japanese history at Indiana University in Bloomington. I received a number of research and travel grants from the Academic Senate of the University of California at Los Angeles and the UCLA Paul I. and Hisako Terasaki Center for Japanese Studies, which enabled me to collect sources and visit archeological sites in Japan. The dedicated librarians of the Young Research Library also facilitated my research. Of course, none of this would have been possible without the California taxpayers' support of institutions of higher learning.

Finally, I want to express my profound gratitude to my family, whose love has sustained me through this long project. My wife, Emily, has always supported me in my work and given me the time and mental space to pursue it wholeheartedly. Our children, Renata and Jonathan, to whom this book is dedicated, passed through their teenage years wondering how one book could take so long to write, never doubting, however, that I would eventually complete it. I am relieved that their confidence was not misplaced.

• • •

Note: The two genealogies of figures 1 and 11 are printed also at the end of this volume on a detachable bookmark for readers' convenience.

INTRODUCTION

This study circles a century and a half of Japanese history, from about the mid-seventh century to around the beginning of the ninth, extending beyond the Nara period (710–784) at both ends. During the last decades of the seventh century, the Yamato kingdom, which had been ruled by unstable coalitions of lineages whose leaders acknowledged one among themselves as their head, was transformed into a rapidly centralizing state, led by an "emperor" (tennō) who extended his rule through a service nobility recruited from old lineage leadership. A bureaucratic structure was put together, comprehensive law codes promulgated, and grand capitals erected in succession, the whole process framed by the drafting of dynastic narratives. Versions of Yamato history appear at this time, although this is also the sunrise of mytho-historical beginnings for the ruling house, reflecting back legitimizing ends.

Several features that today occupy an important place in Japan's national identity were created in the decades straddling the eighth century. In the twenty-first century, a tennō still finds himself at the symbolic pinnacle of Japan's political hierarchy. Nihon, the Japanese name for the country, was adopted around the year 700. Only two generations ago, the Kojiki's mytho-history was officially upheld as factual truth. The poems of the Manyōshū, an eighth-century anthology, are treasured today as the earliest pearls of a national literature. Shinto, upheld by many as Japan's indigenous religion, presumably reaches seamlessly from the ancient past to today's present. The monarch's title, the polity's name, a formula and language for rulership, and an indigenous religion can boast a long history in Japan, or so it seems.

A closer look, however, reveals severe ruptures in the putative continuity governing Japanese history with regard to these national icons. By the ninth century, the Manyōshū poems had already become less intelligible because of the script in which they had been recorded. The Chinese graphs, unstable mixtures of phonetic and semantic signs, constituted a puzzle that, over time, blocked access to clear meaning. The Kojiki, whatever legitimizing role it played at the beginning of the eighth century, was pushed aside by the end of it, replaced in importance by the Nihon shoki, Japan's second preserved history, written in 720, a few years after the Kojiki. Its sequel, the Shoku Nihongi, compiled in the 790s, does not even mention the presumably noteworthy event of the Kojiki's presentation to the court in 712.

Moreover, for over six hundred years, between the early thirteenth and the mid-nineteenth century, no Japanese monarch received the title of *tennō*, not even posthumously. Finally, nowadays more and more scholars are convinced that most of Japanese history lacked "Shinto" if we understand by this term a modern notion of an autochthonous religious tradition in its own right.

The royal house itself constitutes a peculiar genealogical entity since it responds to no family name such as, for instance, the Tudors. Somehow this lack connotes that the dynasty is not of this world and transcends history. Historians dealing with the ancient period often use "Sun line," a title deduced from a component in the names of ancient rulers that refers to the myth of origins, suggesting one single dynasty even though since the late seventh century, two branches have consecutively occupied the throne. The first one, lasting only a century, was the Tenmu dynasty (673–770), followed by the current ruling house, harking back to Tenmu's brother, Tenji (r. 668–671). The image of an unbroken line emanating from the Sun goddess Amaterasu in primordial time was created during Tenmu's reign. Yet historians now suspect that this fabulated pre-Tenmu past covers not one, but three different historical houses that successively ruled the archipelago or parts thereof.

The historic significance of these iconic constructs was altered when recast in the mold of continuity as they have been in modern times. I intend to historicize these and other developments that took place during this early and important period of creative political experimentation, the results of which had differential afterlives. This entails a fine-grained examination of both the power struggles shaping and shaking the newly formed state structure and the representations called into service to mobilize and further state as well as factional ends. Thus, politics and symbolics are the subject of this study. My use of the term "symbolics," now usually understood as the study of symbols, is closer to its older meaning of "use of symbols." It draws attention to the actual adoption or manipulation of symbols, a practice with symbols and parallel to politics, both related to the acquisition or exercise of power, status, or authority. The state enveloped itself in sacralizing symbols — l'État est sacré — while ritualists and managers of the sacred wielded considerable power — l'Église est pouvoir.

I use the image of a "Tenmu dynasty," one that did not last, as a way to start historicizing the time frame. The very term is now being revisited by historians. A close reading of data reveals that the notion of a dynastic line originating with Tenmu was already in dispute in the eighth century. In other words, the idea of a Tenmu ruling house was being contested while under construction, a process that was in part due to flexibility in ways of tracing out lineages and divergent interest groups. Dynasties, as diagramed neatly in family histories and textbooks, appear to be natural and unproblematic. Yet genealogies are more often pieced together with arguably alien symbolic material.

In chapter 1, I examine this process as an ongoing "Bricolage" of constructing a royal line originating in Tenmu by granting posthumous titles to figures who never ruled. A century later, however, much of it is replaced by Emperor Kanmu's (781–806) own configuration of a lineage with his own preferred dynastic personages. Works of genealogical bricolage accompany dynasties as they branch out over time and as founders or successors rearrange their past. They fix history to the extent needed and endeavor to have their own constructs prevail over those of others.

A number of mythological themes in the *Kojiki* anchor the supremacy of Tenmu's descendants and the legitimacy of their rule, which originated in a rebellion. The structure of "Mythemes" in this work is analyzed in chapter 2. More than a tale of origins, this work also presents an exemplar of Yamato's new regime as a *tenka*, a realm extending beyond Yamato's borders properly and acknowledged, to a large extent more in the imagination than in reality, by outsiders.

A divine origin was only one of several "Alibis" (chapter 3) that were devised for Tenmu and his successors to provide their exercise of power with an otherwordly cachet. Tenmu is portrayed in the historical record as a Daoist transcendental, a master of cosmic knowledge, and adept at secret methods of prognostication. These are some of the ways he distanced himself from his predecessors, especially Tenji. The manipulation of signs, portents, and geomancy played an important role in this operation, which culminated in the creation of Fujiwara-kyō, Japan's first capital, along cosmic delineations.

Tenmu personified a master and drafter of signs. No other historical ruler of ancient Japan has been positioned, by himself and his biographers, as personally within the realm of the supernatural to the extent that Tenmu was imagined to be. The *Nihon shoki*'s two chapters devoted to Tenmu begin by stating that "[he] was skilled in astronomy and the art of invisibility."

Keeping control over the field of political semiotics, centered on yin and yang, was essential since the exercise of power was inseparable from the manipulation of symbolics. Tenmu took steps to monopolize yin-yang knowledge, the operational framework of occult knowledge, by declaring it classified information to be housed in a Yin-yang Bureau. The bureau was staffed mainly by men rooted in continental knowledge, refugees from Korean kingdoms or descendants from earlier immigrants. The indispensable contribution by "Allochthons," men who themselves or whose ancestors originated in a "different soil" and were familiar with continental practices, constitutes the topic of chapter 4. "Allochthon" is the term that best covers people who could be aliens, immigrants, refugees, prisoners of war, or their ancestors and who lived in the archipelago but whose official identity (*kikajin*) as originating in a different cultural milieu and geographic soil was consciously maintained by the Yamato state as separate from that of its autochthonous subjects.

The new state assembled by Tenmu and Jitō was a liturgical one. Needless to say, it was amply provided with an infrastructure for taxation and local administration. The Law Codes, however, stipulated a yearly round of ritual events, most of them to secure the ripening of crops and a bountiful harvest. The format for the principal celebrations required that four times a year hundreds of representatives from designated local shrines assemble at the capital, a number that grew to two and three thousand early in the eighth century. These shrine officiants returned home with oblations for their local *kami* (spirits or "gods"). These regular celebratory reunions implemented the reality of a dynamic centralized rulership and spread consciousness of it throughout the land by word of mouth. Those who had been selected to participate experienced, shoulder to shoulder, the throngs of people from far-flung areas, the magnificence of the capital, and the magnanimity of their ruler, the very heart of the realm that encompassed all. These and other ceremonies were Tenmu and Jitō's creations, the subject of chapter 5, "Liturgies."

Daoism played an undeniable role in the symbolics of political ceremony and ritual, even though its presence in the record is elusive at best. Unlike Buddhism, well studied for its obvious contributions to the Nara state, Daoism did not develop over time an autonomous institutional infrastructure. The degree of Daoism's presence in pre-Nara and Nara Japan is a matter of intense debate today. Archeologists have discovered prehistoric evidence such as mirrors and swords that may have been used for Daoist ceremonies, but we do not know for certain. One can find Daoist elements in early historical narratives prior to the period under examination in this study. I consider both archeology and literature, especially the latter, in chapter 6, where allusions to Daoism are treated as "Deposits," left buried in the ground or embedded in texts.

Archeological remains as geological deposits generally date from a time without history. We can surmise the Daoist meanings of artifacts not from

knowledge of their use in the archipelago, but only through our understanding of Chinese Daoism. The narrative fragments, on the other hand,
are deposits having a different sense. As enchanted images, they were *deposited* in the *Kojiki* and *Nihon shoki*, which were compiled at a time when
acquaintance with Daoist texts was fashionable for the court nobility.

Tenmu marshaled a number of Daoist signs to articulate a supernatural
aura for his rulership. They are discussed in chapter 7 as "Articulations."
A court ceremony, later known as the Festival for Appeasing the Spirits
(Chinkon-sai), has undeniably Daoist origins. The New Year receptions at
the court were organized around symbols with "Daoisant" connotations. In
early Heian, possibly earlier, the emperor's ceremonial coat displayed astral
symbolism pivoting around the Pole Star, the heavenly zenith of rulership
in Daoist discourse. Nara-era names are replete with Daoist significations.

Revisionist interpretations by Japanese and Western scholars have lately
repositioned Shinto, denying it a separate religious arena with an indigenous, specific culture and practice. They have reassigned much of its cultic
heritage to Daoism. This question of "Shinto" as an entity in its own right
is also taken up in chapter 7.

The Tenmu dynasty was rife with political intrigue; plots were successful, aborted, or merely alleged. A few armed rebellions erupted, one even
prompting Emperor Shōmu to leave Nara for several years. At almost any
time during the Nara period, there were hundreds of political exiles, many
of them members of the nobility, banned to remote areas of the archipelago. In power struggles, usually around questions of succession, plotters
engaged in black magic, witchcraft, and the manipulation of portents and
supernatural signs, or were accused of having done so. Yin-yang specialists
were even found involved, albeit marginally, in some of the plots. Daoism,
which Tenmu had arrayed to enchant his rule, was, under these circumstances, viewed as a subversive power.

Rifts and rivalries also characterized the field of religion as houses of ritualists, competing purveyors of symbolic power to the throne, jockeyed for
position at the court. A tenuous separation of political authority and ritualist spiritual power was instituted in the 690s by splitting the new Fujiwara
clan into two branches. The Fujiwara were to provide legal experts and career politicians to the court, while the Nakatomi continued to function as
court ritualists. By the mid-eighth century, however, politics and religion
merged when ritualists and Buddhist clerics were appointed to political office. Ise, established by Tenmu and Jitō as the realm's ritual center with a
permanent resident representative from the court in the person of a virgin

princess, became a battleground for Nakatomi ritualists confronting Buddhist encroachments. The internal struggles of the Tenmu dynasty, large and small, political and ritual, are surveyed in chapter 8, "Plottings."

The next chapter focuses on the power of "Spirits" of the dead, often vindictive and vengeful (*onryō*), which came to play an increasing role in the management of power and in its contestation. Emperor Kanmu, in particular, had to placate spirits and was thus forced to operate in a symbolic universe that was significantly different from the one created by Tenmu. In this chapter, I also look into the case of Prince Nagaya, who was accused of black magic in 729, a case that may have provided the occasion for outlawing Daoist magic.

In the final chapter, I pull together strands of elements having to do with the value of "Purity." Toward the end of his life, Tenmu used the notion of purity to signal the central quality of rulership. In the Law Codes, the enthronement of emperors is stipulated to be preceded by a lengthy period of abstinence, far longer than in the Tang model. Nevertheless, Tenmu's use of purity as the preeminent sign for the center of the realm and its emperor has precedents in ancient China; it is a central value in Daoism, and in aspects of Buddhism as well.

Other features of administrative arrangements, such as the distinction between good and base people, appear to have had overtones of pollution. The theme of purity and pollution, however, becomes more pronounced in later centuries that fall beyond the frame of the current study. For Heian political practice, the preservation of purity isolated the emperor, transforming him into a sacred icon encountered by few, untouched, surrounded daily by precautionary ritual. Toward the end of the Heian period, the counter value of impurity became a stigma that was explicitly, although inconsistently, being applied socially.

TWO WORKS IN ENGLISH dealing extensively with early Japanese history, up to and including most or all of the Nara period, are the first volume in the *Cambridge History of Japan*, titled *Ancient Japan* (1993), and Joan Piggott's *The Emergence of Japanese Kingship* (1997) (supplemented by a chapter on Empress Kōken-Shōtoku, which brings the story up to 770). They provide helpful entries into the history of the Tenmu dynasty. Equally important is William Farris's, *Sacred Texts and Buried Treasures: Issues in the Historical Archeology of Ancient Japan* (1998). This work presents an overview of archeology's contributions to our understanding mainly of capital building up to the Heian period. Closer to my theme of symbolics is part 1 of Richard Bowring's *The Religious Traditions of Japan, 500–1600* (2005) and David Bialock's *Eccentric Spaces, Hidden Histories: Narrative, Ritual, and Royal Authority from* The Chronicles of Japan *to* The Tale of the Heike (2007).

Japanese scholars have done an enormous amount of research in all aspects of the history of this period. I would like to mention especially Mizubayashi Takeshi's studies of the *Kojiki* and Shinkawa Tokio's research on Daoism. Both these scholars have assisted me greatly through their writings and willingness to answer inquiries. Equally important has been the dynamic research in Chinese Daoism done by Western scholars such as Anna Seidel, Livia Kohn, and many others. Without their insights, Daoism would remain an amalgam of popular and obscure practices, unrelated to power and politics — the field, we have heard too often, where Confucianism set the tone of discourse and practice.

With this book, I found myself in a place and time far removed from where I started. After my study of Tokugawa village politics of class and status, I intended to explore further the subject of social stigma as it was directed at other marginal classes, even though perhaps less severely than was the case with the leather workers to which I devoted a whole chapter in my *Tokugawa Village Practice*. Curious as to the history and origins of the social disvalue of pollution, I perused a good number of studies until my attention was drawn to the simple statement that Tenmu used "purity" and "clarity" as signifiers for the top ranks of the members of his royal family. Looking for social applications of purity, I found little of it in that early period. Increasingly it became clear, however, that I was dealing with the symbolics of politics — ideology in other words — the terrain of a familiar problematic but with a narrative vegetation more luxuriant than I had found in *Tokugawa Ideology*.

1 BRICOLAGE

It has been a rule in our country since the age of the *kami*
that descendants ["son-grandson"] succeed each other
receiving the Heavenly Rank. Succession between brothers
leads to upheaval.
—696/7/10. Prince Kadono

In 697/8, Jitō passed the government of this country on
to Prince Kusakabe's direct descendant, Monmu, and as
retired monarch assisted him in administering the country
in harmony. Jitō followed a law, established by Tenji as a
never-changing rule to prevail forever, for as long as there
is Heaven and Earth, and as far as the sun and the moon.
—707/7/17. Genmei's Accession Edict

During the second half of the seventh century, three rulers brought
about a regime change in Yamato.[1] They were the brothers Tenji and Tenmu,
and Jitō, Tenji's daughter who was also Tenmu's wife and successor. From
among Tenmu and Jitō's offspring, to the female *tennō* Shōtoku (d. 770), a
line of rulers developed, traditionally referred to as the Tenmu dynasty.[2]
A quick glance at figure 1 reveals that Shōtoku's successor, *tennō* Kōnin, as
Tenji's grandson, restored the line to Tenji.

Dynastic identities revolve around more than bloodlines. Equally important are perceptions of founders, lineage composition, and successions,
issues that were alive throughout the eighth century, as historians are now
discovering. The "Tenmu dynasty" as such was assembled over time, an
incessant work of lineage adjustment. The historical record reveals both the
elimination of family members that were in line to succeed to the throne
and the posthumous addition of relatives and ancestors to lineal positions
of honor with royal titles they never held while alive. I call this construction
of a line of descent with extraneous elements genealogical bricolage.

According to the logic of biological descent, all rulers from Tenji to
Kōnin to the present day, except for Tenmu and Junnin, can be traced, via
Jitō, as a Tenji dynasty. Jitō's political identity is crucial, for she is at once
daughter of the older brother, wife of the younger brother, a successor to the

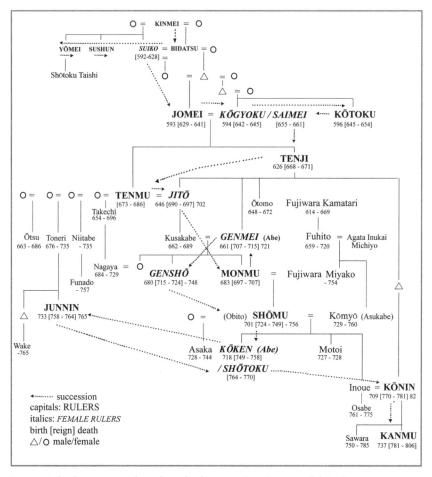

Fig. 1. Ruler lineages in the 7th and 8th centuries. A copy of this chart appears on a detachable "bookmark" at the end of this volume.

throne after her husband, and grandmother of the next ruler, Monmu. Jitō as Tenji's daughter, with Prince Kusakabe her only son by Tenmu (father of Monmu), and others following Monmu, line up as Tenji's lineage rather than Tenmu's. If Jitō's authority is perceived as deriving from her status as Tenmu's consort, the sequence would be Tenmu, Jitō (Kusakabe), Monmu: a Tenmu lineage. I should note right away that female rulers were not exceptional at the time, even though they were never appointed beforehand as crown princesses.[3] Jitō's sex as such did not make her less of a ruler. Anyway, beyond genealogy, it is a matter of emphasizing either Jitō's link with Tenji or opening a distance between Tenmu and Tenji, which Tenmu's biographers do, their work having been made easy by Tenmu's rebellion.

The dramatic history of the Tenmu dynasty evolves from Jitō's maneuvering against a number of other contenders to secure succession for her line down to her great-grandson, the future Emperor Shōmu. He not only passed the throne over to his daughter, Empress Kōken, but made her first crown princess, bypassing a son for the position. She never married, and died childless. Ultimately the political scheming and often violent conflicts around successions spanned the life of the dynasty from beginning to end.

The dynasty is bookended by violence. Tenmu acceded to the throne a year after killing Tenji's son Prince Ōtomo (Tenmu's nephew and son-in-law) in 672. Ōtomo's elimination had been Tenmu's sole purpose for launching the Jinshin War. Tenmu's dynasty ended in bloodshed as well, for exactly one hundred years later, Kōnin (nephew of Prince Ōtomo) cut all ties with the Tenmu line by eliminating his consort Inoue (a fourth-generation patrilineal descendant from Tenmu) and their son, Crown Prince Osabe. In 772, mother and son were accused of black magic and stripped of their royal titles. Held in custody for two years following renewed accusations, the pair mysteriously died on the same day in 775.

Politics, especially when power struggles generate violence, is always in need of stabilizing symbolics to secure its gains. The Tenmu dynasty, unstable from its beginning, resorted to a number of legitimizing strategies. Divine kingship for the Yamato ruling house tracing its lineage as the Sun line back to the Sun goddess Amaterasu is only the best-known device. The *Kojiki* illuminated this mytheme in 712, forty years after Tenmu's military victory in the Jinshin War, and as a written document provided his descendants with the equivalent of a constitutional basis for their rulership.

From the mid-seventh century until the first third of the eighth century, the new dynasty surrounded itself with a new style of bureaucratic state based on the Chinese penal and administrative law codes (*ritsuryō*). The domestic watershed for this consolidation of royal power through these far-reaching reforms was a dramatic assassination that took place in 645. That year, nineteen-year-old Prince Naka no Ōe (Tenji) plotted against and helped exterminate the principal branch of the Soga clan, which had wielded power by providing consorts and ministers to the throne for several generations. According to the *Nihon shoki*, Yamato's official history compiled seventy-five years later by Tenji's nephew Prince Toneri, the Soga had been on the verge of displacing the Yamato Sun line of "great kings" (*ōkimi*). Tenji's preemptive coup inaugurated several decades of the so-called Taika Reforms, which were continued by Tenmu and Jitō, a gigantic project of state building.[4]

Between 645 and 702, the year Jitō died, these momentous transformations necessitated new representations of authority. Nihon, Yamato's new name used in diplomatic exchanges with China, styled itself a *tenka*, an "empire" no longer governed by *ōkimi* but by *tennō* ("heavenly sovereigns" or "emperors").[5]

Government through written laws and a bureaucracy of officials, introduced by Tenji and Tenmu, was continued by Jitō from an actual capital, Fujiwara-kyō, rather than from a royal residence. This also was modeled after a Chinese example. *Ritsuryō* codes were drafted, implemented, and revised during that time, culminating in the Taihō Code of 701, promulgated the following year.[6] That year also, an official delegation left for Changan, the Tang capital, to impress their hosts with evidence of a whole generation's achievements. It had been thirty-three years since the last official embassy had visited China, in the second year of Tenji's reign (668–671).

Tenji held power far longer than his three-year rule as great king suggests. Crown prince in 645, he became officially in charge of the government and reforms in 661, when Great King Saimei died leaving the throne vacant. Tenji's presumptive heir appears to have been his son Ōtomo, a presumption not shared by Tenmu. A year after Tenji's death, it was Tenmu who occupied the throne after defeating Prince Ōtomo. His "succession" therefore raises serious questions of legitimacy for historians, but not for the *Nihon shoki* annalists who, some fifty years after the event, skirt the issue and celebrate the outcome. In that history, Tenmu's achievements, especially military ones, overshadow those of Tenji, his brother and predecessor, burdened during his regency with a crushing military and naval defeat at the hands of Tang China and the Korean kingdom of Silla.

Tenmu's domestic victory allowed him to further consolidate royal power beyond the Yamato basin.[7] Jitō, his main consort for twenty-nine years, succeeded Tenmu in 686. She kept the reins of government in her hands until her own death in 702: the first four years as regent, then as sovereign (690–697), and finally as a powerful retired ruler after abdicating in favor of her fourteen-year-old grandson, Monmu. The symptoms of political undertow during the dynasty's early decades reach across the second half of the seventh century: a spectacular assassination in 645, two regencies (Tenji's in 661–668 and Jitō's in 686–690), the unprecedented retirement of a ruling monarch (Jitō in 697) in favor of an underage prince (Monmu), and his death at a surprisingly young age ten years later.

Broadly speaking, a "long" Tenmu dynasty spans the years 650 to about 800, from the Taika Reforms to the beginning of the Heian period. A year after Emperor Kanmu (r. 781–806), Kōnin's son from a nonroyal consort, came to power,[8] one last plot attempted to reinstate the Tenmu line. Moreover, Kanmu enforced his rule in spite of the critique and symbolic fallout he had caused by eliminating his brother Crown Prince Sawara, who allegedly starved himself to death on his way into exile in 785, and replacing him with one of his own thirty-six children. As dynasties invariably do, the Tenmu line of rulers resorted to bloody adjustments and symbolic strategies, the latter necessarily euphemizing the former. Before we explore these machinations, both violent and semiotic, a word about the nature of the sources.

The Sources

It is important to emphasize from the outset that knowledge of seventh- and eighth-century political developments comes from sources written by and for the state nobility. Thus, the texts historians used as "primary" sources are already themselves effects of a specific narrative organization. They consist almost exclusively of officially produced, retrospective annals that include not only administrative matters but also narratives that are interpretive segments of events.

Yet their official character notwithstanding, these texts also constitute family histories of the ruling and noble houses, making it difficult to disentangle the multiple interests embedded in them. Individuals, factions, lineages, the court, and the state, which were virtually inseparable, inform the creation of facts through data selection. The meaning and significance of these data are presented as well through contextualization, euphemization, juxtapositions, or omissions, and in general through the use of idioms for political symbolization the state is in the process of creating and controlling. Given this nature of the record, interpretations by later historians often cannot venture far beyond arguing historical probabilities. By necessity, using these sources as history cannot be done without a considerable degree of speculation and hedging by the frequent use of qualifiers such as "perhaps," "probably," "most likely," "it seems," and so forth.

Besides two official chronicles, the *Nihon shoki* and *Shoku Nihongi*, there is a court mytho-history, the *Kojiki*. Together they constitute Japan's oldest written record. In 681, Tenmu ordered the straightening out of now lost "chronicles" (*Teiki*, Imperial Chronicles, and *Kuji*, Ancient Dicta). The compilation of the *Nihon shoki* (Record of Japan), finalized in 720 by one of his sons, Prince Toneri, owes its origin to that commission. This work covers Yamato history from its mythological beginnings to 697, the year of Jitō's abdication. Most chapters recount the reign of a single ruler — with two striking exceptions. The *kami* or "gods" are granted two chapters at the beginning of the work, as is Tenmu toward the end: one chapter covering the Jinshin War, which brought him to power, and one covering his reign. A scholar has concluded that Tenmu's rule is covered nearly ten times as much as Tenji's and in more detail.[9] In this and other ways the *Nihon shoki* establishes both a gap and a hierarchy between Tenmu and his predecessor.

The *Shoku Nihongi* (Sequel to the Record of Japan) carries the annals a hundred years further, to 791. After several revisions, the work was finalized in 797. Unusual is the inclusion of part of the reign (the first decade of Kanmu's rule) during which the work was published, an unorthodox practice by Chinese historiographical standards. Kanmu had good reasons for trying to control the future of his past, because the next official history, the *Nihon kōki* (Later Record of Japan), reports that the *Shoku Nihongi* seriously truncated the treatment of the suspicious death of Kanmu's brother, Crown Prince Sawara.[10]

To these two histories one has to add the *Kojiki* (Record of Ancient Matters). Its production and inclusion here raise several questions. One, why would the *Kojiki* shed light on the late seventh century if the last event covered, the death in 487 of the Yamato Great King Kenzō, was considered an "ancient matter" from the perspective of the time the work was presented to the court (712)? Two, what constitutes the "new," implied through contrast with the "ancient": the time up to 487, when the *Kojiki*'s narrative stops, or 628, the end of additional minimal genealogical information concerning the ruling house?[11] Three, why the duplication of history, at least pre-487 history, including the stories of the *kami*? What to make of further complications, the result of diverging narratives not only for the same episodes in the *Kojiki* and *Nihon shoki*, but even of numerous alternative versions, sometimes up to eleven, for many passages within the *Nihon shoki* text itself?[12]

The initiative for producing the *Record of Ancient Matters* is ascribed to Tenmu as well. It was compiled by Ō no Yasumaro, possibly the son of Ō no Homage, who fought in the Jinshin War on Tenmu's side. Yasumaro wrote that he was heavily indebted for tales and legends to the memory of one of Tenmu's *toneri* (lieutenants). The core of the *Kojiki*'s Preface is a panegyric to Tenmu's achievements, especially his victory in the Jinshin War. The work was presented to the court in 712, eight years before the completion of the *Nihon shoki*. Both works were thus in progress together, when the law codes were also being compiled, edited, and revised. It is safe to assume that, at a time when the new state was being fashioned, the composition of its laws, its history, and its ideology, as well as the building of the new capitals, Fujiwara-kyō followed by Heijō-kyō (Nara), proceeded in tandem.

They must have addressed the contemporary political concerns even if they may have done so in different ways, as the existence of two histories leads one to suspect.

The political character of these texts makes for a writing that is alien to a modern curiosity, (theoretically) "disinterested and purely historical," about how things actually happened (the objectivist "wie es eigentlich gewesen war"). However, all history, ancient and modern, claims truth for its reconstruction of the past and is accepted or rejected as such not because that is the way things happened, but because that is the way people choose, or are conditioned to think, they happened. Rather than hard objectivity, plausibility constitutes the modality of historiographical truth.[13]

Both works were actually the end product of a selective editing and rewriting of now lost histories, genealogies, chronicles, legends, and anecdotes. As chronicles, they have their beginnings in Tenmu's order of 681/3/17 to a twelve-man team (among whom were six princes) to "record and fix (*sadameshitamau*) everything pertaining to high antiquity and the Imperial Chronicles (*Teiki, Kuji*)." The assignment is echoed in the *Kojiki's* Preface, where Tenmu is quoted as having wanted "mistakes in the Imperial Chronicles [among other records] erased and the truth fixed (*sadamete*)" with the purpose of providing a correct template for governance: "a basic structure for the state, and a foundation for imperial rule."[14]

Three weeks later, Tenmu ordered the compilation of law codes, which resulted in the administrative code of Kiyomihara-ryō of 689 (named after Tenmu and Jitō's royal residence).[15] That same year of 689, as if still in tandem, a draft "about *kami* matters" was officially circulated, most likely a step in the composition of the *Kojiki*.[16] In 702, Jitō promulgated the Taihō Ritsuryō of both penal and administrative statutes, which was retouched in 718 as the Yōrō Ritsuryō but issued only in 757. The assignment of "fixing" the past, in the sense of establishing and rearranging, even contriving with a purpose, turned the *Kojiki* and *Nihon shoki* into legitimations for a sovereign who was himself above the law but who legislated and thus "fixed" his power over the realm. The mytho-historical narratives in the *Kojiki* and *Nihon shoki* provided the exemplars, descriptions of ruling authority (and sometimes its perilous vicissitudes), and constituted a foundational supplement to prescriptions of the codes.

Besides historic episodes, the *Kojiki* also contains stories beyond history, enchanted tales about the origins of the archipelago and its rulers, supreme and regional, mythological and real, the way the court wanted to hear them or, given the presence of variants, the way factions at the court or among the governing elite were able to get their perspective across. For instance, Amaterasu is not the ultimate progenitrix of the royal line in either account by sending a divine descendant to rule the earth; neither is she unambiguously female. Equally significant, the attention and space granted to *uji*, their origins and structures, varies considerably in the two accounts. (*Uji* were the social names for officialized lineages around the center first and subsequently throughout the country, whose *kabane* titles, attached to their names, indicated their rank and political status, a system given final shape by Tenmu in 684.)[17] In the *Nihon shoki*, about 110 *uji* make an appearance, 45 percent of them linked to the royal house. The *Kojiki*, in contrast, touches upon 201 *uji*, 88 percent of them royalty-related.[18] This constitutes a far greater focus on lineage matters and official sanctioning of more *uji*, especially considering that, with only three *maki* ("scrolls," fascicles, or chapters), the *Kojiki* is about a tenth the length of the *Nihon shoki*, which counts thirty *maki*. Lineage position defined the prestige value of the *uji*, which was legally determined through a revised hierarchical system of *kabane* noble titles.

These two works reflect the ways such lineage groups were "fixed" and officialized. The *Kojiki*, however, brings into the royal fold a far greater section of local notables (176 *uji*) than the *Nihon shoki* (40). The *Kojiki*'s author, Yasumaro, also provides more mythological accounts for the origins of the yearly court ceremonies, listed in the Taihō Codes: he offers twenty tales about fifteen ceremonies, while the *Nihon shoki* provides only seven episodes for seven ceremonies.[19]

The single most important issue around which ancient historical narratives were composed was genealogy. In the newly established state, ancestry, whether divine or noble, determined status, which in turn was linked to rank and office. Unofficial *uji* histories bear testimony to the political importance of lineage position and composition. In the early-ninth-century *Kogoshūi*, the ritualist Inbe Hironari buttresses the position of his lineage in court functions against the Nakatomi by questioning the established lines of descent. Other histories enhanced meritorious feats by ancestors to draw greater recognition for themselves. The *Sendai kuji hongi* (Record of Old Things from Previous Ages) makes a similar attempt for the Mononobe and Owari clans.[20]

That the two historical narratives of the *Kojiki* and the *Nihon shoki* took three to four decades to complete indicates that the historiographical project stalled along the way. Most likely it was a matter of reconciling conflicting status claims by some two hundred lineages that they tried to ground in divine origins and proximity to the ruling house. The multiple variants in the *Nihon shoki*'s mythological chapters are at best accommodations of such claims that received some official acknowledgment. Those of the *Kogoshūi* and the *Sendai kuji hongi* must have survived as private but failed attempts at adjusting the official record to their advantage.

Emperor Kanmu, perhaps alerted by a protracted lawsuit over precedence between two hereditary families that served food at important court ceremonies (the Takahashi and Azumi),[21] decided to check all genealogies and clamp down on unacceptable ones. In 799, he ordered the compilation of a new record of *uji*, the *Shinsen shōjiroku*, completed in 815. Two genealogical records of emperors (no longer extant) that circulated before 809 were proscribed. One was recalled under threat of punishment if not turned in as demanded; written orders were sent to all provinces to have the second one burned.[22] At stake were claims that the rulers in the Korean kingdoms of Koguryŏ and Silla, or the dynastic founders in China such as Emperor Gaozu, founder of the Western Han, also descended from divine ancestors of the Sun line. (These claims may have had something to do indirectly with the fact that Emperor Kanmu's mother had Paekche noble ancestry and that a Korean myth also portrayed a dynastic founder as descending from Heaven.)

Two other texts of a genre we call today "literature" contain enchanting, sometimes touching compositions celebrating the new realm and ruling authority. They date from the mid- and late Nara period but span more or less the century preceding their compilation. The *Kaifūsō*, a collection of 120 poems written in pure Chinese style by sixty-four poets, was compiled in 751. Most important, the late-eighth-century *Manyōshū* contained a collection of over 4,500 poems (the majority *waka*), the last one dating from 759.[23] A good number of these poems were produced for official occasions, and were thus ritually staged. Nearly half of the compositions in the *Kaifūsō* are eulogies given at banquets, laments for a deceased ruler or crown prince, celebrations of a royal progress, and so forth. Reading these poems while imagining hearing them delivered brings one to the scene of the events, all occasions for displaying and playing with the symbolic language that surrounded power.

Lineage Delineation and the Tenmu Dynasty

Lineages, and especially dynastic ones where the stakes are highest, need constant maintenance. Dynasties first of all have to be established, often in violence, then euphemized in later accounts and, most important, accepted by the significant competing power groups. Lineality must often be defended against competing lineage members, especially collaterals, affines of lineage heads and their putative successors. Once a founder is consecrated, which entails distancing him from and above whoever came before him — such is the case with Tenji and Tenmu — as well as those surrounding him, succession rules should ideally smooth out the transmission of power. Even where such rules exist, however, they constantly have to be attuned in an ad hoc manner to accommodate all sorts of contingencies. Without a rule telling when the rules apply and when they don't, such adjustments become issues in dynastic struggles. They can ultimately be settled only by an analogous sovereign authority that fixes the past, secures consensus among elites, sanctions the laws that govern the present, and consecrates the imaginary that consecrates him or her and thus allows him or her to get away with playing with the rules.

Japan's monarchy is even more open-ended. Although one can identify regularities in practice over variable periods of time, there seem to have been only two constants, both negative ones. One is the nonexistence of any legal or agreed-upon rule of succession (until very recently); and two, adoption was never an option for succession.[24]

Japan's monarchy was not bound by legally established rules of succession until the Imperial Household acts of 1889 and 1947 prescribed male primogeniture, a rule the government was seeking to change again in 2006 before the birth of a male, Prince Hisahito. Patrilineal succession, however, has not been custom, law, or even practice since ancient times. In fact, father-son royal succession in the main line is rare throughout all of Japanese history. Such a transmission of power, including the establishment of an intended heir, was actualized only sporadically. In mythological times, *chokkei* transmission flowed until the fifteenth ruler, Ōjin; after Tenmu for about four generations there were vague references to "a rule established by Tenji," precisely the time when the myths were written down; and at three other points during the Heian period.[25] Thus, "the unbroken line" of Japanese rulers is arguably in part a retrospective fabrication (with a purpose), as all genealogies are, on which work is continuing until today. As a case in point, in 1870 the Meiji government inserted Prince Ōtomo as Emperor Kōbun between Tenji and Tenmu.

The actual practice of succession then, only shakily based, if at all, on any sort of principle, left the door open to personal and fierce succession struggles. Regularities and succession patterns, retrospectively constructed in genealogies from a present into the past, "after the game is over" and the outcome known, inevitably narrow the field of contestants and thereby simplify that past.

AT THE FIRST ANNIVERSARY of Tenmu's death (687/9/9), his widow Jitō memorialized her husband by ordering a meager feast to be held "in all the temples of the capital." Later, in article 7 of the Taihō Code's Law of Ceremonial (Gisei-ryō), commemorations for past sovereigns were institutionalized as *koki* (National Memorial [Day]).[26] Jitō's creation of this custom confirmed Tenmu as a founding figure — at least for fifteen years. In 702, three weeks before she died, Jitō added her father Tenji, whose memory had recently been brought to the fore. He had belatedly been given a tumulus, some thirty years after his death.[27] Until then, Tenji had been the only ruler besides Ōjin not to have received either an officially recorded burial or a mausoleum shortly after his death. *Ōkimi* Tenji had been left forgotten publicly on purpose to aggrandize, by contrast, Tenmu, as *tennō*, a ruler altogether of a different magnitude from *ōkimi*. By the end of Jitō's reign, Tenji was being rehabilitated.

Koki, an instrument of commemoration, was a device to accentuate specific nodes of the ruling lineage for the peer audience of the court, pertinent at specific moments, since the links could be changed, erased, or created for the position of "sovereigns of the past" according to present needs. Furthermore, nonruler figures, when they were judged to be politically crucial for lineage strengthening or legitimation, were added posthumously. Kusakabe, Tenmu's crown prince who had died during Jitō's regency, was brought to the fore with a *koki* in his honor in 707. On 758/8/9, with the *tennō* title, Kusakabe was genealogically given full honorary, that is to say political, stature. This kind of symbolic gesture solidified the link between Jitō's only son, Kusakabe, and his son Monmu, who succeeded Jitō as *tennō*. Through Kusakabe, Jitō's importance as a lineage node for the dynasty was therefore elevated at a moment in 758 when Junnin, a grandson of Tenmu through another consort (Toneri's mother), had ascended the throne a week earlier. A signal by ceremony that the legitimate lineage line ran through Jitō's descendants was thus delivered: Junnin's succession was thereby to be understood as only a temporary accommodation. It was brought on by the circumstance that Empress Kōken, forty years old, was not married and was heirless.

Monmu's consort Miyako, Emperor Shōmu's mother, a Fujiwara and the first nonroyal mother of a *tennō*, was also honored with a *koki*, as was the nonreigning empress Kōmyō, Miyako's sister and Shōmu's principal consort: two nonroyal "outsiders" posthumously turned "insiders."[28] Kōnin memorialized his mother as well, undoubtedly one move to consolidate the Tenji line, since Kōnin's father was one of Tenji's sons. Kanmu honored his empress and also his own mother, of Paekche noble birth, in the same way.

Slowly, toward the end of the eighth century, the royal lineage was being redrawn by modifying the list of forbears honored with a *koki* as "former sovereigns." In 791, the genea*logical* conclusion was reached when the Tenmu line was cut out except for Shōmu, who was eliminated in 807. At that point, the lineage consisted in ascending order of Kanmu's empress (deceased a year earlier), Kōnin and his empress, Kōnin's parents (neither of whom occupied the throne), and finally Tenji, clearly signaled as the founder of the line. None of the four ruling empresses — Jitō, Genmei, Genshō, or Kōken/Shōtoku — remained on the list. At no time did Tenji's son Ōtomo, slain by Tenmu in the Jinshin War, or Emperor Junnin, deposed in 764, receive a place under the Sun. Junnin was subsequently referred to as *haitei*, the "abolished emperor."[29]

During the course of the Tenmu dynasty, between the violent elimination of crown princes Ōtomo and Osabe at its beginning and end, rivals were disposed of through a number of assassinations, plots, poisonings, and "sudden deaths" of princes and emperors at a young age, as well as the deposing of an emperor followed by his exile and murder, black magic, bewitching, several large-scale armed rebellions, and many hundreds of banishments, all generated by issues of imperial succession. This relentless violence and bloodshed was a family feud à la *cosa nostra*, typical of dynastic contention in general perhaps, involving generations of collaterals and affines, but no outsiders. In 769, a scheme to have Dōkyō, as Buddhist priest a nouveau arrivé in political circles, ascend the throne was thwarted for just this reason.

The Ritsuryō Law of Succession (Keishi-ryō) dealt only with succession to court rank for noble houses, differential for holders of third rank and above and for those of fourth rank and below.[30] The rule was based on a Chinese-style male primogeniture for the main consort's oldest son, but the question of commoners who had no court rank was left open. Legal provisions were made for cases of adoption also, but only for the ranks of nobility, never for the throne.[31] The *tennō* reigned above court rank and law, being the source of both, and not fettered by either.

SEVERAL NEW STRUCTURAL elements in matters of succession appear during the Tenmu dynasty: the first recorded nonadult crown prince and the only female crown princess ever, the succession backtracking from son to mother, the first abdication, an exceptional number of female rulers, and the temporary disappearance of lateral succession.[32]

Although few pre-Tenmu rulers designated a son for preferential treatment as senior prince (*ōe*), and even fewer as crown prince (*taishi*), these titles, without granting legal right to succession, always went to adults capable of taking over the reins of government. Jitō, however, abdicated in favor of her fourteen-year-old grandson. Shōmu was the first ruler to designate as crown prince not only a youth, but an infant, when in 727 he granted the title to his newborn son, Motoi (who died within a year — cursed?). In 738, Shōmu made his twenty-year-old daughter (Princess Abe, the later *tennō* Kōken) crown princess — the only case in all of Japanese history of a woman's receiving that title. When Genmei succeeded her own son Monmu, the lineage backtracked one generation. Each of these cases of political expediency (except possibly that of Genmei) imply a heightened sense of insecurity in the calculation to lock in succession as soon as possible and a gamble that these preemptive strikes would work and their results be accepted.

Post-Tenmu monarchs introduced retirement in order to secure succession for the next generation. Reigns used to end with the ruler's death. Jitō, however, was the first monarch to abdicate, and five of the seven rulers who succeeded her followed her precedent.[33] This obvious attempt to outmaneuver rivals and prevent succession disputes resulted in the formation of an adjunct site of power in the position of retired sovereign (*daijōtennō*).

The majority of female rulers throughout Japanese history is concentrated in the Tenmu dynasty. Five of Tenmu's seven successors, starting with Jitō, were women. One of them was Kōken, who ruled a second time as Shōtoku. The concentration of female rulership in the Tenmu dynasty, an exceptional phenomenon, also indicates unusual dynastic problems. It should be noted, however, that female rulers elsewhere in East Asia were also concentrated in the seventh century. In Silla, there were Queens Sŏndŏk (634–647) and Chindŏk (647–654);[34] and Empress Wu (690–705) was the only female monarch in all of Chinese history.

This period saw no sibling succession other than Tenmu, who took power by force after his brother Tenji. Earlier, however, lateral succession had not been uncommon. Bidatsu, Yōmei, Sushun, and Suiko, occupying the throne successively between 572 and 628, were all sired by Kinmei; Kōgyoku/Saimei and Kōtoku were siblings. After the Tenmu dynasty, sibling succession revived, with the first three emperors following Kanmu being his sons.

Sixth- and Seventh-Century Successions

The innovations in the succession pattern that developed during the Tenmu dynasty modified the arrangement that had been functioning for about two centuries, one that was fraught with considerable tension and bloodshed. That system itself appears to have been a response to the lack of male successors in the Yamato lineage of great kings when Buretsu died in 506. Keitai, the next great king, may even have started a new ruling house.

The story goes that a few local notables, officials in Buretsu's kingdom, had searched for a male successor with some claim to royal ancestry and, after one candidate declined, they settled, desperately one presumes, for an alleged distant fifth-generation descendant from King Ōjin, a geopolitical outsider as well (see figure 3). He was found in Echizen Province and entered the Yamato basin, possibly by conquest, only twenty years after his coronation as Great King Keitai and married a sister of Buretsu. The intervention by a council of peers for solving a succession problem was often resorted to in times of lineal quandaries.

Subsequently, a pattern of intermarriage developed to close ranks for the ruling line by doubly ensuring royal blood qualifications of successors. This worked as follows. Ideally, the main consort of king B (son of the former king A) was a female of royal blood, which usually meant that she was a half sister of king B (see figures 2 and 3). We shall refer to her as *kisaki* (principal consort).[35] She was, thus, the daughter of the former king A, but through a different consort than king B's mother. As *kisaki* of king B, who was a son of king A's *kisaki*, she would become the mother of king B's successor, C. Thus, in this system of extreme inbreeding, the significant marriages were between a royal half brother and his royal half sister. Royal blood flowed in two parallel channels, through both parents, men and women, to the successor king. Hence the label "double royalty," as some historians have called the practice.[36] Kings had a number of consorts, many of them from *uji* such as the Soga, but at least one was the king's paternal half sister — or so reports the *Nihon shoki*. Only she had *kisaki* status.

Historically, as the broken line in the diagram of figure 2 indicates, a *kisaki* could be a second-generation descendant from a king and an *uji* woman, but kings skipping generations risked diluting the royal family's grip on power through bloodline. An even more critical situation would ensue if the direct line died out as was the case with Buretsu, and later with Shōtoku (see figures 1 and 3). This meant that no adult prince stood ready to succeed. In such an event, collateral branches of the royal house became

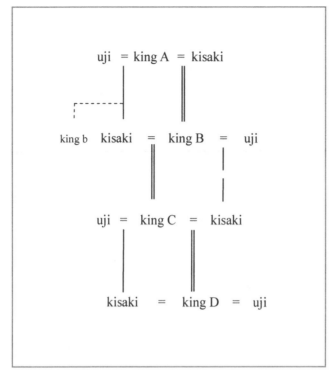

Fig. 2. Double royal succession in the 6th and 7th centuries.
Source: Mizubayashi, *Kiki shinwa*, p. 333, fig. 24, modified.

the pool for a successor, thereby, of course, opening the door for ugly and often bloody struggles by collaterals and affines.

Figure 2 indicates that King b (an interim appointment) could be chosen from a collateral line when king B died while his successor, the future king C, was still a child. In practice and in principle, collateral kings, such as king b, were not or could not be succeeded by their own offspring, but they did or had to return power to the main royal line's king C when the latter came of age. The record's claim that Keitai is a fifth-generation descendant from Ōjin is most likely spurious and covers up the beginning of a new ruling house in the early sixth century (see figure 3). After Bidatsu's death, toward the end of the century, the seat of power passed through two of his siblings and his half-sister and wife (Suiko) before returning to the main male line with Jomei who, although a double royal, was two generations removed from Bidatsu. Kōgyoku and Kōtoku, however, strained the system to its limits, since three generations separated them from Bidatsu (see figure 1).

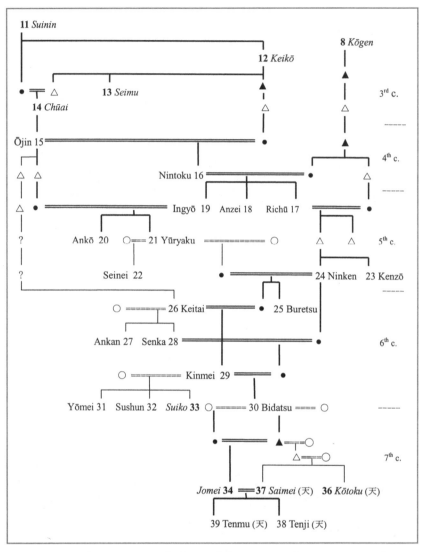

Fig. 3. *Sun* signifiers in names of rulers and their principal consorts or mothers: Suinin (11) to Genshō (43): 270–661. *Sun* (*hi*) appears in all rulers' names (italicized) before Ōjin (15) and again from Suiko to Kōtoku (33–36); also in names of consorts and rulers' mothers (●) crucial for lineage continuity (bold = and –), and occasionally in names of male descendants in that position (▲). *Heaven* (*ame* 天) appears together with *hi* in Kōtoku's and Saimei's names, and displaced *hi* in Tenji's and Tenmu's. Kōgyoku (35) reascended the throne as Saimei, and thus had no separate posthumous title. Jitō, Monmu, Genmei, Genshō (40–43) were styled as *neko* (root child); the latter two had also Nihon in their names. Sources: *Kojiki* (11–33); *Nihongi* (11–39); Mizubayashi, "Ritsuryō tennōsei no shinwateki kosumoroji," p. 25, fig. 2, modified.

The practice of having only a daughter of the former king as the current king's principal consort and mother of the future king protected the core of the royal house from influence by affines since she was not an outsider. In this scheme, *uji* wives could not produce the next king; only his *kisaki* could. Soga politics exploited that possibility for several generations, which was different from the revolutionary practice of Fujiwara wives who, in the early eighth century, became mothers of emperors.

The most ambitious affines in the sixth century and the first half of the seventh were the Soga *uji* who placed their women among the great king's and collaterals' consorts. Gradually infiltrating the inner court, two Soga women were wives of Kinmei, but the throne went to Bidatsu, a son from a non-Soga wife (see figure 1). Bidatsu's death was followed by armed clashes between *uji* supporters of three candidates for the throne. These complications arose in part because after the death of Bidatsu's first *kisaki* (mother of a son whom Bidatsu seemed to have selected as his successor), Bidatsu took the unique step of appointing a second *kisaki*. The three candidates for the throne were the alleged crown prince from the first *kisaki*; a son from the second *kisaki*, a half sister of Bidatsu with a Soga mother (the later Great King Suiko); and one of Bidatsu's half brothers, also from a Soga mother. After a Soga military victory, the throne went to number three, known as Great King Yōmei, who was married to a Soga woman. (Yōmei was the father of Prince Umayado, better known and mythologized as the famous Prince Shōtoku.) A second military victory by the Soga clan following Yōmei's short rule (585–587) resulted in the enthronement of Sushun, another half brother of Bidatsu with a Soga mother, one whom the Soga murdered, however, in 592. The next great king was Suiko (592–628), the first woman ruler and a Soga through her mother. That is probably when Prince Shōtoku became crown prince, because Suiko's son had died. Nevertheless, Shōtoku passed away before Suiko, and no new crown prince had been appointed. A council of notables decided that Jomei, the double royal grandson of Bidatsu would be the next great king. Plotting for power by the Soga clan continued until their main branch was eliminated by Tenji in the Taika coup of 645, two years after the Soga had forced Shōtoku's son, Prince Yamashiro no Ōe, and twenty-two members of his family to commit suicide.[37]

Twice in historical times the possibility arose that the royal line might be transferred to a branch with lesser claims on legitimacy: in 585 following the death of Bidatsu and in 654 when Kōtoku died. Bidatsu's case illustrates the point that a collaterally established king such as Yōmei did not or could not pass the throne on to his son, Prince Shōtoku. After Yōmei died, power remained in his generation with Sushun. Following Sushun's assassination by the Soga, Suiko succeeded in 592. When her son Takeda, with a *kisaki* mother the obvious candidate for succession, died around 600, Shōtoku became *taishi*, or it may have been in 593 because Takeda might have been too young to function as crown prince when Suiko succeeded. Shōtoku Taishi's status as potential successor, even though a collateral one-generation-removed, was enhanced by positioning him as Suiko's coruler. He passed away, however, before succession became an issue. If he had survived Suiko, his own line might possibly have become the main line, but dying as he did in 622, six years before Suiko, he managed no more than a long career as crown prince and coruler, most famous in the legends that surrounded his persona posthumously.[38] With no clear candidate to succeed Suiko, a council decided upon Bidatsu's grandson Jomei as the next great king.

According to the *Nihon shoki*, during the three years between the death of Jomei in 641 and Kōtoku's succession after the Taika coup of 645, Great Sovereign Kōgyoku possibly ruled, 642–645. As Kouchi and other historians have reason to believe, however, the official record may have been tampered with and the throne actually left empty during those years.[39] In any case, one may wonder why Tenji was not crowned in 645 since he was nineteen by then, or at least in 654, instead of Saimei, Kōtoku's sister.[40] In 661, Saimei died and Tenji's position and title moved up, but only from crown prince to regent for another seven years. He finally occupied the throne in 668 at age forty-two for the last three years of his life. Possibly Tenji lacked the necessary backing from factions at court and in Yamato before this time.[41]

Tenji did involve himself deeply in politics and administration to cement his position: participating in the coup of 645, implementing the administrative Taika Reforms, eliminating his half brother Furuhito, reputedly ordering the compilation of the first administrative law code, the Ōmiryō, establishing a university, and so forth. His aim, Kouchi believes, was to supplement his dynastic low value by ruler activities to offset the questionable lineage on his mother's side since Tenji was not precisely a double royal — his mother was only a great-grandchild of Bidatsu — until consensus for his succession was sufficiently strong. Tenji's regency (661–668) and Jitō's (686–690) constituted the last periods in Japanese history that the throne was left vacant for several years, indicating serious divisions over succession and an unsettled state of affairs following the deaths of their predecessors.[42]

The beginning of the *Nihon shoki*'s chapter on Kōtoku's reign (chapter 25) presents the candidates for the throne in 645 as polite gentlemen deferring to each other; most likely, however, they represented contending power groups. Prince Naka no Ōe (Tenji) declined the honor, while Prince Karu wished to step aside for Prince Furuhito, Naka no Ōe's half brother; Furuhito disqualified himself by retiring from the world to the Yoshino mountains. In the end, Prince Karu assumed the throne as Great King Kōtoku.[43] Three months later, however, Naka no Ōe dispatched a posse to kill his half brother Furuhito, and, furthermore, after having framed him with an alleged plot, exterminated Furuhito's family, except at least a daughter who was one of Tenji's wives (see figure 4).

Ishikawa Maro, the third conspirator besides Naka no Ōe and Nakatomi Kamatari in the Taika plot, who had provided the military backup for the coup, had given his daughter to Tenji and was rewarded with a ministerial post. Four years later, however, on 649/3/23, perhaps precisely because of his military clout, he and his family with some two dozen others were exterminated by Tenji. As a disgruntled Soga, he had joined the plot, but in the end he shared the fate of the main Soga line. In the *Nihon shoki*, Naka no Ōe escapes blame for these killings because, allegedly, he had wrongly been led to believe that Soga Ishikawa Maro had been concocting another plot.

In these politics of power, women were used as important assets. As concubines, wives, or consorts, they gained access to the inner court for their *uji*. They were kept even after their *uji* lost out in the power struggles. Naka no Ōe took the daughters of both Furuhito, Princess Yamato, and Ishikawa, Princess Ochi Iratsume, as wives. Princess Yamato became the main consort when Naka no Ōe ascended the throne as Great King Tenji. Ochi Iratsume was Jitō's mother, whom Naka no Ōe had married to entice Ishikawa Maro to join the plot of the 645 coup.[44]

At the end of the tumultuous year of 645, the royal court decamped to Naniwa (Osaka) on the Inland Sea. An office for foreign relations was expanded into a new kingly residence. Kōtoku and his retinue moved in on New Year's eve of 651; all construction was completed in the fall of that year. Then, less than two years later, Naka no Ōe demanded that Kōtoku return to Asuka. Kōtoku refused, but Naka no Ōe moved out anyway, taking with him his mother (the "retired Kōgyoku," Kōtoku's sister), his own sister (Kōtoku's consort), several brothers, and, undoubtedly, his supporting clique at the court. Kōtoku died in his new palace the following year, abandoned and possibly slain or a suicide induced by his unsustainable situation. In fact, by this bloodless coup d'état, Tenji took power, shielding himself with his mother, whom he put on the throne, possibly for the second time, as Saimei.[45]

It was in Tenji's interest, moreover, that Kōtoku's son, Prince Arima, make no claim on the throne. Hence in 658 another plot was "discovered,"

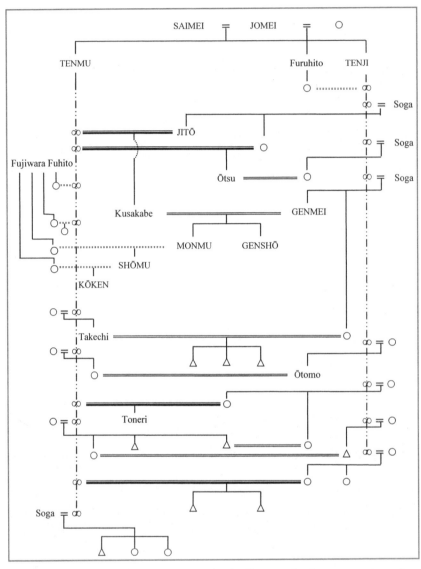

Fig. 4. Endogamous links Tenmu-Tenji. In the figure, rulers' names are in capitals; Tenmu's consort is a Tenji daughter (=); the intermarriage of Tenmu/Tenji offspring (=); marriages of Tenmu, Tenji (∞); male/female (△/○). Design by Christine Schoppe.

resulting in the arrest and strangulation of the presumed conspirator Prince Arima, who was eighteen and old enough to rule. Naka no Ōe conducted an investigation whereupon Arima's alleged coconspirator, son of Soga Iruka (murdered in 645), was banished to a remote post in Tsukushi.[46] When Saimei passed away in 661, the throne was left vacant; Naka no Ōe ruled as regent (shōsei) until 668.[47] The deviations from the pattern of double royal succession after the deaths of Bidatsu and Jomei were unavoidable detours. Female rulers by necessity played an important role in the effort of the ruling lineage to keep a grasp on sovereignty. Affines were needed for alliances with outside uji. The ruler's wives made this possible. However, uji were prevented from taking over the royal line because the inbreeding with kisaki kept succession within the royal lineage.

Close intermarriage bonds between Tenji, Tenmu, and their children had the same purpose. They constituted an attempt to revitalize the double royalty practice. Tenmu received four of Tenji's daughters as consorts, and six of his children married Tenji's offspring, which included Prince Ōtomo (see figure 4).[48] Another indication of the desirability of bilateral royal ancestry can be found in the retroactive enhancement in the chronicles and genealogies given to Tenji's ancestral links to Bidatsu. We do not know for sure whether it was Tenji himself or the authors of the Nihon shoki who bestowed the new prefix title of "imperial ancestor" upon his paternal grandfather, his maternal grandmother, and his mother.[49] Formerly, the title had almost always been reserved exclusively for kami as royal ancestors. This retrospective ancestral upgrade is a precursor to the National Memorial Day of the Taihō Code.

If this interpretation of Tenji's actions and intentions makes sense, then Prince Ōtomo's alleged succession remains a puzzle. How could Tenji have wanted Ōtomo to succeed him since the latter's mother was an uneme, a woman given to Tenji by a local notable, and thus lacking the kisaki status necessary to function as transmitter of ruling charisma?

During his terminal illness in 671, Tenji had signaled his son Ōtomo as perhaps a more preferable successor than Tenmu, who quite reasonably had read other signs pointing to himself as the next great king.[50] The Nihon shoki is vague about whether Prince Ōtomo had actually replaced Tenmu as Tenji's designated successor, and certainly it reveals nothing about Ōtomo having become the next great king. There was ample reason for blurring the issue in the official record. Indeed, if Ōtomo's succession had taken place, the Tenmu dynasty would have been illegitimate — certainly not an interpretation we would expect from Prince Toneri, Tenmu's son in charge of the compilation of the *Nihon shoki,* which refers several times to Tenmu as heir.[51]

The first mention that Ōtomo had actually succeeded Tenji appears centuries later in the mid-Heian *Saikyūki* (Minamoto no Taka'akira's diary), an interpretation adopted by the monumental *Dainihonshi* history of Japan in the eighteenth century and one that received official sanction in 1870. Then the new Meiji government filled in the genealogical time gap between Tenji and Tenmu with Ōtomo as Emperor Kōbun, not unlike the treatment Kusakabe received in 758, as link between Jitō (or Tenmu) and Monmu.[52]

Jitō to Shōmu: Securing the Throne for a Great-Grandson

The first time historical reality actually matches the image of a patrilineal succession through a main line (which had to be constructed) is during the stretch of four generations from Tenmu to Shōmu — where, oddly perhaps, female rulers play an important role (see figure 1). The understanding of these transfers of royal authority as the emergence of the Chinese principle of patrilineal primogeniture simplifies the complexity of the political warfare and the astonishing transformations — both symbolic and real — born of those generations. Of the five successions that took place, three rulers were women (Jitō, Genmei, and Genshō), each no doubt up to the task. They secured the seat by holding the position for a preferred but not yet ready male successor: Jitō for her grandson Monmu; Genmei, Monmu's mother, and Genshō, his sister, for Monmu's son, the future *tennō* Shōmu. Genshō, in particular, was a perfect occupant; as an unmarried woman, thirty-five years old, with no children, there was little likelihood that she might steer the lineage to a side line.

The intention, on the part of Jitō, to secure succession for her great-grandson Shōmu is not in doubt. She engineered these successions of her line. Tradition has also acknowledged this since at least the end of the eighth century by giving her the name Jitō, which means "holding the line."[53] It is possible that Jitō used some principle other than her own lineage claims, her status as Tenmu's queen, or her tenure as *tennō* to secure her grandson's and great-grandson's position.

If there was such a principle, one might expect to find it in the Law Codes. The "norm" of double royal descent, the preferred qualification for kingship since the beginning of the sixth century, however, was not incorporated in the Ritsuryō Code. Moreover, it did not fit the case of Shōmu's succession.

The Ritsuryō Law of Succession set forth the Chinese principle of primogeniture, specifying succession by the oldest son of the principal wife, but not on whether this applied to the monarchy.[54] Succession to court rank for the upper nobility was prescribed by the following order of available candidates: first, the oldest son of the principal wife; next, one generation down to the grandson of the principal wife; then, the full brother of the oldest son; and finally, if none of these were available, the son of a secondary consort. These rules of succession are clearly different from the customary practice of the great kings on two counts: first, all brothers of the assigned heir were also potential successors; and second, if a problem arose with the son of the *kisaki*, the interim king from a side line could not pass the throne to his own offspring. As we shall see, since Shōmu's mother was not a *kisaki*, "in principle" he could not have been the heir.[55]

Jitō's determination and maneuvering made sure that her descendants prevailed against any competitors from Tenmu's other consorts. Jitō had become Tenmu's *kisaki* when Tenmu was crowned in 673. By then, they had already an eleven-year-old son, Kusakabe. Nevertheless, Tenmu had many consorts and offspring, notably Takechi, an older son by another wife, born in 654, and a hero general of the Jinshin War. Jitō's only child, Kusakabe, however, was in 682 maneuvered by Jitō into position as crown prince, twenty years old, with administrative responsibilities — perhaps an echo of Shōtoku Taishi's and Tenji's strategy to increase their symbolic capital.

Seeking to avoid succession problems, Tenmu and Jitō had extracted an oath of agreement from half a dozen of Temmu's sons (brothers and half brothers) in 679.[56] Prince Ōtsu began attending to matters of state in 683/2/1, which implicated his being positioned as heir. Two years later, however, when the court rank system was revised on 685/1/21, he was placed one rank below Kusakabe even though Ōtsu seems to have been the more capable of the two, and Kusakabe appears to have had health problems. The first week after Tenmu's death the following year, Ōtsu was swiftly executed, accused of plotting. The prince reciting the eulogies during the wake (*mogari*) is usually the designated heir. With Ōtsu out of the way, Kusakabe delivered no fewer than six eulogies during the two-year-long wake, yet he is not even mentioned at the New Year's reception of 689. The *Nihon shoki* records his death, possibly due to foul play, just four months later. Instead, after functioning as regent for four years, it was Jitō who acceded to the throne the following New Year's Day.

Although not a double royal, Takechi, Tenmu's oldest son and war veteran, would have been qualified to succeed at age thirty-six. In 697, however, within a year after Takechi died, Jitō installed *her* grandson as *tennō* (Kusakabe's son, Monmu). The year before Jitō herself passed away, her great-grandson (Prince Obito, the future Shōmu) was born to Monmu

(701). In 707, Monmu died at age twenty-four without having acquired a *kisaki*.

Fujiwara Miyako's marriage to Monmu was one of many moves on the part of the Fujiwara clan to engage in an improved version of Soga-style marriage politics, by having a daughter not merely become a royal consort and mother of the next ruler's *kisaki*, but by succeeding in positioning her as *kisaki* even though she was not of royal blood. This move turned into a fierce conflict between "nouveaux bureaucrats" and the royal clan.[57] Fujiwara Miyako did not acquire the title of queen during her lifetime and was not mother to the next *kisaki*, but she gave birth to the prince who would become Monmu's successor.

Miyako was the granddaughter of Fujiwara Kamatari, coconspirator with Naka no Ōe in the coup of 645 and the daughter of Fuhito, who, undoubtedly, was the beneficiary of his daughter's prestigious union as *tennō* Monmu's royal spouse (*fujin*).[58] Kamatari belonged to the Nakatomi family of court ritualists but was granted the Fujiwara name on his deathbed in 669. Thus, the Fujiwara was a new and small *uji* without a long pedigree, but Fuhito had already succeeded in placing two other daughters, ranked as "spouses," among Tenmu's ten wives (see figure 4). In 689, the year before Jitō became *tennō*, Fuhito, at age thirty, became a judicial officer (*kotowaru tsukasa*), holding the lowest court rank of the middle officialdom, the equivalent of the later fifth junior lower (sixteenth rank on a scale of thirty; see figure 10). The number of *uji* whose members filled the ranks of middle officialdom was probably less than 150.[59] The last twelve years of his life (708–720), Fuhito functioned as minister of the right on the Council of State, holding second senior rank. He died, having placed four sons in important administrative posts. Before 689, however, there is no record of this still rather insignificant *uji* as having taken sides in the Jinshin War (Fuhito was only thirteen then). His father's cousin, Nakatomi Kane, who had functioned as minister of the right under Ōtomo, was even executed on 672/8/25 and his children banished. Under Tenmu, Fuhito received training in Chinese legal and administrative matters from Tanabe Fuhito Ōsumi to emerge in 689 as a judicial official.

Jitō turned the Fujiwara into a politically important ally after Takechi's death in 696 when she promoted Fuhito to fourth rank junior lower.[60] This was a year before Monmu succeeded to the throne (697/8/14) and took Fuhito's daughter Miyako as royal spouse a week after his coronation (8/20). No doubt, it was Jitō who arranged the marriage between Monmu and Miyako. When Monmu died, with their son Prince Obito only six years old, the throne was secured by Monmu's mother, Genmei. She abdicated

in 715, a year after Prince Obito was officially made crown prince. Her unmarried and childless daughter Genshō (Monmu's sister) held the throne
for another eight years and in turn left it for Obito, who succeeded her as
Emperor Shōmu in 724. These women held on to power by physically occupying the throne while Obito grew up. This necessity they hid by turning
it into virtue, as Pierre Bourdieu would phrase it, which in this case took on
the guise of "law."[61]

During the eighth century, four succession edicts by Genmei, Shōmu,
Kōken, and Kanmu (respectively in 707, 724, 749, and 781) maintained that
a "law (nori/hō) whereby Tenji had established a forever unchanging rule
(nori/ten)" was being followed. Many modern scholars interpret this "law,"
not without controversy, as referring to lineal succession.[62] When recover-
ing the throne after Monmu's death, his mother Genmei referred to this
rule of lineal succession, which, she stated, "was received and implemented
by Jitō" at the time when Jitō abdicated for her grandson Monmu. Thus
Genmei's succession, an unusual one that backtracked one generation from
son to mother, was represented in the light of a Tenji law, followed first by
Jitō. Tenji's authority was invoked, revealing his increasing importance in
legitimating succession, superseding that of Tenmu, since Tenmu, having
killed Tenji's son, loomed large as the counter-exemplar for patrilineal succession. To make it appear as if Monmu's imperial predecessor, for both
symbolic and political reasons, was not Jitō but Kusakabe (Monmu's father), Genmei's edict of 707/7/17 was preceded by a declaration on 4/13 establishing a National Memorial Day for Kusakabe, transforming him into
the equivalent of a memorialized tennō.

The first celebration of a National Memorial Day took place on the first
anniversary of Tenmu's death. Then, three weeks before Jitō died, she declared that a yearly Buddhist Memorial Day be established on the anniversary of the deaths of Emperors Tenmu and Tenji (702/12/2).[63] Thus, it was
virtually on her deathbed that Jitō signaled to Tenmu's sons Toneri and
Niitabe and his grandson Nagaya, all potential collateral contenders for the
throne, that Monmu (and by extension the latter's son, Obito) stood in a
three-generational male line: Tenmu, Kusakabe, Monmu. Genmei stated
that Jitō had wanted it that way, because Tenji had laid down the principle.

Shōmu's as well as Kōken's mention of a "Tenji's norm" may have had a
similar purpose. Neither Shōmu nor Kōken had royal mothers, and with no
surviving sons from Shōmu, Kōken's succession may also have been questioned because past practice would have dictated succession shifting to a
side line (which happened anyway when Junnin took over after Kōken's
abdication in 758 and when Kōken died unmarried and childless in 770).

Fujiwara Fuhito did not rest even after Miyako had borne Monmu a son. Monmu was survived by two concubines from other *uji*, and at least one of them had another son by him. On 713/11, both concubines were stripped of their *hin* rank (of low-ranked consort); six months later (714/6) Prince Obito was officially made crown prince. With Obito as the only child by any consort, the others demoted, and the son from one of them thereby doubly disqualified, Miyako was de facto in a position of *kisaki*, even though she could not be and was not sanctioned as such.[64] Nevertheless, tensions around the crown prince's legitimacy continued — hence an official plea in an edict of 719/10/17 to Princes Toneri and Niitabe to support the succession of the crown prince, a plea that did not stop Prince Nagaya's fierce opposition to making Shōmu's Fujiwara consort a *kisaki* but that eventually cost him his life in 729.

Each succession during the seventh century was surrounded by crises. The violence and assassinations in the years following Bidatsu's reign were followed by the seven years during which Crown Prince Naka no Ōe was in power but without any great king on the throne. There was also the Jinshin War and the execution of Prince Ōtsu a few days after Tenmu's death, followed by another four-year interregnum while Kusakabe was crown prince and before Jitō ascended the throne.

At her abdication, Jitō was in need of some consensus, especially since she had waited until Prince Takechi, the obvious successor, had died. On 696/7/10, according to an introduction to a poem in the *Kaifūsō*, she apparently held a meeting to discuss the problem.[65] Prince Kadono opined that "succession between brothers leads to upheaval." As the oldest son of Prince Ōtomo who might have been crown prince or *tennō* had his father, and not Tenmu, succeeded Tenji,[66] he spoke from experience. "And," Kadono added, "as a rule (*nori*) of our country, succession has been lineal since the age of the *kami*." Jitō succeeded in solving the issue to her advantage, preventing the succession from sliding toward one of Tenmu's numerous sons from other wives by abdicating in favor of her grandson, Prince Karu (Monmu). His father, Kusakabe, was the only child Jitō had with Tenmu.[67]

Kadono's appeal to the "age of the *kami*" according to the *Kaifūsō* is possibly an anachronistic embellishment from the mid-eighth century when the work was published (751). If historically accurate, however, it must have been a reference to the genealogy that eventually became recorded in the *Kojiki* in 712, a partial draft of "*kami* matters" having been circulating officially since 689. The *Kojiki*'s final version presents a historically unverifiable succession pattern for the first seventeen mythological Yamato rulers as patrilineal, father-to-son transmission. Kadono's "old example" from Yamato antiquity was more likely of recent vintage.

Thus, a proposal for a practice, lineal succession, was buttressed by two arguments: a "Tenji norm" and a "Yamato exemplar," an agreement in principle to prevent succession struggles, but one that in practice would lead to divergent interpretations. Ultimately, political power play was the decisive factor directing the dynastic flow from one generation to the next.

2 MYTHEMES

The Gods took council together:
The Plain-of-Reeds
Should be
For the August God
Who was sent down to earth:
The High-Illumining
Sun Prince,
At his palace Kiyomigahara
In Asuka,
He established firm his reign
In all his godhead.
—689. About Tenmu in a lament
for Kusakabe. *Manyōshū*.

Before identifying divine emperorship too readily as a singularly Japanese mytheme, one should remind oneself that, as a rule, power becomes accepted only when sacralized. Rulership without religious sanction is power without legitimacy. As Gilbert Dagron remarks, "Tout pouvoir de fait ne devient pouvoir de droit qu'en se sacralisant: l'État est sacré, l'Église est pouvoir."[1] It is not that some cultures sacralize authority and others don't; all do somehow and often in similar ways. In the fifth century, for instance, Koguryŏ kings appealed to Heaven and the Sun, as Yamato kings did later.[2] The differences between traditions called upon for conjuring up an enchanted world for political power can be reduced to a question of modality, as a matter of what sort of symbolics is put to the task of such a world-making enterprise.

This modality is never monological, although we customarily label it Buddhist, Daoist, Shinto, because all traditions are composites. The symbolic in action is always promiscuous, within and among traditions. Robert Heine-Geldern speaks of a "plural symbolism" as being common in Buddhist Southeast Asia,[3] but a multilayered borrowing is shared throughout Asia and China, and in Japan as well. We are confronted with a web of superimposed modalities rather than with a coherence of single-strand ideas.[4] The operating logic of this symbolics is one that groups together tangles of meanings rather than a discriminating one that separates through argumentation acceptable and unacceptable alternatives. For political power, the sacred is fungible.

Cosmogonic Groundings

Kōnoshi Takamitsu has demonstrated that what we unreflectingly refer to as the Shinto mythology, recorded in the texts of the *Kojiki* and the *Nihon shoki*, did not, at the time of their compilation, exist as such. Rather, these two works present two separate cosmologies that ground Yamato rulership in significantly different ways.[5] Moreover, to further complicate textual interpretation, the inclusion of numerous original commentaries, annotations and alternate versions (*aru fumi ni iwaku*) to the main text, indented and written in small type in the oldest manuscripts, have produced the *Nihon shoki* as a laminated text. For instance, scholars have charted six variants (the *Kojiki*, the *Nihon shoki*'s main text, and four different versions) regarding the details of the descent of the Heavenly Grandchild Ninigi to the Central Land. The variations concern the identity of who ordered the descent, the nature of the regalia, Ninigi's companions, and the site where they landed.[6]

Kōnoshi's interpretation constitutes a radical break with a centuries-old hermeneutics guided by the unquestioned aim to clarify "the" Japanese mythology, thought to be retrievable as a single-strand ideology from a number of variants, some contradictory, others almost repetitious. Omissions in the "Age of the *kami*" chapters of the *Kojiki* (the first of three) and the *Nihon shoki* (the first two of thirty) were filled in, and variations glossed over as insignificant. Working within a chronological framework of a discourse that would have evolved from earlier and simpler oral tales to later and more complex texts, scholars developed, as early as the ninth century, a hermeneutics that collapsed the differences into an evolving but single narrative. Thus, according to Kōnoshi, not one but at least two mythologies were at work in the seventh and eighth centuries, and side by side.

Amaterasu, whom the monological version of Japan's origins puts forth as the divine ancestor, protector, and guarantor of the Yamato house, is mainly a product of the *Kojiki*, and even there that role has to be qualified. In the *Nihon shoki*'s mythological chapters, Amaterasu plays no part in the important episode of the descent to earth by the divine grandchild Ninigi, and Amaterasu does not function as founding ancestor. For the compilers of the *Nihon shoki*, that important function is reserved for the *kami* Takamimusuhi, whose daughter married Amaterasu's son and produced Ninigi.

Takamimusuhi is the one who wants to send his grandson down to the Central Land of the Reed Plains, which, however, was in chaos. Several dispatches of *kami* were needed, each time preceded by a meeting where Takamimusuhi consulted with Amaterasu and all the gods, before Ninigi could be sent and the Central Land pacified. No mention is made of the mirror, sword, or jewel, regalia that tradition has always considered the sacred emblems for the legitimate rule over Yamato. According to the *Kojiki*, however, Ninigi received these indispensable guarantees of rulership from Amaterasu, who, in this version, is in charge of the whole affair.[7]

The numerous parallelisms between the events of the late seventh century and mythological episodes constitute symbolic causal reversals as memory of recent events converted into sacred stories of origin that thereby bestow their legitimizing halo on these events. After the founding narrative of Jinmu as Yamato's first ruler, he is never mentioned again in either the *Kojiki* or the *Nihon shoki*, except in the latter, when Tenmu goes to worship at his grave after his Jinshin victory. In the twenty-eight chapters of the *Nihon shoki* dealing with rulers, Amaterasu is virtually absent. She helps Jinmu in his eastward conquest of the Yamato region, and once makes an appearance during a military campaign by Jingū. As well, both the *Kojiki* and the *Nihon shoki* report that Yamato Takeru made a detour to "worship at the shrine in Ise" at the start of his campaign to subdue northeastern Honshū.[8] The next time we meet Amaterasu is five centuries later, when Tenmu is leading another campaign in the east at the beginning of the Jinshin War.[9]

Tenmu's story begins in the summer of 672. In great haste and with only a small entourage, he rushed eastward from Yoshino to the strategically important Fuwa Pass in Mino (near Nagoya), some 150 kilometers away. On the morning of the third day (6/26), Tenmu paused at the Asake River and worshipped from afar, in the direction of Ise, "toward Amaterasu." Reaching the pass in a record time of four days, he blocked Prince Ōtomo from reaching and mobilizing mounted warriors in the east. Tenmu counterattacked with the eastern cavalry and defeated Ōtomo within one month.

It is during the reigns of Tenmu and Jitō that Amaterasu and Ise gained prominence. At the beginning of his rule (673/4/14), Tenmu chose one of his virgin daughters to become *saiō* priestess at Ise, a custom, the record makes a point of telling, that had lapsed for over fifty years.[10] On that occasion, the Ise shrine was referred to for the first time as *daijingū*, "great shrine." In a *Manyōshū* poem from 696, Tenmu's Jinshin victory was attributed to a *kamukaze*, a divine tempest that blew in from Ise.[11] On the eighth memorial of Tenmu's death (694), Jitō composed a poem to his memory suggesting that, as "son of the Sun," he had returned to Ise.[12]

Two years earlier, on 692/3/6, Jitō had visited Ise, a unique event for a *tennō* and not repeated again until Emperor Meiji in the nineteenth century. When Emperor Shōmu left Nara in 740, in the midst of Fujiwara Hirotsugu's rebellion in Kyushu, he retraced Tenmu's campaign route. As a gesture to the Sun *kami*, perhaps inspired by Tenmu and the by-then-created mythic exemplars Jinmu and Yamato Takeru, Shōmu sent a delegation with offerings to the Ise shrines.[13]

At the heart of the matter, however, is that shrines and temples represented the powers via patronage of the various *uji*, families, and factions at the court. Jitō's visit was so extraordinary that it met with strong objection from Ōmiwa Takechimaro, caretaker of the Miwa shrine, the traditional site (some five kilometers northeast of Fujiwara-kyō) for the court's cult of the Sun. He resigned, returning his court rank in support for a social cause "because rulers should not travel at a season when it hampers work in the fields." Takechimaro, however, may have felt personally threatened because Jitō's trip to Ise may have signaled the official transfer of the Sun cult from Mount Miwa to Ise.[14]

TWO MYTHOLOGICAL accounts present the flow of events framed by two separate worldviews. In the *Kojiki*, Amaterasu presides over the creation of the Japanese archipelago, and guarantees order both in heaven and on earth. If Amaterasu is not manifest, as when she hides in a cave, chaos erupts in the Central Heavenly Plain (Takamanohara) as well as in the Central Land of the Reed Plains.[15] In the *Nihon shoki*, Amaterasu is simply placed in the sky as the Sun without the attributes of ruling mana.[16] The *Kojiki* foregrounds Amaterasu as the progenitrix of the royal line, and portrays her occasionally as a warrior, armed to the teeth.[17] The *Nihon shoki* provides the only evidence of Amaterasu's female gender in an interchange with Susanoo, her trouble-making brother calling her "sister."[18] Also, according to the *Nihon shoki*, Amaterasu takes the role of servant weaver maid for a ritual garment, possibly Takamimusuhi's, while in the *Kojiki* Amaterasu charges others with the task.[19] In the *Kojiki*, Amaterasu represents the strong, warrior ruler, in great contrast to the *Nihon shoki*, which portrays a female, subordinate Amaterasu, creating the impression that, in some respects, the *Nihon shoki* is an anti-*Kojiki* work regarding Amaterasu's status and role.

Izanagi and Izanami present another case of diverging roles in these two narratives. In the *Kojiki*, the creative (*musu*) energy of Takamimusuhi and Kamumusuhi infuse Izanagi and Izanami with the sexual power to bring the world into being, a task that, however, is left incomplete after Izanami dies.[20] Ōkuninushi eventually finishes the task, and passes the land on to Ninigi, the grandson of Amaterasu and Takamimusuhi.[21] In the *Nihon shoki*, however, Izanagi and Izanami receive no orders, and proceed all on their own. Although their names are mentioned at the beginning, the creation of the world flows in a natural unfolding, a consequence of the *Nihon shoki*'s authors identifying these two *kami* with the female and male cosmic forces of yin and yang from Chinese cosmology. The creation comes to a smooth completion (Izanami does not die in this account) and without the direction or protection from *kami* in the Central Heavenly Plain, as told in the *Kojiki*.[22] There is even no Central Heavenly Plain in the *Nihon shoki*, only a Heaven.[23] The *Kojiki*'s Amaterasu is a transparent double of the female *tennō* Jitō whose second posthumous title includes a reference to Takamanohara, Amaterasu's realm: Takamanohara hirono no hime (Princess High-Heaven-Plain).[24]

The *Kojiki*'s second chapter begins with Jinmu, the first human albeit mythological ruler and great-grandson of Ninigi, the grandson of Amaterasu and Takamimusuhi. The scene has irreversibly shifted to earth. The Central Heavenly Plain, not mentioned, remains the guarantor of Jinmu's task of building not a *kuni*, a country or land, but a *tenka*, a "realm under Heaven": in other words, Tenmu's story. Jinmu ponders "Where [would it be best] to dwell in order to carry on the government of the kingdom (*tenka*) peacefully?"[25] —words that could have been scripted for Tenmu when, following his victory, Tenji's and Prince Ōtomo's royal residence in Ōtsu had turned into smoldering ashes, and he was about to establish his palace (Kiyomihara) and eventually a capital (Fujiwara-kyō) elsewhere.

The line of rulers following Jinmu is anchored in origins that are the essence of a mythology with two ideologies, one centered on divine creative energy and the guarantee of *musu*, the other in cosmogonic forces of yin and yang. This dual mythology was not woven into a singular narrative until much later, in the Heian period, mainly through a series of exegetical court lectures on the mythological opening chapters of the *Nihon shoki*. This aroused interest in and the composition of a third, unified mythology not found as such in either the *Kojiki* or *Nihon shoki*.[26] Kōnoshi's close textual reading of each text as a separate, self-contained, structured unit has enabled him to substitute a complex, plural origin for a single one. His rigorous hermeneutics, however, keeps him from venturing beyond the texts, out of what he calls a refusal "to read what one wants to read in them."[27]

Nevertheless, the question remains: why two different stories? Kōnoshi's answer stays within discourse analysis by falling back on style (and psychology). For Kōnoshi, the *Kojiki* is closer to the spoken language of the time than the more sinicized, official language of the *Nihon shoki* possibly because it preserved a Yamato self-identity during a time of massive cultural change. This explanation, however, addresses the question of the difference of the medium, hardly that of the message.[28]

Mizubayashi Takeshi dispenses with the difference in style between the two works in a summary and bold way. The *Nihon shoki* was written in the official logographic "Chinese style" (*kanbuntai*), as was the *Kojiki*'s Preface. In the body of the *Kojiki* text, graphs were used not only semantically, to signify the meaning attached to them originally as in the Chinese script, but also in a "modified" way (*hentai kanbuntai*), namely to express the spoken language of the Yamato capital area phonetically. To be more precise, the language of the *Kojiki*'s narrative parts is something artificial, falling between the Chinese of the *Nihon shoki* and the purely phonetically written songs (113 of them) that interlard the *Kojiki*'s text. This archaizing medium, Mizubayashi points out, led Motoori Norinaga and others after him into positing an indigenous culture of semantic and phonetic simplicity for which Chinese graphs were an ill-suited medium. By this ploy, the author of the *Kojiki* presented new ideas in the guise of the old and venerable, and thus with a semblance of the real and the authority of the past, "just like movie directors in an age of color movies resort to black and white film when they want to present something as old and belonging to a bygone era."[29] The question whether these two cosmologies had divergent political orientations, left open by Kōnoshi, has also been taken up by Mizubayashi, a legal historian, and not a student of literature.[30]

The *Kojiki*'s Story of Origins

The writing of the *Kojiki* and the compilation of a series of legal codes were parallel and interrelated developments. Tenmu's decision to "fix the record" and the order to produce the Kiyomihara Code were announced within three weeks of each other, early in the year 681. Eight years later, on 689/6/29, the Kiyomihara Code was promulgated, and a month later (8/2), a draft on *kami* matters was circulated (both in time to increase Jitō's credit as a ruler worthy of ascending the throne the first day of the first month of the following year).[31]

The legal codes of Kiyomihara, Taihō, and Yōrō, as well as the mytho-histories of the *Kojiki* and *Nihon shoki*, reflect back upon the new administrative state structure that Tenmu and Jitō had established.[32] These documents represent a view of their worldly realm in two avenues, the legal has-to-be and the legendary has-been, the latter a legitimizing exemplar for the former. The codes were patterned on the rationally organized Chinese codes of the Tang, and even earlier ones like the Northern Wei's.[33] The mytho-histories of both the *Kojiki* and *Nihon shoki* present a meandering and complex but nevertheless structured narrative of *kami* (281) and Yamato rulers (33).[34]

Indeed, it is the structured character that makes myths have sense. The way to the meaning in myths leads through structure: the individual episodes, when combined, say something else and more than what they convey separately or simply juxtaposed. Multiple correspondences are established through a narrative, which the structure unifies. Thus the first step, rather than looking for meanings, should be to find structure.[35]

The three chapters of the *Kojiki*, a rather short work, present the establishment of rule in the archipelago in three phases, a process that in important ways reflects and refracts the building of *ritsuryō* state authority and the establishment of a *tenka* ruled by a *tennō* during the late seventh and early eighth centuries.[36] The opening chapter is devoted to the birth and activities of the *kami*, first in the Plain of High Heaven, then in the archipelago after its creation as the Central Land of the Reed Plains, and to the decision of the *kami* to send one of their own down to pacify the land and establish a ruler. After several failed attempts, Ōkuninushi completes the process and hands over the land to an emissary from Amaterasu, who feels that the time is ripe to send Ninigi down. Amaterasu's first choice had been her son, Ame no oshiho mimi, magically produced through a gift exchange with her brother Susanoo. Instead, her grandson Ninigi (son of Ame no oshiho mimi and Takamimusuhi's daughter) descends, Ninigi's great-grandson becoming the first ruler, Jinmu, human with a divine pedigree (see figure 5).

One may wonder why it took so many generations to reach the royal lineal founder, Jinmu: three generations removed from Ninigi, five from Amaterasu. This generational sequence, however, must have presented less of a puzzle for the nobility of the time, for it held a mirror to events at the court: Ninigi had a great-grandson Jinmu, and so had Tenmu, the future Emperor Shōmu, born in 701. Twenty-two years before the *Kojiki*, in 689, a ruler's descent from heaven had been sung about on a very public occasion, in a lament (*banka*) for Crown Prince Kusakabe, Tenmu's anticipated successor, who died that year, during Jitō's regency. The reference, however, was not to Jinmu, but to Tenmu:[37]

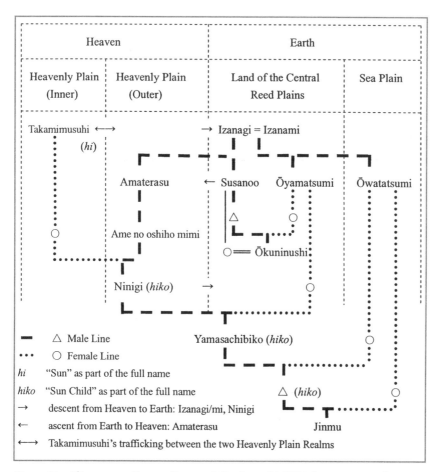

Fig. 5. *Kami* lineages to Jinmu. Source: Mizubayashi, *Kiki shinwa*, p. 247, fig. 18a, modified.

> Him who was sent down
> In godly descent to earth:
> The High-Illumining
> Sun Prince,
> At his palace in Asuka,   *Tobu tori no* [Asuka]
> Kiyomi of the Flying Bird   *Kiyomi no miya ni* [Kiyomihara]
> He established firm his reign.
> In all his godhead

Had Kusakabe succeeded and been alive in 711 when the *Kojiki* was finished, Jinmu would probably have been Ninigi's son.

A number of other mythological episodes can be historically reframed (reversing the actual signifying process). Amaterasu's first choice, her son Ame no oshiho mimi, to put someone in charge of the land did not work out, but she recovered the position with her grandson, Ninigi, in a clearly recognizable parallel with Jitō, who, after her son Kusakabe failed to gain the throne, held on to power with grandson Monmu.[38]

The second chapter of the *Kojiki* reports the establishment of *tenka* through the efforts of fifteen rulers, from Jinmu to Ōjin. The term *tenka* appears for the first time in the chapter's opening line when Jinmu ponders where to establish a capital from where to rule the *tenka*, literally meaning "[all] under Heaven." *Tenka* was not yet a generic term meaning "realm" when it was adopted from Chinese use. Rather, *tenka* was the name of a specific and unique polity, an empire that included satellite, tribute-paying border kingdoms. It was a political term of rulership. Of the ninety times that it is used in the *Kojiki*, it appears seventy-seven times in the phrase "governing the *tenka*."[39]

Through conquest, Jinmu, his descendants, and the hero Yamato Takeru claimed all of the territory entrusted to them, including "barbarians." Queen-regent Jingū's military expedition further extended it on the continent by forcing the "kingdoms of Silla and Paekche" into a tributary relationship.[40] The story is found in both the *Kojiki* and the *Nihon shoki*, with a slight difference. The *Kojiki* treats the two kingdoms as "natural" extensions of Yamato by giving Jingū a royal Silla ancestry through her mother. In the *Nihon shoki*, the kingdoms express their "vassal" status of dependency by referring to Yamato with the honorific appellation Nihon.[41] China, the actual model for *tenka*, is never mentioned in the *Kojiki*, and hardly in the *Nihon shoki*,[42] possibly because there was only one *tenka* under the sky. On the other hand, Kaya, an ancient and important trading partner for Yamato and the subject polity of the narrator's mainly imaginary *tenka* in the peninsula, is mentioned 215 times.[43]

YAMATO'S *TENKA* existed predominantly in the minds of Yamato rulers, a political imaginary with only a fleeting foundation in reality. After the collapse of the Eastern Han, upstart emperors sought to enhance their legitimacy by conferring titles of rulership to kings on outlying border areas, buying their alliances with gifts. Although theoretically vassals to a Chinese emperor, and as such enhancing their own status and protection against their own subjects and rival neighbors, petty rulers often actively requested official affirmation of titles (civil, military, or both) after having bestowed them upon themselves and some of their subjects.[44] The reception of such titles signaled that their holders had joined the Chinese empire as "outer subjects" of the Son of Heaven, a sovereign–vassal relationship beneficial to both parties.

Rulers in Yamato also actively sought such consecration of their authority for domestic consumption, beginning with Himiko (238) for several decades, and again more intensely throughout the fifth century, when a Yamato kingdom was taking shape, especially with Yūryaku (456–479). He coveted titles to legitimize military interference in Paekche — a request denied several times by China.[45] According to the *Nihon shoki*, Yamato established a tribute relationship with the southern peninsular states of Paekche, Kaya, and Silla, a relationship that, however, did not involve investiture or the granting of titles. Needless to say, Korean scholars reject this "history" as pure fabrication, and for good reason, it seems.

When the Yamato court established relationships with the newly unified China (first the Sui, then the Tang dynasty) in the early seventh century, the Yamato great kings did not seek titles any longer. With no domestic rivals other than the northern Emishi clans, they may have had no further need for the borrowed authority from China.[46] The official correspondence taken to Sui China by a delegation from Suiko in 600, the first one in over a century, abandoned the reference to her as "King of Yamato," which Chinese protocol would have required since it held the connotation of "border land vassal king." Instead, the term *Ōkimi ametarashi hiko* was used, which reads phonetically in Japanese as "Great King, Son Coming from Heaven," something the Chinese officials would have objected to if they had not read the phrase as Suiko's personal name.[47] The next delegation, in 607, conveying wishes from "The Son of Heaven of the land where the sun rises to the Son of Heaven of the land where the sun sets," took the stance of peer equality, causing a diplomatic row. Eventually, the Yamato court agreed to abide by Chinese protocol, accepting, for the time being, China-centered diplomatic language, yet without investiture.

THE AMBITION FOR the title and status of heavenly ruler was domestically pursued nevertheless, as witnessed by Tenmu's adoption of the *tennō* title toward the end of the century, as well as the idea of a *tenka*, a world-class realm having subservient vassal states. *Tenka* had already been used to signal domestic rule as early as the fifth century,[48] but Tenji took advantage of a unique opportunity to wield its symbolic power over Paekche, however briefly as it turned out.

After the Tang and Silla conquest of Paekche in 660, Tenji, still as Crown Prince Naka no Ōe, responded to a plea from a Paekche minister to return Prince P'ung, a refugee for several decades, who would lead a resistance movement against the Tang and restore the Paekche kingdom.[49] Tenji sent an escort of five thousand troops (661/9) after granting P'ung the highest court rank, essentially making him a Yamato subject. A year later (662/5), Tenji ordered the Yamato general in charge of the fleet at the walled town of Soryu (Aston: Sonyu) in Paekche to bestow upon the prince investiture as king of Paekche.[50] A kingdom near Yamato's borders was established, ruled by a king who was both Paekche royalty and a Yamato subject. For a very brief moment, no doubt of great importance for matters of political self-image, Yamato was a genuine *tenka* with a duly invested border king. It was only a fleeting moment, however, for in 663/8, a Yamato naval force with 27,500 troops was sunk, and with the resistance crushed, the hope of restoring Paekche was lost, but not the dream of a Yamato *tenka*.

The text of the *Kojiki* makes it clear that behind the process of state building, the *kami* were at work, especially Takamimusuhi but also Amaterasu. Takamimusuhi appears as a creation *kami* in the first lines of the *Kojiki*, immediately to "hide," like the initial dozen *kami*, in the wings of the Heavenly Plain. Most members of this backstage *kami* family are never heard of again. Takamimusuhi (High Generative-Force Deity) is one of the original trio of single *kami*; the other two are Ame no minakanushi (Central Lord of Heaven, never mentioned again), and Kamumusuhi (Divine Generative-Force Kami, who reappears once to produce seeds). Although single, both *musuhi kami* have offspring, as it turns out later.

Takamimusuhi functions as the ruler of the world of manifest *kami*, and he remains active, true to his name, as the vital energy of creation. When he comes out of hiding into the world of manifest *kami* at crucial moments, he enlists Amaterasu's assistance to summon *kami* each time a decision has to be made. The heavenly court, not unlike the Yamato court, relies on consensus among peers to send someone down to the Reed Plains, to scout the land, to pacify, rule, or help conquer it. Takamimusuhi provided Jinmu with a crow to guide him in the conquest of the east, and it is an oracle by Amaterasu that prompted Jingū to invade Silla.[51]

Succession events and lineages of rulers, the descendants of the *kami*, form the final chapter of the *Kojiki*.[52] The story is one of treason, murder, and bloodshed nonetheless, events that were part of known history as well. The Sun line of rulers prevails through perilous times, and the realm flourishes, as the great number of songs suggests (sixty, versus forty-three for the second chapter and ten for the first). All this travail is presented as the internal problems of a single dynasty, although historians believe that there were at least two breaks in the line of rulers. "Three dynastic regimes" rather than one royal line might more accurately reflect the early historical reality.[53] The Sendai *kuji hongi*, argued by one scholar to be a pre-*Kojiki* text — a thesis hard to prove or disprove — is structured also in a way that suggests three successive royal lineages, founded by Jinmu, Ōjin, and Keitai.[54]

The *Kojiki's* Model of/for a *Tenka*

The scholar Mizubayashi Takeshi has argued for a story in the *Kojiki* with a political message far more complex than the sacralization of the Sun clan. Since the *Kojiki* was produced for the ruling house and the court nobility, the version of sacred origins and the distribution of political power had to be made acceptable to powerful *uji*. In fact, the Sun line of Yamato rulers was not the only one to claim heavenly origins in the archipelago or even the peninsula. As early as the beginning of the fifth century already, as mentioned, Koguryŏ kings made legitimacy claims through reference to Heaven and the Sun.[55] In Yamato also, a number of important *uji* assumed *kami* founders, even *kami* from the hidden part of the Heavenly Plain, Takamimusuhi's realm. The Fujiwara *uji* and the Nakatomi house of ritualists, originally the same lineage, affirmed their descent from Kamumusuhi, the (probably female) counterpart of Takamimusuhi.[56] The Inbe ritualists and the Ōtomo clan of warriors and ritualists shared Takamimusuhi with the Sun line as their originating ancestor. These claims, it should be noted, were not always consistent; neither did they go uncontested. A sacred origin, even from the highest *kami* who ruled the most elevated sector of the Plain of High Heaven, the realm of the hidden *kami*, was by no means a monopoly of the Sun line. Besides her son, progenitor of the Sun line, Amaterasu had two other children with multiple offspring, consisting of nineteen *kuni no miyatsuko* (country chieftains).[57] Sharing sacredness of the highest order was built into the tale of origins, reflecting possibly centuries of intermarriage and suggesting a manner of shared governance of the land among peers. The lineal narrative was lateral as well.

The Plain of High Heaven where the *kami* dwell is not a uniform space. A division that is not mentioned as such in the *Kojiki* has an undeniable function in its narrative.[58] Namely, one must posit an Inner Plain of High Heaven, a place where the first seven single *kami* and four subsequent pairs of *kami* retire. The most important among them is Takamimusuhi. The myriad other *kami*, which follow the fifth pair, Izanagi and Izanami, dwell in an Outer Plain of High Heaven (see figure 5).

Izanagi and Izanami descend to an amorphous primordial world, which they bring into shape as the Central Land of Reed Plains, where they produce the multitude of creation filling the world. Most important are the two siblings, the Sun *kami* Amaterasu and the Moon *kami* Susanoo. Amaterasu, born on earth, ascends to the Outer Plain of High Heaven and takes her place there as ruler under the guidance of Takamimusuhi, who directs her from the Inner Plain of High Heaven and occasionally appears in the Outer Plain. This inaugurates a progressive structure of intertwining dependencies that inform the creation of the cosmos, the formation of the earth, and the establishment of a *tenka* ruled by a *tennō*, guided by unseen but everpresent *kami*.

This structure of interdependencies follows a logical course. The first interdependency consists of the Earth complementing Heaven, an arrangement ordered and directed from the Inner Plain of High Heaven. The Earth produces the ruler for the Outer Plain of High Heaven, Amaterasu, who provides light for the Earth, her birthplace, and for her abode, Heaven. Eventually the *kami* traffic between Heaven and Earth stops, and the two realms are closed off from each other. The second interdependency links the land and the sea. The land produces the ruler of the sea, and the sea provides water for the earth; then, access to the sea world of *kami* ceases.[59] Lastly, the Land amidst the Reed Plains is dependent on the Land of the Dead (Yomi no kuni), which controls death in the Reed Plains but also renews life, since an alternate name for this realm is Land of Firm Roots (Ne no katasu kuni). Access to this world also comes to an end.[60] Thus the Land amidst the Reed Plains receives the life force (whereby things grow) from Ne no katasu kuni, water from the Sea Plain, and the sun from the Plain of High Heaven, behind all of which is at work the generative energy of Takamimusuhi.

This interdependency of the various realms contrasts sharply with other interpretations (including Kōnoshi's),[61] which lay out a transcendental position for the Plain of the High Heaven in general and for Amaterasu as its ruler in particular. This vision does not take into account that Amaterasu came from Earth and functioned in Heaven as Takamimusuhi's right hand. The ontological interdependency, however, establishes a peer relationship, more lateral, horizontal, or "equal" — parts complementing each other — than vertical and transcendental. Furthermore, the interdependency structures the acquisition of the necessary magic and power to rule, as well as alliances between Heaven and Earth, linked through important marriages. The two phenomena are related; here, again, the dependency of Heaven upon Earth may be surprising.

Takamimusuhi left very few progeny, a daughter who married Amaterasu's son and, most important, Omohikane. This *kami* thinks (*omoi*) for the gods when they gather in council each time one has to be sent to the land below, and he accompanies Ninigi down to the Central Land of the Reed Plains. He is Heaven's counterpart to the counselor behind those in charge, a relationship that develops at the Yamato court between Fujiwara Fuhito and the first *tennō*, from Tenmu to Genshō. Izanagi and Izanami, the first couple of the Outer Plain of High Heaven, descends to the Central Land of the Reed Plains where, sexually, magically, and ritually they create the world and beget Amaterasu, Susanoo, and Ōyamatsumi.

The marriages between *kami* of the three realms create occasions for stealing magical power for the Heavenly Grandchild, and once secured, the realms are closed off from each other. Offspring of Susanoo (a sixth-generation descendant or, according to a *Nihon shoki* variant, his son) and Ōyamatsumi (the *kami* of the mountains) produced Ōkuninushi, who, through a number of trials, becomes the land's final pacifier, a task that is facilitated when his eighty brothers cede their lands to him.[62] Through his wife, a daughter of Susanoo, Ōkuninushi steals Susanoo's three magical treasures: his sword of life, his bow and arrow of life, and his heavenly speaking *koto* musical instrument.[63] Eventually, Ōkuninushi hands the land over to Ninigi, himself the result of a union between *kami* from both parts of the Heavenly Plain and married to another daughter of the *kami* of the mountains, producing Yamasachibiko, the mountain hunter (see figure 5).

Yamasachibiko travels to the sea palace of Ōwatatsumi, whose daughter he marries.[64] Through her, he receives water and acquires the magical power of its control. Jinmu, his grandson, also marries a daughter of the ruler of the sea. The Heavenly Plain and the Central Reed Plains are thus linked through two marriages, as are the Central Reed Plains and the Sea Plain (Jinmu and his grandfather). The magical powers over life and water have been acquired. Everything is ready for Jinmu to establish his *tenka*. With the marvelous secured, the political could be taken on.

Jinmu's ancestors, going back to Takamimusu*hi*, form a Sun (*hi*) line, as the signifier *hi-ko* (sun child) in their long names indicates (see figure 5 and table 1). Jinmu, the first human founder of the dynasty has "divine Yamato" in his official name. "Yamato" appears in the names of a number of rulers, while *kami* ancestry was emphasized through the fourteenth ruler, Chūai, as well as in the names of later principal consorts, indicators of double royalty (see figure 3). A new element, signifying earth, *neko* (root child) was added to *hiko* for rulers seven through nine, paralleling its presence in the posthumous titles of rulers Jitō through Genshō (see table 1).[65] The

Changes in symbolic signifiers within rulers' names in the *Kojiki*

Hiko (sun child) is used for Jinmu's ancestral *kami* and earthly rulers from the *kami* Ninigi to the ruler Chūai (no. 14), with other prefixes added occasionally: *amatsu-* (heavenly young man/sun child): Ninigi to Jinmu's predecessor; *Yamato-* (Yamato sun child): Jinmu and his next five successors (nos. 2 to 6); *Yamato neko-* (Yamato root child sun child) for the next three (nos. 7 to 9).

Marriages of all *kami* after Ninigi and rulers down to number 7 were "exogamous" to female *kami* of the soil ("earth") or the sea (see figure 5 for Ninigi to Jinmu), or to women from local magnates of the soil ("root child"), or from founders of their clans. Marriages of rulers 8 and 9 were to *kami* from the Heavenly Plain.

Hi (sun) is present in names of consorts of rulers Chūai to Jomei (270–641); see figure 3, numbers 15–34. With very few exceptions, all principal consorts of male rulers had a *hi* component in their official names, sometimes with the sun character as the phonetic sign for the *hi* of *hime* (princess); Jomei's consort name follows this pattern in the *Nihongi*. Consorts were seen as carriers of the Sun-line charisma after a son became ruler. Their names must be a fabrication of the sixth or seventh centuries. A number of consorts whose offspring did not continue the Sun line had no *hi* component in their names, for instance, the consorts of Ankan, Yōmei, and Sushun.

Source: Based on Mizubayashi, *Kiki shinwa*, 248, fig. 18b; and idem, "Ritsuryō tennōsei no shinwateki kosumoroji," 20–26, modified.

names sketch the progression of alliances. Prior to Jinmu, the domestication of nature and control over the land are secured through marriages between the Sun line and *kami* from different realms. About Jinmu's first half-dozen ruler successors, the only thing known is their marriage alliances with daughters of local *kami* or ancestral *kami* of local strongmen. In the mythology, through their wives, Yamato's first rulers solidified their power.

For Mizubayashi, this development demonstrates that in the *Kojiki* model of the polity, local rulers contracted a share of power through marriage alliances linked to a ruler whom they further acknowledged by "hand-ing over the land."[66] As mentioned, the *Kojiki* establishes genealogical links to the ruling house for far more lineages than the *Nihon shoki* does (176 versus 40). Tenmu's victory in the Jinshin War was due to the military assistance he received from *uji* outside the Yamato region, who were "rooted in the local soil" (*neko*).[67] Through a modified ranking system, by making it reach beyond the Yamato central area, Tenmu incorporated them into his new state structure.

Jitō and her immediate successors, Monmu, Genmei, and Genshō — three women and a very young ruler — were given posthumous names having the component *neko*, possibly indicating support from local power holders, which they needed and received. *Tennō*, however, signaled a rulership from above, rooted in Heaven, Tenmu's idea. Thus the *Kojiki* supplemented this notion of supremacy with a message that a *tenka* is established through interdependencies between Heaven and Earth and between ruler and *uji*, a dimension that is also strikingly different from the Korean myth of heavenly ancestry of their ruler Tan'gun.[68] The *Nihon shoki*, however, deemphasized the *Kojiki* model. By the time it was compiled, in 720, the transition from Tenmu to an adult male *tennō* seemed secure. Prince Obito was nineteen then, had been crown prince for several years, and was to assume the throne four years later, hopefully as a strong *tennō*.

Major contributions to the Yamato political culture were made by *kikajin*, a term borrowed from China referring to uncivilized *jin* (people), who are beyond *ka* (civilization), but can *ki* (come home when becoming part of the realm). Its referents were modified to signify Yamato's relation to its internal "others," or allochthons (people "generated in a different soil") in contradistinction to autochthons (sprung from the ground they inhabit), terms I prefer to "aliens," "immigrants," or "non-Japanese," which all strongly imply a modern nation and state apparatus.[69] As Michael Como has clearly documented, many allochthon transplants and their descendants had a virtual monopoly on continental knowledge and technology, and their understanding of the way rulership could be represented and sacralized in pre-Nara Yamato made many of them important advisers (*sakashihito*) at the court. The *Nihon shoki* displays them in this capacity, as advisers to several of Yamato's mythological or historical "sage kings."[70] These allochthon *uji* such as the Kusakabe, Abe, and Hata clans also entered into important marital relationships with the ruling house. Comparable to the political and military power of local strongmen, some of whom were allochthons, their skills in governance and technology became indispensable for the consolidation of the ruling house. The trope of "interdependency" in the mythological narrative of the *Kojiki* (Mizubayashi), along with the supportive and sacralizing role in the *Nihon shoki* (Como) may represent their relationship to rulership in these two texts.

Universal Rulers

Two changes took place in the representation of royal authority in the mid-seventh century, decades before the *Kojiki* was written. For one, the shape of four of the royal tombs was modified, and second, the posthumous names of four important rulers made reference to Heaven (*ten, ame*), namely Tenji, Tenmu, and their two predecessors Kōtoku and Saimei (table 1), culminating in Tenmu's title heavenly ruler (*tennō*). Both modifications express the idea of universal rule.

The emerging Yamato court of the fifth century had displayed the power and status of their great kings by their sheer ability to mobilize and fund master craftsmen and the labor force necessary to build monumental tumuli (*kofun*). It is estimated that construction of some of these royal keyhole-shaped mounds required the equivalent of a thousand laborers a day for four years.[71] Toward the end of the sixth century, the keyhole layout was being replaced by large round tumuli. Size, however, was no longer the distinguishing marker for royal tombs, since *uji* leaders were being consecrated in similarly impressive mounds. Octagonal tombs, covered with round earthen mounds, were the royal solution in this competition for posthumous distinction: Saimei, Tenji, Tenmu, and Jitō were all buried in the new type of octagonal tomb, which was reserved solely for Yamato's supreme rulers.[72]

Traditionally, Japanese historians have interpreted the octagonal shape as a sign of the influence of Buddhism, the prime example being the famous Yumedono chapel of the Hōryūji, a temple built in the early eighth century and long admired for its architectural combination of the octagonal and round shapes.[73] More likely, however, Buddhism and the royal tombs both turned to the same font of symbols to express universal stewardship. Octagonal tombs were built for only four rulers.[74] The abrupt appearance of these radically different mausoleums projected the sudden interest of these four sovereigns for the power of Chinese symbols of political culture.

The Tang reconstitution of the empire in China revitalized the deployment of symbolism to express sovereignty. A Tang edict of 652 refers to the octagonal shape of the upper platform of the Mingtang (Sacred Halls), allegedly created by Emperor Wu of the Former Han, for the emperor to preside over important cosmic ceremonies.[75] The Yamato mission of 665 to the

Table 1. Patterns in symbolic signifiers within posthumous names of rulers

Suffix in name	Meaning	Ruler
hiro kunioshi	wide land ruler	Ankan (535)
hiro kunioshi	wide land ruler	Senka (539)
ame kunioshi	heaven land ruler	Kinmei (571)
hi, hime	sun, princess	Suiko (628)
tarashihi	suffice, sun	Jomei (641)
ame, hi	heaven, sun	Kōtoku (654)
ame, hi	heaven, sun	Saimei (661)
ame	heaven	Tenji (671)
ame	heaven	Tenmu (686)
neko	root child	Jitō (702)
neko	root child	Monmu (707)
neko	root child	Genmei (721)
neko	root child	Genshō (748)
ame	heaven	Shōmu (756)
ame	heaven	Kōnin (781)
neko	root child	Kanmu (804)
neko	root child	Heisei (824)
neko	root child	Junna (840)

Suffixes are components of elaborate posthumous names for deceased rulers, a custom possibly started under Jitō. Rulers are listed in the order they died, with the year of death given in parentheses. Two-syllable Chinese-style names for rulers by which they are referred to today were introduced in the mid-eighth century. There are some breaks in the sequence because rulers who reascended the throne have only one posthumous name, and only clusters of suffixes are listed.

Source: Adapted from Mizubayashi, *Kiki shinwa*, 302–303, fig. 25.

Tang may have been in time to witness the very theatrical and rare imperial ceremonies at Mount Tai (Taishan), performed on an octagonal platform the following year.[76] Reports of this event by the returned embassy may even have inspired Tenji and especially Tenmu and Jitō to devise political rituals. The octagonal shape symbolized the eight directions, which, in turn, signified universal rule over the polity. Another contemporary Chinese ruler, Empress Wu, built a version of the Mingtang in 695, and erected an octagonal cast-iron pillar 105 feet high to celebrate her short-lived restoration of the Zhou dynasty.[77] She is credited with the creation of a new graph for *guo* (country), written with the two graphs for "eight directions" within a square enclosure 圀.[78]

The association of the magic number eight with universal political stewardship was sufficiently well known to Yamato literati who employed it in official poetry to celebrate lords and rulers. Some twenty *Manyōshū* poems use the pillow phrase *yasumishishi*, meaning "who rules the eight corners in all tranquility," for *waga ōkimi* (our great lord). [79]

The Taika Reform edict of 646 (3/22), in seeking to regulate symbols of social and political distinction, legislated in minute detail the size of tombs and the kinds of material goods that could accompany the dead, all of it calibrated to the rank and status of the deceased. Only four years earlier, Soga Emishi's preparation of "outrageously" large tombs for himself and his son (using illegally conscripted labor) and performance of an eight-row dance were interpreted as transgressions revealing intentions of usurping the throne.[80] Graded distanciation through levels of distinction were stressed further during Jitō's rule to ensure the supreme status of the ruling house above all other *uji*. Eighteen noble families were ordered to submit their house records of family tombs (691/8/10), undoubtedly with sumptuary regulations in mind. Royal tombs were awarded the honor of being assigned service households as guards (691/10/8).[81]

After the end of the seventh century, no more tumuli for *uji* leaders or octagonal tombs for rulers were built. Jitō's ashes were deposited next to Tenmu's remains in the tomb she had built for him; hers was the first documented cremation in the archipelago. The tumuli's disappearance and the adoption of cremation resulted in the quick discontinuation of the long wakes (*mogari*) during which succession matters were settled. This, in turn, created a need for swifter transitions of power.

The second modification during the mid-seventh century is the appearance of *ten* in postmortem royal names and, starting with Tenmu, in the title of *tennō*. In Japanese, *ten* is read *ame*, or *ama* as in *Amaterasu*. Since Takamimusuhi is the *kami* to whom the rulers of the Sun line trace their origin, and whose presence and authority prevailed over those of Amaterasu (in the *Kojiki*'s cosmogony), scholars think that rituals were originally directed to the sun, rather than to Amaterasu. They now believe that worship of Amaterasu by the Yamato ruling house may not go back further than the late seventh century, when *ama* was given prominence in the great king's posthumous names (see table 1).[82]

Amaterasu emerges in the *Nihon shoki* twice during Tenmu's reign, once when Tenmu performed a ritual "toward Ise" and a second time when he renewed the practice of sending a virgin princess to reside at the shrine (673/4/14). The last time Amaterasu had been mentioned was some five centuries and more than twenty-five reigns earlier. Nevertheless, for the dozens of rites and ceremonies performed on numerous occasions during

Tenmu's reign, Ise or Amaterasu are not among them. Neither does the shrine seem to have been singled out as special by Jitō's reign. On one occasion (on 692/5/26) offerings were sent to four shrines, Ise among them, but without being singled out as special. Starting on 698/12/29, during Monmu's reign, however, the tradition of referring to Ise as the Great Shrine of Ise took hold.

The Chinese conflation of cosmology and rulership is lit from within through Daoist significations such as *ten* (= *ama, ame*), *tenka, tennō*. Ancient concepts embodied through Daoist symbolics occupied and naturalized political emblems, and bestowed the very meaning of rulership itself. It is not clear, however, to what degree the Daoist signifieds of these signs were still perceived as such in China, a fortiori in Japan. Nevertheless, it has become increasingly accepted that Daoist elements were privileged and used by Tenmu and the compilers of the *Kojiki* and the *Nihon shoki*. This suggests that, before the institutionalization of court ritual as regulated in the Taihō Code of 701, and before the creation of mythological exemplars in the *Kojiki* (712) and the *Nihon shoki* (720), Daoist elements were present, presumably understood, and put to use during the formative decades of the *ritsuryō* state.

The sequence of the posthumous titles of four rulers, Kōtoku, Saimei, Tenji, and Tenmu (645–686), are styled by reference to *ten* (Heaven), followed by *neko* for the next four: Jitō, Monmu, Genmei, and Genshō (686–724) (see table 1). *Ten* carries the light of the transcendental, Heaven, a quality of rulership thought by these rulers and their successors to best represent their reigns. *Neko* suggests the Earth, Heaven's companion and sustainer of life. Posthumous titles reflected perceptions not just of how a sovereign governed, but also, and probably more so, of the quality through which she or he was remembered.[83]

The posthumous titles bestowed on Jitō and Monmu (on 703/12/17 and 707/11/12 respectively) were subsequently changed. We know this from Jitō's modified title heading the last chapter of the *Nihon shoki*, and for Monmu from the first line of the *Shoku Nihongi*.[84] It appears that the *neko* component was removed some time before 720, the year the *Nihon shoki* was finished, and replaced by references to Heaven for Jitō, "Takamanohara" hirono no hime (Princess [or Daughter of the Sun] of the Wide Field of the "High Heavenly Plain"), and for Monmu, "Amenomamune" toyo ōji no sumera mikoto (Heavenly Ruler with Venerable Ancestry of the "Real Lineage of Heaven"). Possibly, *neko* came to be considered inappropriate for the authority of *tennō*.[85] The reason may have been Prince Obito's position around that time. The change probably was made after the prince became crown prince in 714. A new Law Code, the Yōrō Ritsuryō, was also being drafted, starting in 718, no doubt in anticipation of his rule.

This prince's status needed shoring up. Although his official appointment as successor was a dream of Jitō come true, it constituted an abomination for those who were offended by a breach in the practice of double royal ancestry for principal consorts-mothers of *tennō*. Prince Obito's mother, a Fujiwara, was not of royal stock. The issue of succession became a political tug-of-war between the factional alliance of (Jitō)-Genmei-Shōmu and a cohort of princes of the blood like Toneri and Nagaya. The *neko* faction, as expressed in the *Kojiki*, would have been connected with powerful local *uji*, some of which must have been Tenmu's allies during the Jinshin War, and from beyond the Yamato region, while the *ten* party may have sought to strengthen Shōmu's position, without necessarily supporting the Fujiwara's marriage politics.[86]

Mythemes of another kind were introduced later. The last two *tennō* of the Tenmu dynasty, Shōmu and his daughter Kōken,[87] used Buddhist imagery to symbolize their authority as "servants of the Buddha." When Kanmu, by far the most forceful ruler of the eighth century, who solidified the Tenji line, sought stronger symbols of authority just as Tenmu had done, he also turned to Heaven by introducing Chinese-style ceremonies to Heaven. Moreover, he jettisoned *akitsukami* ("*kami*-in-the-present" or "manifest *kami*"), which disappeared from imperial edicts. The *Kojiki* was being abandoned as an authoritative political text and replaced with a reinterpreted *Nihon shoki*, a development that paralleled the increased sacrality and distant character of imperial authority.[88] By the mid-ninth century, yin-yang masters had gained great visibility at the new capital Heian, insinuating themselves into the court by multiplying rites and purification ceremonies; the Ise *kami* ritual was elaborated considerably; new Buddhist sects provided the court with their own yearly round of complex rituals. The symbolic bricolage with ever new mythemes and the multiplication of sacralizing modalities did not let up.

3 ALIBIS

In a eulogy, Chitoko Takima no Mahito recited the succession to the throne of the imperial ancestors. Following this ritual, formerly called the Sun succession, Tenmu was buried in the Ōchino Royal Tomb.
—688/11/11. *Nihon shoki*

Great Kagu Mountain:
    At the sunrise-facing great eastern palace gate,
    A spring mountain stands luxuriantly dense;
Unebi, that lush mountain:
    At the sunset-facing great western palace gate,
    A lush mountain rises mountain-perfect;
Miminashi, green-sedge mountain,
    At the back-facing great northern palace gate
    In full splendor stands in godliness;
The Yoshino mountains, lovely in their name,
    From the sun-facing southern palace gate
    Lie far off in the cloudland of the sky.
—Anonymous poem on Fujiwara-kyō
    from Jitō's reign. *Manyōshū*

Tenmu, Yamato's last great king and Nihon's first *tennō*, is portrayed in the *Nihon shoki* as an extraordinary military strategist, institution builder, and ruler: powerful, charismatic, and numinous. Prince Toneri, the final editor of the work, allotted to Tenmu and his consort Jitō more attention (15 percent of the total volume) than given to any of the thirty-nine other rulers chronicled. Eight years earlier, the *Kojiki's* Preface had already celebrated Tenmu's Jinshin victory in panegyric, epic, and even cosmic terms.[1] The *Manyōshū*, ancient Japan's earliest monumental compilation of poetry, was finalized by Ōtomo Yakamochi (718–785), grandson of the leader of the Ōtomo forces, Tenmu's allies during the Jinshin War.[2] It offers the earliest representation of a Yamato ruler as *kami*-in-the-present in a poem about Tenmu, composed while he was still alive. These texts, the oldest extant compositions of history, mythology, and lyrics, date from the time of Tenmu and Jitō, and they are about them as well, in direct or oblique ways.

Yet we are left in the dark regarding the year this celebrated figure was born, or his age when he died, routine entries for all historical rulers in the *Nihon shoki*.[3] On the other hand, equally unusual is the absence in the *Nihon shoki* of Tenji's wake and burial. For at least three decades, Tenji was denied the honors befitting a Yamato great king. The *Shoku Nihongi*, completed in 797, a century after the *Nihon shoki*, tells us that Jitō had a tumulus built for Tenji toward the end of her life. Until then, Tenji's place in history had been usurped by Tenmu's achievements in war and peace and by the image constructed around him.[4] What ancient records and poems tell us or are silent about and the images portrayed therein are closely related. They feed each other: images halo achievements, which in turn shape memorialization. Tenmu came to possess power he seized by force, the highest one in the land, which is represented as if power, the highest one in the cosmos, had come to possess him — ruling power's perfect alibi, providing its holder an alternate identity wherein to hide.

From the Margin to a New Center

We encounter Tenmu first as crown prince. He is referred to as such in the *Nihon shoki* (inconsistently) and also in a Fujiwara Nakamaro house history (*Tōshi kaden*) of his *uji*, written in 760–762. Nakamaro suggests that considerable tension marked the relationship between the two brothers, if one may extrapolate from one important incident. At Tenji's coronation banquet in 668, a possibly tipsy, probably jealous younger brother ("crown prince" in the text) threatened the new great king by plunging a long spear into the floorboards right in front of him.[5] Startled, Tenji reached for his sword, but Fujiwara Kamatari prevented him from striking down the crown prince. This anecdote casts Nakamaro's great-grandfather in the Fujiwara's role (by the 760s paradigmatic) of protector of the crown and throws an unflattering light on Tenmu's uprising five years later as one rooted in personal ambition.[6]

Next we meet Tenmu as rebel. When in 671, the last year of his life, Tenji appointed his son Prince Ōtomo to the position of *daijōdaijin* (prime minister),[7] he sparked the succession issue that triggered Tenmu's uprising. Tenmu left the court, retreated to the Yoshino Mountains, and from there launched his military campaign against Prince Ōtomo in the middle of the following year. Emerging victorious and with Tenji's royal quarters in Ōmi destroyed, he built his own in Asuka. In hindsight, however, Tenmu was a transient in his own palace, for soon after he occupied it, he started planning Yamato's first capital, Fujiwara-kyō. Ultimately, he created a "realm" because he fashioned a center by mobilizing cosmic notions of centrality. Tenmu did not simply replace Tenji as the next great king. Presided over by a *tennō*, Tenmu's regime was of a different order.

After his victory, Tenmu incorporated local leaders from the Yamato provinces and beyond into a realm structured around him and a center that he conceived and Jitō eventually realized as Fujiwara-kyō. Historians have attributed Tenmu's victory to careful planning, swift action, and the support he rallied outside the Yamato basin proper from lords in Ise, Mino, Owari, and elsewhere, some as far away as the northeastern region along the Japan Sea. Most allochthon *uji* from the Aya and Hata warrior clans joined him.[8] Ōtomo's camp included Yamato magnates and several Paekche generals, asylum seekers following Tenji's failed attempt in 662 to restore the Paekche king after that Korean kingdom had been run over by the Tang and Silla.

Once in charge, Tenmu broke off official relations with the Tang (only to be resumed in 702). By 675, Unified Silla was in control of virtually the whole peninsula after driving out the Tang armies. Tenmu followed through with the state-strengthening efforts Tenji had launched in the context of these emerging powerful states by adopting continental models of statecraft with considerable help from Paekche refugees and through yearly contacts with Silla, a policy continued under Jitō and Monmu.[9] During the thirty-five-year rule of these three monarchs, a total of thirty-six embassies crossed the sea to or from Silla.[10]

Silla sought to prevent Yamato from an alliance with the Tang, and the Yamato court was eager to learn Chinese methods of governance and state building from Silla, which had demonstrated the effectiveness of the model by considerably tightening domestic rule and effectively reorganizing its military. In the face of Tang threats, Koguryŏ had already taken similar measures after a coup in 642 had brought Yŏn Kaesomun (?–665) to power as a military strongman. He was spectacularly successful in resisting the Tang armies for twenty-five years. Silla's own reforms had started with an adaptation of the Tang Code in 651, and scholars have argued that Tenmu and Jitō's Kiyomihara and Taihō codes were patterned not directly on the Tang Code, but on Silla's modified version. The committee of eighteen officials who drafted the Taihō Code, headed by Fujiwara Fuhito, included eight allochthons, several of whom had studied in Silla. Only the Yōrō Code, drafted between 718 and 722 with further modifications later on, was written with firsthand knowledge of Tang China to which effect, according to some historians, traces of Silla's modifications were removed.[11]

Tenmu recast royal family members (holding ranks two and three) as qualified for top positions, and relied on *uji* holding middle-rank positions in pre–Taika Reform times (*maetsukimi*) for filling posts reserved for holders of fourth and fifth rank. Many of the latter came from among his personal followers in the war and those of his sons, Princes Takechi and Ōtsu.[12] They were subjected to merit evaluation and organized in an expanded multitiered ranking system. The granting of titles drew allegiance from local elites in control of districts, including them in the prestige emanating from Tenmu's charisma as a victor in war. In return, an interdependency was cultivated, goods, women, and entertainers for the court being exchanged for degrees of distinction. This system functioned like a domestic variation of China's tribute system, resorting to a "liturgical" way of providing for the ruler's needs: Heaven in the person of a *tennō*, supported and nourished by men with their roots in the Earth (*neko*).

The focal point for this political liturgy was initially Tenmu's palace of Kiyomihara in Asuka. It was larger than any previous royal residence (approximately 150m by 200m), built immediately after his victory in 672 on the site where Jomei, Kōgyoku, and Saimei had previously established their residences. Kiyomihara was thus like previous royal palaces, except for its scale and the presence of a Daigokuden (Hall of State). Within four years, however, and possibly earlier, the idea emerged to develop something altogether different, an actual political center with officials positioned near the ruler. Jitō realized it some twenty years later, in 694, as Yamato's first palace-city, Aramashi no miyako, better known as Fujiwara-kyō. Using Chinese techniques and allochthon designers, it was positioned according to cosmic and geomantic coordinates and laid out with perpendicular avenues and streets and special residential wards for officials. Kiyomihara was, from the beginning, a temporary residence, to be replaced by a magically situated center, appropriate for a heavenly ruler.

The decision to proceed with a capital appears for the first time in the *Nihon shoki* on 676/11/23. Two visits to a possible site, one by Tenmu himself, took place in 682. On 684/2/28, Tenmu dispatched a committee that included a prince, a middle-rank official, judges, clerks, artisans, and yin-yang masters to various Home Provinces to determine by divination the optimum site. By the time Tenmu died in the fall of 686, the final decision had been reached. The building of the capital itself was delayed during the four years of Jitō's regency, but she visited the site several times from 690, when she became *tennō*. She moved into the new palace at Fujiwara-kyō in 694. One of the immediate effects was to impress the envoys from Silla, which also had built a new capital in 670. Their almost yearly embassies were talked about in Yamato as tribute missions. Starting sometime before 700,

Royal Residences and Capitals: Asuka to Heian: 600–800

Asuka, today a rural village with a population of about seven thousand, located toward the southern end of Yamato province in the valleys of the Yoshino mountain foothills, constitutes a small area, some three kilometers north-south and east-west. These green hills rise to a height of between 150 and 250 meters, while the Yoshino mountain chain ranges from 600 to 1,400 meters. This cul-de-sac, open to the north, is where the Yamato great kings, starting with Suiko, established their residences in various spots. Kōtoku is the first one to have left the area when in 651 he established his court for a few years in Naniwa, some forty kilometers to the northwest (in present-day Osaka). Tenji moved from Asuka in 667 some sixty kilometers north to Ōtsu on the southern tip of Lake Biwa. After his victory in 672, however, Tenmu returned to Asuka, where he erected his Kiyomihara royal quarters. Subsequently, genuine (Chinese-style) capitals were built, gradually farther north in the open plain: first Fujiwara-kyō, planned by Tenmu and finished by Jitō in 694, just outside Asuka proper; then Heijō-kyō or Nara (710–784 except for five years, 740–744, when Emperor Shōmu moved his court to Kuni), twenty kilometers to the north of Fujiwara-kyō. After Nara, it was Nagaoka, twenty kilometers farther north, for ten years (784–794), and finally Heian (795–1868), only five kilometers north, nestled against mountains that rise on three sides to a height of over 500 meters.

For details on the pre-Fujiwara-kyō royal residences, see Harris, *Sacred Texts*, 146–147.

Silla envoys lined up at the New Year ceremony outside the Daigokuden, together with Emishi and tribal leaders from the southern islands, as "outside subjects" of Yamato's *tenka*.

IN THE NEW REALM, wealth accumulated in two places, each with its own separate symbolic structure: the bureaucratic center, which controlled grants of land, labor, and goods attached to court rank and office, and the religious establishments of Buddhism (Fujiwara-kyō alone counted thirty-three temples), with power over supernatural forces. Buddhism held great value for rulers because it claimed access to protective and preventive powers against natural calamities, illnesses, and wrathful *kami* through

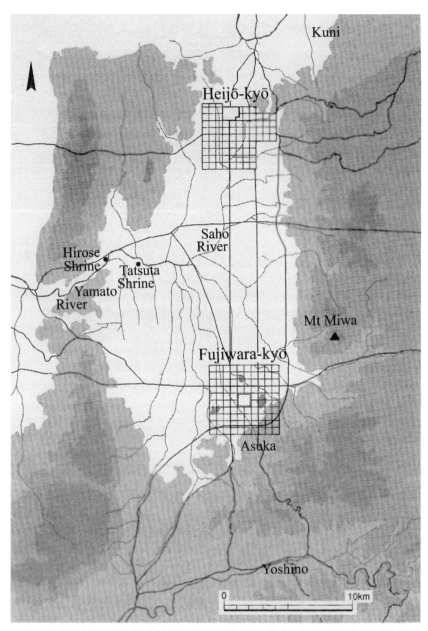

Fig. 6. Yamato basin with Fujiwara-kyō and Heijō-kyō. Source: Ozawa, *Nihon kodai kyūto*, 20, fig. 1, modified.

practices such as the transcription and recitation of sutras, the building of temples, and the dedication of statues. Men and women, sometimes in considerable numbers, were occasionally commanded to take Buddhist orders in the hope of healing a ruler stricken with a serious illness. On 614/8/8, for example, an ailing Soga Umako ordered a thousand people to renounce the world, hoping thereby to regain his health; during his final illness, Tenmu did the same with seventy people on 686/7/28, and he added another eighty three days later. Both institutions, the state and Buddhism, were alike in that they relied on rituals to provide them with a liturgical structure to direct the flow of goods and services.

The set of rituals Tenmu and Jitō created to provide their power with a fitting symbolics was not indebted to Buddhism. These rituals were mostly new, and if not, they were put to new uses. Most famous, perhaps, is the regular, twice-yearly Great Purification, incorporated as such in the Taihō codes, but already mentioned under Tenmu's rule.[13]

Great Purifications and Other New Court Rituals

Ritual removal of sins and pollution was not unknown before Tenmu. One encounters it occasionally in the record, sometimes undoubtedly dated anachronistically such as the one mentioned under king Chūai in the year 200.[14] In this case, its setting was the "country" (kuni; province of a later date) of Tsukushi where "expiatory offerings" (ōnusa) were collected. In 469/3 the Mononobe, ritualists like the Nakatomi, were in charge of purifying an offender who had to provide horses and swords.[15] These "offerings" may have had combined meanings of punishment, compensation, expiatory offering, and haraetsumono (physical objects for the transfer and removal of pollution), for which the Kojiki provides exemplars, whether historical or planted ones is hard to decide.[16] Tenmu's innovation consisted of orchestrating Great Purifications on a pan-tenka scale. He ordered expiatory offerings as a form of "religious" tribute to be made at various administrative levels, leading up to the center, eventually renamed Kiyomihara (Palace on the Pure Plain), by implication the residence of the Great Purifier.

We know of two such Great Purifications under Tenmu. For the first one, held on 676/8/16, he requisitioned one horse and one piece of cloth "per province," it being unclear how far outside the Yamato area such orders were followed. These offerings had to be delivered by the country chieftains (kuni no miyatsuko), while each district official (kōri no mikotomochi) contributed one sword, one deerskin, one mattock, and so forth. In addition, each household was to provide a bundle of hemp.[17] These Great Purification rituals brought the realm's new administrative structure literally into play, at least in the Home Provinces, and possibly beyond.

On 681/7/30, Tenmu ordered another Great Purification throughout the land without any specifics except for the supply of one slave per province; perhaps an unusual *haraetsumono*, or was this a survival of an older custom involving actual sacrifice? A wooden tag (*mokkan*) has been discovered in excavations of Fujiwara-kyō with inscriptions on both sides: on one, a magical rainmaking spell addressed to the powers of the Dragon Kings of the Four directions (a reference to the Tantric Mahāmāyūrī sutra); on the other, the name of a slave girl, possibly a *haraetsumono* or scapegoat.[18] Whether such victims for purification/exorcism or rainmaking ceremonies were actually killed or functioned as live sacrificial substitutes, for which later small human effigies made out of wood or metal (*hitogata*) or paper (*katashiro*) were used, is a matter of speculation. Two separate rituals were performed during Great Purifications. A *kami*-related one was conducted by the Nakatomi court ritualists, and a Chinese, Daoist one by allochthon diviners (*urabe*), most likely from the Fubito clans of Yamato and Kawachi.[19]

Local officials and lords at the provincial and district level functioned, at least in principle and on particular occasions, as ritualist intermediaries between the households of the realm and the *tennō*. It was in 686 that Tenmu renamed his royal residence Asuka Kiyo(淨)mihara no miya (Palace on the Pure Plain of Asuka).[20] Only deliberate intention can explain this name change a dozen years after the construction of the palace. Not a place name, like those of earlier royal residences, it had an unmistakable metaphoric message. Thus, the diseases of Tenmu's body politic were being transferred as impurities to substitute carriers of sins and ills, gathered and disposed of at the center. On 686/7/28, a week after he had given his palace the new name, Tenmu ordered seventy men of pure conduct (*jō*(淨)*gyōsha*) to retire from the world, and he sponsored a Buddhist meager feast (Ch. *zhai*; Jp. *sai*). Purity was being mobilized as the central value to represent the politico-religious realm as Tenmu conceived it.

Qualifying rites as Daoist (purification/exorcism), Buddhist (meager meals), or Shinto raises the question of terminology. To avoid substantialist misconceptions about "traditions," one best desist from using such terms — which, however, is nearly impossible. Most problematic of these is "Shinto." Capitalizing the term "Shinto" misleadingly suggests an indigenous practice framed by a unitary institution — which, however, did not exist. Without historical referent, its meaning dissolves. It is preferable to use *kami* because *kami* worship was practiced, and *kami* ritual was performed in innumerable local variations.

The term is even absent from the *Kojiki*, where one would expect it most. In the *Nihon shoki*, it appears only a few times: first in 585, in the introductory paragraph to the chapter on Yōmei ("The Emperor believed in the law of the Buddha and revered *the way of the kami*"); a second time, in 645, as an opening line for Kōtoku's rule ("He honored the religion of Buddha, but despised *the way of the kami*"); and again, in an edict of 647/4/29 by Kōtoku, where there is talk about "following *the way of the kami* or possess in oneself *the way of the kami*."[21] Years ago, Kuroda Toshio proposed that "way of the *kami*" refers to the activity of spirits, but not to an institution that one could call "Shinto," which, properly speaking, emerged only in the nineteenth century when Buddhist and *kami* practices were forcibly separated.[22] Moreover, the term shares, with many others, a Daoist ancestry, to be discussed later.

Under Tenmu and Jitō, court ritualists designed a yearly cycle of rituals to enhance the supramundane character of their ruler over the new realm. The existence of *uji* with ritualist expertise such as the Mononobe, Nakatomi, or Inbe going back to before the seventh century, however, does not signify continuity between folk religious practices for *kami* and the court ritual.[23]

THE ENTHRONEMENT CEREMONY, as traditionally reconstructed from eighth-century and later texts, consisted of three parts: the accession ritual performed by two ritualist families — the Nakatomi, who pronounced a prayer (*yogoto*), and the Inbe, who handed over the two regal emblems, the mirror and sword; the Daijō-sai we have come to know as the Great New Food Festival;[24] and a ceremony for all the *kami* of Heaven and Earth (*sōtenjinchigi-sai*) held in conjunction with the two most important festivals, the accession ceremony (*sokui*), and the court's Spring Festival (Toshigoi). The difference of these rituals before and after Tenmu is as follows. Until a few decades before Tenmu, the regalia that certified ruler legitimacy were handed over by a council of local Yamato leaders, expressing a political trusteeship rather than a *kami*-based mandate; the Daijō-sai's meaning was unrelated to a harvest celebration of first-fruit tasting; and the all-*kami* ritual did not exist.[25]

The Daijō-sai's meaning of harvest festival was added later under Kanmu and thereby fundamentally altered.[26] As a harvest festival close to the winter solstice, it takes place too late for being a celebration of first fruits. More-over, the Kanname festival performed in Ise in the ninth month was the court's official Harvest Festival. The Daijō-sai's original meaning of a meal was a ritual of submission to a higher authority for which there are mytho-logical and historical examples.

A religious component was added later as a celebration of a hierogamy, a reenactment of the union of Amaterasu's son with the daughter of Takami-musuhi, which produced the children of the Sun. Given Amaterasu's rather late association with royal ancestry, however, the hierogamy element can-not be very old.[27] Ise's cultic function for Amaterasu as ancestor of the im-perial line may, at the earliest, go back to Tenji's time; some scholars date it even as late as Jitō's reign. The shrine was revitalized by Tenmu, possibly in part as reward for support during the Jinshin War: its ritual rebuilding every twenty years and the institution of the Saiō princess in permanent attendance near the shrine were firmly established during his rule.

Aside from the enthronement ceremony, when the ruler received homage from the whole country through two representative provinces, Tenmu and Jitō connected center and periphery through ingeniously staged harvest-related ceremonies that involved a gradually expanding number of selected shrines. These ceremonies took place four times a year at the Jingikan (Of-fice of Kami Affairs) in the capital and required the presence of representa-tives from these "state" shrines (*kansha*). On these occasions, *hafuri* ser-vants of local shrines received offerings they brought back as "disbursed oblations" (*hanpei: han*, "distribute"; *hei* or *mitegura*, "royal oblations") from the *tennō* to their *kami*. This important pan-*tenka* institution constituted a vertical appropriation of selective local ritual personnel of *uji* that were institutionally unconnected laterally.

The point of Tenmu's and Jitō's ideological constructs was invariably to elevate the rulers and their descendants beyond the realm of political power in a center "out of this world." They achieved this through a promiscuous use of symbols. The "plural symbolism" manipulated by Tenmu included being turned (by himself and others) into a descendant of Takamimusuhi and Amaterasu and being referred to as a living god (*akitsukami*), which has a great family resemblance with Daoist, and thus Chinese, notions. In addition, he styled himself a heavenly ruler (*tennō*, a Chinese title) and a transcendental immortal (*senjin*), a ruler savior (Daoist signifiers), possibly even a recipient of the Mandate of Heaven.

This potpourri of symbols should not surprise. Most traditions are not entities that police themselves through a sharp sense of orthodox purity against internal deviations or outside competitors. Such assembled symbolism fails the test of the internal coherence of concepts, anchored in separate traditions that one expects to be mutually exclusive. Rather, it is governed by a superimposition, in practice, of models or symbols, by grouping rather than sorting out along a true-false dichotomy.[28] What was thus reiterated in various symbolic idiolects was the value of supremeness, which, it seems, could not be overemphasized enough. The sacred idioms of supremeness for rulers were fungible.[29]

Rulers were not rulers because they were thought to be sacred. It is much simpler. They were sacred, many times over, because they were rulers. The multiple figures of Tenmu's public persona rearranged local symbolic elements with appropriated continental ones and ultimately functioned, among other things, as alibis obscuring Tenmu's past as a rebel while consolidating greatly his position with and above powerful *uji*, and if nothing else, glorifying his regime by wrapping it in enchanting tales or origin.

Tenmu as Origin, Tenji as Beginning

Yasumaro, the compiler of the *Kojiki*, is clear about his ideological purpose in his Preface. He intends to trace the *kami* lineage of Yamato's dynasty of *tennō* as a Sun line of rulers and thereby present a correct exemplar for rulership unlike past histories, riddled with mistakes that thwarted such purpose. This lineage as syncopated in the Preface culminates in Tenmu, whose leadership in the Jinshin War Yasumaro celebrates in heroic and flowery terms. Understandably, this was in honor of the one who had originally ordered the *Kojiki*'s compilation, Tenmu, both uncle and brother-in-law of Empress Genmei, who requested its completion in 711. Yet the narrative of events in the body of the text stops in 487, two centuries before Tenmu's time, although a bare-bones genealogy that runs until 628, the end of Suiko's reign, is tagged onto the narrative proper.

This is the *Kojiki*'s way of setting Tenmu apart from his predecessors, which the *Nihon shoki* achieves in a different way, namely by leaving us in the dark as to when Tenmu was born and by omitting a closure for Tenji's rule. In addition, no historical Yamato ruler is surrounded in the *Nihon shoki* with as many signs of the supernatural as Tenmu is. The suggestion appears to be that Tenmu had no beginnings worthy of the record, for he was origin.

The *Kojiki*, as the title suggests, is a record about "ancient matters," which were endowed with distinction and authority in good measure precisely because they were ancient. A contrast being implied, one wonders when the "new" or "present" age started. Was it after Great King Suiko's rule, which is about the time that Tenmu must have been born? What does this imply for positioning Tenmu in this scheme? If Tenmu had been the climax of the narrative, as he was in the Preface where he figures as origin, why not carry the story through to him or Tenji?

Tenmu as Origin

The Preface, composed in the official script of logographic Chinese, is replete with borrowed elements from Chinese sources that inflate the rhetoric. The effect, however, reaches beyond mere grandiloquence. Political allusions are prominent, forming a cluster of connotations linking the notion of dynastic founder, Daoist knowledge, and warrior power. Tenmu's image as dynastic founder, contrary to what one might expect, overwhelms his position as one ruler in a succession of Sun-line kings.

He is compared to two legendary Chinese founding figures: Huangdi, the Yellow Emperor of mythological pre-Shang times, who, during the Former Han dynasty (206 BCE–25 CE), was consecrated as the fountainhead of Daoism; and King Wu, military founder of the Zhou dynasty (1122–255 BCE).[30] This impression is reinforced further by a throwaway remark at the end of Tenmu's life, the day his remains, after a two-year wake, were being entombed. The *Nihon shoki* reports that one of the eulogists recited in succession the names of Yamato's previous supreme rulers, clarifying that "in the past, this was called the Sun Succession" — a surprising statement, suggesting that Tenmu's identity (as *tennō*?) was different from that of his predecessors, who had ended their posthumous names with a reference to *hi* (sun), Jomei, Kōtoku, Saimei.[31] Moreover, this was more than two decades before the *Kojiki* was being confabulated precisely around a Yamato Sun line of rulers.

Admittedly, Tenmu's portrayal in the *Kojiki*'s Preface was Yasumaro's image of Tenmu. The *Nihon shoki*, however, mentions an incident that suggests that Tenmu also positioned himself, at least on one public occasion, at a distance from his predecessor(s). In the summer of 673, several months after Tenmu's enthronement, delegations from the peninsula disembarked in Kyūshū, some intending to convey congratulatory messages for Yamato's new ruler, others with condolences for the death of his predecessor. They had come from Silla, Koguryŏ, and the island of Chejudo (Tamura). The islanders, however, were not allowed to proceed to the capital with their condolences since Tenmu "did not invite any other envoys than those who came to convey congratulations." Instead, they were sent back with an expression (ironic?) of paternalistic concern about their health: "The weather is cold and the waves are mountainous. . . . You would therefore do well to take your departure without delay" (Aston's translation). (After all, having received neither wake nor burial, Tenji was not a deceased great king since he had not been officially mourned that way.)[32] Thus, on several occasions in the record, Tenmu's dynastic linkages as legitimizing factors are underplayed. Foregrounded instead is an unmediated identification with the realm of the supernatural: he himself *is* a *kami*, he himself manipulates cosmic forces.

Details about his transcendental persona will follow in the next section. First we have to address the question of the chronological end to the period of "ancient matters." Why not conclude the *Kojiki* narrative with Tenji, which would definitely signal Tenmu as the first nonancient, "modern" ruler?

Tenji as Beginning

Although the *Kojiki* registers no events for the reigns of rulers from Kenzō (485–487) to Suiko (592–628) but only elementary genealogical data such as length of reign, age at the year of death, and names of consorts and offspring, the last ruler mentioned in the text is not Suiko, but Jomei (629–641).[33] He appears under Bidatsu (572–585) as the son of a "crown prince" (named Hikohito, "Man Sun-child"). The names of Kōgyoku/Saimei (Jomei's consort; 642–645/655–661) and Kōtoku (646–654) are absent, but a son of this crown prince, Chinu no miko, whom we know as their father, appears in the text (see figure 1).[34] Thus, Jomei is the last ruler of ancient times mentioned in the *Kojiki*. Would Kōgyoku then be the first ruler of the new age? The honor of inaugurating a new beginning belongs to Tenji. Why?

The reason has to do with a distinction to be made between fully blood-vested rulers and others one could call transit rulers, "holders of the line," as Jitō's name suggests. As explained in chapter 1, starting with Keitai (507–531), double royalty (a father ruler and a royal mother) was the condition in practice for being fully blood-vested, which entitled one to pass on the crown to a (fully vested) descendant of one's offspring (Kinmei, Bidatsu). The son of a crown prince and a princess would qualify also (Jomei's father was a "crown prince" according to the *Kojiki* and thus destined to succeed, a situation that enhanced Jomei's qualification). However, offspring from a ruler and an *uji* consort (Ankan, Senka, Yōmei, Sushun, Suiko) or from relatives of rulers with even thinner royal blood in their veins could only be transit rulers (Kōgyoku/Saimei, Kōtoku). Both of Tenji's parents had been great kings, yet according to this genealogic, his qualification for succession was weak since the royal blood of his mother, Saimei, was very thin. She could have been seen as the end of the line, and Tenji, by implication, as the first postancient ruler, as a new beginning.

By not including Kōgyoku/Saimei and Kōtoku, Yasumaro avoided references to Jomei and Kōgyoku's marriage and their son, Tenji, which would have positioned the latter in "ancient" times. He was a beginning in at least two ways. During the reigns of Kōgyoku/Saimei and Kōtoku, Tenji as the actual architect of the Taika Reforms, drafter of laws, and creator of the new Fujiwara lineage, steered politics into uncharted terrain. Moreover, he was seeking to secure the future of his house by endogamous ties with his brother Tenmu, unprecedented in their redundancy (see figure 4). How else would one explain that ten of Tenji's fourteen children (by nine consorts), Ōtomo being one of them, wind up married into Tenmu's household: four as Tenmu's wives (among whom Jitō) and six as spouses of Tenmu's children (out of seventeen, produced by ten consorts)? In contrast, only one of Tenji's consorts was of royal stock. She was the daughter of Prince Furuhito, Tenji's half brother, a son of a Soga mother and Great King Jomei (and killed by Tenji, who made her his main consort when he became great king in 668), but by the time he died three years later, she had borne him no children.[35]

The Kojiki's chronological ending implicitly rests upon the understanding that Tenji was an out-of-the-ordinary, new kind of ruler, not "ancient." By the time the Kojiki was written, Tenji's rehabilitation was well under way. It had started with the building of his mausoleum in 699, honoring him on a par with Tenmu by celebrating his koki in 702, and endowing with his authority an "inalterable rule" of succession, mentioned for the first time in Genmei's accession edict of 707 and repeated several times throughout the century. Tenji was even praised in an edict (719/10/17) by Genshō and years later (757/i8/17) by Fujiwara Nakamarō for establishing, through his Ōmi-ryō one assumes, Japan's "eternal laws that remained fundamentally unchanged," while no mention was made of the Kiyomihara-ryō, ordered by Tenmu, or of Jitō's comprehensive Taihō-ryō. Also, research has revealed that of all the national memorial days in the eighth century, Tenji's was more observed (or more mentioned in the record) than any other.[36]

Tenji had an unabashed admirer in the anonymous compiler of the Kaifūsō, Japan's first poetry anthology, put together in 751, the year before the inauguration of the Great Buddha of Tōdaiji. In his Introduction, he traces in broad strokes the history of writing, culture, and poetry in Japan. From his perspective of an age when rulers had embraced Buddhism (introduced by Shōtoku Taishi, he notices in passing without any enthusiasm), he bemoans the loss of a golden age of "culture," centered on Tenji's court in

Ōmi. Tenji is extolled as a culture hero-ruler who administered the realm through the written word (of the first Law Code), thereby opening space for "nonaction," which was filled with poetry. This came to a brutal end, however, with Tenmu's Jinshin War: "time passed, bringing chaos, reducing all exquisite writings to ashes, a heart-renting destruction if one thinks of it."[37] The Introduction, like the poems themselves, is replete with allusions to Chinese poems or historical episodes. One scholar has detected in this phrase an equation of the Jinshin War with the Qin burning of books (213 BCE).[38] Tenji dons the mantle of state builder and cultural leader, leaving Tenmu as a destroyer of culture, a total reversal of the persona Tenmu and Jitō had fashioned. It is hard to avoid the conclusion that the *Kaifūsō*'s editor was a Tenji admirer, while the *Manyōshū*, especially its first books, celebrated Tenmu.

Clearly, the eighth-century rulers and some of the culture elite perceived themselves as a Tenji dynasty, as Japanese historians are now acknowledging. It is only a question whether, and to what extent, this was the prevailing view at the time. Let me close this discussion by drawing attention to the fact that Tenji's rehabilitation from the very start appropriated a Daoist symbol of supreme rulership, which Tenmu had introduced. His mausoleum was probably not built on the location where work may have started thirty years earlier before being interrupted by the Jinshin War. The reason is that it was positioned astronomically straight north (55 km, with a deviation to the east of only 3' or 4.5 km) from the Hall of Ceremonies of the Fujiwara capital, the Daigokuden (also read Daikyokuden 大極殿, Hall of the Great Culmen), which in 672 was not even on the drawing board. It is as if, like the Pole Star (Tenkyoku 天極, Heaven's Culmen) in the Heavens, Tenji were guiding the evolving order of the realm below him.[39] His posthumous name, Ame mikoto hirakasu wake tennō, which includes the graph *ten* (天 *ame*), could be read as meaning "The *tennō* who received the Mandate of Heaven (天命 *Ame mikoto*) to open or start the imperial revolve"[40]—a title anachronistically bestowed upon Tenji, the last of the great kings, since it had been his successor, Tenmu, who had started the line of actual *tennō*. Most likely, Tenji's posthumous name was given when his tumulus was built, at the time when *tennō* had already been used for Tenmu and Jitō during their lifetimes.

Tenmu, Transcendental

In the *Kojiki*'s Preface, Yasumaro portrays Tenmu in similar terms as a master of cosmological knowledge: "Following correctly yin and yang, he arranged the order of the Five Phases." This, in my mind, not only tells us of Tenmu's special power but also points to the ideology for his regime: Chinese/Daoist ideas of yin-yang, the Five Phases, directional and celestial magic, teachings, and lore. Tenmu, the *Nihon shoki* reports, launched his campaign against Prince Ōtomo after consulting Heaven through a divination he himself conducted.[41] Thus, Tenmu came to understand that success would eventually be his. Yasumaro, however, expands: "The time of Heaven had not yet come." Heaven's timing is a not-too-veiled allusion to the Chinese theory (Confucian and Daoist as well) of a ruler's heavenly mandate to rule. Tenmu's accession to power is construed here as preordained, what Goodman calls "the reckoned and automatic aspect of fate."[42]

The rhetoric of this Preface is heavily intertextual with Chinese sources. Informed readers or listeners of the time would have recognized some if not all of the mainly Daoist connotations. Yin and yang are the cosmic forces that control everything, and here Tenmu is portrayed as understanding and following them when aligning the realm along their dynamic coordinates as the Five Phases. This political cosmology dates from "the Qin-Han period" when, Goodman notes, "intellectual constructions used by founding dynasts and their courts moved increasingly toward metaphysical theories and the creation of a high religion surrounding the dynastic and other cults."[43] Tenmu, by following yin and yang, performs as a *tennō*, and he is described in cosmic terms when said to have "arranged the order of the Five Phases."

In Chinese lore, Taiyi (Jp. Taiitsu) was the Great One, who controlled yin and yang and, positioned above them and beyond Heaven, was held to transcend them because they emanated from his cosmic vapor. He appears as the single origin of the universe in texts of the fourth century BCE.[44] This is the numinous entity around which Emperor Wu built his new sacrificial cult in 113 BCE, a perfect associate in the heavens for a theocrat famous for his ambitious centralizing statesmanship. Tianhuang (heavenly ruler; Jp. *tennō*) and Di (emperor; Jp. *tei*) became associated with Taiyi,[45] an identification that had already been made in works like the *Huainanzi* (ca. 130 BCE).[46] Taiyi resided near the polar center and rode his carriage, the Great Dipper, around the sky as a great time- and space-ordering contraption, a paradigm of supreme rulership.

Yasumaro's line "The time of Heaven had not yet come . . ." continues with "and cicada-like he shed his wrappings in the southern mountains" (line 24 of Philippi's translation). The cicada is a commonplace metaphor for the transformation of Daoist practitioners into immortals. The "southern mountains" are those of Yoshino, a short distance south of the palace,

Tenmu's refuge from where he launched his rebellion. Indeed, Yoshino was a special region, which along with other sites forms a sacred geography imbued with Daoist themes and motifs one finds often in writings of the time. Here, the enhancing power of this enchanted site is borrowed to metamorphose Tenmu from a rebel into an immortal. Thus Tenmu and his regime are enveloped in Daoist signifiers that were available at the time.[47]

By exhibiting Daoist metaphors, Yasumaro no doubt displayed his learning for an audience that must have appreciated his rhetorical panache, but he was also in tune with Tenmu's image as revealed in Tenmu's posthumous name. Such names, if not constructed anachronistically for past rulers under Jitō, were either chosen by the deceased or created for him or her by the close circle, and reveal the way royal authority was conceived for a specific ruler.

Tenmu's impossibly long posthumous title — Ama no nunahara oki no mahito no sumera mikoto — heads the two *Nihon shoki* chapters devoted to him.[48] This bewildering concatenation of signifiers, rendered as "Emperor the Perfected Man of the Offing in the Central Marsh of Heaven," relies on Daoist terms for effect: the perfected man (*mahito*), offing (*oki*), and probably even the Central Marsh of Heaven (*ama no nunahara*).[49]

The unusual graph used for *oki* refers to Yingzhou, one of the three Isles of the Immortals in the "Eastern Sea."[50] Since ancient times, Chinese imagined the archipelago as the Islands of Immortality (Fusang). The image is here appropriated by or for Tenmu as ruler of this enchanted realm (Yamato/ Fusang).[51] *Mahito* (perfected one) means immortal.

Mahito are the *zhenren* of the *Zhuangzi* (composed possibly as early as the fourth century BCE), who eventually became deified and worshipped during the Han dynasty as *xianren/senjin*, Daoist transcendentals having achieved immortality.[52] As the most perfect of beings, these saints (hermit-wizard-ascetics), also called *shenxian/jinsen* (spirit wizards), served the heavenly emperor in his Jeweled Palace, which constitutes the innermost part of his Purple Palace. This heavenly emperor (*tennō*) is the Pole Star, the regulator of heavenly portents, the calendar, the seasons, master of yin and yang.

Tenmu's posthumous name signals that his rule, imprinted with Daoist supernatural style and values, had become the epitome of perfection as presented in continental learning, and must have resonated positively with the Yamato elite. His title (*tennō*) expressed it, sacred geography (Yoshino) localized it, and poets (Kakinomoto Hitomaro of the *Manyōshū*) celebrated it. He had succeeded in making others imagine and experience himself and royal authority in general in a new way: a legacy of the marvelous, as important as the bureaucratic reforms he implemented and the law codes he had ordered, but outlasting these whether as metaphor or as mere allegory — one, however, whose power to morph again in metaphor has never faded.

Kami-in-the-Present

As is well known, Japan's oldest record, the *Kojiki*, traces the story of the Yamato rulers' divine genealogy to a *kami* origin. Accordingly, we have been accustomed to the idea that all Japanese rulers, until the current one's father, were held to have been living gods. Yet there was a time when the *Kojiki*, this "oldest record" was the "newest," and earlier when multiple versions were circulating, and earlier still when even these may not have been extant even in draft form. In other words, "*kami*-in-the-present" or "manifest *Kami*" as one of several titles for Yamato rulers has a history — that is to say, a beginning, an end, and even interruptions in between.

In the *Manyōshū* one can trace the emergence of Tenmu's *kami*-fication.[53] This anthology of poetry was given its final form by Ōtomo Yakamochi. The poetic attribution of numinous qualities to Tenmu, Jitō, and occasionally some of Tenmu's sons seems to have been mainly the work of Kakinomoto Hitomaro. A poet and panegyrist during the Tenmu, Jitō, and Monmu reigns, Kakinomoto (active ca. 685–705) has some eighty poems in the *Manyōshū* under his name that were part of a now lost "Hitomaro collection" of several hundred poems.

The first reference to a Yamato ruler in *kami* terms is found in a short poem composed by Ōtomo Miyuki, Yakamochi's granduncle and also a war veteran, allegedly shortly after Tenmu's victory in the summer of 672. Miyuki celebrates Tenmu's palace, later called Asuka Kiyomihara no miya, which Tenmu built on the Asuka plain the fall and winter following his victory:[54]

Our Great Sovereign	(ōkimi wa)
Is a very god indeed	(kami ni shi maseba)
Where red-roan stallions	
Once rubbed their bellies in the paddy fields	
He has made his capital.	

Poetic freedom allows great fluidity of terms, opening several registers at once.[55] *Ōkimi* is written here with the graph *kō*, *sumeragi* meaning emperor. The poem following this one in the anthology, similar in structure with lines three and four altered to evoke "waterfowl gabbling in the marshes," uses two graphs for great king. On the other hand, in the lament for Crown Prince Kusakabe, Tenmu's title is written with the graphs for heavenly sovereign, *tennō*, but read *sumeroki*.[56] The lament was composed in 689.

More prevalent and typical of *Manyōshū* poems for Tenmu, Jitō, and some of their offspring is the pillow phrase *kami ni shi maseba*: "who is a god." It is used the last time in 699 for Prince Yuge. This term would fit the image of a transforming process ("cicada-like") that took place for Tenmu and his entourage in Yoshino and during the month-long military campaign, a process marked by several encounters with the supernatural.[57] Within one year, Tenmu turned from a rebel with a following of no more than perhaps two dozen into an emperor who was building his palace and planning a capital patterned on a Chinese model, with an audience hall called Daigokuden. Some members of his immediate family were made to share the numinous limelight, no doubt in order the shore up the Tenmu dynasty's hold on the future, especially, perhaps, because its past was rooted in rebellion.[58]

Empress Jitō also was ascribed *kami* status in the following verses by Hitomaro with regard to raising a (possibly Daoist star-gazing) tower at Yoshino:[59]

Our Great Sovereign	*yasumishishi*
Who rules the land in all tranquility,	*wa ga ōkimi*
She who is a god	*kamunagara*
In action godlike has ordained . . .	*kamusabi sesu to*

Ōkimi and *kamu* are here juxtaposed to *yasumishishi*, the Chinese marker of universal rule: "who rules the land/earth (*yasumi*, 'the eight corners') in all tranquility." In a poem composed for her dead husband, Jitō compares Tenmu to an immortal drifting away as a blue cloud beyond the moon and the stars.[60]

Hitomaro's poetic skills endow Tenmu with a spirit/*kami* aura that spills over to his successors in two laments, read on the occasion of the death of each of Tenmu's sons who had been destined to succeed him on the throne: Prince Kusakabe, who died in 689; and Prince Takechi, who died in 696. Fully half of each long poem is devoted to Tenmu. The first one marshals the land-bestowing myth and the story of creation, twenty years later to become part of the *Kojiki*. Tenmu is identified here not as a descendant of Jinmu, the mythological founder of the lineage, but as the divine ancestor who descended from Heaven, the role Ninigi was to occupy in the *Kojiki*. In other words he is portrayed as origin, his own and that of the beginning of the lineage. He is called "the High-Illuming Sun Prince" and he re-ascends to Heaven in a godly ascent (*kamuagari*), a feat befitting a Daoist immortal.[61] Another sacral register may have been opened here as well, for Cranston remarks that the first twenty-four lines "resemble the rhetoric of the *norito* [prayer to the *kami*] ... and are particularly close to a passage in 'The Great Exorcism of the Last Day of the Sixth Month.'"[62]

The occasion for the second lament was the death of Prince Takechi, Tenmu's oldest son and a war hero. The first half of this poem, the anthology's longest, a "poem of superlatives" where "the full mystique of imperial rule" is created, celebrates Tenmu as a *kami* (*kamunagara*) "who now, god-like (*kamusabu*), hides within the stone [of his burial chamber],"[63] evoking Amaterasu's withdrawal into a cave. The dark cloud, in the *Nihon shoki* the occasion for Tenmu's resort to divination about the future of the realm, is here a *kamukaze* that arose from Ise to confuse the enemy.[64] In a poem for another son of Tenmu, Hitomaro describes Prince Niitabe as "Our Great Lord who rules the land in all tranquility (*yasumishishi wa ga ōkimi*), the Divine Child of the High-Shining Sun (*takahikaru hi no miko*)."[65]

The theme of *kami*-in-the-present is ubiquitous in the celebrations of Tenmu, Jitō, and some of their offspring. Henceforward, starting with Monmu's enthronement in 697, the divine ancestry is evoked in accession edicts of new monarchs. The *Kojiki*, brought out years later, eventually functioned as the official charter for such hallowed legitimacy claims. Its Preface follows this line of homage to Tenmu as the source of the inspiration for the imagery of divine rulership.

It was the generation coming to power with Tenmu that celebrated his achievements in supernatural terms, starting with his victory, and memorialized his prematurely deceased assigned successors. This discourse evoking a long past, expressed at different points in time on various occasions in poems, posthumous names, and accession edicts, was not so much about the past as each time about a critical present moment.

By the beginning of the second decade into the eighth century, Tenmu's descendants were two generations removed from his reign. To secure for the future this discourse of legitimacy anchored in his persona and image, to "fix" it, must have been one of the reasons for commissioning the completion of the *Kojiki* in 711, and, although with significant variations, the redaction of the *Nihon shoki* in 720 as well: documents meant to transcend time by securing future time. Instead of the tombs of the past, first gigantic keyhole mounds, then round, then octagonal tombs, these two textual monuments were to serve as legitimizing memorials for future generations.

In slightly later *Manyōshū* poems by Kasa no Kanamura, celebrating the occasion of Empress Genshō's and Emperor Shōmu's visits to Yoshino, in

723 and 725 respectively, the nature of divine rulership of these sovereigns is no longer mentioned.[66] Sacralizing the rulers through a *kami* ancestry was about to be supplemented and in part displaced by Buddhist constructs. When gathered in an anthology in the late eighth century, the *Manyōshū* poems discussed above acquired a new identity, different from the one they had at the time of their composition. Although, as mentioned, the early books of the anthology specifically constructed a sacral legitimacy for Tenmu, by midcentury the poems may have been viewed more as literary monuments from the past. The original political effect, while not lost, was probably dulled, in part because this was the heyday of state patronage of Buddhism when Shōmu had declared himself "servant of Buddha," a stance to be taken also by his daughter four years later when ascending the throne as Empress Shōtoku. Prominent now was a Buddhist panoply of sacralizing symbolizations.

There is no denying that Hitomaro was the one who versified Tenmu's *kami*-like status. Yet it would be incorrect to ascribe this deification solely to his creative genius. Tenmu (or Jitō) may very well have commissioned the theme. After all, when Emperor Wu of the Western Han had decided that he himself was a "perfected man," he ordered scholars to compose poems on transcendentals and perfected ones.[67]

Through Tenmu, a politico-religious discourse and practice was set up, one that could accommodate a number of enchanting idioms. The full potential for the development of sacred rulership was to be realized later during the Heian period. Then a value already present during Tenmu's reign came to the fore with the force of an obsession: purity, a mytheme keyed to an entire topological discourse and practice constructed by yin-yang specialists, intended to set imperial rule apart from the rest of society to an unprecedented degree.

THE NUMINOUS STATUS of Yamato rulers that they and their entourage envisioned toward the end of the seventh century was expressed in several ways. *Arahitokami*, the best-known term, signifying that the emperor is a *kami* appearing (*ara*) as a human (*hito*), seems to be more recent than "manifest *kami*" (*akitsukami*).[68] In China, the compound *arahitokami* is associated with Buddhism and is related to the notion of avatar. It appears in the *Shoku Nihongi*, the sequel to the *Nihon shoki* covering the years 697–791 and completed in 797. *Akitsukami*, manifest *kami*, is used for emperors in the *Nihon shoki* and the *Ritsuryō*, compiled in the early 700s, and also in the opening formulae of a number of imperial edicts (seventeen out of the *Shoku Ni-*

hongi's sixty-two edicts).[69] However, the term disappears from documents after 809.[70] In the *Manyōshū*, the modifier *akitsukami* is found only once in a rather late poem, celebrating Kuni, the place where Emperor Shōmu had moved his capital from 740 to 744; it is probably an isolated adoption, in a laudatory poem, of the formula for imperial pronouncements.[71]

Akitsukami 明神 has a family resemblance with Tenmu's posthumous name's *mahito* 真人 (Ch. *zhenren*), a term similar to *shinjin* 神人 (Ch. *shenren*, "spirit man," written with the graphs for spirit or deity [*kami*] and man), the Daoist perfected men of the *Zhuangzi*, worshipped as *senjin* 仙人 (Ch. *xianren*), immortal transcendentals, during the Han period. Hermits, wizards, and ascetics were also called *jinsen* 神仙 (Ch. *shenxian*), "spirit wizards."[72]

In the world of the immortals, as elaborated during the sixth century in China by Tao Hongjing (456–536), the transcendentals (*xianren/senjin*) occupied the lowest rung; the perfected ones (*zhenren/mahito*) had a place at the top. The latter were ranked in the nine palaces located in the eight directions of the compass and the center, and were placed under the four perfected ones of the great culmination (*taiji/daigoku*) or purple palace (*zigong/shikyū*). Above them presided the *tennō*, supreme ruler of the numinous realm of all transcendentals.[73]

Master of Sign Language

One of the first things one learns about Tenmu in the opening lines of the first of two chapters devoted to him in the *Nihon shoki* is that he had mastered the arts of astronomy and invisibility. If introductory paragraphs of reigns, such as those for Yōmei and Kōtoku ("venerating the *kami* and respecting the Buddha"), have meaning as summations of their "spiritual orientation," then Tenmu is associated with secret, semi-occult knowledge. Books on *tonkō* (invisibility) prognostication were on the list of "secret books" whose circulation was later prohibited in the Taihō Code.[74]

Books on calendar making, astronomy, geomancy, "recipes and techniques" (*hōjutsu*), and the "art of invisibility" (*tonkō*) had been brought over in 602 by Kwallŭk (Kanroku), a Paekche monk. *Hōjutsu* refers to various divination methods, mantic and magical arts, knowledge of cures. It includes *tonkō*, which uses prognostication as protection against ill omens, a technique for morphing following *ki* flows of energy, and thus becoming impermeable to evil forces. This art figures prominently in books on military strategy.[75]

With the influx of continental knowledge in subsequent decades, the world became richly articulated with signs. The creation and interpretation of signs and their use through divination and prognostication were of vital importance for rulers, perceived as charged with synchronizing society and cosmic forces. In China, Kuang-wu, the founder of the Later (Eastern) Han dynasty and possibly Tenmu's model, had claimed the mandate on the basis of "omens and prognostications" that, one scholar writes, "virtually constituted a kind of national religion centering on the emperor as defender of legitimacy."[76] Such a mandate is hinted at in the *Kojiki*'s Preface with the words "The time of Heaven had not yet come." Scholars have found reasons to propose other candidates such as Liu Bang, founder of the former Han, as models for Tenmu, or at least for his chronicler. Interestingly, such comparison would cast Tenmu as founder of a new dynasty.[77] Prince Toneri may very well have skillfully planted signs in the *Nihon shoki* narrative that could be read several ways. After all, Tenmu's political persona, developed as it was through various numinous overlays, was sufficiently fluid that he could be portrayed as founder, restorer, recipient of the mandate, and more.

According to the *Nihon shoki*, Tenmu practiced divination personally from before the Jinshin War and put it to strategic use during his campaign.[78] He must have learned it from yin-yang specialists at Tenji's court, which in 667 was moved to Ōtsu in Ōmi near Lake Biwa. When four years later Tenmu, still Prince Ōama then, withdrew in great haste to the Yoshino Mountains, he probably came to rely on his own divination skills.[79] At least, the record pictures him that way, analyzing situations, predicting victory (which came swiftly within one month) like a yin-yang master, and even stopping thunder and lightning, like a Daoist immortal. Tenmu is thus presented as combining in his person a proficiency in both divination and military strategy, the two being intimately connected since strategy entailed gauging and engaging movement (of troops), and divination is a skill to decipher cosmic forces in flux through a mastery of signs.

Fire and the color red were Liu Bang's emblematic signs. Tenmu, allegedly similarly inspired, chose red as the distinguishing color for his army. In addition, a number of fire-related symbols in zodiacal components of significant dates, including the declared day of his death and the proclamation of the first era name ever, announced by Jitō around Tenmu's death, mark his rule.

The historian Yoshino Hiroko has gone out of her way to argue that the manipulation of yin-yang symbols endowed Tenmu's rule with cosmic significance. This becomes evident, she suggests, when one reads the record with an eye for such symbolism, never mind that in such matters one often winds up finding what one is looking for. Since Yoshino's reasoning, like the original theory, is an imaginative application — admittedly loose, but not totally arbitrary — of a system of signs that yields some plausible surplus meaning, it should not be dismissed offhandedly as ahistorical.

Yamato rulers after the Taika Reforms can be associated with zodiac signs in an ordered sequence that in Han China had been applied to successive regimes.[80] The theory was definitely known during Jitō's rule through the *Wuxing dayi* (The Great Meaning of the Five Agents; Jp. *Gogyō taigi*).[81] When applied to reigns of Yamato rulers from the second half of the seventh century, the water symbol (associated with the mythological Chinese emperor Zhuan Xu and the North Pole) might have been Emperor Kōtoku's sign, followed by wood for Tenji, fire for Tenmu, and earth for Jitō.[82] The zodiac coordinates of the dates of important events (coronations, moves of residences, major appointments, and even *recorded* moments of deaths) that could be manipulated through divination do relate to the signs of the rulers in question.[83]

As far as Tenmu goes, most significant are the three zodiacal components (year, month, date) of the official date of his death (686/9/9). They are overdetermined as they express the complete trajectory of the fire sign (birth, flourishing, death expressed through the fire-senior, horse, and dog signs), and numerically (9/9) express a full yang.[84] Thus, Yoshino points out, the era name change to Vermilion Bird (related to fire) partakes of the same cosmic valence and was therefore chosen as the day his death was announced — or reported in the *Nihon shoki*.[85] This, however, was only the continuation of a great number of supernatural measures taken during Tenmu's final illness, many of them informed by Buddhism, others by Daoism.[86]

The enhancement of Tenmu's narrative was achieved in other ways indebted to Chinese models as well. Some of the *Nihon shoki*'s descriptions of battle scenes in the Jinshin War were lifted from the decisive battle that brought Kuang-wu to power. Moreover, toward the end of the Former Han, the Confucian notion of the changing of Heaven's Mandate had been greatly intensified by a widespread "Daoist" millenarian belief in the imminent epiphany of a supernatural savior, styled as a *mahito*, the perfected man of Tenmu's posthumous name.[87] I call it "Daoist" because it certainly was not Confucian, and it is pre-Buddhist. "Daoisant" would probably be more appropriate, like "marxisant," since strictly speaking "Daoist" themes as such can be identified only after Daoism became an organized religion, nearly two centuries later.

A Daoisant synthesis of early Han thought, written by Liu An, king of Huainan, and presented to Emperor Wu in 139 BCE, and as mentioned ear-

Wuxing dayi / Gogyō taigi
(The Great Meaning of the Five Phases)

This mega synthesis of cosmology and divination was compiled by Xiao Ji (c. 530–614), a member of the Board of Rites, and presented to the first Sui emperor, Wen, in 594. The Xiao lineage had formerly produced founders of the Southern Qi (479–502) and the Liang (502–557) dynasties. Emperor Wen was extremely interested in omens, in part with regard to a posteriori legitimation of his new dynasty through a synthesis of the Chinese heritage with the idealized Han dynasty of the past.

Xiao Ji collected writings concerning the theory and application of yin-yang, which included hemerology, calendar making, physiognomy, methods to achieve longevity, and exorcisms. Scholars have concluded that half of the text of the *Wuxing dayi* refers to 160 texts through 700 identifiable citations. Only 227 citations are from the Confucian canon in the broad sense; more than half (119) are from apocrypha. Xiao Ji also refers to some thirty post-Han mantic texts, a number of Daoist writings, the classics, and liturgical texts of the celestial masters from the time of the Six Dynasties. He relies on Daoism especially for his treatment of mythological emperors and the emblematic discourse on the body. His ultimate purpose was a restoration of a Han-style rulership in which divination played a key role in governance. The *Wuxing dayi* is thus not a manual for prognostication or geomancy as such.

In China, the *Wuxing dayi* was hardly referred to after the Tang, yet it exerted a great influence in Japan for a millennium (ca. 700–1700). A wooden tag (*mokkan*) dating from 705 found in an excavation at Fujiwara-kyō suggests that the work was most likely available during Tenmu's or Jitō's time. On 757/11/9, the *Shoku Nihongi* lists it as one of four works (which included the *Yijing*) as essential for the students of yin-yang at the official Yin-yang Bureau (Onmyōryō). Well known in Fujiwara circles, the *Wuxing dayi* also played a significant role in Buddhist sects such as Tendai, Shingon, and Jōdo. Practices at Ise and later in fourteenth-century Yoshida Shinto belie its influence. In the latter, the work constituted the only Chinese text used in the "internal teachings" of Yoshida Shinto.

In Japan, this condensed systematic treatment of the vast theoretical literature on the Five Phases provided the basis for entry into the prolific world of Onmyōdō.

This information was gleaned from Cd, 11–14, 17, 20–23, 36–37, 40–50 passim; on the Sui search for a cultural synthesis, see Wright, "The Formation of Sui Ideology," 71–104.

lier known to someone like Tenmu's grandson Prince Nagaya (684–729),[88] may very well have played a role in wrapping Tenmu in such otherwordly nomenclature. This is the *Huainanzi*. It presents a picture of the perfected man that is poetically amplified, thoroughly mystified, and politicized at the same time. Wondrous and magical, such a text lends itself to a reading for its own marvelous sake only if one overlooks the political allegory that is its point.

The image of a mystic who can return to the origin, a state of nondifferentiation, is combined with that of the perfect ruler, the sage, clearly a Confucian ideal, but a notion over which Confucianism had no monopoly.[89] (The term *mahito* is not to be found in Confucian texts.) Moreover, such a perfect statesman who is pure and rules through tranquility and nonaction was said to arise as the one who would restore the Mandate of Heaven in a world threatened with imminent chaos.[90] This image of a ruler as political savior became fairly widespread during the last decades of the Former (Western) Han and its restoration as the Later (Eastern) Han around the beginning of our era.[91] Such rectification of the world through the establishment of the mandate from above, far removed as it is from the Mencian notion of a change of mandate, is easily reconcilable with Tenmu's self-presentation as a state builder claiming divine prerogatives.

The narrative of the Jinshin War also sends symbolic messages in a different direction. In one episode, the implicit reference is to the most heroic legendary figure of Japan's past, Yamato Takeru no Mikoto. At the start of this war, during his four-day forced march from Yoshino to the Fuwa Pass, on 672/6/26, Tenmu found time to worship Amaterasu in Ise from a distance. In the *Kojiki* (chapter 82) and the *Nihon shoki* (on 110/10/7), Yamato Takeru no mikoto similarly sets out to the east to wage war, and on his way stops in Ise to worship Amaterasu (and when he later died, his spirit flew away in the form of a white bird — a Daoist way of journeying to the other world). One month later, at the end of the campaign, on 7/23, the day Prince Ōtomo "committed suicide," Tenmu had offerings brought to the grave of Jinmu, the founder of the Yamato Sun line, in Asuka.[92] This is the first time Jinmu is mentioned again in the *Nihon shoki*, twenty-five chapters after chapter 3, which is devoted to him. Thus the threads of Tenmu's legitimizing links to the Sun line, *kami*, and Ise, which he was to continue spinning during his rule, were being woven — in part no doubt posthumously — in the narrative of the Jinshin War.

Fujiwara-kyō: Numinous Fulcrum

The manipulation of symbols to buttress Tenmu's regime through supra-mundane means intensified toward the end of his life and continued under Jitō. Concurrent with this trend were succession problems that started to emerge during these years and continued to plague the dynasty for decades to come, problems that may have contributed to these symbolics. One high point in these ideological efforts was the building of Fujiwara-kyō in 694.

Tenmu's initial moves to elevate the status of the royal core were being reformulated en route. First, on 684/10/1, he revised the court rank system into eight classes, reserving the highest one, which he called *mahito* or the perfected ones, for royal lineage members. Then, on 685/1/21, the *mahito* title was dropped, possibly because he reserved the title for his own posthumous use: Tenmu's final year-long illness was mentioned the first time on 9/24, and he died on 686/9/9. China's first emperor, Shi Huangdi of the Qin, had taken a similar step. As recorded in the *Shiji*, he allegedly told the *fangshi* ("recipe master" of the arcane and occult) Lu Sheng, who had described to him the immortality ideal of the perfected ones, "I hope to become a Perfected Man. I shall refer to myself henceforward as 'The Perfected One,' rather than as 'I.'"[93] In any event, the eight-class court rank system was replaced in 685 with a far more complex one, reserving for princes the top two ranks, *myō* 明 (bright/sacred) and *jō* 浄 (pure). Later in the year, on 7/26, when colors were assigned to ranks, they received the yang color red.

The graph *myō*, for the upper rank of the imperial relatives, is none other than the *on* Sino-Japanese reading for the graph *akarui* (sacred-royal), the *akitsu* of *akitsukami*, manifest *kami*, the title used for emperors in enthronement edicts starting with Monmu's in 696. The record mentions no recipients of that rank on the day that it was established. Tenmu may have intended to create a distance between his elevated persona and the rest of the inner court. *Jō*, apparently reserved for potential successors since five princes received it then, is the Sino-Japanese reading for *kiyomi* (pure/purity).[94] These two rank titles for royal relatives were the only ones carrying symbolic Daoist connotations. Purity became the privileged signifier for the center of power.

On 686/7/22, two months before he died, Tenmu gave the palace he had built immediately after the Jinshin War where the *jō* (and presumably the *myō*) ranks of princes also resided the name with which it has been known since: Asuka no *Kiyomi*hara no miya, the "palace/shrine on the *Pure* Plain of Asuka." Moving inward from the pure plain were first the "pure" rank holders, then the "sacred" ones, and finally, in the center, the heavenly ruler. Earlier royal residences had been named after their location within Asuka, usually as soon as they were built. Kiyomihara no miya marked the first time a symbolic signifier was chosen as a palace name, and this naming took place only after the palace had been occupied for fourteen years. That this designation was meant to inaugurate a new beginning and secure the future during Tenmu's final illness was further made clear through a new era name, possibly the first in Yamato,[95] announced the same day the new identity of the palace was created. Time and space were being synchronized in a new order of the sacred.

The era was now to be known as Akamitori (Shuchō), Vermilion Bird — red, the yang color of Tenmu's victorious army and the sartorial ceremonial attire for princes. This bird, a pheasant, as the *Wuxing dayi* explains, is also the directional bird for the south, with a martial character, associated with the agent Fire. Vermilion birds, like phoenixes, are signs of a great, auspicious conjuncture of the cosmic forces.[96]

Meanwhile, the planning for Yamato's first palace-city of Fujiwara-kyō, built eventually a few kilometers north of Kiyomihara, was proceeding apace. Much time and thought went into its design, a process that must have started almost as soon as Kiyomihara was completed. The idea to create an actual capital appears in the *Nihon shoki* four years after Kiyomihara was built, but it may have been around earlier. Divination was used to help choose the propitious site on 684/2/28, and the resident spirits of the large swath of land to be used were pacified on 691/10/27.

Archeological excavations in 1990 have revealed Fujiwara-kyō's expanse to have been wider than previously thought: not 3.2 by 2.1 kilometers, but "as large as Nara or larger," measuring 5.5 kilometers east-west and 4.5 north-south, almost square rather than rectangular like Nara and Heian, its successor capitals.[97] The layout followed a checkerboard grid of avenues and streets, with a palace that for the first time was more than a residence for the great king. It featured a Daigokuden where public ceremonies were conducted. Special residential wards were set aside for court officials and bureaucrats. Their presence near the great king helped centripetalize the realm and convert the site of the royal court into an actual capital.

Fujiwara-kyō's layout was inspired by Chinese models, yet with its palace right in the center of the city and its shape close to a perfect square, it resembled no Chinese capital that was ever built. Scholars have concluded that its model most likely was the ideal capital described in the *Rites of Zhou*.[98] This may seem peculiar since firsthand knowledge of Changan by

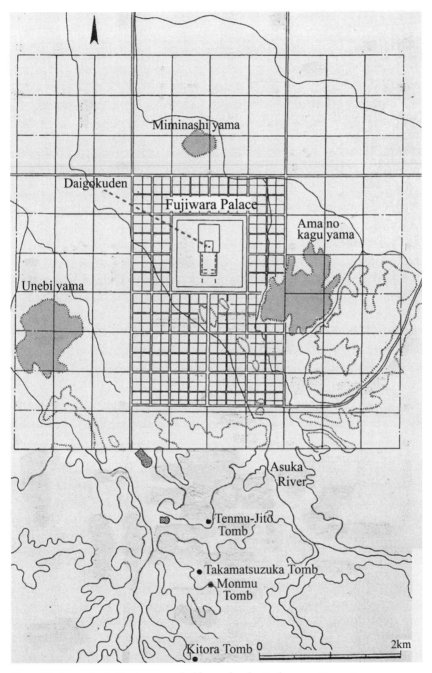

Fig. 7. Fujiwara-kyō. Size as revealed by archeological excavations since 1990; earlier, it was thought to consist only of the central area with the dense grid of streets between the wide roads running north-south and east-west. Source: Ozawa, *Nihon kodai kyūto*, p. 214, fig. 19; p. 243, fig. 24, modified.

Yamato delegations from Tenji's time must have been deliberately set aside in preference for an ideologically perfect design based on textual information. The *Rites of Zhou* prescribes a palace-city that, like Fujiwara-kyō, is square with a grid of nine major perpendicular arteries north-south and east-west and the palace in the center.[99] (This Classic was also relied upon strongly in archaizing reforms in mid-sixth-century China; to be discussed in chapter 6.)

The hypothesis of a model that is textual and ideological rather than historical and architectural is quite plausible since Tenmu and Jitō were creatively experimenting with power symbolics. That is why they valued yin-yang knowledge, indispensable for managing the topographical flow of cosmic forces, and had established a Bureau of Yin-yang (Onmyōryō) and an astronomical platform (*senseidai*).

Topomancy was used to find a proper site for the capital, which, it turned out, was finally situated less than two kilometers north of Kiyomihara. Tenmu was personally involved in the process. He himself visited a possible location on at least one occasion, and it must have been he, the *tennō*, apparently knowledgeable about geomancy and matters of cosmic ether, who made the final decision where to place the center inasmuch as the precise location of the Daigokuden was known before Tenmu died (which was years before building on the capital even started), and his tomb is on a line astronomically straight south (about three kilometers) from the center of the Daigokuden, one kilometer beyond the hills outside Fujiwara-kyō (see plate 1). Jitō's ashes were deposited in the same grave, and Monmu's tumulus was built one kilometer further on the same south-to-north axis, as "the celestial meridian writ small"[100] of cosmic importance, the south being associated with yang, the firebird, and rulership. (The symbolic emphasis on a north-south axis was something quite new in Yamato.)[101]

The search for a site entailed, two years after Tenmu had personally rejected one possibility, the dispatch of a committee, including yin-yang masters, "to various Home Provinces." One may wonder why it took several years of looking far and wide before settling ultimately for a place right next to Kiyomihara. From the two subsequent capitals of Nara and Heian, we are accustomed to believe that topomantic stipulations consisted mainly of having a capital surrounded on three sides by mountains and open to the south.[102] The requirements for Fujiwara-kyō may have been more complex, possibly because Yamato's first heavenly ruler needed to be cosmically centered. The considerations that follow lead to that hypothesis.

The centrality of the *tennō* in the Daigokuden was existential and cosmic foremost and had to be expressed as best as possible through a topographic location, experientially signifying the articulation of Earth with Heaven in a center that thereby became sacrosanct. *The Book of Documents*, Nancy Shatzman Steinhardt reports, formulates "the ruler's association with heaven, his central position, and the necessity of heavenly satisfaction through divination — the ideology, in other words, of imperial city building"; this means, as a poem of the *Book of Songs* puts it, "Orienting them [the buildings] by the rays of the sun."[103]

Mountains that on three sides protect capitals like Nara and Heian from the outside against adverse currents of cosmic forces were, in the case of Fujiwara-kyō, traditionally thought to have been the Yamato *sanzan*: Yamato's three mountains. The archeological research of the 1990s, however, has revealed these mountains to have been located within the perimeters of the large palace-city, not outside it. They thus cosmicize specifically the palace and Daigokuden. These three hills — hardly "mountains" at a height of between 70 and 130 meters — rise abruptly above the south Yamato plateau: Miminashi yama, only some 700 meters north of the palace; Ama no kagu yama, mentioned in the *Kojiki* as a mountain in Heaven, to the southeast; and Unebi yama to the southwest. Situated in the center of these mountains and "oriented by the rays of the sun," the Daigokuden cosmically symbolized the center of All under Heaven (see plate 2).[104] The epigraph from the *Manyōshū* at the beginning of this chapter celebrates the cosmic location of these mountains over which Jitō *tennō* performs a *kunimi* (viewing of the land).[105]

Viewed from the spot where the Daigokuden once stood, the sun on the day of the winter solstice sets right over Unebi yama, and it rises that same day over Ama no kagu yama. This day is of major symbolic importance in the Chinese and specifically Daoist worldview. It is the pivot in time when the cosmic forces, having reached their seasonal lowest point, start their life-generating cycle. It played an important role during Tenmu's final illness, and enthronement rituals are timed around it.

The winter solstice sight line from the Daigokuden over Unebi yama across the archipelago reaches Hyūga — ancient pronunciation *himuka*, "facing the sun" — on the eastern coast of Kyūshū, where Ninigi was said to have landed with the regalia.[106] About six kilometers in the exact opposite direction, northeast, one faces the much taller Mount Miwa (467m), the traditional place of sun worship for the Yamato rulers before the elevation of Ise to that position under Jitō. Extended across Honshū to the shore in the northern Kanto, the endpoint for this line is Hitachi, "sun standing or rising," the spot where the sun rises on the day of the summer solstice. Tenmu's geomancers had found the right site, suffused with cosmic and centralizing significance, sufficiently sublime for a Heavenly ruler from where to rule all under Heaven, or, one could say, "from sea to shining sea."[107]

Hitomaro renders further homage to Fujiwara-kyō's numinous halo by opening a different register in a *Manyōshū* poem that he puts in the mouth of the conscript laborers ("we") who built it:

> To the gates we build,
> The lofty Gates of the Sun,
> Let unknown lands
> In obedience draw near: from Kose Road,
> Bearing on its back
> Strange markings that proclaim
> Our land the Deathless Land (*Tokoyo*),
> A sacred tortoise has come forth,
> Foretelling a new age.[108]

The turtle of the poem, a sacred and symbolic emblem of immortality and also used in geomancy, carries on its back the legendary three mountains of the Land of the Daoist Immortals. As part of a sacred landscape or re-creation thereof, Fujiwara-kyō seems supported (rather than surrounded) by three mountains, resting on a turtle, as an Everworld or "Deathless Land," a Land of Immortals.

Two Nara Palaces

If the ideological background for Fujiwara-kyō was cosmic, Daoisant, and historiographically perhaps somewhat controversial, the matter is even more complicated for the two consecutive palaces of Nara (Heijō-kyō), the new capital from 710 to 784 with an interruption of five years, 740–745. The reason is that the palace and administrative center were rebuilt at one time, the date of which may or may not coincide with Emperor Shōmu's return to Nara in 745 after a nearly five-year absence. The court officially moved from Fujiwara-kyō to Heijō-kyō in 710, even though construction was far from completed. Some essential buildings including the Daigokuden and the Suzakumon main entrance to the palace precincts were finished only in 715. The Daigokuden, this functionally and symbolically most central structure, was probably brought over from Fujiwara-kyō. A mere twenty-five years later, Shōmu moved out, dismantled the Daigokuden, reassembled it in Kuni, and left it there when in 745 he returned to Heijō-kyō, where he built another one, but positioned it differently within the palace structure. Shōmu's rebuilding upon his return, at least, is the hypothesis I am following.

There are a number of theories for the two palaces and Daigokuden, all relying on bits and pieces of evidence, archeological and textual, that have led only to inconclusive hypotheses so far.[109] I choose to rely on one recent theory advanced by Mizubayashi Takeshi because he brings to the debate issues of rulership symbolics, relating the change in architectural layout to one in the function and conception of political authority.[110]

Legitimation of rulership started out in early Nara reflecting a dual notion of governmental authority, textually grounded in the *Kojiki*, which Genmei ordered to be finalized in 711, the year after the move from Fujiwara-kyō to Heijō-kyō. On the one hand, the title of *tennō* stood for ruling authority over the realm; on the other, as *tenshi* (heavenly descendant) the emperor expressed a sense of ruling solidarity with the nobles and *uji* leaders through a common *kami* ancestry. This commonality was expressed in a Festival for All the *kami* of Heaven and Earth (*sōtenjinchigi-sai*). Emperor Shōmu would have moved away from this model, without abandoning it, after his return to Nara in 745. This move would have reduced considerably the second component, initiating a process of lessening the ideological role of the *Kojiki*. His interest in Buddhism was one element in this shift.

Jinmu, the first human ruler, was referred to in the beginning of the *Kojiki*'s first section of book 2 as *amatsukami no miko* (child of the heavenly *kami*), but this *tenshi* nomenclature (the *ama* and *ko* of his title) changed to *tennō* once his successors started ruling the *tenka*.[111] In the *Kojiki*, rulership entailed expressions of both taking charge of governing (*tennō*) and of divine descent (*tenshi*), which entailed a lateral dimension.

Tenmu and several great kings before him who pursued a strong program of governmental reform and state strengthening anchored their authority metaphorically and genealogically in Heaven (*ten, ame/ama*) or the Sun (*hi*). This is characteristically a pre-*Kojiki* notion of the mid-seventh century. The next four rulers, Jitō to Genshō (690–724), supplemented Heaven with Earth (*tenchi*), also expressed through the metaphor of rootedness in the soil (*neko*), highlighting an additional essential ingredient of rulership, namely the need of localized support (from *uji*) for a central authority that had made transcendental claims of supremeness. This is the political philosophy that informs the structure of the *Kojiki* narrative, the composition of which coincides with the planning of Heijō-kyō.[112]

Although Heijō-kyō was undoubtedly patterned on Changan, the layout of the palace expressed this particular form of rulership, which rested on the two important but separate institutions of the Daijōkan (Council of State) and the Jingikan (Office of the Kami) — the latter absent in the Chinese model. The palace compound consisted of a western half, where government was conducted, and an eastern counterpart, where, among other buildings, the Jingikan was situated.

From the central gate of Suzakumon in the south of the western half, an empty space led straight to a second gate that opened onto the Morning Gathering Halls (Chōdō), where officials assembled every morning. Behind it lay a second large open ceremonial ground, the Morning (or Palace) Garden (Chōtei), an Audience Plaza where the high officials gathered in front of the Daigokuden for all important state events such as accessions to the throne, changes of era names, the issuing of edicts, New Year's greetings, and banquets.[113] All the buildings in the western part, constructed according to Chinese construction techniques, had tiled roofs, red lacquered walls, and a foundation of large stones.

The eastern half of the palace consisted of three areas with mainly traditional Yamato-style buildings with thatched roofs, the supporting wooden pillars resting in postholes. In the far northern end, roughly parallel to the Daigokuden, was the residential palace; the space at the southern end, as large as the Chōdō, housed the Jingikan somewhere although we do not know exactly where. The nature and function of the buildings in a third small area in between are also unknown. Thus, the western half constituted the Daijōkan's jurisdictional area for government affairs while the eastern half was mainly the domain of the Jingikan.

Fujiwara-kyō's administrative buildings, including the Daigokuden, had also been erected using the new Chinese techniques, except for the residential palace proper, built in the traditional style,[114] also used in Ise and, as to be discussed in chapter 8, bearing resemblance to the materials prescribed for the Mingtang. Thus, it appears first of all that the old style was reserved for religious spaces, including the inner palace, residence of the *kami*-in-the-present, and the Jingikan where pan-*tenka* ceremonies were held four times a year, honoring local *kami* through several thousand representatives from official shrines (to be discussed in chapter 5). These delegates received oblations to be brought back to their shrines. Second, architecturally there is continuity between Fujiwara-kyō and the early Heijō palace, but not with the second one, which would be the work of Shōmu after 745.

In the second palace, the western half was abandoned, except possibly for a Western Palace, which along with a great number of other small buildings may have been in the northern area where the Daigokuden once stood. The residential palace remained where it used to be, in the northern end of the

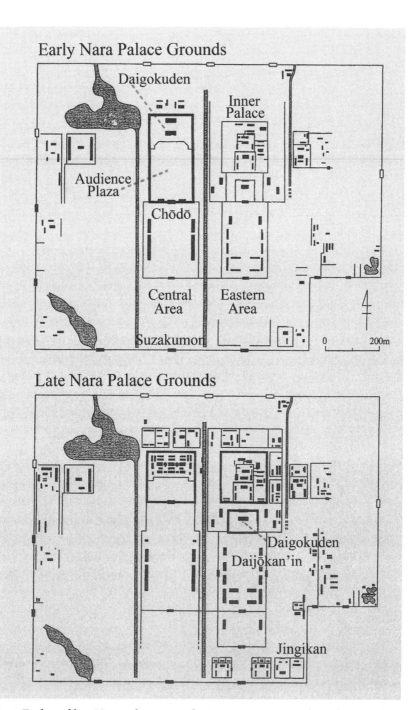

Fig. 8. Early and late Nara palace grounds. Source: Tateno, *Kodai toshi Heijō-kyō*, 31, modified.

eastern half. The new Daigokuden was placed south of it, having lost, however, its large ceremonial plaza. Further south were a number of buildings, called in some texts the Daijōkan'in, the Council of State Compound.

The significance of this change is as follows. The architectural style was now unified. All buildings were built according to the Chinese formula. The maintenance of the traditional style for some specific structures in Fujiwara-kyō as well as the early Heijō palace, even though "more advanced technology" was available, was probably meant as a visual expression of sacred spaces, an element that was lost in the second layout. So was the architecturally marked spatial separation of the Jingikan and the Daijōkan (the offices and the Morning Gathering Halls).

In the thanksgiving edict of 749 for the discovery of gold in time to gild the Great Buddha at Tōdaiji, Shōmu is referred to as the servant of the Buddha, another indication of quietly deprioritizing Kojiki-based political nomenclature. A network of Buddhist provincial temples was established, and a few years later a nun, Empress Shōtoku, occupied the throne. Buddhism penetrated into the central political issue of the day: Princess Abe's appointment as crown princess, her succession as Empress Kōken first, then as Shōtoku.[115]

In the past, only males had held the title of crown prince. Female rulers had come to power as princesses, daughters, or consorts, not as designated successors. Between the years 735 and 752, a period encompassing the rule of Shōmu's eventual successor first as Princess Abe, then as Crown Princess Abe (749), and finally as Empress Kōken (749), five Buddhist ceremonial events were staged (consisting of a sai-e, "frugal repast," and several transcriptions of sections from the Konkōmyō-kyō) to turn her, the royal successor of the Sun line, into a transmitter of the royal protector role for the Law of the Three Treasures. (In China Emperor Wu from the Liang dynasty had self-ordained himself as a bodhisattva in 519, as had Empress Wu from the Zhou dynasty in 694.)[116] Shōtoku Taishi was also invoked, not as crown prince, but as someone who had been transformed into a holy man and high priest. The dynasty was in the process of moving away from Sun line symbolism to adopt a transmission of kingly roles as successive protectors of Buddhism. The Kojiki began to be sidelined.

The reversed order of spiritual powers as they are invoked in royal edicts between 757 and 769 reveals this ideological turnabout. The kami of Heaven and Earth and the spirits of imperial ancestors move from first and second place in 757 to fifth and sixth (last) place in 769, when the first three invocations were to Roshana Nyōrai, the Konkōmyō-kyō, and Kannon Bosatsu.[117]

This context may help explain why the Jingikan of the second palace, according to Mizubayashi, was probably smaller than the first one, with a courtyard that would have accommodated only with great difficulty the two or three thousand delegates from across the country, together with Nara's officialdom and a display of great numbers of gifts, that would have gathered for the most important yearly ceremonies.[118] It certainly was small in comparison to the audience plaza of the first palace, which was intended to accommodate a large number of people. As we shall see, somewhere in the 740s, the first signs of faltering participation were recorded. Ultimately, toward the end of the century, the scale of these large festivals was curtailed considerably. The reason for the small Jingikan may have had to do with the dwindling interest in these ceremonies already by the time it was built.

Finally, the *sōtenjinchigi-sai* was an important festival that symbolized the "common origins" in myth of the emperor and all significant local power holders. The codes prescribed that it be held at accession ceremonies and the yearly court Spring Festival of Toshigoi.[119] By the end of the century, as far as the former is concerned, this pan-*kami* festival was absorbed into the accession ceremony, overshadowed by the installation of a new emperor, and thereby losing its distinctive character, and the size of the latter was reduced by 75 percent.[120] This was also the time that the *Kojiki* was lost sight of and replaced in importance by the *Nihon shoki*.

These and other developments lead to the conclusion that the *Kojiki's* life span as an effective political document in ancient Japan was limited to a half century, namely the decade or two while being composed (690–710) followed by some thirty years until the last years of Shōmu's rule. It established the mythological beginnings of the ruling house, made a case for nonroyal women to acquire queen status, and presented the ruling elite as bound together through *kami* the emperor also was venerating. The all-important genealogies that structured the prestige hierarchy of the ruling group through the narrative lineaments of the *Kojiki's* mytho-history did not lose any of their importance, but they had to be reexamined and certified anew in the early Heian period when the *Shinsen shōjiroku* (A Record of the Clans Newly Compiled) was completed and presented to the throne in 815.

4 ALLOCHTHONS

During the Kōken years [749–757], several edicts were issued, granting requests by a number of allochthons (*shoban*)
for [new] *kabane* titles [attached to *uji* names]. Thus the old
kabane titles [the highest ones unobtainable by allochthons]
and the new ones became indistinguishable. One could no
longer determine whether an *uji* family was allochthon or
authochthon (*banzoku wazoku*). Everywhere, commoner *uji*
distorted their status, claiming to be offshoots of high nobles; allochthon residents from the Three Korean Kingdoms
called themselves descendants from the *kami*.
—815. Introduction, *Shinsen shōjiroku*

The emperor's supreme role in the Chinese model of rulership consisted of keeping the realm's human affairs in sync with cosmic forces, and
thus promoting the welfare of all under Heaven. This task required special
knowledge and expertise concerning the operation of the yin and yang syn-
ergies, the flow of cosmic *qi* (ether; *ki* in Japanese), and portents and the interpretation of signs. How did this knowledge cross over to Yamato? Where
did the specialists who controlled it come from? How did Tenmu secure
both this culture and the practice, especially since contact with China was
discontinued for a whole generation during his and Jitō's rule?

Continental Knowledge

The application of continental learning in Yamato reached a thus far all-
time high in the second half of the seventh century. It had a long history.
During Japan's two prehistoric periods (first Jōmon, then Yayoi) ending
around 250 CE, local chiefdoms in a wide region — which included besides
the western part of the archipelago, China's southeastern coastal regions
and the Korean peninsula — shared many elements of material culture and
ritual practice.[1] As evidence of cultural commonality, archeology points
to pottery patterns and square burial mounds, evidence buttressed further
by a few Chinese texts.[2] Needless to say, the *Kojiki* and *Nihon shoki*'s "historical" record of this period of prehistory cannot be tapped for exemplars

that might have inspired later rulers such as Tenmu. The information is too scarce and rudimentary, and, as far as they would be present in Yamato's chronicles, they would be inserts from a later age.

The *Nihon shoki* reports that as early as 205, skilled laborers were brought over from Silla as war captives. In 463, Great King Yūryaku's military expedition would have returned with "tribute" from Paekche in the form of potters, saddle makers, painters, brocade weavers, fleshers, and an interpreter; and in 493 tanners from Koguryŏ were delivered. These men, however, were not carriers of the kind of knowledge that would be serviceable as a political ideology.

Continental culture, which contributed to the ideas through which Tenmu reimagined himself and his rulership, is identifiable as such when we read about the transfer of books and learned people. They arrived sometimes as "gifts" from one ruler on the continent to another on the archipelago, at other times as loot or captives from raids into the peninsula. During the sixth century the information regarding the transfer of culture becomes specific in the record.[3]

Scholars versed in the Five Classics on loan from Paekche were being rotated in and out of Yamato in 513, 516, and 553, the year when Buddhism in the form of Buddhist monks and statues from Paekche officially "arrived."[4] A year later, specialists in divination, calendar making, and medical knowledge as well as herbalists and musicians were brought over or rotated, per request or command of the Yamato ruler to the king of Paekche. The monks themselves were carriers of all varieties of knowledge including yin-yang, divination, and Daoist magic.

Starting in 600, the Yamato court went straight to the fountainhead of all this learning when it established direct contact with China. Prior to Tenmu in the seventh century, four missions traveled to the Sui court, followed by six embassies to the Tang capital.[5] It was not unusual for members of these delegations to remain in China for protracted periods of time, sometimes thirty years — that is to say, half a lifetime. Tang officials eventually dealt with long-term residents by ordering those who were staying more than nine years to reregister with the Office of Daoist Worship.[6]

A considerable number of these envoys from Yamato were allochthons who themselves or whose ancestors had come over from Paekche, Silla, Koguryŏ, Kaya, some possibly from China itself. Over time they formed *uji* such as the Aya, Kawachi no fumi, or Hata. These *uji* names, however, stand for many rather than one single *uji*. The Yamato no Aya, for example, split into three groups, totaling ninety-one *uji*.[7] Some, like the Yamato no fumi, were specialized scribes. In the mid-sixth century, the Hata were said to have counted over seven thousand households, possibly an exaggerated figure. Nevertheless, their influence was considerable through the culture and knowledge they had brought with them from overseas.[8]

From the start of Tenmu's rule, centralization of continental knowledge had a high priority in his blueprint for a bureaucratic state. In 673/3 within days of his enthronement, Tenmu brought scribes together for transcribing the "whole Buddhist Tripitaka." This pious exercise was repeated later many times in the course of Japanese history, often in the context of political crises as a meritorious deed of expiation for bloodshed. Emperor Shōmu established a sutra-copying department in his consort Empress Kōmyō's household after Prince Nagaya's "plot" of 729, and Empress Shōtoku ordered the distribution of one million wooden mini pagodas (hyakumantō) and the copying of the Tripitaka after Fujiwara Nakamaro's rebellion of 764.[9] Certainly, after the bloodletting of the Jinshin War there was a sufficient amount of guilt, pollution from bloodshed, or both to justify expiation. Yet, in this first-of-its-kind undertaking, another motive may also have been at work, for the enterprise provided an opportunity to get hold and take stock of arguably the largest body of knowledge available in the archipelago, "nationalize" it, and secure control over it. The sutras had first of all to be collected. On 675/10/3 messengers were sent in all directions precisely for this purpose.

More essential than Buddhism for deciding on the course of government on the Tang model, however, were the interpretation of portents, the manipulation of divination, and astronomical knowledge. With the erection of an astronomical observation platform and the establishment of the Yin-yang Bureau (Onmyōryō) and a university (possibly founded by Tenji) early in his reign, staffed and operated mainly by allochthons, Tenmu centered crucial information that had been available for a couple of generations in a scattered fashion.[10] A "tower," possibly for astronomical and Daoist ritual star-gazing purposes — we do not know — had already been built by Great King Saimei (655–661).[11]

The various domains of continental knowledge were organized through elaborate discourses framed by yin-yang hermeneutics and pragmatics based upon the Yijing (Book of Changes). This Chinese cosmology was structured through correlations and correspondences. The scholar Aihe Wang describes it as

> an orderly system of correspondence among various domains of reality in
> the universe, correlating categories of the human world such as the human
> body, behavior, morality, the sociopolitical order, and historical changes, with

categories of the cosmos, including time, space, the heavenly bodies, seasonal movement, and natural phenomena.[12]

As far as the record shows, yin-yang knowledge came over sporadically from Paekche to Yamato during the sixth century. Its transmission took place with the ceremonial presentations of books and men of learning, usually Buddhist monks from Paekche, to the great Yamato kings in 513 and 553. Portents started to be exploited for political purposes in the beginning of the seventh century by the Soga clan, which had since the mid-fifth century maintained close relations with *uji* claiming Paekche roots.[13]

The Soga, themselves possibly of peninsular origin, constituted the major royal in-law group from the time of Kinmei (539–571). Toward the end of the sixth century, they functioned as kingmakers. They used the allochthon *uji* of the Aya as their private militia. After they massacred their enemy the Mononobe military *uji* in 587, the Soga became the unchallenged patrons of Buddhism (which continued to be Soga Buddhism until 645)[14] and through it, of continental learning. That is why the Soga took the monk Kwallŭk under their wing and housed him in their lineage temple, the Hōkōji. They used his knowledge of portents as a trump card in the new game one could call portentous politics.[15]

During Suiko's reign, omens were used as a new weapon of political critique that the ruling house and the Soga, whom Suiko was attempting in vain to control, wielded against each other. These dueling portents were generated on the Soga side by Kwallŭk, who provided the most potent ones, and on the opposing side by anonymous court diviners who launched their critiques against Great Minister Soga Umako (?–626).[16]

In 632, Min, a Buddhist monk, returned from China with several others who had been sent there by Suiko twenty-four years earlier, bringing new hermeneutic ammunition for the court. Min soon started lecturing on divination, counting among his students Nakatomi (Fujiwara-to-be) Kamatari and Soga Iruka (victim-to-be of Kamatari in the Taika coup). He seems to have been able to turn the tables and gain the upper hand in the portentology field, defending Emperor Jomei and critiquing Great Minister Soga Emishi's handling of the government. (A generation later Tenmu's Yin-yang Bureau, set up to monopolize this knowledge, was busily applying it left and right. The *Nihon shoki*, our only source for this information, records no fewer than seventy-two omens for the fifteen years of his reign. No wonder that, with a average of some five portents a year or almost one every other month, Tenmu was celebrated as a master of yin and yang.)[17]

The competition between the Soga and the court also concerned interventionist knowledge of a "magical" ilk. A severe drought struck in 642. On 7/25, people were sacrificing cattle and horses at shrines, a very common practice at times of drought or incessant rain, hoping to induce meteorological change.[18] Soga Emishi ordered excerpts from "the Great Cloud Sutra"[19] chanted in the temples, and on 7/27 he adorned Buddhist statues in the Hōkōji garden and was seen personally offering incense, with minimal efficacy, however: merely a light drizzle the following day. Then, Great Sovereign Kōgyoku stepped in, ordered a halt to the sutra chanting, and went on a pilgrimage to the river source of Minabuchi on 8/1. There she bowed to the four directions and, on her knees, offered prayers to Heaven, Tang style, a ritual performance with obvious Daoist overtones — an alternate source of continental knowledge to the Soga's Buddhism. The record — undoubtedly one maneuver in this contest — states that the response was "instantaneous in the form of thunder and rains that did not stop for five days."

During another drought under Tenmu, all religious traditions were again resorted to. In the summer of 676 (6th through the 8th months), priests and nuns were invited to offer supplications to the Buddha, the Law, and the Priesthood (the so-called Three Precious Things); captured and caged animals were ordered to be released (a meritorious practice based on the Buddha's prohibition of taking life); punishments were mitigated, criminals pardoned, the gods of Heaven and Earth prayed to; and a Great Purification (more Daoist than anything else) was held, involving district officials "throughout the realm."

Before the end of the same year, Tenmu sent emissaries throughout the land to expound on the *Konkōmyō-kyō* (Golden Light Sutra) and the *Ninnō-kyō* (Sutra of the Benevolent Kings), two politically important sutras that remained the state's staple protection against natural disasters and political crises for centuries to come. Later he had sutras deposited in Buddhist chapels "in all the provinces" for purposes of worship. Jitō had one hundred copies made of the Golden Light Sutra and ordered them to be read every New Year, again "in all the provinces."

This effort in the second half of the seventh century to seek protection for the realm against natural calamities was clearly a multimedia undertaking, at least in as far as Buddhism, "Shinto," and Daoism could be identified as separate providers of remedies in the domain of the supernatural. The great purification/exorcism (*ōharae*), institutionalized under Tenmu and later known as one of the most important Shinto ceremonies, was first referred to in the record (8/2/676) with the Daoist term for great exorcism (*dajiachu/daikaijo*),[20] and its purpose here was no different from that of other rainmaking solutions tried.

Containing Symbolic Production

Wealth through state power and access to the supernatural through knowledge were two separate assets in the beginning of the seventh century. As the state developed its bureaucratic reach, however, and the world of Buddhism expanded, the state sought to align Buddhism along its own interests. This entailed some supervision of the Buddhist institution, but most important, it required measures to control the relevant knowledge Buddhist adepts possessed for interacting with that other world, believed to greatly influence what happened in the realm.

During this turbulent seventh century, Buddhism grew into a formidable institution. In 624, we are told, there were forty-six temples, mainly in the Kinai region,[21] the Soga functioning as the primary sponsor of Buddhism. By the end of the century, during Jitō's reign, court supervision had replaced Soga sponsorship. Moreover, the Buddhist establishment had grown tremendously (possibly in part through the registration of already existing temples). Jitō is said to have dispensed alms to 545 temples in the Kinai region.[22] The recitation of sutras by order of the great kings became a common feature of government activity in times of crisis.[23]

The Soga functioned as sponsor of Buddhism for about seven or eight decades until the mid-seventh century, when support of some important temples was taken over by the court, and oversight of Buddhist personnel started to take shape with the establishment of a Clerical Office (Sōgō). Jitō eventually placed the office under the umbrella of the Genbaryō, the bureau for the administration of alien relations and the registry of monks and nuns.[24] The specific regulations for the Buddhist clergy and nuns that form part of the Taihō Code of 701 most likely reflect practice from Tenmu's and Jitō's time.[25]

Following the Taika coup of 645, Min and a lay scholar, Takamuko (Kuromaro) Genri (an Aya *fuhito* or scribe, later ambassador to Silla and China) joined eight others to form a brain trust of ten newly created national scholars (*kuni no hakase*). Through these "state employees," the court began to lay claim to the new continental knowledge from China. On the Tang model, three lay supervisors for Buddhism were appointed next to the ten national scholars.

As had become evident in the first half of the seventh century, prognostication, divination, and omen interpretation could be manipulated in political wrangles and, as acquaintance with the vast domain of yin-yang knowledge grew, were essential tools to conduct government in a world now understood to be at the mercy of cosmic forces. Tenmu took several measures to marshal this knowledge, corral it, and declare it the equivalent of classified information. His Yin-yang Bureau had offices for astronomical observations, prognostication and divination, calendar making, and timekeeping. Judging from the dramatic increase in the number of omens reported during the twenty-four years of Tenmu's and Jitō's reigns (673 to 697) compared to the preceding seventy-three years of the seventh century, the Yin-yang Bureau must have been very busy.[26] The thirteen auspicious and eighty-six inauspicious omens reported during the first three quarters of the century increased to thirty and ninety-one respectively for the last quarter alone.

Under Tenmu, auspicious happenings followed each other at a rate of more than one a year, possibly to counterbalance the inauspicious signs that were far more numerous. The latter appeared at a rate of almost five a year (an all-time high for both the seventh and eighth centuries), revealing perhaps a continuous state of alert to which the internal reforms and state-building efforts, undertaken in the face of the expanding Tang empire, may have contributed. Under such circumstances, auspicious auguries may have been welcome, but inauspicious ones must have increased support for action to prevent disastrous outcomes, in other words, for Tenmu's state strengthening: rule by fear. Containment and control over the interpretation of such signs (that is to say, their production) to orient action was of utmost importance. Hence the restriction on the circulation and use of prognostication (specifically targeted at Buddhist specialists). There was ample continental precedent for such measures.

Linking prognostication and divination with political events had been prohibited in the Northern and Southern dynasties in China (fourth through sixth centuries), and prognostication books were even burned during the Sui dynasty (581–618). In the eighth century, under the Tang, astrology or fortune-telling figured several times in accusations brought against alleged plotters.[27] Thus, it is not surprising that article 20 of the *Shikisei-ritsu* (Office Penal Laws) in the Ritsuryō Code, a virtual copy of the Tang Code of 624, stipulated that books on divination, prognostication, and astrology could not be owned privately:

> The private possession of the following items is forbidden: astronomical instruments, maps of the heavens, [divination manuals such as] the River Chart [*Hetu*] and the Lo Writing [*Luoshu*], books predicting the future, books on military strategy or dealing with the calendar, prognostication books such as the Methods of the Great Monad [*Taiyi*] or the Methods of the God of Thunder [*Leigong*]. The punishment will be one year of penal servitude [Tang: two

years]. The prohibition and penalty applies to the private study of these materials. However, apocryphal interpretations of the *Five Classics* and the *Book of History*, as well as prognostications based on the *Analects* are exempt.[28]

The court sought to be in control of divination and prognostications. To prevent combustion when fused, the fields of astronomy and divination were to be kept separate. Astronomers were not allowed to engage in divination. We know of one incident in 767 when Ōtsu Ōura, a yin-yang master and astronomer, twice involved in plots, was demoted, ordered into exile, and had his "books of astronomy, yin-yang, etc." confiscated, but who nevertheless four years later became head of the Yin-yang Bureau.[29] All matters related to strange natural phenomena had to be reported to the ruler through the Yin-yang Bureau (article 8 of the *Zō-ryō* [Miscellaneous Administrative Laws]):

> Manuals on divination, maps of the heavens, astronomical instruments shall not circulate. Students of astronomy cannot read books on divination. Astronomical observations shall not be leaked. Any event of good or bad omens, or strange natural phenomena, when detected, shall be reported to the emperor through the Yin-yang Bureau. These reports will be sealed after each season, and forwarded to the Ministry of Central Affairs, where they will be included in the National Histories. Oracular statements of divination shall not be part of the reports.[30]

Punishments for violations of these prohibitions were stipulated in article 21 of the *Zokutō-ritsu* (Penal Laws for Theft):

> All cases of making magical inscriptions or magical spells are punished by maximum banishment [Tang: 3,000 miles]. "Making" means to fabricate by oneself stories about auspicious and inauspicious events or spirits and ghosts, and thus engage in reckless explanations involving good and bad omens that counter official authority. Cases of written or oral fabrications by others, used to lead more than three people astray, shall be dealt with in the same way. For fewer than three people, the penalty will be mitigated one degree. If the content of what was communicated was reasonable and no harm was done, the penalty is 60 strokes of the cane [Tang: 100]. For the private possession of magical inscriptions, even if they are not distributed, the penalty is 80 [Tang: 2 years incarceration]. If the content was reasonable, 40 strokes [Tang: 60].[31]

Since Buddhist adepts were most likely to know about matters of yin and yang and divination, the same restrictions were repeated in the first half of the very first article of the *Sōni-ryō* (Law for Monks and Nuns). They could not falsely expound on good and bad omens based on observations of astronomical phenomena, discuss affairs of state, bewitch and mislead the people, and study or read books on military strategy:

> All monks and nuns, who from the observation of astronomical phenomena falsely expound on the nature of omens, discuss imperial affairs, bewitch and mislead the people, a fortiori if they read or study books on military strategy, are to be taken to officials and punished according to the law.[32]

These prohibitions precede as more serious, infringements of monastic discipline that follow in the second half of the same article (murder, marriage, stealing, and false claims to enlightenment).

To a large extent, state control was maintained over these various fields, although yin-yang specialists were sometimes found in the circles of plotters, a development to be discussed later. Yet unlike in the Heian period, commoners seem to have had no access to this knowledge. Only in early Heian does certain almanac making on the part of folk astrologers appear for the first time as a problem in the record. In 807 a prohibition was issued to eliminate geomantic notations from almanacs.[33]

The Continental Connection

To staff his Yin-yang Bureau, which played the major role in the semiotical overlay of the political landscape, Tenmu relied virtually exclusively on foreign talent, abundantly available among continentals of long standing, recently arrived Paekche refugees, and Buddhist monks. The allochthons with a long pedigree in Yamato could be called continentals, but those upon whom Tenmu relied most were actually refugees. This change in terminology reveals a dramatic story.

The Paekche refugees were the third and largest wave of transplants to have come over from the Korean peninsula. The first wave lasted through the final decades of the fourth century into the first ones of the fifth century. It was in part occasioned by the beginning warfare on the peninsula between Koguryŏ in the north and Paekche in the southwest (Silla, in the southeast, constituting the third of the Three Kingdoms). Sandwiched between Paekche and Silla in the south lay Kaya, a league of six tribal groups. Since the mid-fourth century it was in commercial contact with the emerging Yamato state, which maintained a post there until 562. In this enclave, Paekche and Silla offered tribute-like gifts to Yamato, perhaps with the aim to secure their southern borders to better confront the Koguryŏ threat in the north, which forced Paekche in the fifth century to move its capital farther south more than once.

The claims of Chinese descent made by the two main groups that came over then, the Aya and Hata, is unverifiable. However, they may have been displaced residents from the Chinese commanderies in the peninsula that had disappeared during the warfare of the fourth century. They could have found their way to Yamato, perhaps via Yamato's post of Mimana (Imna) in Kaya.[34] Their role during the next three centuries, until the early Heian period, was crucial in the transmission of Chinese culture, and very important in a number of political struggles. Put succinctly, they could write and fight. They became comptrollers for the great kings, and introduced mounted archery in the archipelago.[35]

The Aya were the Soga's military ally for a century and a half. It was an Aya who, on Soga Iruka's orders, assassinated Great King Sushun in 592. When, ready to fight for the Soga after Iruka's murder in the coup of 645, they were instead persuaded to lay down their arms, this signaled the beginning of the end for the main Soga line. During Tenmu's war, they rallied overwhelmingly to his cause (which is why Tenmu, on 677/6/14, overlooking their long association with the Soga, decided to forgive their "past misbehavior"), for which they continued to be praised and rewarded into the Nara period. When in 740 Emperor Shōmu left Nara, traveling first in the direction of Ise, then to Fuwa, following Tenmu's campaign trail, he was escorted by a combined force of four hundred Aya and Hata mounted warriors.[36] Still later, in 764, the Aya helped put down a rebellion, and the leader of the Sakanoue main Aya house played a decisive role as shogun in campaigns against the Emishi around the turn of the century. In 815, one half (163) of the 324 *uji* in Heian and the five Home Provinces of the Kinai with declared continental roots claimed Chinese descent. It is important to add that these 324 *uji* in turn constituted one-third of the Heian nobility's 1,059 *uji*.[37]

A type of new arrivals (*imaki*) started coming over toward the end of the fifth century, continuing throughout the sixth. They were men who brought the accouterments of Chinese learning (beyond writing). Some of them were "on loan" from Paekche. Others settled permanently in Yamato, where they were put under supervision of the first wave of continentals, mainly the Aya. Their hereditary service groups, organized as *be*, had leaders (*tomo no miyatsuko*) who became incorporated into the administrative structure of the Yamato state. These leaders and their close kin were granted hereditary titles (*kabane*) by the Yamato court, which simultaneously indicated the special tasks these service lineage groups performed and created among them a sociopolitical hierarchy. Thus, for instance, including Aya, there were forty *uji* that held the *kabane* title *fuhito*, marking them as scribes, thirty-seven of them allochthons.[38]

When Great Sovereign Suiko decided to open direct relations with the Sui court of the newly unified China in the beginning of the seventh century, it was predominantly allochthons who were sent over as students of government techniques, institutions, laws, culture, Confucianism, and Buddhism. The embassy of 608 counted eight allochthons among its members. Three of them were prominent figures: the monk Min, and the scholar-monks (*gakumonsō*) Takamuko Kuromaro and Minabuchi Shōan.[39] They remained in China several decades, experiencing firsthand the Sui-Tang transition of 618. Min, an Imaki Ayahito, returned in 632; the other two, both Yamato no Aya, eight years later. They tutored the future Yamato leaders. Minabuchi taught Confucianism to Prince Naka no Ōe (Tenji) and Kamatari, the future founder of the Fujiwara *uji*. Min lectured on divination to them and to Soga Iruka.

These three scholars, no doubt, helped formulate the Taika Reforms, launched in 645, following Iruka's assassination. The next year, Kuromaro was sent on a mission to Silla, and in 654, as head of the embassy, he returned to Tang China where he died soon after his arrival. These allochthons were critical to the court for the dual purpose of the pursuit of international relations and the attempt at political reform, two initiatives that were launched in the first half of the seventh century. Toward midcentury, both of these efforts were infused with a new urgency, given international developments in East Asia.

The political turmoil of warfare on the peninsula involving the Tang and the so-called Three Kingdoms constituted the source of the problem, and also, in a much unforeseen way, provided the solution with a third wave of highly educated refugees from the upper echelons of Paekche nobility. They eventually helped Tenmu and Jitō accelerate and bring to fruition the transformations that Suiko had initiated.

A Twin Birth: Korea and Nihon

Evidence does not corroborate the story that the Three Kingdoms of the Korean peninsula originated between the years 50 and 10 before our era, allegedly after the Chinese commanderies, established in 108 BCE, started to loose their grip on territory north of the Han River (running through today's Seoul). Koguryŏ was the first to emerge on the historical horizon during the first century CE, when it established itself separate from the Tungusic Puyŏ, centered in Manchuria, and against China. This was some three centuries before Paekche and Silla came into being. Koguryŏ was a warrior state raiding its neighbors and raided by them. Eventually the last Chinese commandery fell under Koguryŏ pressure in 313.[40]

A few decades earlier, in the southwestern part of the peninsula south of the Han River, Paekche had developed into a confederated kingdom out of a number of castletown states. Toward the end of the fourth century, Paekche pushed northward into Koguryŏ and sought to strengthen its international position by establishing contact with the Eastern Jin state in China and kings in the archipelago. Koguryŏ's response, after Paekche had raided its capital and killed its king, was to modernize its institutions through sinicization, including the adoption of Buddhism. King Kwanggaet'o (391–413) dramatically succeeded in reversing Koguryŏ's fortune by expanding in all directions: he conquered the Liaodong region in the west, Manchuria in the northeast, and pushed south of the Han River into Paekche territory, crushing a Yamato force that had advanced against Silla. This is the period when the first groups of émigrés from the peninsula settled in Yamato.[41]

Chinese sources report that Yamato, which saw its fate linked to that of Paekche, sent eight missions to the Southern Song in China during the fifth century.[42] The threat by Koguryŏ, however, was not the only motive for the Yamato king's interest in Paekche. Metallurgy and the abundance of iron ore in Paekche also played a role, as did their advanced technology in matters of administration, the organization of specialized tribute groups (be), silkworm rearing, and weaving, among others.

Silla, like Paekche, developed from confederated walled-town states and petty kingdoms into a single sovereign state. Kaya followed a similar path, with a less secure autonomy as outcome, however. Its economy was dependent on maritime trade, which explains its close connection to Yamato. Politically, it became caught in the mid-sixth century in a new rivalry between Paekche and Silla, which had been allies for some 120 years. Yamato forces became involved again, as they had once long before. Eventually, however, Silla absorbed Kaya, in 562.

Silla was the last of the Three Kingdoms to adopt Chinese culture around the turn of the sixth century and went even as far as creating its own era names in 536 instead of following China's, which, as tribute payer to the Central Kingdom, it should have. Around that time, Buddhism was also established as state religion. In 551, Silla, with the help of Paekche, expanded into the southern part of Koguryŏ, the region of the Han River basin. Subsequently Silla turned on Paekche and drove it out of the conquered territory. The result was a change of roles. Paekche now allied itself with Koguryŏ in a number of attacks against Silla, its new enemy.

Elsewhere on the continent, other tensions were rising in the latter half of the sixth century. The Sui dynasty succeeded in unifying the Chinese empire in 589, only to be threatened by Turks in northcentral Asia. Koguryŏ, which extended far into Manchuria, sought a rapprochement with them against the Sui. Silla, now spread across the center of the peninsula, wary of this alignment of power in the north and pressured by Paekche and Yamato in the south, joined forces with the Sui. A series of large, unsuccessful battles against Koguryŏ weakened the Sui, which were replaced in 618 by the Tang, a dynasty closely related to the Turks. Starting in 645, the Tang launched a number of large-scale invasions into Koguryŏ with no more success than the Sui.

The Tang then agreed to enter into an alliance with Silla. The plan was to first get rid of Paekche and then launch a combined attack against Koguryŏ, China advancing from the north, Silla from the south and east. The strategy succeeded all too well. In 660, while Silla attacked from the east, China landed a force at the mouth of the Kŭm River, some 70 kilometers from the capital of Sabi, where the king surrendered. This was the end of Paekche, but not for everyone. A member of the royal family led a three-year-long resistance movement. This is where Yamato entered into the picture once more.

(At least twice before this time, members of the Paekche royal family had sought residence in Yamato. In 461, during a new outbreak of hostility with Koguryŏ, the king had sent his mother as "hostage" or guarantee to the Yamato court, asking for military assistance. Paekche was quite desperate, and for good reason. In 475, Koguryŏ routed its army and killed its king.[43] The second time was in 642 or 643,[44] when Prince P'ung had been sent as a hostage.)

After the Paekche king's abdication in 660, the restoration leaders brought P'ung back across the sea and installed him as king. The Yamato court, quite understandably worried about the Tang-Silla alliance that had crushed its ally Paekche, was willing to support the restoration militarily. Accompanied by Crown Prince Naka no Ōe and Nakatomi (later Fujiwara) Kamatari, Great Sovereign Saimei personally went to Tsukushi in Kyushu to supervise preparations for an expeditionary force. When she suddenly passed away there, Naka no Ōe took over as regent.

The Tang forces, withdrawn from Paekche after the king's abdication, had started the invasion of Koguryŏ from the north, but the restoration movement and Yamato's involvement made them change course. They returned with their fleet to the mouth of the Kŭm River where, joined by Silla forces, they sank the Yamato fleet of some four hundred ships sent by Naka no Ōe in 663. The Tang established a puppet king in Paekche. Yamato had no choice but to accept the fait accompli, and two years later reestablished relations with all the parties involved: the Tang, Paekche, and Silla.

The final scene of this drama opened with the Tang's third invasion of the peninsula in 667 (after the first one in 660, which liquidated Paekche, and the second in 663, which destroyed the restoration movement and sank the Yamato fleet). One year later, Koguryŏ was obliterated. Thus, in 668, only the Tang and Silla were left on the peninsula. The Tang, however, acted as if they were the sole power, and considered both the former Paekche and Silla as new provinces of the expanding empire. They established commanderies in the former Paekche, appointing the son of the abdicated Paekche king as one of its governors, and Silla's king as the governor-general of the Great Commandery of Kyerim, through which Silla would be ruled.[45] In P'yŏngyang, they set up a Protectorate-General to Pacify the East, with jurisdiction over the former Koguryŏ, Paekche, and Silla as well. Then, in 676, the third year of Tenmu's rule, Silla drove the Chinese forces out and established a unified rule over the peninsula roughly south of the 39th parallel.

Silla's dominion lasted until 935. North of its border soon another kingdom, Parhae, formed in 698 from the remnants of Koguryŏ and Tungusic tribes (it was overrun by the Khitan in 926). Silla's single rule over most of the peninsula until its surrender to Koryŏ constitutes for some nationalist historians the birth of Korea, which for others took place only when Koryŏ incorporated the northern third of the peninsula beyond Silla's borders.

THESE DEVELOPMENTS on the peninsula had a major impact in Yamato one can call the birth of Nihon, presided over by Tenmu. The year 645, when the Tang forces launched their massive attack on Koguryŏ, was the year of the Taika coup d'état, which ushered in reforms that strengthened Yamato rule internally. This was one of several coups on the peninsula and in Tang China, several of them witnessed by foreign visitors.

Three years earlier, a coup in Koguryŏ in the face of Tang threats had brought Yŏn Kaesomun (?–665) to power as a military strongman who was spectacularly successful in resisting the Tang. His strengthening program included a persecution of Buddhism and promotion of Daoism.[46] He had come to power "after a wholesale slaughter of the king (Yŏngyu) and others who opposed him."[47] In 645, Koguryŏ envoys witnessed a similar event in the audience hall of the Yamato court where Naka no Ōe and Kamatari murdered Iruka, the prelude to the Taika Reforms. On the other hand, Yamato students must have been present in the Tang capital earlier when, in 626, a son of the Tang founder succeeded to the throne only after he killed his brother the heir apparent, had another one slain, and forced his father to abdicate.[48] In Silla, King Muyŏl (r. 654–661) came to power after crushing the rebellion of Pidam, which greatly strengthened his hand against the aristocracy. He succeeded in passing the throne to his lineal descendants and kept the pressure on Paekche.[49]

During the seventh century, especially its latter half, rulers and would-be rulers in the major regimes in East Asia, as a response to the Tang threat, were experimenting with new formulae to strengthen their rule, increasing their autocratic character. The coup in Yamato, the Taika Reforms, and Tenmu's rebellion and administrative innovations should be understood in this context.

Around the Jinshin War, the situation was as follows. Tenmu left Ōtsu in a hurry after his meeting with ailing Tenji on 671/10/19. Before Tenji died on 12/3, the governor of Dazaifu in northern Kyushu received a messenger from Tsushima on 11/10, warning that a Tang delegation of extraordinary size was on its way to Japan, all in all two thousand men on forty-seven ships, but that they should not be engaged in order to avoid hostilities.

This Chinese garrison remained in Dazaifu for months, not unusual for delegations, but this time certainly creating a good amount of anxiety.[50] On 672/3/18, they were informed of Tenji's death and conveyed appropriate expressions of condolence. This was fully three and a half months after Tenji had passed away. Was there some fear that the Chinese would take advantage of the situation? Two months later they were still there. On 5/12 they were presented a number of gifts, and they finally left on 5/30. Three weeks later, on 6/22, Tenmu launched his rebellion. Thus the Tang threat may also have functioned as an alibi for Tenmu to seize power under the excuse of a much-needed regime strengthening, or a regime change, which is what he eventually realized if one pays attention to the symbolics accompanying his politics.

By this time, one should recall, it looked as if the Three Kingdoms, including Silla, had disappeared from the map and had become provinces of the Tang empire; but only four years later Silla drove the Tang out. Thus, the Tang "delegation" could no doubt be read as a signal that Yamato would become the next addition to the empire. The Chinese military commander of the former Paekche sent five missions to Yamato, the first one in 664/5, nine months after the debacle of the Japanese fleet.[51] Diplomatic relations intensified over the next two decades, with delegations from Koguryŏ still arriving years after it had been conquered (679, 680), and seven from the large island of Chejudo (some 250 km west of Kyushu and 75 km south of Korea), formerly part of Paekche, which started contacting Yamato after Paekche had fallen. In addition, delegations came from the Mishihase (or Ashihase, the Su-shen of Aston's translation), which were either Tungusic tribes that may have been part of Koguryŏ and later of Parhae, or possibly Emishi.[52]

During one generation, between 630 and 669, Yamato had sent six embassies to China. The next generation, however, had none; contact with Tang China was resumed only in 702. Yamato's diplomatic relations during those decades were limited to Silla and the remnants of the upheaval on the peninsula who seemed to have pinned their hopes on Yamato for reversing the course of history. Ignorance of events in China must have been thorough if we are to believe the story Awata no Ason Mahito, the ambassador of the 702 mission, told upon his return on 704/7/1. When disembarking in China, he was surprised that he had arrived not in the "Great Tang," but in the "Great Zhou." "Why the name change?" he reportedly inquired, and learned that for the last twenty years, a new dynasty under a female ruler, Empress Dowager Wu, had ruled China. "In 683," he was told, "the Great Heavenly Sovereign and Emperor (*tenkō taitei*) [Gaozong] had died and the Great Imperial Empress (*kōtai gōkurai*) [Empress Dowager Wu] succeeded him on the throne; she took the title of Saintly and Divine Empress (*seishin kōtei*) and called the country the Great Zhou."[53]

The formidable institution building that Tenmu and Jitō engaged in during those years (673–702), undoubtedly in part a repetition of defensive moves against the expansionist Tang first taken by Koguryŏ, then by Silla, was carried out without the benefit of direct contact with China. This is when the new and largest wave of foreign talent, driven out of Paekche by the Tang and Silla conquests, played a crucial role (together with the frequent exchange of embassies with Silla that continued). The number of refugees is impressive.[54]

AFTER THE NAVAL DISASTER of 663 killed the restoration effort, Prince P'ung fled to Koguryŏ by ship, while his wife, successor, and other children together with a number of aristocrats and office holders crossed over to Japan. The size of this group is not known, but two years later, more than four hundred men and women from Paekche were settled in Ōmi and granted fields (665/2). The next year, more than two thousand who had been supported by the Yamato government for the last three years were moved to the eastern provinces (666/10).

A considerable number of these refugees were well educated and cultivated members of the Paekche nobility and officialdom. In other words, they constituted in embryo a government in exile. In 671, about seventy of them who were first- or second-rank holders in Paekche's rank system of sixteen tiers were given Yamato court ranks ranging between the equivalents of fourth and seventh junior rank of the later *ritsuryō* system of 701.[55] Two of them were appointed to the Law Office that may have produced Tenji's Ōmi Code (if it was ever written); one became the head of the University Bureau, created around that time. Others included specialists in military matters, medicinal cures, the Confucian classics, and a yin-yang master. The military experts were immediately set to work building fortifications against an anticipated Tang invasion. Many of them were soon to be employed in Tenmu's bureaucracy. The Yin-yang Bureau was staffed by refugees who often taught other refugees. Some names show up in the *Kaifūsō* as guests of Prince Ōtomo's salon of Chinese poetry in Ōmi.

Around this time, a number of technological innovations are mentioned in the record and sometimes explicitly linked to allochthons. Prince Naka no Ōe is reported on 671/4/25 to have built a clepsydra (water clock) that was activated several years later. Twice a Buddhist priest from the Yamato no Aya is recorded as having presented a compass to the court (658 and 666). In 670, a new method for smelting iron, using water power, was introduced. On 671/3/3, a man of peninsular ancestry presented a water level to the court.

Eventually, after one or two generations, these refugees were given Japanese *kabane* titles. Toward the end of the Nara period and the beginning of the ninth century, we find allochthons among the upper echelons of the nobility. Fujiwara Kadonomaro (755–818), middle councilor on the Council of State and eventual ambassador to the Tang in 804 and son of the great councilor Okuromaro, had a Hata mother. Some of them, like Sakanoue Tamuramaro (758–811), were third-rank holders. Tamuramaro had perhaps one of the most eye-catching careers. Between 791 and 804, he led several victorious campaigns against the Emishi. Heian's founder, Emperor Kanmu, whose mother was of royal Paekche stock, counted one of Tamuramaro's sisters and one of his daughters among his consorts.[56]

By the early ninth century, as mentioned, one-third of all *uji* were listed as allochthons: 324 out of the 1,059 *uji* in Heian and the five Home Provinces according to the *Shinsen shōjiroku* (Newly Compiled Record of Clan Names), compiled between 799 and 815. (A modern scholar who has traced the *uji* of all of Japan has come up with the same percentage: 710 out of 2,385).[57] From its Introduction, cited at the opening of this chapter, it appears that this compilation purported to halt the "naturalization" of allochthons who, by changing their surnames, were obliterating evidence of their continental origin and even claiming kinship with noble families.[58] It was a testimony both to the degree they had succeeded in penetrating the circles of the nobility and to the threat they seem to have constituted to that nobility.

How had this happened? The census of 670 was supposed to have fixed all surnames and required official permission to change them. In 684 a hierarchy was introduced for surnames of officials by adding a *kabane* suffix to them. The top three prestige ranks (*mabito*, *ason*, and *sukune*) from a total of eight, however, were not available to allochthons.[59] Empress Kōken changed this. On 757/4/4, possibly in a political move to build a loyal clique, she decided to grant all requests for changes of name and title from allochthons of Koguryŏ, Paekche, and Silla stock. Within the next four years, about two thousand applicants were absorbed into some fifty *uji*.[60] The *Shinsen shōjiroku* of 815 appears to have been a reaction to this policy, which had resulted in obscuring the alien origin of many allochthons. Anyway, with the record straightened out and the origins of all *uji* clarified once and for all, the term *kikajin*, which I have translated as allochthon, henceforward lost its function as a marker of either an occupation or roots. The term disappeared until modern times, when it was revived as the administrative term for "naturalized alien."

The refugee population, however, was not limited to people fleeing Paekche. There were also over a hundred Chinese captives sent over by a Paekche general with a request for military assistance (660/10). They were settled in two districts in Mino (Nagoya area), one of them at the Fuwa Pass. Tenmu may have relied on their expertise during his Jinshin campaign. The main architect for the new capital of Nara was an Aya, as were two members of the committee of nineteen charged with the composition of the Taihō Code.[61] Others, as hinted at before, must have contributed to the earlier (now lost) versions: Tenmu's Kiyomihara-ryō (and possibly Tenji's Ōmi-ryō).

On 685/2/14, Tenmu gave cap rank to 147 people from the former Paekche, Koguryŏ, and China. In 716/5, some 1,799 people from Koguryŏ who had been settled in seven provinces of central Honshu and the Kanto region were resettled in Musashi's Koma district (part of today's Iruma district in southern Saitama prefecture). The Yamato and Nara courts did not lose track of the allochthons.

Silla was also represented. Between 714 and 766, a total of 417 men and women, 74 households, 32 monks, and 2 nuns from Silla were settled in the frontier regions of the northern Kanto plain.[62] These settlements obviously played a role in the imperium's expanding frontier against the Emishi.[63]

In hindsight it is as if Tenmu and his wife-successor Jitō had a thirty-year post–Jinshin War plan. The overarching aim was to "modernize" under the threat of the Tang. In 702, they had reached their goal and were ready to show off their achievements. Before Jitō died that year, a new Penal and Administrative Code was promulgated, and an embassy was sent to the Tang (actually the Zhou) to announce, among other things, that a new political entity had taken shape across the sea: Nihon, as Yamato was to be called henceforward.[64] Nihon, moreover, was more than ready, as mentioned in chapter 1, to style itself a Small Central Kingdom, ruled by a heavenly sovereign.

Tenmu and Jitō were able to put Nihon on the East Asia map as a serious player thanks to the allochthons, the recent refugees, and the knowledge they embodied. Buddhism played a well-known role in this process through its overwhelming institutional presence. So did yin-yang learning, far less identifiable even though it had a bureau, and Daoism, which lacked any institutional framework. Both of these traditions provided a rich variety of symbols that could be put into the service of rulership. To understand this role requires that one peel away the Buddhist layer of culture and historiography from this period, which I shall attempt to do in the following two chapters.

5 LITURGIES

Presents were distributed to all who had provided service at
the Ōnie Great Offering: the Nakatomi and Inbe, the people
from the Jinkan (Kami Office), the district governors from
the two provinces of Harima and Tanba, and all the laborers
under them.
—673/12/5. *Nihon shoki*

Amaterasu and Takamimusuhi imparted upon Ninigi the
magatama jewel, the mirror, and the Kusanagi sword.
—712. *Kojiki*

The Heavenly Ancestors presented the Heavenly Grandson
with two Sacred Treasures, together with jewels and a spear.
—807. *Kogoshūi*

No country can be governed without grains ["millet"]; the
essence of government for the ruler, and the fundamentals
of life for the people consist only of the task ["duty"] of working the land.
—852. *Directive of the Council of State*

Food has played a crucial role in the life not only of individuals, but
of political regimes as well in East Asia. Through ritual, people have forever sought to secure its production against the elements, and when states
developed, perceiving themselves equally vulnerable to the political consequences of natural disasters, they created public rites or liturgies for the
same purpose. China, the first state emerging in East Asia, understood that
its survival depended on success with the weather, called Heaven, an awareness that took root in Yamato concurrently with the establishment of a state
there in the late seventh century. We find this understanding succinctly
expressed in the above Directive of the Council of State from 852 (see epigraph) and in a memorial presented to the throne in 914 by Miyoshi Kiyoyuki, adviser to the Heian emperor Daigo. The memorial appropriately
opens with a quotation from a Chinese source:

For the state, the people are the most important, for the people their livelihood is what is most valued. Without people, what would the state rest upon?
Without livelihood what would the people build upon? Therefore, the right
way to appease the people, and the secret to secure their nourishment consist only in that the fruit of the year ripens without catastrophic flooding or
droughts. That is the reason why the Imperial Court celebrates each year on
the 4th day of the 2nd month the Toshigoi festival, and on the 11th days of the
6th and 11th months the Tsukinami festival in the Jingikan.[1]

In China, the emperor was ultimately coresponsible with Heaven for
abundant crops through rituals that sought a measured rainfall avoiding
the extremes of floods and droughts. As far as the record shows, this performative dimension of royal power developed rather late in Yamato and
remained underdeveloped. Great King Kōgyoku constitutes an early, but
isolated, example of a successful Chinese-styled rainmaking intervention
with Heaven in the middle of a drought in 642. A century and a half later,
Emperor Kanmu is also credited with a similar feat in 788. In between these
two dates, the record does not present Yamato monarchs directly interced-
ing personally as ritual actors. It was mostly religious specialists who came
to be relied upon to prevent and stop natural calamities.

In Yamato food and harvest were the focus not only of one, but of all
important yearly state rituals (three of them mentioned by Miyoshi), and
even of the enthronement ritual. Some of the terminology ("Kinen-sai,"
for instance, the original name for Toshigoi) and structure (offerings to the
spirits and at royal mausoleums) were adopted from China by Tenmu and
Jitō, and the ceremonies were ultimately fixed by law in the Taihō Code of
701. Most likely, these rituals were already part of the Kiyomihara Code,
begun drafting in 681 and promulgated eight years later.

Ritual and Food

Half of the yearly state festivals, six out of thirteen, listed in the Jingi-ryō
(Law of the Kami of Heaven and Earth) of the Taihō Code dealt with crops
(table 2).[2] Four of these were major festivals involving the whole realm: the
Toshigoi festival (Tenmu's Kinen-sai, held on 2/4), by far the largest; the
Tsukinami festival (duplicating the former and held twice: on 6/11 and
12/11); and the Niiname festival (First Fruit Tasting, held on variable days
in the eleventh month).[3] During the two additional minor harvest festivals,
oblations were sent from the court for celebrating the Kanname festival in
Ise and the Ainame festival held at shrines in the Kinai capital area, mainly

Table 2. Calendar of the *ritsuryō* state liturgies

Festival	Date	Oblations	Description
Toshigoi	2/4	distributed at Jingikan	prayer for year's harvest
Hanashizume	3/31	Jingikan	protection against contagious disease
Ōimi (Rain)	summer/fall	court sends to Hirose	for harvest, moderate wind, and rain
Saikusa	summer	Jingikan	protection against contagious disease
Kazakami (Wind)	summer/fall	court sends to Tatsuta	protection against storms
Tsukinami	6/11, 12/11	distributed at Jingikan	for year's harvest
Hishizume	summer/winter	Jingikan	protection of capital against fire
Michiae	summer/winter	Jingikan	protection of capital against spirits
Kanname	fall	emperor sends oblations	harvest: oblations sent to Ise *kami*
Ainame	fall	Jingikan	harvest: oblations sent to to Yamato *kami*
Chinkon	before Niiname	Jingikan	strengthen emperor's spirit
Niiname/ Daijō-sai	11th month	distributed at Jingikan	harvest thanksgiving
Ōharae	6/30, 12/31	Suzaku palace gate	great purification of pollution

Source: Adapted from Nishimiya, *Ritsuryō jingi saishi*, 17, table 1.

the Yamato and Kii provinces — fourteen by 737, increased to forty-one by 920, but reduced considerably later that century.[4]

Three peculiar aspects of the four greatest of these festivals are relevant for the discussion that follows. One, curiously perhaps, food offered to the monarch and officials and consumed by them played an important role in the ritual expression of ruler jurisdiction and officials' acceptance thereof.

Offering food was a gesture of seeking to ingratiate oneself with someone more elevated: district officials with provincial governors, they with the monarch, and he or she with the *kami*. The consumption of rice by the monarch together with the *kami* (offered by two provinces representing the whole realm) constituted the essence of the enthronement ceremony, which was combined with the Niiname harvest festival (on such an occasion called Daijō-sai). Two, most strikingly, a peculiar circulation of foodstuff and goods was highlighted as much as its plentiful production, this through the disbursement of great amounts of products, natural ones from the fields as well as man-made ones, from the center outward to the *kami* of local shrines — conceivably an exemplary enacting of sorts for the *kami* of what was expected from them and a promise of more if they responded in kind. Three, somewhat surprisingly, the emperor's direct role in these rituals (aside from the enthronement ritual) was virtually nonexistent. Miyoshi's Memorial, to which we shall return, even though addressed to the emperor, is neither about him nor his role in securing ritual efficacy.

Consumption of food offered to the ruler played an important symbolic role in the Yamato polity. Traditionally, the king's realm was referred to with a term for eating: *osukuni* or *osukuni tenka*, which can be paraphrased as "the realm or country [which supplies the food for] consumption [by the ruler]." *Osu* is the honorific form for eating, *kuni* means country, and *tenka*, realm ("[all] under Heaven"). One encounters the term in the *Kojiki* and the *Manyōshū*, but it continued to be used in official documents such as royal edicts recorded in the *Shoku Nihongi* even after the adoption of Tang political nomenclature.[5]

This conception of authority and submission was also enacted in royal progresses when local leaders presented natural products from their area to the visiting monarch.[6] The offering of food and other goods, and their acceptance, expressed a relationship whereby the recipient acknowledges the assistance, support, and service presented to him by the gift giver, a practice that is homologous to oblations made to *kami*. From *mokkan* we also know that at least since the 730s, during the night following the Tsukinami ceremony, the emperor was isolating himself to have two ceremonial meals with the *kami* in a ritual called *jingonjiki*.[7] First fruits from tribute (*nosaki*) were also offered to the *kami*, followed by others to the spirits of former rulers at their mausoleums, and then to the current ruler.[8] Tribute to the state, gifts to rulers, and offerings to *kami* took the form of oblations.

The offering and acceptance of food, sealing the hierarchical relationship between the ruler and his officials, and by implication the realm — commoners as such were irrelevant in expressions of the arrangement of power

— played a central role in the enthronement ceremony of the Daijō-sai (Great New Fruit Festival). This rite was a modification of the Niiname-sai. The new monarch accepted and consumed rice offered by two provinces chosen by divination, standing for all provinces east and west (first enacted at Tenmu's enthronement in 673).[9] In the mature *ritsuryō* state, it was preceded by the distribution of *mitegura* (royal oblations for the *kami*) to all shrines chartered by the government (*kansha*), a flow of counterofferings in the opposite direction from tribute offerings to the ruler: this time from the monarch nominally to local *kami* but actually honoring local elites associated with important shrines, who were thus reincorporated under the politico-ritual aegis of each new ruler.

State ceremonies were ranked. The Daijō-sai was the only one classified as "great," but all four middle-ranked ceremonies of the Nara yearly calendar had a similar structure of disbursed royal oblations, and all were related to food and harvest.[10] These celebrations, especially the Toshigoi festival, were gigantic productions in the form of distributed oblations (*hanpei*).[11] Staged four times a year, and downscaled on some other occasions as well,[12] they combined a number of aspects, religious and political. Gifts by the state to the *kami*, they were also counter-gifts to local notables who had been instrumental in forwarding tribute to the center, some of which was thus brought back into circulation. Subtle enticements on the one hand to render tribute as expected, on the other they were also tribute in the form of offerings to the local *kami*, supplications to the *kami* for more and signs to the realm that the center took care of its welfare by placating the *kami*.

These rituals took on the format of national conventions because they required that delegates from designated shrines all over the country gather in the capital. Initiated by Tenmu on a small scale in southern Yamato province, they developed over time as assertive new rituals demonstrating the preeminence of the center in an ever-widening reach, under Jitō probably enlisting selected shrines first in all of Yamato province, then the surrounding provinces, and eventually, by the time the Taihō Code was issued, involving shrines throughout Yamato the country.

The Liturgical State

Tenmu and Jitō fashioned the *ritsuryō* state as a liturgical state, a church-state. They gave the state a liturgy without grafting it on a full-grown religious institution or creating a state-church. By establishing harvest liturgies at the center, they selectively built connections with an expanding number of shrines and *kami* serviced by local *uji*. Max Weber writes about a "*liturgical* meeting of the ruler's political and economic needs" through "specific services and contributions" where "it is natural to view the subject as existing for the ruler and the satisfaction of his needs."[13] While certainly applicable to the *ritsuryō* state (and many others), the term is even more apt than Weber's metaphorical use suggests, because actual religious liturgies were created for a state where contributions for ritual purposes and regular taxes often merged into each other. Offerings one usually thinks of as voluntary gestures were ordered by the state, and taxes were spoken of in the religious language of service donations. Terminology is important here, for it presents practice in a skewed manner.

Taxation is a term that is best avoided for premodern levies since it is calibrated to wealth and income, is monetary, and most important, has a quite open connotation of imposed burden, a dimension absent from the ancient terminology. "Tribute," although undeniably like taxation and no doubt a burden, is preferable because it refers almost exclusively to material imposts ("taxes in kind," used often as "stipends in goods"); "tribute," however, shifts the emphasis to an expression of submission and even homage of subjects to their rulers, as in today's metaphorical use of "paying tribute to someone's achievements." Levy contributions were presented as offerings (*nie*) to the Yamato rulers.[14] I propose "oblation," especially for the discussion of the festivals that follows. "Oblation" resonates with meanings that include connotations of solemn offering, token of respect, or voluntary gift to a monarch or god even when obtained as a levy.

Oblation elides obligation from the representation of the relation between the provider of goods or services and their recipient. What we spontaneously would call taxation was referred to in seventh- and eighth-century Japan with an official vocabulary akin to "oblation" used in relation to human superiors and *kami* alike. A relationship of dependency, simultaneously to rulers and *kami*, was expressed by offering samples of first fruits from the harvest (i.e., tax/tribute) to important *kami* shrines, at the tombs of deceased rulers, and then to the monarch, in that order. Since tribute from abroad (i.e., taxes collected by foreign rulers brought as presents by overseas delegations, mainly Silla) was channeled, like domestic tribute, to the ruler and "as a tribute" to the *kami*, such tribute signaled, at least for the Yamato officials, a subservient relationship of these countries toward Yamato.[15] Not only levies, but also the execution of duties by state or court officials was expressed in that language whereby officeholding became service offered to the sovereign.

My focus on representation and language, at the expense of the actual practice of surplus extraction, should not be interpreted as a downplaying of the exploitation of commoners. It was undoubtedly elite language that represented tribute paying as the offering of oblations. The commoners' understanding of "service" was expressed without words when they fled the imposed corvée labor for projects such as the building of the palace in Nara.[16]

Maruyama Masao is one of many scholars who have argued that *matsurigoto*, "matters of governance and ritual" (my translation), and other related terms such as *osame-matsuru* (ruling/offering-service) express a particular ancient representation of government, not as something a ruler does to people below, but as services or offerings rendered to him or her (by officials). A superior's position, especially the emperor's, is thus configured as one of passive recipient of services offered by subordinates paying homage to him or her.[17] Unquestionably a euphemism of domination, an ideological function Maruyama acknowledges in passing,[18] the position of the great king or heavenly ruler nevertheless seems to lack the absolutist dimension often associated with the term "emperor" — certainly in its representation vis-à-vis lesser powerholders.

Beyond their important function of providing a palpable experience of the center to thousands of locals, disbursed oblations, the structural core of the four most important ceremonies, revealed the tenor of rulership as finalized by Jitō. Indeed, if the presentation of offerings, gifts, and foodstuff expresses a relationship of submission to the recipient of these goods, as exemplified on numerous occasions by rice offerings from provinces at enthronement ceremonies or of regional products by the Emishi and delegations from the "southern islands," a similar but reversed significance accompanied the presentation of oblations to local *kami* by the Jingikan.[19]

The distributed oblations were ostensibly destined for local *kami*, but what the several thousand participants at these events witnessed with their own eyes, four times a year, was a gigantic flow of gifts outward from the center, which thereby, according to the cultural logic, adopted a relatively subordinate posture. The connotation of some manner of dependency by the center upon the supernatural but through the local must have been communicated by the very form of the rituals. The message of these staged events was homologous to the one encapsulated in Jitō's posthumous name where, even as heavenly ruler, she presented herself as *neko*, "child with roots" in the soil.[20]

Moreover, in the Jingikan's courtyard, delegations from far and wide saw, piled high, tribute that had come from a variety of places unfamiliar to them. The state, embodied in its hierarchically lined up ministers and officials, was there in front of them. The emperor, however, was present only as the hidden reality behind the displayed tribute, referred to in the *norito* prayer formula as "precious oblations from the August Descendant [of the Sun *kami* Amaterasu]."[21]

The shrine representatives were *hafuri*. Originally, they functioned as mouthpieces for *kami* in village rituals, as a few episodes going back some two centuries before Tenmu's time indicate. One *hafuri* also played a role during the Jinshin War.[22] Through their state-related function, which appears to have been mainly in connection with these harvest-related celebrations, they gradually received a professional cachet. In the Taihō Code they are mentioned as a *be*, an official functional group.[23] Later in the Nara period they are identifiable as the bottom rank of shrine personnel, classified below *negi* (prayers) and *kannushi* (shrine priests). By then, they had become mostly ritual assistants, perhaps best understood as the equivalent of sacristans or sextons, caretakers of ritual paraphernalia.

The mixing of political and religious domains in the terminology (offerings as levies, and tribute as oblations) was also realized in administrative matters. Other departments of state besides the Office of Kami Affairs were involved in the great annual state rituals conducted in its courtyard.[24] For each celebration, several lists of needed items were drawn up at the office. One list with the specific amount of supplies in fruit, other foods, and drink was submitted for approval to the highest administrative organ, the Council of State. Separate lists went to provincial governors to check, verify, and approve the amount of tribute requested from the provincial storehouses: special *kami* taxes levied on sustenance households attached to shrines called *kami* households (*jinko* or *kanbe*) and regular tribute.[25] Following approval, these lists were forwarded, via the head of the controllers (*benkan*), to the Ministry of Popular Affairs (Minbushō) and back to the Office of Kami Affairs. The goods for the festivals were stored with the tribute at the Department of the Treasury (Ōkurashō), or they were specially manufactured (items such as offering tables and sword cases) at the Bureau of Carpentry (Mokuryō), one of the eighteen bureaus and offices of the Ministry of the Imperial Household (Kunaishō). When needed, the Imperial Stables delivered sacred horses.

THE JINGIKAN (which had no counterpart in the Tang bureaucracy) and the Daijōkan formed the two most important state organs. The latter formulated policies, while one can conceive of the former as maker of the polity. Indeed, this seems to have been not only a side effect of the state rituals orchestrated by the Jingikan, but its principal raison d'être.

Tenmu, followed by Jitō, created the liturgical state and its central institution, the Jingikan, as eventually defined in the Taihō Code. On 692/9/14, under Jitō, this office made its first appearance under that name, but very early in Tenmu's reign already (on 673/12/5), a Jinkan (another term for Kami Office) was mentioned in the context of Tenmu's first court-initiated celebration, Ōnie (Great Offering, later called the First Fruits Festival), which was coordinated with his coronation.[26] Thus, when Tenmu, a year after his rebellion and military victory, was ready to officially consecrate his position with a proper enthronement, he combined his installation with a Harvest Thanksgiving Festival, where he accepted rice from two representative provinces symbolizing the allegiance of the whole realm and signifying his regime as benefiting the country and himself as the supreme ritual intermediary with the *kami*.

In a comparative vein, Robert Ellwood has noted that "The *Daijō-sai* is the only major *accession* rite which is definitely and unambiguously tied to the Harvest Festival."[27] This connection, however, stems more from political necessity than from some cultural need or affinity, or perhaps more accurately, its initial political function was subsequently overlaid with cultural interpretations. In linking the two, Tenmu must have perceived an opportunity to substitute his stature as conqueror and usurper for an image of intermediary with cosmic forces, and the legal codes subsequently froze this connection into heralded tradition.

Since a Kami Office is mentioned for the first time at the time of Tenmu's enthronement, it must have been created sometime during the first year of his rule, possibly even specifically for that purpose. Evidence is scarce, but it appears that under Tenmu, the members of this office (consisting most probably of *hafuri* and other diviners) did not yet include the Nakatomi and Inbe ritualists since they were mentioned separately on this occasion. These two ritualist *uji* were at that point most likely personal-service *uji* to his court and not yet incorporated as full-fledged officials into the administrative structure. Most of these offices were staffed by *maetsukimi*, middle-rank office lineage members, harking back to pre-Taika times, when they had served ministers (*ōmi, ōmuraji*). It seems that it was Jitō who installed the Nakatomi and Inbe as officials of the newly created Office of Kami Affairs, which by 694 (3/23), two years after the record reveals its existence under its Jingikan name, counted a staff of 164, half of whom were probably *hafuri*.[28]

These *hafuri* on the Jingikan's staff were the lowest-ranked "state employees" (without having court rank), as were those attached to the chartered shrines in the provinces. The latter also were registered on Jingikan rosters.

They constituted the deepest point of direct penetration of the center in local matters, but they were most probably not linked horizontally except when they stood together in the courtyard of the Jingikan four times a year. They were either chosen from *kami* households attached to shrines (maximum two or three, mostly no more than one) or appointed from commoners for shrines lacking such households.

Before these state rituals were established, plentiful harvests had been secured through local rituals. Prior to Tenmu, however, the court had not been involved in them, and neither did the *ritsuryō* state legislate, after their establishment, that all local harvest festivals be uniform and synchronized. When attendance at these state rituals in the capital began to falter, about three-quarters of a century after they were established, the number of shrines expected to participate was reduced drastically, revealing perhaps that the state, to extend its dominion, which it succeeded in doing in part through these rituals, had overreached itself or that it had achieved its goal.

The Jingikan's political role was not limited to regularly displaying and orchestrating, albeit selectively, the integration of the realm. It also hierarchized that integration by establishing a ranking order for the various *kami* and shrines, calibrated to the differential importance (which was thereby displayed) of the local magnates associated with these shrines in the districts, below the provincial level. The *Engishiki* distinguished six classes of state shrines. To my knowledge, the first indication of hierarchizing the *kami* world is to be found on the day the Jinshin War ended, for on 672/7/23 (the very day Prince Ōtomo "strangled himself"), three *kami* who had served Tenmu's army well through oracles were ordered to have their ranks raised.[29] (No time was wasted to signal *kami* cooperation for what had just happened.) The texts do not mention earlier rankings, but since this was a promotion, ranks must have already been in existence, although it is unlikely that they went back earlier than the time when court ranks were created at the beginning of the century.

This political manipulation of shrines and through them of local strongmen was particularly crucial in the decades following Tenmu's accession to power, when the center in Yamato province was seeking to solidify its stature as the center for the Yamato realm. By the 770s, however, the costs entailed to yield this political profit were beginning to be felt unwarranted, as was the effort to enforce attendance at the rituals. By the end of the century the extension of the center's ritualistic reach had been drastically reduced.

Yet even then, four times a year, the liturgical character of the centralizing state was acted out at the capital and at all provincial headquarters in large gatherings of *hafuri*, its spiritual foot soldiers. In the process, the *hafuri* had become a constituency. In many enthronement edicts starting in 714, they figure as recipients of celebratory donations. In ten out of the seventeen edicts between 714 (Genshō) and 884 (Kōkō), they appear as "the *hafuribe* from all shrines in the realm" together with "the monks and nuns of all the temples in the capital and the Kinai." Initially they were referred to after the monks and nuns, but starting in 758 (Junnin) they were mentioned in first place, before the Buddhists.[30] Around the turn of the century, their positions were further institutionalized with six-year appointments.

Oblations

In principle and initially, the goods used in these ceremonies seem to have been generated by a rice levy, tagged "*kami* tribute" (*shinzei*), the beginnings of which, like so many aspects of the liturgical state, go back to Tenmu's early years. On 677/5/28, he issued a decree that marked for liturgical use the regular rice levies from *kami* households (*jingo*) attached to chartered shrines, one-third of the amount intended as offerings to the *kami* and two-thirds going to the shrine's chief *kannushi*.[31] The provision of this special tribute was incorporated twenty-four years later in the Taihō Code (article 20 of the Jingi-ryō). This tribute was not a supplementary levy but the regular rice tribute of these *kami* households that was set apart at the provincial storehouses and was eventually exchanged for other goods. Actually, however, it appears that this *kami* tribute was also often used for other than the originally intended purposes. Complaints were registered that all of it went to the local *kannushi*. At times, part of it was also being used to support the central staff of the Jingikan.[32] Occasionally one finds stipulations that regular levies could be used for liturgical purposes.

By 701 already, 4,876 households were registered as supporting 172 shrines.[33] This amounts to an average of 29 households per shrine, but that may be a distorted picture. In 806, 40 percent of such shrines had only one or two *kami* households, and more than half had fewer than five.[34] Whatever the case may be, these figures pale by the number of prebend households attached to Buddhist shrines. That year, Tōdaiji counted 5,000 supporting households, while the largest shrine, Usa Hachiman, had 1,660.[35]

When these tribute articles were (selectively) released back into limited circulation on these ritual occasions, they changed character. When the *hafuri* shrine ritual assistants received them to offer them to their *kami* at home, the articles became *hanpei*, "distributed oblations from the emperor to the *kami*." These liturgical events were fundamentally political because the exchange transformed the things exchanged into signs of recognition.

The ritual itself at the Jingikan was rather simple. A Nakatomi ritualist read the *norito* prayer, and the head of the Inbe clan of ritual assistants distributed the offerings to the delegates one by one. Taboo restrictions were supposed to be observed by all involved. The whole of the capital's officialdom was present, but not the emperor. At the stage of their full implementation, several thousand people must have been lined up for these events, the whole a visual display of the lineaments of the state. Miyoshi's memorial, quoted above, continues with a brief evocation of the Toshigoi and Tsukinami festivals:

> Purification and abstention rules are strictly observed, the *kami* of Heaven and Earth are worshipped in all four directions, prayers are said for a luxuriant ripening of the crops, and thanks offered when the prayers are fulfilled. For this ceremony, the Board of Controllers and all other officials, preceded by the nobles, proceed to the Jingikan which prepares for each shrine one batch of *mitegura*, one bottle of clear sake, one iron spear. These are displayed on tables. If shrines are additionally accorded sacred horses (one horse for the Toshigoi and two for the Tsukinami festival), officials from the Left and Right Stable Bureaus bring them out and line them up. Then an official from the Jingikan reads the *norito* prayer. Subsequently, the above-mentioned oblations are distributed to the *hafuri* of all the shrines, who bring them back each to their own shrine.

The *Engishiki*, a compilation of procedures from the first two decades of the tenth century, provides lists of shrines, their *kami*, and what they received on these occasions. By then, the selected shrines had been divided into those serviced at the center by the Jingikan (737), further subdivided into four classes and provincial shrines (2,395), and composed of large and small ones. Before the downsizing that took place in 798, all chartered shrines, most likely a lesser number than that mentioned over a century later in the *Engishiki*, participated in the ceremonies at the capital. The amount of the material outlay for these four ceremonies is staggering. A sampling from the yearly total equivalent of some of the thirty-two categories of oblations, from which each *hafuri* received allotted portions according to the rank of his shrine, includes textile items (comprising ten categories) such as 2,250 meters of pongee, approximately 309 kilograms of hemp, 5,288 meters of tax cloth; weapons (also ten categories): 1,649 shields, 594 bows; sake: 2,000 (or 666) liters; sea products (seven categories, including varieties of seaweed): 111 kilograms of abalone and bonito each; and salt: 427 (or 142) liters.[36] Starting in the fourth and fifth decades of the eighth century, many of these goods were items that local magistrates had acquired through an official barter (*kōeki*, "exchange" or "trade") of tribute rice. Local tax personnel, using regular tribute grains and rice, could thus purchase a variety of goods, from silks to hoes, demanded in the capital.[37]

Caution is needed to interpret these figures. First of all, they come from a document compiled more than two hundred years after the system was established. Moreover, the *Engishiki* is a normative text, prescribing what was expected, not necessarily reflecting implementation, which had run into difficulties by then. Miyoshi Kiyoyuki, who eventually joined the staff charged with compiling the *Engishiki*, was appalled by the way *hafuri* handled their oblations. He continued his report as follows:

> Now, the *hafuri* should actually observe a fast,[38] take the offerings humbly in custody, and deliver them to their own shrines. Instead, right in front of the highest officials, they take the offerings of silk and stuff them in their satchels, throw away the shafts of the spears taking only the heads, cant the bottles of sake, and empty them in one gulp. Hardly anyone walks out of the gate of the Jingikan with all the offerings. Not to mention the sacred horses! They are sold off to dealers waiting at the Ikuhōmon [palace gate next to the Jingikan]. How could the celebrated *kami* take pleasure in the oblations? When the *kami* do not rejoice, how can we expect a rich harvest?

A few decades later, in 979, the courtier Fujiwara Sanesuke described a similar scene of ritual insouciance, not by lowly *hafuri*, but by the highest officials. That year, he wrote, not a single high official was present at the Great Purification, which the court, the ministers, and the rest of officialdom were expected to attend.[39] Around that time, the state's income from tribute having worsened gradually over the last two centuries, a measure was taken to safeguard funds for ceremonies by setting aside 10 or 20 percent of the yearly tribute to finance oblations to Ise and the main shrines.

Through the measure of 798, 75 percent of the then total of some three thousand shrines were henceforward to dispatch their *hafuri* not to Heian (founded four years earlier) but to the provincial headquarters, where they would receive the oblations. For these shrines, the financial burden was thereby completely shifted from the center to the provinces, which had to dip into their own regular tribute (*shōzei*) to cover the costs, a practice started already in the 730s and 740s.[40] Evidence of faltering compliance appears clearly in the record in the 770s, but it may have started earlier if Mizubayashi, whose theory I discussed in chapter 3, is right about the size of the second Nara Jingikan being actually too small to accommodate the large crowds that apparently gathered earlier in the century. *Hafuri* who did not show up at the festivals were ordered to be dismissed and replaced (775); complaints were registered that travel was too arduous for *hafuri* from outlying regions (798). In the 810s, several admonitions notwithstanding, many *hafuri* still failed to show up at the capital for the Toshigoi, even though by then the number of those expected to make the trek had been drastically reduced. At one point, 142 offerings (nearly 20 percent) had not been picked up.[41] One wonders whether these surplus offerings were not rerouted to noble houses since they are reported as recipients of *hanpei* in 807.[42]

IT WAS AGAIN Tenmu who initiated (on 675/1/23) the practice of ordering offerings (*mitegura*) to be made, repeated on some dozen recorded occasions, not to a particular *kami* as was done in the past, but to "several" or "a number of" *kami* or shrines (*shojingi, shosha*), indicating an expanding relationship of the court to local Yamato shrines, a practice that amounted to a differential distribution of honor among shrines and their supporting *uji*.[43] Of particular importance here are two shrines that appear also that year (on 4/10) for the first time in the record: the Hirose and the Tatsuta shrines dedicated to *kami* of water and wind respectively (see figure 6).

Tenmu had these shrines built downstream along the Yamato River, the principal waterway of the southern Yamato region. The Hirose shrine was situated near the point where the rivers of the basin, including the Saho River from the north (where Nara was to be built) and the Asuka River from the south, converge before flowing westward as the Yamato River, which works its way a few kilometers farther between the Ikuma and Kongō mountain ranges and flows into the Osaka plain. The Tatsuta shrine, honoring two wind *kami*, was at this opening in the mountains (see figure 6).

The agriculture of the Yamato plain depended on the reliability of the water supply provided by rainfall, rivers, and ponds. Crops, however, did not simply have to grow. They also needed protection against inclement weather, mainly storms. At the break in the mountain range where the Yamato River flows east out of the Yamato basin, storms could blow in from the west. This explains the geocultic prominence of these two shrines, which in addition also protected the important transportation route between Asuka and the Inland Sea.

It may very well be that the establishment of these shrines by Tenmu, who was styling himself as a Yamato *tennō*, can in part be explained by his awareness of the Chinese state's role in securing a bountiful harvest. Ritual-istic meteorological control (wind and rain) may have been part of Tenmu's self-image. During the Jinshin War he allegedly warded off a thunderstorm. The importance of these two shrines to Tenmu and eventually to the court is clearly signaled by the exceptional dispatch of two princes (holders of between sixth and third rank) to each shrine for twice-yearly celebrations, a tradition that, modified, continued until well into the Heian period. Partici-pation and contributions by other shrines in the area were also requested on these occasions, starting in 675, making these two shrines contact points between the court and a number of additional shrines.[44]

The expanding territorial range of Jingikan-centered ceremonies, some-what parallel to administrative rearrangements, culminated in the years 701–702, Jitō's last years as retired monarch, coinciding also with the com-pletion and implementation of the Taihō Code.[45] Not surprisingly, Tenmu's incorporation of ritual sites developed here in the southern part of the Ya-mato plain, principally Asuka, via participation in the Niiname Festival. It seems that a group of sixteen shrines, an additional cluster of fourteen Yamanokuchi shrines, and the six shrines of the *miagata* districts that sup-plied foodstuff for the royal kitchen were the first to be incorporated into servicing the new state in a regular and official capacity.[46] One scholar has connected some of these shrines with notables who supported Tenmu in his Jinshin War.[47]

On 690/1/23, after her coronation, Jitō had *mitegura* distributed to *kami* of Heaven and Earth in the Kinai, followed on 7/3 by another distribution, this time without specification, probably indicating shrines beyond the Kinai. During the last year of her life, Jitō, as retired monarch, further saw to it, on 701/11/8, that an office was established specifically for making "*mite-gura* for a large distribution," undoubtedly in preparation for the Toshigoi festival to be held a few months later. On 702/2/13, messengers went out to all provinces to summon "all *kuni no miyatsuko* [provincial chieftains] to the capital for a large distribution of *mitegura*." One month later (3/12), all *mitegura* were distributed to the shrines of the whole country ("the Kinai and the Seven Circuits"). Interestingly, this was followed on 4/13 with an important straight-lining of provincial leadership when henceforward the title *kuni no miyatsuko* would be restricted to one *uji* per province, which was to supply the provincial governor.[48]

The format of the four main yearly festivals as grand gestures of royal largesse through the disbursement of oblations to the *kami* throughout the country via gathered *hafuri* was finalized during Jitō's rule. Harvest-related rituals, either to pray for an abundant crop at the beginning of the year (with the prayer repeated twice, in the sixth and ninth months) or to give thanks for the first fruits, do not go back further than the reigns of Tenmu and Jitō as court-sponsored ceremonies.

THAT THE EMPEROR officiated only at the thanksgiving festival and not at the supplicatory prayers for abundant crops is intriguing. In China, the emperor as intermediary between Heaven and the realm was held responsible (and thus accountable) for the welfare of the people, which he secured through ritual. The *Wuxing dayi*, the great sixth-century synthesis of knowledge of yin-yang and the Five Agents, known in Yamato since the time of Tenmu as *Gogyō taigi*, expresses this role as follows: "The Son of Heaven performs the ceremony of spring cultivation, which will produce the fruits used for ritual offerings [for the ancestral spirits], while his royal spouse honors with her presence the opening of the season to cultivate silkworms, which will produce vestments needed for the cult [of the ancestors]. The gods and the spirits of the dead will respond to such signs of respect by granting great prosperity";[49] otherwise disasters will ensue.

A Broom and a Plow

The Shōsōin treasure storehouse in Nara, which originally housed a large number of precious objects from the eighth century, has preserved two sets of a ceremonial hand plow and a pearl-studded broom. One set was actually used by Empress Kōken on 758/1/3, proof, one might think, of the existence at the Nara court of the Chinese ritual, where the broom was used for sweeping the silkworm platforms.[50] The scene as evoked in the *Manyōshū* by Ōtomo Yakamochi, who witnessed the event, however, was one of joyous entertainment for the court, rather than ritual adjuration by the monarch:

> In the second year [758], spring, on the third day of the first month, the Empress summoned her chamberlains, pages, princes and ministers, assembled them at the foot of the enclosure of the eastern pavilion in the palace, provided them with jewel brooms, and held a banquet. The palace minister, Fujiwara no Asomi, received the imperial command and declared: "Princes and Lords, pray compose Japanese and Chinese poems as your thoughts direct you in accordance with your several preferences." Thus they composed both Japanese and Chinese verses in response to this command, giving expression each to his own thoughts.[51]

Ceremonial events at the Yamato court related to agriculture, aside from Chinese ritual, very early on turned into entertainment even if their origins lay in *tamai* (rice paddy dances). Such a *tamai* dance is mentioned briefly under Tenji (671/5/5) and under Shōmu (742/1/16), each time accompanied by a banquet and entertainment. Shōmu's event was called *gosechi no tamai*, "the rice paddy dance of the five changes of seasons," a practice expressing hope for a plentiful harvest. The celebration, however, seems to have separated from the agricultural part. The following year, on 743/5/5, a *gosechimai* dance was held at the court (the *ta* or rice paddy part having been dropped), a grand event on which the *Shoku Nihongi* dwells at great length, presenting it as a new celebration.[52]

The dance was performed by Princess Abe, who had become crown princess five years earlier at age twenty-one and was to succeed Shōmu as Empress Kōken six years later. Although we have here an important member of the royal family, albeit not the emperor or empress, involved in a performance that appears to be related to generating agricultural blessings — there was also a drought at the time, which had prompted the sending of offerings to shrines in the Kinai two days earlier — the thrust of the event was actually a public declaration of Abe's legitimacy as the next ruler.

Minister of the Right Tachibana Moroe offered an official enunciation (*mikotonori*) to Retired Empress Genshō, linking the happening to Tenmu, who, knowing that rites and music brought peace to the land, had instituted this dance, which had been transmitted through the generations and which Princess Abe had mastered and had now performed. Genshō responded by concurring, in most flowery language, with the view Moroe had voiced, adding that this dance was not merely play (*asobi nomi*) but intended to teach the principles of hierarchical deference between rulers and ministers, and parents and children. This was followed with a song and another *mikotonori* by Moroe, declaring that he could not agree more with Genshō. Finally, the episode closed with the announcement of rank promotions for a long list of officials.

It is probable that this elaborately staged event, highlighting the maintenance of hierarchy, was intended to enhance the legitimate status of Princess Abe as *taishi*. In this, it may not have been much different from the Chinese ceremonial plowing which, even though ideologically of utmost importance, was "observed with noticeable infrequency during early imperial times."[53] Kōken is the only female monarch in Japanese history to have been appointed crown princess before acceding to the throne, the result of complications with Shōmu's succession plans and maneuvering by court factions that will be detailed in chapter 8. It was not that Shōmu had no male child. Prince Asaka, a half brother to Abe, was ten years old when she, at age twenty, became the designated successor. The dance performance, however, notwithstanding the accompanying gloss, may not have been sufficient to hold Asaka at bay. Fortunately for Princess Abe, her half brother died suddenly and mysteriously about six months later.

This series of "dances" is of interest for two reasons. First, one is led to conclude that the relationship of the court and its principal players with performative ritual to boost agricultural production is virtually nonexistent. The *tamai* part drops out of sight, and Genshō's admonition notwithstanding, *asobi* sets the tone. Even the physical traces (broom and plow) of the adoption of Tang ritual, if that is what we should call the event, seem to have been "asobized." On the other hand, if indeed Kōken handled both plow and broom, she was positioning herself as both emperor and empress at the same time — in other words, fully capable of securing all aspects of providing what a *tenka* needed: agricultural and textile products. Such a hypothesis, however, is too far-fetched.[54] In the *Shoku Nihongi's* lengthy disquisition on Crown Princess Abe's dance performance of 743, the drought, recorded in the preceding entry, is not mentioned at all. It was taken care of by other means: the sending of *mitegura*. Second, it is striking that Tenmu is appealed to when a new ritual having to do, however tenuously, with governance and ritual management is introduced. This may be an indication that Tenmu was more committed to the combination of both than his successors had been, possibly that he had initiated the formula.

To conclude this discussion, one looks in vain for a personal performative side to the ritual role of the *tennō*. Emperor Kanmu, an emperor with a puissance extraordinaire, political as well as sexual, was perhaps the first one (since Kōgyoku) to actually have tried and succeeded to make it rain. After having purified himself through water ablutions, he stepped out in the palace yard and successfully prayed to Heaven for rain (788/4/16). On 797/8/18, he was personally involved in the "Southern Garden" when messengers were sent to bring *mitegura* "to the famed *kami* of the provinces in the Kinai and the Seven Circuits."[55]

Kanmu's ritual interventions, including sacrifices to Heaven in Katano near Heian in 785 and 787, give his rule a pronounced Chinese cachet, including the adoption of a new ceremonial coat, which used to be white but became patterned on the Tang emperor's by 820. However, it is important to note that the symbols of ritual significance, the Great Dipper and the Star of the Weaver Maid on the sleeves, representing the ritual functions of the emperor and empress to protect agriculture and sericulture, were replaced with dragons.[56] The Great Dipper found a new place in the top center of the coat, symbolizing cosmic rule patterned on the Pole Star, while the Weaver Maid was dropped, a visual acknowledgment that the *tennō* positioned himself differently than did his counterpart in Tang China, notwithstanding the many important state rituals semantically related to harvest (see plates 3, 4).

The liturgical state that was established through the Taihō Code evokes the image of a political structure imposed uniformly from above upon regions that had now become equalized as provinces participating in the pan-realm liturgies. Yet the reality was quite different. Traces of its origins in the kingship as structured by Tenmu, localized in Yamato province, remained embedded in the structure after it was reduced at the end of the eighth century. Ultimately, therefore, the *ritsuryō* liturgical state as established under Tenmu and Jitō turned out to be a form of local kingship with a remaining disproportionate importance granted to the Kinai and Yamato, even after the capital moved away to another province, Yamashiro, when Kanmu built Heian.[57]

An analysis of the geographic distribution of the shrines participating in the Tsukinami and Niiname festivals, as stipulated in the *Engishiki* in 927 (the same number for each), shows that 264 shrines from a total of 304 were in the Kinai (231), the palace (30), and the capital (3). Of the 71 shrines benefiting from *hanpei* at the Ainame festival, 65 were Kinai shrines (half of them in Yamato province).[58] The harvest festivals were more important around the center, even the old center, than throughout the rest of the country because the crop they secured was, after all, predominantly political.

Enthronement Implements

Being persistent and mutable at the same time, cultural memory is selective and cunning. On the one hand, it links the Japanese ruling house's legitimacy, "since the beginning of time," to the possession of the three "regalia": mirror, sword, and jewel. On the other hand, one of the two founding mythological texts, in the main text the *Nihon shoki*, does not mention them at all. Moreover, for several centuries, only the sword and mirror were transmitted to the new monarch in his enthronement ceremony, which, far from simply being a "Shinto" liturgy, changed drastically over time and was even discontinued for over two centuries.

The creators of the *ritsuryō* state and its founding documents, the Taihō Code, *Kojiki*, and *Nihon shoki*, were not bothered by variability, most probably because the degree of uniformity we assume indispensable for unitary states was neither attainable nor necessary then (nor perhaps ever anywhere). Unitary states can exist having no unified ideology of origins even when they make gestures in that direction without, however, being able to push monology or monopractice further because of the strength of secondary powers. In ancient Japan these powers were of two kinds: one, *uji* who needed to agree on acknowledging one among themselves as primus inter pares, and for all significant others, degrees of privilege and proximity to their leader; and two, competing ritualist lineages when the enthronement ritual was on the drawing board (which it never left). The latter phase starts under Tenmu and Jitō and introduces a creative mutability that has characterized enthronement rituals throughout Japanese history.[59]

Of the three imperial insignia, the sword (the only one that originated on earth) has had a colorful career all its own. Susanoo retrieved it from the tail of a dragon he slew in Izumo and presented it to his sister Amaterasu in Heaven. Called Kusanagi, it was sent down with Ninigi together with the mirror and curved jewel (*Kojiki* only) and wound up in Ise, where the princess-in-residence gave it to her nephew, Yamato Takeru.[60] He used it to conquer enemies east and west for his father, the legendary twelfth emperor Keikō. An instrument of destruction, the sword was also a guarantee of strength and life for its bearer because after Yamato Takeru left it with his wife in Owari, where it remained, he succumbed in no time to a debilitating illness and died (although enjoying a Daoist nondeath since his spirit escaped from his corpse in the form of a white bird).[61] At one point under Tenmu, a monk from Silla tried to steal it but failed to smuggle it across the sea, and during Tenmu's final illness a divination revealed it as the source of a curse put on Tenmu, whereupon it was promptly returned to the Atsuta shrine in Owari (without any explanation of what it was doing in the palace in the first place). To bring the story up to date: in the last days of the Pacific War, word has it that it was whisked away out of fear that it might fall into the hands of the Occupation.[62]

During the fifth century, three accessions of great kings were accompanied by their reception of unspecified "symbol(s)" of power. With Great King Keitai in the early sixth century, however, the transmission of a sword (not specified as the Kusanagi) and mirror to the new great king was added to the enthronement procedure, which since Yūryaku (456) had consisted of stepping onto a raised platform to be acclaimed by Yamato magnates.[63]

With Keitai's acceptance of the royal throne in 507, after first declining it, a sword and mirror make their entrance as emblems of royal authority, granted by powerful local leaders (whose offer of rulership had been turned down earlier a first time by someone else). The claim that Keitai was a fifth-generation descendant from King Ōjin is tenuous at best. He most likely started a new royal line. Two magnates, an Ōtomo and a Mononobe, located him in Echizen on the Japan Sea coast; he did not move to Yamato province until twenty years after his enthronement, which took place on 507/2/4. One suspects that *uji* rivalry, armed clashes, and ultimately conquest of the center may have played a role in the delay. The new element of certification of kingship through the sword and mirror may have been added because of Keitai's sinuous path to succession.[64] By the seventh century, swords handed over to *uji* heads, to leaders of missions to the Tang, or to shogun campaigning against Emishi symbolized royal appointments to positions of authority.[65]

Mirror and sword were used at Jitō's enthronement in 690, and the Taihō Code stipulates that these two royal insignia be handed to the new monarch by the head of the Inbe, the *uji* in charge of ritual paraphernalia. This was supposed to be accompanied by the chief of the Nakatomi reading a *norito* prayer (Jingi-ryō, article 13), a new element introduced by Jitō, possibly Tenmu.[66] The Inbe reassert this function and claim it as their prerogative in the *Kogoshūi*, a document they submitted to the throne in 807 seeking redress against the Nakatomi.

Among the many eighth-century treasures preserved in the Shōsōin in Nara, there is an intriguing document regarding a sword that belonged to Emperor Shōmu. The storehouse's north section (one of three) houses objects personally used by Shōmu that his widow, Empress Kōmyō, dedicated to Tōdaiji in 756 on the forty-ninth memorial day after his death. The catalogue of the dedicated articles, composed on that occasion (*Tōdaiji kenmotsu-chō*), records the history of the sword, which reaches back some seventy years to Crown Prince Kusakabe, Shōmu's grandfather.[67] Before he died in 689 at the young age of twenty-seven, Kusakabe would have "entrusted the sword that he always wore to Fujiwara Fuhito," who was thirty at the time, holder of the lowest rank of the middle tier of official servants (junior fifth lower). Yet even that early in his career as legal expert, Fuhito must have had a very close relationship with the ruling house, a continuation of the commitment to the throne his father Kamatari had demonstrated as coconspirator in the Taika coup. "At Monmu's enthronement," the text continues, "Fuhito passed the sword on to Monmu, and he received it in trust again when Monmu died. The day Fuhito himself died [720], he handed the sword to Crown Prince Obito [i.e., the future Emperor Shōmu]."

This story, whatever its veracity, is of interest for several reasons. It purports to be an early indication of the unquestionable role of crown protector that came to cement a close relationship between Fuhito and Jitō following the latter's accession the year after Kusakabe died. (Fuhito's daughter was to become consort to Jitō's successor and grandson, Monmu, another seven years later, and less than three weeks after his accession to the throne; two other daughters had already been added earlier to the list of Tenmu's wives — see figure 4.) Even as a fabrication, the legend may also testify to the need for Empress Kōmyō to express the special bond between herself, her father Fuhito's *uji*, and the throne (or concretely between her and her nephew Fujiwara Nakamaro) at a precarious juncture in 756 when the rivalry between the Fujiwara and Tachibana was about to reach the breaking point. The years 756–757 witnessed in close succession: Retired Emperor Shōmu's death and, the same day (756/5/2), the appointment by the Tachibana clique of a non-Fujiwara crown prince, Funado, intended as eventual successor to Kōken; Kōmyō's gifts to Tōdaiji forty-nine days later; the deposition of Funado and his replacement by Prince Ōi (grandson of Tenmu, later Emperor Junnin) on 757/4/1; Tachibana Naramaro's rebellion, put down by Fujiwara Nakamaro (757/7); and the death under torture-interrogation of Funado.

Nakamaro's grandfather Fujiwara Fuhito had assisted the throne when the Tenmu dynasty met its first test as dynasty, namely during the transition from Tenmu to Jitō. After Kusakabe's death, the situation faced by the forty-three-year-old widow Jitō was, although less dramatic, certainly filled with dynastic uncertainty. When, a year after Kusakabe's death (and four years after Tenmu's), Jitō ascended the throne, she was in dire need of support against Tenmu's sons (especially Takechi, the former Jinshin war general, thirty-seven then) if she wanted her royal line to continue — support that Fuhito, entrusted with Kusakabe's sword, seemed ready to provide. Kusakabe had been Jitō's only son, and his consort, the future Genmei, was now a widow. Among their children, the future Genshō was not married (and was to remain single), as was Princess Kibi, later to marry Prince Nagaya; and then there was Prince Karu (the future Monmu), seven years old. The watchdog role of Fuhito, symbolized or not as the case may be through his informal function as keeper of the sword while the throne was not occupied by a male successor, may help explain the rivalry between his *uji* and its allied branch of Nakatomi ritualists on the one hand and the Inbe caretakers of ritual who handled the sword and mirror regalia at enthronement moments on the other.

THE NAKATOMI and the Inbe disagreed on the nature and number of the regalia, and the *Kojiki* and *Nihon shoki* were of no help in settling the matter since the dispute was incorporated in these very texts. The *Kojiki* states that three regalia (including the jewel) rather than two were part of Ninigi's travel kit, courtesy of Amaterasu, when she sent him down to earth. The *Nihon shoki*, on the other hand, omits any reference to insignia of any kind in its main text, but mentions the *Kojiki* version in what appears to us today as the equivalent of a footnote (NSK 1: 146; Aston 1: 76).

A quick explanatory comment on the phenomenon of variants to the main narrative. The *ritsuryō* state held together only as long as the *uji* that constituted its service core agreed to its arrangement of power. They jockeyed for their status through claims of august ancestry, preferably going back to important *kami*. One of the reasons the projects of the *Kojiki* and *Nihon shoki* were stalled for decades must have been the difficult decisions regarding the proper allocation of distinction among *uji*. For instance, no fewer than forty-one *uji* succeeded in making official their claims of ancestry to the highest *kami*, Takamimusuhi, to whom the Sun line traced its origins.[68] Others tried to have their founding ancestors among those sent down with Ninigi to protect and serve his Sun line.[69] The *Kojiki* names twelve while the *Nihon shoki* lists none. On the other hand, the *Sendai kuji hongi*, a manuscript tapping into older competing genealogies and drafts of both official mytho-histories but obviously never gaining the official stamp even as an alternate tradition, presents Ninigi as having had a brother, and being assisted by no fewer than thirty-two clan ancestral *kami*.[70] The *Sendai kuji hongi* reveals a perspective that leans toward favoring the Mononobe warrior and ritualist *uji*. The *Kogoshūi* is yet another private document of the house of Inbe ritualists.

Factional rivalry between ritualist lineages lurked behind the versions of two versus three regalia. One party consisted of the two related clans of the Fujiwara and Nakatomi, which acquired powerful positions respectively in political and ritual matters during the 690s, after Jitō's accession. Not yet in power when the Kiyomihara Code, later amplified into the Taihō Code, was compiled in the 680s, they prevailed when the *Kojiki* was being composed under Jitō and Genmei.[71] Unable, however, to modify the precedents set by Jitō's enthronement and the Taihō codification, both of which practiced and stipulated the transmission of a sword and mirror, but strong enough not to be ignored, their viewpoint was acknowledged as an alternate version in a *Nihon shoki* footnote. The Inbe, needing a *kami*-based justification for their version (and for the clan's professional occupation), which neither the

Kojiki nor the *Nihon shoki* provided, simply stated in their attack on the Nakatomi in the *Kogoshūi* (807), that "the Heavenly Ancestors [Amaterasu and Takamimusuhi] presented the Heavenly Grandson [Ninigi] with *two* Sacred Treasures, *together with jewels and a spear*."[72]

The reason that the issue of two versus three regalia was so important has to do with the nature of the jewel, the only one that was kept in the palace. (The mirror, used to lure Amaterasu out of the cave where she had ensconced herself against her brother Susanoo's rambunctious behavior, was supposed to remind Ninigi, when down in the Central Land of the Reed Plains, to worship her.[73] It was eventually transferred to the Ise shrine and a copy installed in the palace.) The jewel's documented role in enthronement rituals appears rather late, in the ninth century, even though archeological excavations of prehistoric tombs have discovered many sets of mirror, sword, and jewel, apparently magically potent symbols of rulership. It is worth noting in passing that the myth of Tan'gun, the oldest Korean founding myth, also mentions the bestowing of three regalia, unspecified, on the son of a ruler in Heaven, thereby appointing him to go down and rule the earth.[74]

Whether or not these regalia kept their inherent power in historic times as well is a question that has no simple answer. First of all, the mirror and sword used in the enthronement ceremonies were not the originals, which were kept in their remote locations in Owari and Ise; they were duplicates. The protestations by the Inbe in the *Kogoshūi* for the divine origins of only the mirror and sword seem to have been a last skirmish in a power contest with the Fujiwara and Nakatomi, a contest they were losing because the transmission of regalia by the Inbe ceased altogether after 833.[75] Instead, already starting at Kanmu's death (806), it appears that the two items that were transferred from Kanmu's death chamber to his successor the moment he died were the jewel and a sword case (presumably in lieu of the genuine article, which was in Owari), an activity (hardly a ritual) referred to as *kenjitogyo* (transfer of sword and jewel).[76]

In the Taihō Code, the article concerning the duties of the director of the Palace Storehouse Bureau (Shōzō), one of twelve bureaus of the Rear Palace, all staffed by women, refers to her duty as "keeper of the seal(s)" ("sacred sign/jewel[s]"), which, another article specifies "does not refer to the two symbols used at the enthronement ceremony."[77] These two entries, one scholar argues, concern the jewel. While the sword and mirror were used at public enthronement ceremonies, the jewel played a role in the private appointment of the successor (which is why there is no record of it, at least before 806) that took place in the interior of the palace and preceded the public ritual.[78] It settled the issue of succession as an in-house affair, perhaps in a fashion similar to Kusakabe's sword.

Until 828, the directorship of the Storehouse Bureau of the Rear Palace was monopolized (with one exception in 774) by Fujiwara-related women, wives of high-ranking officials.[79] The next fifty years, however, the women holding that position were far less well-connected, with only one Fujiwara among them. These data, and two obscure entries in late-Heian writings (the *Saikyūki* and *Hokuzanshō*), leads to the conclusion that the Fujiwara (and Nakatomi)'s support for three regalia was an anti-Inbe strategy, which succeeded with the removal of the Inbe from the accession ceremony around 830, leaving only the Nakatomi as ritualists on that public occasion, reciting the *norito*. Control of the directorship of the Palace Storehouse Bureau was, therefore, no longer needed for the Fujiwara, whose northern branch henceforward was concentrating its efforts on securing the position of in-law to the ruling monarch by controlling marriages of crown princes.

Before the ninth century two terms were used indiscriminately for the enthronement that took place during the Daijō-sai: *senso* and *sokui*. During the Heian period, however, they came to refer to two separate ceremonies, perhaps best rendered as succession (*senso*) and accession or enthronement (*sokui*). Thus, the transmission of royal power took place three times. The *kenjitogyo* still took place in the interior of the palace upon the death of the former ruler. This was followed several days later by a public proclamation (*senso*) to all assembled officials in front of the Daigokuden, an event patterned after the New Year ceremony. Then, in the fall (of the same year or, if succession took place after the eighth month, of the following year), the accession proper (*sokui*) was held during the Niiname-sai, called Daijō-sai on such an occasion.

Buddhist Supplements and Substitutions

Cultural memory has been exceedingly flexible with regard to the Daijō-sai, which one thinks of as the most important rite of the three succession procedures, the one indispensable "Shinto" ceremony for making emperors. The ruler known since 1870 as Emperor Chūkyō was until then remembered as *hantei* (half emperor) because he was deposed in 1221 before acceding to the throne in a Daijō-sai. This three-year-old crown prince, who succeeded (*senso*) his father, Emperor Juntoku (exiled by the Kamakura warrior government [*bakufu*]) was deposed by the same government after seventy days without ever acceding to the throne (*sokui*). Only in 1870 was his official status as a legitimate emperor established by the Meiji government. Nine other rulers, however, over a span of 220 years after Gotsuchi-mikado's accession in 1466 until Higashiyama's in 1687 never performed a Daijō-sai, without the issue of their legitimacy ever being raised.[80]

Moreover, a Buddhist consecration of the new emperor was added to the accession ceremony in 1288 and was performed uninterruptedly for half a millennium, from 1382 until 1847.[81] This was the *sokui kanjō* (eso-teric enthronement; Skt. *abhiṣeka*) of a *cakravartin*, the Buddhist universal monarch. Regular *abhiṣeka* consisted of "sprinkling water [from the four directions] on the top of the head," the meaning of *kanjō*. Originally an Indian enthronement ceremony, it became the procedure by which Bud-dhist masters or abbots consecrated and certified one of their disciples as privileged recipient of their teachings.

At the Heian court, however, the procedure was simplified in order to eliminate the hierarchical relationship of dependency implied for the recipient. The new emperor applied it to himself without clerical assis-tance. While proceeding during the succession ceremony in front of the Daigokuden toward the platform from where, seated, he faced the assem-bled court, he formed a fist mudra and recited a brief five-syllable mantra. He was given information about these esoteric Buddhist formulae before the ceremony — not by monks, however, but by the chancellor or regent, who by definition was the emperor's servant.[82] Supremeness was always salvaged, no matter what the ritual idiom.

The rituals that the emperor performed or took part in personally were mainly if not exclusively oriented toward his persona, to set it apart or pro-tect it. In 839, the Buddhist esoteric Shingon Rite of the Supreme Marshal (Daigensui no hō), which only the emperor could order to be held against his enemies, was introduced, and yin-yang masters and Buddhist monks created a number of protective rites during the Heian period. A monk re-sided at night in a two-mat room adjacent to the emperor (mid-tenth cen-tury), and three other monks each performed a daily ritual (mid-eleventh), all to protect the emperor.[83]

By the eleventh century, Buddhism also started to play an enormously important role in legitimizing a second type of imperial power, away from Fujiwara control, namely, that of retired emperors. Its importance is clear from the frequent pilgrimages to the Buddhist sacred site in Kumano that retired emperors and their consorts undertook, from the tenth century through the first decades of the thirteenth. During these three centuries, near one hundred such pilgrimages were undertaken. They were elaborate, requiring at certain times up to eight hundred men and two hundred horses from each province on the road to Kumano, and laborious, since they consisted of a nearly one-month round-trip by sea and over mountains covering 700 kilometers.[84] Although no reigning emperor set out for Kumano, and none, except Jitō, set foot in Ise, the intense association of the court with Buddhism as dramatically expressed in these pilgrimages in late antiquity clearly overshadows the significance of the most important rituals Tenmu and Jitō had created with the institution of *hanpei* at their center.

6 DEPOSITS

Yamato Takeru emerged from his tomb, morphed into a
white bird, and flew toward the land of Yamato. The ministers accordingly opened the coffin, looked, and only the
empty clothing was left, and there was no corpse.
—110. *Nihon shoki*

Succession problems after Suiko, who died in 628, were serious
enough for a council of officials to convene and decide on a new sovereign.
Their choice fell on one of Bidatsu's second-generation descendants, Jomei,
who was in turn succeeded by Kōgyoku/Saimei and Kōtoku, both three
generations removed from Bidatsu (see figure 1). The brothers Tenji and
Tenmu, as sons of Jomei and Saimei inheriting the throne on shaky genealogical grounds and, in addition, having the blood of eliminated rivals on
their hands, appear to have attempted restoring some sort of double royalty
through a dense web of endogamous marriages for themselves and their
offspring (see figure 4). If the *Kojiki* had been finalized not in 712 but some
thirty years earlier, one suspects that Tenji and Tenmu would have been included for their effort at reestablishing double royalty, the prevailing practice described in that text. By 712, however, the dynastic issue had changed
drastically. It had been turned upside down. Now, the establishment of a
future *tennō* from a *non*-royal mother, a Fujiwara, needed legitimation. This
new problem may help explain several developments: the very timing of
having the *Kojiki* presented to the throne, the absence of full genealogical
data for the post-Suiko rulers in the *Kojiki*, and the introduction of *neko*
elements as patterns in prehistorical times and postmortem signifiers for
contemporary deceased sovereigns (Jitō, Monmu, Genmei, and Genshō).

One additional reason for not formally including post-Suiko rulers in
the *Kojiki* may have to do with the shifting ground of rulership. From the
Nihon shoki, we know that Chinese elements were being highlighted from
around mid-century (Kōgyoku, Kōtoku). Kōgyoku personally conducted
a Chinese/Daoist-style rainmaking ceremony that proved more effective
than a Soga Buddhist attempt. Kōtoku's Taika edict of 646/2/15 (admittedly in the midst of Chinese-style reforms that, like the edict, may have
been dated anachronistically) explicitly refers to Chinese mythological

rulers: the Yellow Emperor and his Mingtang and Yao, Shun, and Yu and the administrative measures they and the founders of the Shang and Zhou dynasties introduced. Moreover, when the nature of royal authority had to be symbolized publicly at the end of the reigns of the four consecutive mid-century great kings Kōtoku, Saimei, Tenji, and Tenmu (r. 642–686) (or whenever their history was written), Heaven (*ten* or *ame/ama*) was chosen as the first character for all their posthumous names (see table 1). This trend culminated under Tenmu in the change of the ruler's nomenclature from *ōkimi* (great king), to *tennō* (heavenly ruler).

The subsequent move away from *ten* to *neko* in posthumous names must have signaled a shift in the concept of authority, from transcendental and supreme to one less imposing and more conscious of needed acceptance by the leading clans. The strong notion of ruling authority under Tenmu was articulated by Daoist signifiers, the subject of the next chapter. To understand the significance of Tenmu's constructs, one needs first to examine the pre-Tenmu history of these symbolics, which I shall do in this chapter.

Daoist elements lie dispersed across the written record about pre-Tenmu Japan. Traditionally, some historians have gathered them as deposits from the past, embedded in layers of native custom, and have mined them for traces of Daoist practices in the archipelago. Others considered the ore too poor to yield anything of substance. I take the position that these elements are often less traces of the past than deposits in a different sense, that they were deposited in the record by the compilers of the texts in the late seventh and early eighth centuries.

A Historiographical Conundrum

Identifying Daoist elements in seventh-century Japan has become an increasingly important endeavor in current Japanese scholarship, frequently a tricky exercise on slippery hermeneutic terrain. Such identification usually occurs at the expense of previous explanatory references to Buddhism or "Shinto." Thus, for instance, arguments are being made for the predominantly Daoist iconographic components of the preserved fragments of Japan's oldest embroidered tapestry, the *Tenjukoku shūchō mandara*, allegedly woven around the time of the wake (*mogari*) for Shōtoku Taishi and his mother in 622.[1] Traditionally understood to be a visual representation of the Buddhist Pure Land as the realm where the prince, a legendary pillar of early-Yamato Buddhism, and his mother had migrated, there is no denying that it is replete with references to Daoist and Daoisant symbols such as turtles with graphs on their shells, a three-legged crow in the sun, and the alchemical hare in the moon holding a flask of the elixir of immortality next to the tree of life.

It is arguably easier to separate Buddhist emblems from Daoist signs and Chinese cosmology than to disentangle the latter two from each other. Such may be the case, for example, with the directional animals in the two seventh-century stone burial chambers of Takamatsuzuka and Kitora: are they generically Chinese or specifically Daoist? Questions of this kind are particularly complicated because by the sixth and seventh centuries Daoism in China had succeeded in positioning itself right near the center as its purveyor of political symbols and practices. Assuming the existence of "original" Daoist significations of some of these symbols — admittedly problematic because some have pre-Daoist "Chinese" careers — their meanings may by then even have abraded over time. In addition, as Anna Seidel warns, " [w]hat many authors . . . call Taoist practices at the Japanese court — divination, five-element sciences, time-keeping, calendar-making, astrology, prognostication, omen-lore, etc. — were Chinese traditions cultivated at every Chinese court. . . . These traditions [called *onmyōdō* in Japan] . . . exerted a great influence on Taoism; but they are a pan-Chinese branch of learning with its own chain of transmission distinct from Taoism."[2] Nevertheless, Seidel's warning notwithstanding, the argument to be developed in the next chapter can be made that political symbolization at Tenmu's court was not a piecemeal operation producing disparate Daoist elements — or, as suggested earlier, "Daoisant" fragments — but amounted to an articulation of such elements as constituent moments of a fairly comprehensive political symbolic whole.

Many students of Japanese history in the West still imagine Daoism as a hodgepodge of magico-religious practices marginal to the mainstream "traditions" of "Shinto" and Buddhism. It may, thus, be surprising to read about Daoism as an essential component of the Yamato *ritsuryō* state's ideological underpinnings. Hence the need to make two detours: one to highlight the political side of Daoist teachings and ritual, the second to document the presence of dispersed Daoist elements around Tenmu's time. Only then will one appreciate Tenmu's arrangement of them as articulated moments of a religio-political construct.

IT IS UNDENIABLE that Daoist writings, concepts, and practices were known in Japan during the seventh and eighth centuries, the result of intense contact with China and Korean kingdoms. In China, the eighth century in particular is considered to have been the heyday of Daoism. By midcentury, all-out imperial support for Daoism was clearly outpacing the sponsorship Buddhism had enjoyed in the past.[3] The historical trajectory is clear: one hundred years later, in 845, Buddhism was to suffer severe persecution in Tang China.

The first two Tang rulers, Emperor Gaozu (r. 618–627) and Emperor Taizong (r. 627–650), even used Daoism in their diplomatic relations with other countries while domestically following a fairly balanced approach to both religious "Ways." The *Daode jing* was translated into Sanskrit and allegedly taken to India by the monk Xuanzang, not an official ambassador, however, because he sneaked out of China illegally.[4] Following an official request by Koguryŏ, however, Daoist missionaries were sent to that Korean kingdom. In the early eighth century a missionary attempt may have been made in Tibet, and Yamato envoys also actively inquired about Daoism with Emperor Xuanzong (r. 712–756) in 735.[5]

Until rather recently, the main historiographical issue for ancient Japan with regard to Daoism had been where, how, and to what extent a Daoist presence in the archipelago could be argued. Japanese historians were either minimalists or maximalists. In the last twenty years or so, however, they have started to question why Daoism never established an institutional foothold in Japan.[6] The commonsense answer that Yamato, having Shinto, had no need for Daoism is no longer satisfying. Scholars have come to understand that Shinto as such was not around when cultural borrowing from the continent started in earnest in the seventh century. *Kami* worship, as Shinto is better called, acquired the beginnings of some historically traceable identity — *pace* the essentialists and antiessentialists — only with the accretion of continental elements (Daoist, yin-yang, and even Buddhist) to whatever it was before it became what we have traditionally referred to as Shinto.[7] Using the traditional terminology, we are thus confronted with an odd paradox: Daoism as such did not exist in the archipelago and neither did Shinto when the two met there in the seventh and eighth centuries.

Chinese Daoism

In theory and practice, Daoism pursues the twin goals of longevity and non-death ("immortality") and has developed many ways to achieve them, both in reality and metaphorically, even though interest in such methods preexisted Daoism as such, in the second century BCE among the elite and by the end of the first century among the people at large.[8] Daoism, however, offered a full spectrum of such techniques, a rich choice of multiple practices — meditative, alchemical, medicinal, shamanistic, ritual, liturgical, and magical — all of them integral to a wondrous world of the marvelous, informing cosmological and ideological representations and developing both sectarian divisions and state institutions, notably during the Tang empire (618–907).

Daoism went through a long gestation period before it grew into an identifiable movement, and it fed on a variety of practices and teachings. The two oldest texts appropriated by Daoism and linked since the Han period are the *Daode jing*, most likely dating back to the fourth or third century BCE, and the somewhat later *Zhuangzi*. They acquired canonical status only during the third and fourth centuries CE.[9] The *Yijing*, which antedates both by several centuries and has occupied a central place in all intellectual movements and religious practices throughout Chinese history, came to be elevated in the third century aside the *Daode jing* and the *Zhuangzi* as one of the three mystery texts (*sanxuan*).[10] This set was particularly treasured by Fujiwara Muchimaro (680–737).[11]

During most of the Former or Western Han dynasty (206–8 BCE),[12] various theories of a correlative cosmology developed, premised on the correspondence of all forces animating humans, nature, and Heaven. Dong Zhongshu (179–104 BCE) advocated this cosmology as the proper foundation for statecraft against the mantic and magical practices to control spirits and conquer death, favored by the imperial court of Emperor Wu (r. 140–86 BCE).[13] Yin-yang, Dong's tool to reformat Confucian knowledge, as a theory of homologies[14] combined with that of the Five Phases as well as numerous divinatory and mantic practices, came to constitute a phenomenon that had no name until Sima Tan (d. 110 BCE) called some of their practitioners Daojia, "experts in the Way."

Tan elevated the practice and ideas of the Daojia above those of five other groups of specialists that together represented schematically all varieties of political proposals for the newly created Han empire. Although Tan and his son the historian Qian[15] considered the Daojia politically the most useful of these groups, they excluded from their definition practitioners of the occult, the *fangshi* whose only preoccupation was to prolong life, and who were much sought out by Emperor Wu.[16] They also rejected the Huang-Lao teaching of the early Western Han, which combined emperor and sage (the lore about the Yellow Emperor Huangdi, and Laozi's teachings).[17] *Fangshi* promoted the idea that Huangdi, as an immortal, had ascended to heaven. In his capacity as an absolute ruler-god, Huangdi played an important role in legitimizing and amplifying the authority centered on the first emperor of the Qin dynasty and Emperor Wu of the Han dynasty.[18]

Daojia adepts "would adopt relevant policies from any quarter" in overseeing all aspects of government.[19] Weeding out the occult, Tan retained as important for this group the knowledge of the great rhythms of the cosmic Dao because good governance consisted in following these rhythms.[20] The *Huainanzi* (139 BCE), known to Prince Nagaya in the early eighth century, can be understood as a similar private synthesis of ideological and symbolic techniques informed by a cosmic view of the Dao.

Tan's configuration of specialists by constructing a taxonomy of their ideas rather than through names of teachers was a first step toward the creation of "-isms" or "schools" whose identity jelled around specific texts and lineages of practitioners. In the *Hanshu* (History of the [Western] Han), written in the first century CE, some two centuries after Tan's creation of Daojia, the term became a comprehensive name for a school with a distinct tradition, texts, and practices.[21] Tan probably aimed his Daojia at Dong's rival synthesis of Confucian learning and the Five Phases theory. In other words, the former Han was a time when various discourses spun their own versions of a unified field of knowledge, applied to the practice of government, which not only integrated ideology with politics but gave the group whose vision would prevail great power.[22]

Emperor Wu's obsessive interest in mantic practices made him institutionalize the study of the *Yijing* in the state educational system that he established.[23] This, in turn, "led to a bifurcated system of transmission" of mantic practices: the official one and numerous nonofficial ones.[24] The latter were often perceived by the state, not without reason, as dangerous. Popular eschatological movements during the final decades of the Western Han, often led by *fangshi* or shamans, were driven by predictions of the impending fate of the dynasty.[25]

The movements associated with these amorphous and idiosyncratic practices and writings sprouted the first Daoist religious mass movements and even outright rebellions during the Eastern Han (25–220): the Yellow Turbans or Great Peace (Taiping) movement of 184 in eastern China, crushed soon after; and the Way of the Celestial Masters or the Five Pecks of Rice sect in Sichuan, the southwest, which was dispersed in the third century. Messianic movements inspired by the Celestial Masters developed in the south. During the four centuries between the fall of the Eastern Han and the rise of the Sui immediately followed by the Tang, a time when some twenty-five dynasties, thirteen of them non-Han Chinese,[26] ruled over parts of China in rapid succession, it was "the messianic dream of the Taiping that kept the vision of a unified Chinese Empire alive," Anna Seidel writes. "Again and again, throughout the period of disunion, the messianic prophecy: 'The Han will rise again!' resounded as the battle cry of the rebels." It was a popular Daoist religion that supported the rebels' claim that the Mandate of Heaven had passed to them.[27] One of the legitimizing devices used by the first emperor of the Southern Wei, Cao Zhi, was an inference that he, as a transcendental, qualified to take over from the Eastern Han (220).[28] In the Northern Wei dynasty (386–535), a churchlike Daoism was proclaimed for a few years (444–450) as the official religion of the Tuoba rulers, and their empire was in part directed at the last of numerous populist Daoist-inspired rebellious movements.[29]

Eventually, the founder of the Tang dynasty benefited greatly from popular prophecies for establishing his regime over a unified China, just as the Eastern Han had. Based on a prophecy, the Han house had claimed a special link with the Li clan, which traced its origin to Laozi. The Tang founder adopted the name of the Western Han's founder, Gaozu, for himself, and similarly claimed Laozi as the ancestor of his house, throwing his full support behind Daoism.[30] By then, as Anna Seidel puts it, "Taoist priests had long since transformed the Perfect Ruler into an otherworldly god."

Prophecies and omens often played an important role in Daoist movements. This started with "omen weft" texts (Ch. *chenwei*; Jp. *shin'i*) at the end of the Western Han. Prognostic omen weft "apocrypha" (*wei*) were a period-specific genre of writing of that time, "esoteric complements attached to the [Confucian] classics (*jing*) like the weft or woof (*wei*) to the warp (*jing*) of a fabric."[31] As Tsuda Sōkichi noted long ago, the term *tennō* originated in one such esoteric, portent astrological text, the *Weft* [interpretation of the] *Spring and Autumn Annals* (*Chunqiu wei*). Other political terms that eventually emerge in late-seventh-century Yamato are *mahito* (perfected man; Ch. *zhenren*) (a component of Tenmu's posthumous name) and *huangdi* (sovereign emperor; literally, "august god"). These names were also used by rebel leaders during the Eastern Han.[32] Daoism was thus fully implicated in deploying a vocabulary of political enchantment, both celebratory and subversive. It was capable of charging a Confucian polity with religious intensity and had the power to legitimize and delegitimize rulers.[33]

Daoism as a Source of Legitimacy in China

Even from its prebeginnings, "Daoism" was about a perfected polity. The Huang-Lao movement of the early Western Han linked the teachings of Laozi with the rule of the Yellow Emperor, a political ideal that can be identified as "Daoist," but only retrospectively.[34] An ideally ordered society formed the core of the Great Peace, Taiping, a notion that goes back to the

Zhuangzi.[35] The emergence of prognostication texts around the fall of the Western Han, however, was the catalyst for the development of politico-religious Daoist movements.

During Emperor Cheng's reign (32–7 BCE), a "recipe master" presented him with a text revealing that the heavenly emperor had sent a perfected man (a first-step immortal on a scale of three) to renew the Han's Mandate. Sichuan province, in the southwest and bordering on Tibet where the first organized form of religious Daoism took root, was an important center for the production of prognostication texts by recipe masters about likely dynastic destinies.[36] Anna Seidel has put it forcefully, "[T]he organization and the priesthood of Taoism [is] a recreation, on a spiritual level, of the lost cosmic unity of Han. . . . Without the downfall of the Han dynasty there would be no Taoist religion as we know it."[37]

The celestial masters of the second Daoist religious movement were purists. They modeled their religious practice on Han court ritual and interacted bureaucratically with the life forces of the Dao, namely through written petitions. The animal sacrifices of popular and state cults were condemned. Rejected also was the state's reliance on diviners and popular shamanistic rites.[38] The celestial masters intended to rule through purity, and were zealous proselytizers, targeting rulers in particular.

It should come as no surprise that the use of the apocrypha, these privately generated political portents heralding dramatic political change in cosmic terms, temporarily sanctioned during the early Eastern Han (by correlating them with Confucian classics), became "diverted" as Daoist delegitimating strategies and were therefore proscribed. The first prohibition dates from some time before 217, toward the very end of the Eastern Han. It was repeated at politically turbulent moments at least nine times during the next dynasties up to and including the Tang, and then in Yamato as well.[39]

Laozi, deified as the Dao of good government during the first two centuries, was believed to have appeared throughout history in the guise of known teachers to dynastic founders. With the celestial masters, however, these epiphanies ceased. Taking over the mantle of imperial preceptors, they maintained that each dynasty needed Daoist sanction in order to be legitimate.[40]

The Northern Wei, a model for the Yamato of Tenmu, Jitō, and for Nara as well, plays an important role in the political use of Daoism by imperial authority. The Tuoba emperor Taiwu (r. 424–452) of the Northern Wei underwent a full-fledged Daoist ceremony of investiture and declared Daoism the state religion and himself and his era "Perfect Lord of Great Peace

(Taiping)."[41] This development had a very specific, if complex, political purpose, for Daoism and Buddhism were being manipulated in internal struggles between Xianbei Tuoba and Han factions. In a complicated scenario, a non-Han Tuoba ruler was using Daoism explicitly as an autochthonous religion against the Han nobility, identified with Buddhism, depicted as alien, in order to implement a Confucian-inspired reform![42] Eventually, Cui Hao, the adviser who had been the architect of these reforms, was executed in 450, and state patronage shifted to Buddhism. However short-lived this experiment with Daoist state ideology may have been, it had long-lasting effects. Whether state sponsorship would go to Buddhism or Daoism, or both, and to what degree were issues that were raised repeatedly after the precedent established by the Northern Wei. After all, this dynasty had shown how a reformed Daoism could be put to use for the state, supplementing Confucianism's bureaucratic contributions with a religious dynamism. It could even be marshaled against rebellious Daoism, which disappeared altogether after the Northern Wei. Moreover, state support for Buddhism did not mean the end of Daoist investiture ceremonies.

A closer look at these important rituals shows how Daoism moved center stage in Chinese political ideology.[43] This development started in 442 when Celestial Master Kou Qianzhi transmitted to Emperor Taiwu lists of Daoist spirits and deities, together with talismans that granted him power over them. His successor, although reversing policy and supporting Buddhism as the state religion, also received the registers and talismans at the start of his reign in 452, and so did the next emperor in 466. When the capital was moved to Luoyang in 493, a Daoist altar was built south of the city. A general statement in the record reports that the practice of investiture was continued by the Tuoba rulers of the Later Zhou (557–589).

Emperor Wu (561–578) of the Later Zhou organized a debate between representatives of Daoism and Buddhism in 570 and "abolished" both, but ordered the collection of all Daoist scriptures in a newly built state Daoist temple and the creation of new official rituals. He tried to appropriate Daoist ideology or at least reshape and control it without interference by the Daoist establishment. This, I suggest, is what happened in Yamato also, particularly under Tenmu. He appropriated Daoist or Daoisant symbols, which by his time had proven useful to Chinese emperors, to build an ideology unencumbered by a Daoist religious establishment (nonexistent in the archipelago). Archaizing reforms in the Western Wei, the Later Zhou's predecessor, in the 550s were inspired by a new interest in the *Zhouli* (Rites of Zhou), which presented an ideal template for a system of perfect rulership. Tenmu also relied on this classic for designing his capital, Fujiwara-kyō. In the first couple of years (554–559) of the Later Zhou dynasty, the founder adopted the title Heavenly King (*tianwang*).[44] (Fifty years before the debate in the Late Zhou dynasty, in 519, Emperor Wu from the Liang dynasty had made an analogous move by personally devising for himself a bodhisattva ordination ritual, bypassing the monastic order, *sangha*.)[45] Clearly, during the last century of disunion before the Sui unification of 589, many rulers in China were creatively experimenting with a variety of legitimizing symbols, Daoism being one of them, as would Tenmu and Jitō.

Another indication that, starting with the Northern Wei, Daoism moved to the ceremonial and political center is the building of a *Daoist* Mingtang. The Mingtang was a complex of ceremonial halls, originally built by Emperor Wu of the Former Han in 109 or 106 BCE, after he ascended Taishan, where he performed the elaborate *feng* and *shan* sacrifices to report to Heaven about the state of the realm. He allegedly repeated the *feng* ceremony from the roof of the Mingtang.[46] Wu's ceremonial and architectural innovations were part of the construction of an emperor cult.[47] In 425, the year after Celestial Master Kou appeared at the Wei capital of Pingcheng, he built a Daoist temple allegedly modeled on the Mingtang, an unverifiable claim because the precise layout of the original one, which had long since disappeared, was unknown. The building of the empire's most important ceremonial site under the auspices of Daoism was a visible sign of Daoism's importance for political ritual. Daoism had become a supplier of public ritual and legitimacy and, with a few interruptions (notably the relatively brief periods of the Sui dynasty in the late sixth century and Empress Wu's reign at the late seventh), would continue to function increasingly in that way.[48]

Public debates continued to be staged during the Tang (in 621–623, 626, 637), resulting in continuously shifting modes and doses of differential state sponsorship for Buddhism and Daoism.[49] In 637, an isolated official edict even squarely attacked Buddhism as a foreign religion that was deluding the masses.[50] Starting in the 720s and reaching a peak around 750, the situation changed drastically. Then, Daoism became a full-fledged imperial institution. Ten copies of the Daoist canon were made in 749, and five more in 751; a number of imperial princesses even became Daoist nuns.[51] In 753, a Japanese delegation was given permission by Emperor Gaozong to return home with a famous Buddhist monk only if Daoist missionaries would be given an equal opportunity to spread their teachings there. The delegation refused to comply with the emperor's condition and had to smuggle Ganjin out of China as a stowaway, an episode we shall revisit in chapter 9.[52]

In the first half of the eighth century, when Japan resumed direct contact with China, Daoism was reaching its peak of state support there. In Yamato, however, the *tennō* Shōmu and Kōken/Shōtoku (724–770) declared themselves servants of Buddha and promoted the construction of a realm-wide Buddhist establishment fully supported by the state. This may explain the ambassadors' response to Gaozong in 753: "The Lord King of Japan does not venerate the Law of the Followers of the Way" (to be discussed in chapter 9). Indeed, Daoism had not developed an institutional base or official support in Japan. Its role was more elusive, yet significant in several ways, especially in the decades when Tenmu was creating Yamato's *ritsuryō* state.

Disparate Daoist Elements in Yamato

Japanese scholars have taken great pains at arguing the presence or absence of disparate Daoist elements in pre-Nara (and Nara) culture. In part, political stakes are involved because these positions entail visions of national identity. (Korean scholarship on Daoism is struggling with analogous issues.) Denials of the historical significance of Daoism at the beginning of recorded history would lead in Japan to conclusions about a homogeneous indigenous religious heritage to which the name Shinto has customarily been applied. In the last couple of decades, however, "internationalization" has helped highlight Japanese culture's heterogeneous beginnings and, with regard to Daoism, has even sometimes led to strained interpretations beyond what the historical record warrants. Nevertheless, even if there is no consistent pattern, then at least a quilt can be stitched together from scattered data.

Artifacts related to Daoism uncovered by archeology in the archipelago have been mainly limited to swords and mirrors. It was during the Northern Wei, a dynasty that exerted a certain fascination for Yamato rulers, that they came to symbolize imperial power, although sets of them had already been described in apocrypha of the second and third centuries as magical tokens of heavenly rulers.[53] They are found in Japan from ancient times as well. The Shōsōin in Nara and Osaka's Tennōji temple treasure such ceremonial swords. Some have star symbols of the Great Dipper similar to those found engraved on the blades of swords used in Daoist ceremonies in China, and much later in Japan.

A famous passage in the *Record of [the Southern] Wei* (*Wei zhi*) reports that Queen Himiko received one hundred bronze mirrors in 239.[54] Three hundred fifty-one such mirrors have been unearthed in Japan, and not only in the central region of Yamato. In the early Yamato state of the third and fourth centuries, bronze mirrors functioned as symbols of authority for the kings; they distributed them to local leaders, who may very well have traded in them.[55] They were, at least originally, magical mirrors decorated with Daoist emblems such as directional animals and zodiacal signs. The *Baopuzi* (Book of the Master Who Embraces Simplicity) ascribes special potency to large ones measuring more than 9 *cun/sun* (21 cm) in diameter. These were meant to summon spirits, reflect the future, and show what was happening hundreds of miles away. In general, mirrors were believed to provide protection against evil spirits.[56] Very few large mirrors have been found in China, but 40 percent of those discovered in Japan were of that type.[57] There is no evidence that they were used in Yamato other than for symbolizing a political relationship of sorts between the giver and recipient of them, perhaps limited to an exchange of prestige goods. The Sujin "dynasty" (rulers 10 to 14), centered on the ceremonial center of Miwa in the third and fourth centuries (a few kilometers northeast of where Fujiwara-kyō eventually would be built), distributed bronze mirrors to local rulers. They carried images of sacred animals and also of the Queen Mother of the West and the King Father of the East, a "talisman of cosmic bliss."[58]

The nonarcheological data have as their main source the *Nihon shoki*, the *Manyōshū*, and to a far lesser extent the *Kojiki*. These works were compiled, however, in the early eighth century, when Daoist writings were eagerly read in learned and "literary" circles. Therefore, it should come as no surprise to find Daoist-styled allusions, metaphors, or episodes introduced in narrative fragments of these sources in order to selectively enhance the numinous character of some traces of the past. To disentangle rhetoric from trace in each instance would require detailed monographic analysis, an empiricist project altogether different from the present study, and largely pointless. I shall limit myself to present a few examples to better delineate the meeting ground of politics, power, and Daoism.

Reading Immortals between the Lines

A legend about Shōtoku Taishi is recorded in the *Nihon shoki* and with a slight variation in the *Nihon ryōiki*.[59] It is a wonder tale that turns this prince, famous for his alleged support of Buddhism, into a Daoist immortal.[60] On 613/12/1, Shōtoku passed by a starving man, lying by the road, to whom he handed out food, drink, and a garment of his own. The following day, he sent someone to check on the beggar, but the man was found to have died and already been buried. Several days later, however, Shōtoku declared that this beggar was no ordinary person. "He must have been an upright man" (Aston). A messenger was sent, who opened the tomb under an undisturbed mound, but found no corpse. The tomb was empty, "the garment folded up and laid on the coffin." Shōtoku got his garment back "which he continued wearing as before." The people then commented: "How true it is that a sage knoweth a sage. And they stood more and more in awe of him."

The graph for the term Aston translates as "upright man" is *mahito*, the implication of the story being that it takes a perfected man/Daoist immortal to know one. Shōtoku Taishi is here presented as an enchanted immortal recognizing one of his kind, a type of encounter one can also find in the third-century *Wei zhi*.[61] The transcendence of the beggar took the form of "deliverance from the corpse and being transformed by escaping" (Ch. *shi-jie dunbian*; Jp. *shikai tonben* 尸解遁変). After seeming to die, the undead's corpse (*shi*) vanishes, leaving only clothes, a stick, or sword behind.[62] The spirit of the great hero Yamato Takeru similarly lifted from his grave mound in the form of a white bird, leaving only his clothing in his coffin.[63]

Such enchanting themes must have been familiar to a late-seventh-century literate audience. "Corpse deliverance" is one variety of the "art of invisibility,"[64] which the Paekche monk Kwallŭk brought in 602 from Sui China. This was a system of Daoist calendrical calculations around which tales of invisibility were spun, an art mastered by Tenmu and another exceptional Paekche monk.

Processes of metamorphosis, which are central to Daoist tales of religious practice, were often referred to metaphorically through images of molting snakes or carapace shedding by cicadas.[65] These striking metaphors could be made to carry other messages as well such as the entrance into a realm of purity from a defiled and polluted world left behind, messages one would be inclined to label Buddhist but which in the *Manyōshū* could be taken for granted without doctrinal references.[66] In the *Kojiki*'s Preface, the cicada metaphor is used for Tenmu's transformation into a ruler with supernatural powers and eventually to his status as *tennō* during his lifetime, and *mahito* after death.

Most tales of immortality in the *Nihon shoki* are wonder tales that are divorced from Daoist practice, but appear in contexts exalting kingly ("imperial") rule.[67] Such snippets of free-floating lore may have originated in allochthon communities as well as in texts brought over for scholarly use and literary enjoyment. Yet in the historical narrative, Daoism was also linked with destabilizing events. An episode from around the mid-seventh century, and therefore more historically reliable, provides a Daoisant context for subversive developments. An outbreak of millenarian hysteria brought on by a belief in immortality forced the authorities to intervene and slay the leader to restore public peace.

In 644/7, a man from Azuma (today's Shizuoka), supported by shamans, caused a commotion that spread quickly by persuading people to worship a particular insect to obtain long life and riches. Dancing and singing that the new wealth had arrived, people threw away their belongings. The insect was called Tokoyo no kami (God of the Everworld, a Daoist term for the realm of the immortals). The social disruption in the country and the center was so great that the leader had to be slain. Although this particular kind of worship has nothing to do explicitly with Daoism per se, the focus on prolonging life and the presence of an insect that was probably a huge caterpillar,[68] the morphing creature par excellence, feeding on orange trees (*tachibana* perhaps, the legendary tree from the Land of Everworld),[69] makes one wonder.

There is an intriguing context for this millenarian episode. This is part of the *Nihon shoki*'s narrative buildup toward the slaying of Soga Iruka, followed by his father Soga Emishi's suicide in 645/6. The last entry for 642 (Aston, 178) reports royal ambitions by Emishi: he had tombs prepared for himself and his son, and most shockingly, he had sponsored the performance of an eight-row dance. In book 3 of the *Analects*, called "The Eight Rows," on the subject of usurpation of royal rites, chapter 1 refers to the royal privilege of conducting the eight-row dance in the king's ancestral temple. Emishi performed the dance in his newly constructed ancestral temple. The next year (on 643/11/1) Iruka exterminated Yamashiro no Ōe, former prince Shōtoku's son and long-time candidate for the throne, together with twenty-two members of his family. A half year later, in 644/6, all the "shamans [*kamunakira*] of the realm" surrounded Emishi when he was "crossing a bridge" (going too far?) and bombarded him with obscure prognostic warnings. The people said that "this was a sign of changes." The next entry of a month later reports the shaman-incited millenarian hysteria. Another four months later, the Soga built two fortified residences, but they nevertheless were killed on 645/6/12. (It was a Hata chief who killed the leader of the movement, while the Aya took up arms, ready to defend Emishi in his last hour.)

The grassroots movement, the Soga plots, and their interpretation as "signs of change" put in the mouths of the people most likely refer to actual events and real persons. Weaving the foreboding supernatural in the form of shamans and Daoist lore into these developments enhanced their momentous character. It is relevant to note here that the legitimizing use of Daoist imagery by Tenmu notwithstanding, Daoist magic came to be associated with subversive plots in the eighth century as well.

Recipes for Immortality

Less than a year before Tenmu died on 686/9/9, a Buddhist monk and a lay helper were sent to Mino (the Nagoya area) to fetch the medicinal plant *okera* (*Atractylis ovata* belonging to the chrysanthemum family), which they used to prepare an infusion for him on 685/11/24. Knowledge of the medicinal qualities of herbs and minerals, intimately related to Daoist practices for maintaining and strengthening one's vital force (*ki*) and prolonging life, was available in seventh-century Japan.

The *okera* is a plant whose benefits are described in Daoist Chinese medicinal texts as lightning the body and prolonging life (and being a "famine food"). Its preparation in the form of powder, pills, or infusion had become widely known in South China through the *Collected Commentaries on the Canonical Pharmacopoeia* (Ch. *Bencao jing jizhu*; Jp. *Honzō-kyō shūchū*), written by Tao Hongjing (456–536), the founder of the Daoism of the Highest Clarity.[70] The work was known in Yamato by the late-seventh century, as indicated by a reference to it on a wooden tag (*mokkan*).[71] It was part of the "medicinal" literature brought from Paekche, and its distinguishing feature was the annotation of Daoist longevity-producing qualities of plants, trees, and minerals.[72]

Mercury, the famous alchemical substance, was believed to induce immortality — but certain death if consumed pure. Various recipes such as those for golden elixir (Ch. *jindan*; Jp. *kintan*) and golden liquor (*jinye*; *kin'eki*), described in the *Baopuzi*, the oldest of such texts, prescribe a lengthy process (taking one hundred days) to liquefy gold and mercury, but also an easier method refining mercury from cinnabar.[73] The "safest" way of ingesting the allegedly life-prolonging substance, however, was thought to be by drinking the water from a mercury-rich area, bathing in its springs, and consuming fruits, herbs, and animals that had absorbed mercurial elements. The Katsuragi and Yoshino mountains east and south of Asuka may have become associated with Daoism because of the natural mercury in the soil. The Uda plain, north of Katsuragi, was most likely chosen for the yearly herbal gathering parties for the same reason.[74]

The custom of designating the fifth day of the fifth month for "medicinal hunting" (*kusurigari*) parties did exist in Yamato by the time of Suiko's reign, in the early seventh century. Men went hunting for young deer, as their horns were believed to have medicinal qualities, and the ladies gathered herbs.[75] Most likely, this ceremony was a modification of a continental (Chinese and Korean) practice directly related to the Daoist *waidan* tradition of external alchemy.[76] However, these parties were not held just any-where. The collection of medicinal herbs took place in areas such as Mino, where allochthons had settled who presumably lent their knowledge about medicinal plants.[77] Chinese prisoners brought over in 660/10 had been moved to two districts there: Fuwa, of strategic importance for Tenmu in the Jinshin War, and Kata-agata.

Mino's connection to Daoist lore came also to play an important role in 717 for Empress Genshō, who had succeeded to the throne under difficult circumstances two years earlier.[78] The change of the Yōrō (Nurture Aging) era name in the fall of 717 was preceded and framed by an imperial progress to Mino.[79] There, the empress met with the assembled provincial inspectors (*kuni no mikotomochi*) of nineteen central and eastern provinces who entertained her with local "ethnic" songs and dances, a ritual of allegiance and submission especially welcome in difficult times. Subsequently, she "discovered"[80] a miraculous "sweet" spring with rejuvenating and life-restoring qualities, which is mentioned as a particularly auspicious augury in her edict and prompted the change to the Yōrō era name a month and a half after her return to Nara.

The foregrounding of Daoist elements in this sequence of events may be related to an increased need for legitimacy in the face of the expanding power of the Fujiwara, supported by Genshō against contending royal kin. Two weeks after Genshō's return from Mino, where Fujiwara Muchimaro (one of Fuhito's famous four sons) had been provincial governor for two years, Fuhito was joined on the Council of State by another son, Fusasaki, even though no two members of this governmental body of eight could come from the same *uji*. Thus the omen of the "sweet spring" may have been intended to consecrate "unconstitutional" political developments opposed by a faction of the nobility.

Enchanted Yoshino, Daoist Paradise

Ōtomo Yakamochi, the compiler of the *Manyōshū*, sings the praises of Yoshino as a natural paradise in compositions occasioned by some of Jitō's many visits.[81] In poems of the *Kaifūsō*, Daoist metaphors suggesting mystery celebrate Yoshino as the land where immortals dwell. That the Yoshino Mountains, no more than some fifteen kilometers from neighboring Asuka, also sheltered the Kuzu, an isolated group of primitive mountain dwellers written about as a different people, must have added to the mysterious aura of the area.[82]

No fewer than seventy poems in the *Manyōshū* and sixteen in the *Kaifūsō* relate to Yoshino.[83] In the former, the purity of nature, rushing waters of mountain streams, freshness of snow, luxuriant verdure, mysterious mists, clear river beaches, and cherry blossoms are celebrated, often with the recurring qualifiers *kiyoki* and *sayakeki* ("clean" and "fresh"), mostly written with the graph *sei* 清 of *seimei* 清明.[84]

The *Kaifūsō* supplements this picture with a pronounced sense of mystery, *yū* (*kasokeshi*) 幽, grafting allegory onto natural beauty. *Yū* alludes to what is mysterious, dark, dim, and deep. The compound *yūmei* juxtaposes darkness and light, the other world and the present.[85] The season most mentioned is autumn with its faint, dim, mysterious light (poems 32, 80). Almost all poems portray Yoshino as the land of immortals (for instance, poems 45, 73). The immortals are spiritual beings that fly from Yoshino to the stars on cranes, sliding back to earth on rafts (poem 32).[86] They reside in the woods near the Detached Palace (poems 48, 73) — Daoist material, no doubt, but without explicit textual referents. The land of the immortals, usually located in the ocean near China, is here close at hand as soon as one "enters Yoshino" (poem 31).

Jitō took a total of thirty-two trips to a detached palace in Yoshino, each averaging eight days.[87] Some years, she went as many as five times, even in the heart of winter. The purpose of these frequent excursions is unknown. Participation in a Daoist practice, either medicinal or ritual, is a reasonable explanation. As mentioned, the area was rich in mercury, and some sources also speak of a tower that could have been used for star cults.[88] Hitomaro celebrates Jitō's building of such a tower.[89] Poem 46 of the *Kaifūsō* refers to one such a structure as a site where the spiritual beings congregated.

The aura of mystery and wonder that envelops the Yoshino Mountains is also directly connected with several critical moments in the political history of the Sun line during the seventh century. When Prince Furuhito disqualified himself as a candidate for the throne in 646, he retired there "to devote himself to Buddhism." Naka no Ōe (Furuhito's half brother), another candidate, did not trust this symbolic retirement and made sure that it was final: three months later, he dispatched a posse to kill the prince, possibly having framed him with an alleged plot, and exterminated Furuhito's whole family. Tenmu also fled there in 671 to "engage in ascetic practices," and "cicada-like" shed his profane identity as rebel and followed Heaven's path. On 679/5/6 Tenmu and Jitō returned to Yoshino (Tenmu's only visit as *tennō*) with half a dozen princes "from different wombs." Seeking to prevent succession struggles, they extracted oaths of loyalty from the princes who swore that, regardless of their blood relationship or seniority, they would "obey orders, assist each other, and avoid contention." Yoshino was a site for tapping Daoism's legitimizing potential to secure political futures.

En no Gyōja

East of Asuka lay the Katsuragi Mountains, where the shaman En no Gyōja (Ozunu)[90] was active around the year 700. A century later, he was remembered as a magician and Daoist immortal.[91] Much later, toward the end of the twelfth century, mountain ascetics and shamans (*yamabushi*) became an organized religious group known as Shugendō. They claimed En no Gyōja as their founder.

Little is known about En no Gyōja.[92] In the service of the Kamo house, he was in charge of a deity important to the court. Accused by a disciple, Karakuni Hirotari, of putting spells on gods and spirits — a frightening reversal of supernatural power — En no Gyōja was exiled to Ōshima off Izu in 699 (whence, as an immortal, he flew to China), while Hirotari became employed in the Bureau of Medicine as a *jugonshi*, a spell master with knowledge of medicine, acupuncture, and spells.

Gyōja may have been the victim of two circumstances. One, around the turn of the century, the government was trying to bring under control spiritualist and divinatory free entrepreneurs especially within the Buddhist establishment, with which Gyōja may have had some marginal association. Two, internal rivalries within the Kamo house may have led to En no Gyōja's removal from Yamato. Hirotari, even though not a monk, was adept at both Buddhist and Daoist magico-religious practices he had probably learned from En no Gyōja. Eventually, he dropped the Daoist variety, possibly because it became proscribed, an issue to be taken up later.[93]

Another Kamo, namely Kibimaro, who was part of the embassy to China in 702, has been claimed as the founder of the lineage in charge of the important Kamo shrine in Heian. Most likely, he too was versed in magical practices. The Kamo line of yin-yang specialists also considers him as their ancestor, a lineage that, much later through Abe no Seimei, formed the Heian house of Abe yin-yang masters.

Several magico-religious traditions that have incorporated Daoist practices locate their origins in the late seventh century. For instance, Shugendō practitioners have adopted rites and formulae described in Ge Hong's *Baopuzi*.[94] The work is quoted twice in poems by Yamanoue no Okura, a member of the 702 China mission, which is when he may have brought it over, if it was not known earlier.[95] Ge Hong (283–343) was a central figure

The *Baopuzi* and the *Zengao*

Ge Hong (283–343), an alchemist who lived in the country of Wu in South China, wrote a biography of immortals, the *Shenxian zhuan*, and, in 317, the *Baopuzi* (Book of the Master Who Embraces Simplicity), an important work in the development of the Lingbao (Numinous Treasure) school of Daoism. This was just before a wave of northern celestial masters emigrated from the north after Luoyang fell to non-Han invaders. Ge Hong absorbed many local beliefs and practices of South China in his writings. In the *Baopuzi*, he clearly distinguished between longevity, which can be achieved through various practices such as gymnastics, the consumption of herbs, plant medicine, and immortality, attainable only through alchemical elixirs.

In chapter 17, Ge Hong quotes several sources on the subject of *dunjia* (Jp. *tonkō*, "invisibility"), a form of Daoist calendrics and ritual practice that, judging from the *Suishu* (History of the Sui), was widely used in those days. Numerous works on its subject were connected to the name of Ge Hong. *Dunjia* consists of a form of hemerology, the art of determining auspicious days for certain activities, and was especially needed when entering the mountains (literal and spiritual ones) for communicating with spirits, for protection, and for guidance in the collection of herbs and the planning of military strategy. From ch. 17, "Into Mountains, Over Streams": "Without knowing the secret technique of *dunjia*, the great mountains cannot be entered. . . . If you do not pick an auspicious day and an auspicious time, you will be punished by the spirits. Never enter the mountains lightly."

In the 360s, in the same region where Ge Hong lived, the brothers Yang Yi and Yang Xu were visited by perfected men who had descended from the Heaven of Highest Clarity or Supreme Purity (Shangqing) and handed them scriptures. Their visions were sorted out and systematized by Tao Hongjing (456–536) from the Liang dynasty (502–557) in his *Zengao* (Declarations of the Perfected).

Hongjing became the founder of the religious school of Shangqing, where the immortal Ge Xuan, a great-uncle of Ge Hong, was a major figure. The Shangqing school eventually absorbed the Lingbao school and became the dominant school of Tang Daoism.

Information on *dunjia*, including the quotation, are culled from Sakade, "Divination," 547–548; for a translation of the *Baopuzi*, see Ware, *Alchemy* (and 279–280 for a variant translation of the quotation).

in the development of Daoist alchemical disciplines of the Taiqing (Great Clarity) tradition in China.[96]

A section of the *Baopuzi* on a book on invisibility discusses precautions, based on the proper zodiacal coordinates, to be taken when "making one-self invisible" by entering the mountains. One historian, detecting correspondences between these prescriptions and details in the *Nihon shoki* regarding the timing of Tenmu's flight to Yoshino in 771, has argued that Tenmu did not "enter Buddhism," but "Daoism."[97] By Tenmu's time, there stood deep in the Yoshino Mountains the Detached Palace of Amatsu miya (a name with Daoist connotations), built by Saimei (655–661). Jitō's building of a "watch place" (Ch. *guan*; Jp. *kan*) or tower, used in the Daoist ritual observation of the stars, is also mentioned.

In sum, a variety of disparate elements, Daoist and Daoisant, were present in the historical narrative of pre-700 Yamato (the *Nihon shoki*) and the poetry of that time (the *Manyōshū* and the *Kaifūsō*). In the former, the political context in which they appear alludes to Daoism's transformative and enchanting power, subversive in the case of the millenarian hysteria, divinizing when applied to figures like Shōtoku Taishi; and in the latter, culturally enhancing the circles of the ruling nobility. Its rich metaphoric language, extended by the yin-yang potential of infinitely expanding correlations and correspondences, relying on a rhetoric of "aggregation,"[98] made possible its diffuse presence throughout late-seventh–early-eighth-century culture.

The Daoist Way from China to Korea and Japan

The reason for Buddhism's role in the transmission of these bodies of knowledge, which greatly complicates things for historians averse to dealing with messy matters, has to do with the place Daoism acquired on the Korean peninsula during the centuries of intercourse between Paekche and Yamato before Yamato's missions to Sui and Tang China in the 600s.[99] Written records inform us that Daoism was transmitted formally twice to the peninsular kingdom of Koguryŏ, the first time (in 624) in the form of two Daoist priests and a statue sent by Gaozu, the Tang founder; the second time (in 643), when eight Daoist priests were imported to stem the power of Buddhism, which had been introduced in 372.[100] Archeological evidence, however, clearly points to an earlier presence of Daoist beliefs and practices, in the sixth century according to an English article by Jung Jaeseo (or the third century, if one reads him in Japanese).[101] Silla opened its doors to

Chinese culture rather late. Buddhism was adopted there in 535, around the same time the Yamato court officially sanctioned its presence in the archipelago. Daoist lineages appear in Silla only toward the end of its rule over a unified peninsula (668–935). Paekche constitutes yet a different case, quite similar to Yamato's.

The transmission of Daoism to Paekche is mentioned nowhere in any written record, but archeological evidence such as mirrors with Daoist motifs excavated from the burial mound of King Muryŏng, who died in 523, point to the presence of Daoist cultural elements from at least the late fifth century.[102] Moreover, the manner in which knowledge regarding the calendar, divination, and astrology was brought over during the sixth century by Buddhist monks to Yamato from Paekche, where no institutional Daoism existed, must have been similar to the way it originally entered Paekche from China, namely through Buddhism (officially adopted in Paekche in 384). Several Chinese histories written in the first half of the seventh century report the presence in early-sixth-century Paekche of various techniques marginally related to Daoism (calendrical, medicinal, divinatory knowledge, physiognomy prognostication), and two of three similar texts add that Paekche had "many monks, nuns, temples and pagodas, but no Masters of the Way (*daoshi*)."[103] The same description could accurately portray Japan's situation in the seventh and eighth centuries.

Yet it is not only a matter of the way Daoism was transmitted first to Korea and then to Japan. The Daojia who formulated Daoism's doctrinal beginnings in China were active in a highly syncretistic intellectual environment where, "power derived from an ability to master not one but all fields of politico-intellectual practice, and to render them into a unified field of knowledge."[104] Regarding the intellectual field in China around the beginning of our era "it makes no sense to speak of Taoists, Legalists, or even of Yin-Yang/Five Phases cosmologists as distinct groups," one historian writes.[105] It is important to keep this in mind when discussing yin-yang and Daoism in ancient Japan, where these bodies of knowledge and practice, hard to differentiate to start with, were introduced from Paekche through a third cultic vehicle, namely Buddhism.

The abundant use of visual imagery in Daoist texts, in some measure the result of visualization practices, lent itself easily to the enchanting manipulation of language in poetry and belles lettres and the celebration, in the modality of the marvelous, of remarkable accomplishments by a pair of rulers in the last quarter of the seventh century. Tenmu and Jitō were victorious in war, building Yamato's first palace-city, transforming local leaders into a court nobility, giving Yamato an official history, constructing a *tenka* ruled by a *tennō*, a new Central Kingdom, and, as poets in Yoshino and at banquets, sometimes in the presence of envoys from Silla, occasionally put it, Everland itself, which one should therefore not seek anywhere else.[106] In addition, Daoism was richly panoplied with images, representations, and concepts that generated power, whether legitimizing or subverting, but always enchanting, a fount Tenmu and Jitō were eager to tap and the subject of the next chapter.

7 ARTICULATIONS

Tenmu was skilled in astronomy and the art of invisibility.
— *Nihon shoki*

The group of four consecutive rulers from Kōtoku to Tenmu are memorialized in the *Nihon shoki* with posthumous names opening with a reference to Heaven such as Ame yorozu toyohi and Ame toyo takara ikashihi tarashi hime, "Heaven Myriad Abundant Sun" and "Heaven Abundant Treasure Grand Sun Bountiful Princess" for Kōtoku and Kōgyoku. The new practice continued with Tenji and Tenmu's posthumous names. In addition, almost a century later, when the court in late Nara allocated two-graph names to all past rulers, Heaven was further highlighted in the names of the brothers Ten-ji and Ten-mu ("Heavenly Wisdom" and "Heavenly Warrior"). Also, Emperor Kanmu, whose powerful and long reign (781–806) overshadows in importance that of his predecessor, Emperor Kōnin (r. 770–781), the restorer of the Tenji line, paid particular ritual attention to Heaven (*kōten jōtei*) to the point of offering Chinese-style animal sacrifices (*gisei*) to Heaven on two occasions at the winter solstice.[1] One has the impression that the appeal to Heaven coincides with the troubled beginnings of both the Tenmu and Tenji dynasties.

Of course, this focus on Heaven became most prominent in the new identity of rulers during their lifetime as *tennō*, starting with Tenmu. *Tennō* owes its origin in good part to Daoism, where the cosmological heaven of the asterisms occupies a prominent place. The new form of royal power constructed in the late seventh century was an articulation of Daoist mythemes.

Tennō

Three stages mark the development of the *tennō* title and its association with astral symbolism in China: the Western Han, the Daoist Taiping movement of the Eastern Han, and the Tang dynasty. Sima Qian (?–85 BCE), in a famous passage, used the Pole Star region as a metaphorical field to understand the central cosmic role played by the emperor (*di*):

The Northern Dipper is the wagon of the emperor. It moves around the center and thus governs the four cardinal directions; it separates the yin and the yang and regulates the four seasons; it maintains the Five Elements in equilibrium; it moves time forward across its periodic divisions and determines all regular movements. All this is connected to the Northern Dipper.[2]

Slightly later, toward the end of the Western Han, "heavenly ruler" made its appearance in the weft texts of the apocrypha. There, it refers to the supreme cosmic deity that resides in the Purple Palace, located in the handle of the Little Dipper, from where he controls the four directions.[3] By then, the Heavenly Ruler Great Emperor (Tennō taitei) had been further identified with the Great One or Great Monad (Ch. Taiyi; Jp. Taiitsu).[4]

Toward the mid-second century, under the Taiping, religious identifications were believed to be achieved by ascetic practices of transcendentals. They were transformed into perfected ones, then into spirit people (Ch. shenren; Jp. shinjin), and finally, as Sovereign Heaven (Ch. Huangtian; Jp. Kōten), acquired the same shape as the Supreme Ruler of Heaven in the Purple Palace.[5]

Traditionally, we are accustomed to think of Chinese emperors as sons of Heaven (tianzi/tenshi), not heavenly rulers. There is one intriguing exception, however, when rulers in both China and Yamato, at the same time, used tianhuang/tennō. A mokkan constitutes hard evidence that in Yamato tennō was used during Tenmu's reign. In 674, however, the year following Tenmu's accession to the throne, Gaozong, the third Tang emperor (r. 650–684), changed his title from huangdi (Jp. kōtei)[6] or "august emperor/god" to tianhuang (Jp. tennō), and that of his main consort from huanghou (Jp. kōgō), "august queen," to tianhou (Jp. tenkō), "heavenly queen."[7] Gaozong's posthumous title was Tianhuang dadi (Jp. Tennō taitei) (Heavenly Ruler Great Emperor/God), which is the title that Emperor Xuanzong bestowed on Laozi, the legendary founding father of the Tang ruling house of Li.[8]

There are three possible sources for the Japanese tennō: the Han weft texts, the Taiping religious texts, and the Tang emperor's adoption of the title. The Han weft texts are the most likely candidate, but the possibility remains that the contemporaneous adoption of tennō by the Tang and Yamato rulers might point to Gaozong as the inspiration for Yamato. Even though between 669 and 702 no embassies left for China, there was a monk who had crossed over to China in 653 and returned via Silla in 678, and others in 684 who might have brought back news of the new title.[9]

One other textual analysis points in the same direction of Daoist connotations for Tenmu's rulership. This concerns the Festival of Appeasing
the Spirit or Chinkon-sai. By 702, this ritual was listed in the Taihō Code
together with the Niiname-sai as the only two festivals to be performed
by the *jingihaku*, the head of the Bureau of the Kami, a Nakatomi, and the
only two in the court's yearly ritual cycle centered on the persona of the
emperor.[10] The Niiname-sai is held the day after the Chinkon-sai.

Chinkon-sai

The *Nihon shoki*'s terse entry for the first Chinkon-sai, held for Tenmu on
685/11/24 reads, "Fire-Senior/Tiger [i.e. 24th],[11] Hōzō, priest, and Konshō
present [Tenmu] an infusion of *okera*; on this day, the calling back the spirit
(*shōkon*) was held for the heavenly ruler [Tenmu]."

That this *shōkon* ceremony was the same as the *chinkon* court ceremony
was established much later. There is some difference, however, in the meaning of the two terms. In *shōkon*, the spirit is called back, being an effort to
make it return, or prevent it from leaving. *Chinkon*, on the other hand, means
"appeasing the spirit(s)." Furthermore, the phonetic side marks (*kana* gloss)
for these graphs suggest the reading *mitamafuri*, "shaking the spirit." Both
the interpretation and names of this festival, "calling back," "appeasing," or
"shaking," were a work in progress over several centuries. *Shōkon* was used
only once, in 685, and is a Daoist term (*zhaohun* in Chinese). *Chinkon*, from
the Taihō Code of 702, does not occur in the *Kojiki, Nihon shoki, Fudoki*, or
Manyōshū.[12] It also is a Daoist term.[13] *Mitamafuri* is an interpretive reading added in the thirteenth century by Urabe no Kanekata in the *Shaku
Nihongi*, his commentary on the *Nihon shoki* in which he identified *shōkon*
as *chinkon*.[14]

To understand Tenmu's ceremony of 685, scholars have traditionally
fallen back on the first description of the festival, found in the *Sendai kuji
hongi*. This text is unanimously believed by Japanese scholars to have been
composed in the mid-ninth century. In 2006, however, John Bentley presented a linguistic analysis that led him to date it around 700 as a pre-Kojiki
text against scholarly consensus.[15] This work is a genealogical history centered on the Mononobe lineage of professional ritualists who maintain
that the Chinkon-sai originated with them at their Isonokami shrine. As
described in this text, the ceremony was a ritual elaboration on the shamanistic dance by the female *kami* Ame no Uzume that enticed Amaterasu out
of the cave where she was holed up, thus restoring the sun to the sky.[16] This
mytheme was also linked to the Chinkon-sai in the *Kogoshūi* (Gleanings

from Ancient Stories), written in 807 by Inbe Hironari, a member of the Inbe lineage of ritualists.[17]

In 685, at the time of the first "Chinkon-sai" (*shōkon*), the ancient narratives were still in flux, and court ceremonial, if we can judge from later texts, was not fixed yet.[18] Consequently, it remains an open question whether, as the texts of the ritualist lineages suggest, Tenmu's *shōkon* constituted a ritual enactment of the myth of Amaterasu's "rebirth" from a cave. The narrative incorporates the cooperation of the *kami* ancestors of three lines of ritualists, the Nakatomi, Inbe, and Sarume, which explains its legitimizing importance for these three houses. By 702, however, court ceremony had become principally the Nakatomi's domain. The Inbe felt that they had been pushed aside, as they complain through the *Kogoshūi*, where they remind the emperor, the addressee of the work, that their divine ancestor-founders had been equal partners in the ritual that brought Amaterasu out of her cave.[19] The Mononobe claimed that the Chinkon-sai was originally theirs. The Sarume, whose ancestress played a central role in the mythical episode according to the *Kojiki* (passed over in silence by the *Nihon shoki*), had been reduced to a minor ritualist house by Heian times. One is left with the impression that the Chinkon-sai as related to the Amaterasu myth developed over time as an arena for competing ritualist houses.

More recent studies relate the Chinkon-sai to extremely ancient ritual practices having to do with *tama* (spirits and their powers).[20] By Heian times, the ritual's function was to prolong the emperor's life and, according to some texts, that of the empress and crown prince as well. The reconstruction of the festival around narrative mythological episodes would thus constitute an effort by Heian scholars, exposed to Chinese culture and Daoist writings, to make new sense of a ritual that was no longer understood, a ritual, moreover, that had also changed over time. Originally, according to this line of interpretation, the ceremony had been a rite for the pacification of *tama*, those of a peer group of kings whose presence at the ceremony signaled their acceptance of a new paramount's authority as great king before his enthronement the next day. Thus the Chinkon-sai of 685 was not a "calling back of Tenmu's spirit" (*shōkon*) as the Chinese graphs in the *Nihon shoki* suggest, but a "festival for appeasing the spirits" (*chinkon*) of *uji* leaders and their ancestors.

There are problems with this argument. The first Chinkon-sai was not held after the Jinshin War's end in 672, a perfect opportunity for having local leaders acknowledge Tenmu's authority. Neither did it take place before his enthronement in the spring of 673 (2/27), but near the winter solstice many years later toward the end of his life. Since with the new secure authority structure of the Ritsuryō Codes, acceptance of a king of kings by the other kings had lost its meaning, Tenmu's Shōkon-sai would have been a moment of transition, in a process of hermeneutic entropy, when the ceremony was supplemented by Daoist elements.

A MORE THOROUGH historicization of this Shōkon-sai leads in a different direction if one does not lose sight of the Shōkon-sai's context, namely Tenmu's illness, the manifold attempts at restoring his health, and the symbolism surrounding his new title of *tennō*. Tenmu's intake of the *okera* infusion and the ceremony were held the same day.[21] That particular day, the zodiacal calendrical marker was Fire-Senior/Tiger. Less than twenty years later, the Taihō Code fixed the day of the Tiger closest to the winter solstice for holding the yearly Chinkon-sai.

Earlier I discussed the strong likelihood that the winter solstice played an important role in determining the location of Tenmu's and Jitō's new capital and its Daigokuden. Celebrations at court of this particular day took place unrelated to the Chinkon-sai or Daijō-sai. They are mentioned occasionally in the historical record especially under the reigns of the *tennō* Shōmu and Shōtoku.[22]

The winter solstice marks a pivotal time of seasonal transition and reversion that has been overlaid with multiple strata of meaning in many cultures. The *Yijing*'s twenty-fourth hexagram, Return or The Turning Point, marks it as the pivot of the cycle of the year and of life.[23] This solstice has also been linked to a recurring climax in the cosmic struggle between yin and yang, the latter expressing the sun, light, and generational potency, about to fade away, but which gradually expands its life-giving force toward the coming renewal of spring.[24]

Daoist writings from the Northern Qi and Zhou (550–589), and the subsequent Sui dynasties, recommended in general and sometimes specifically for rulers, the taking of certain herbal medicines or elixirs and summoning back the yang soul (*hun/kon*) in the eleventh month. Like the fading yang of the cosmos, the yang soul was believed to be in danger of leaving its yin (*po/haku*) soul mate and rising to Heaven. If this were to happen, death would follow.[25] Regardless of the time of the year, however, calling back the soul from the rooftop of the house immediately after or just before a family member's last breath was an ancient custom going back at least to the Western Han, one that was also practiced in Japan even until modern times.[26] There are many Chinese references to the practice.

In the *Chuci*, a collection of poems from about 300 BCE predating Daoism proper by some five centuries, a shaman calls upon the departing soul to return after describing the perils awaiting in the five directions, the underworld, and the beasts blocking access to Heaven.[27] The *Baopuzi* mentions that *zhaohun* can be achieved through minor elixirs.[28] A *Scripture of Calling Back the Soul* (*Zhaohun jing*), late fifth century, incorporates practices of recuperating and protecting the souls of both Buddhist and Daoist followers, the latter having to deal with no fewer than three *hun* and seven *po* souls. This text was used by yin-yang diviners in Japan.[29]

The combination of the impending flight of the ruler's soul and the winter solstice brings into play dramatic correspondences between the supreme celestial body of the sun, the physical body of the ruler, and his body politic: the cosmic macrocosm, the social microcosm, and their bodily double in the ruler share the same critical point of either impending termination or transition to rebirth. Daoism, amplified with yin-yang elements, contributed to the understanding of ritual intervention capable of securing the continuation of the ruler's two bodies by synchronizing it with the seasons' revival of life.

Yin-yang knowledge was well established in Yamato during Tenmu's reign, as witnessed by the establishment of a Yin-yang Bureau and an Outer Pharmacy. As we know from *mokkan*, the *Wuxing dayi* was available at the time.[30] This work, later officially adopted as one of the Yin-yang Bureau's four canonical works, can thus serve as an appropriate guide to the symbolism in the timing of Tenmu's Shōkon-sai and all later Chinkon-sai on the day with the zodiac sign of the Tiger.[31]

Geomantically, the astral figure of the white tiger standing for the West, decay, darkness, opposite the green dragon of the East is ancient. Archeologists have uncovered a skeleton from the Yangshao culture (5000–3000 BCE) along the Yellow River with a dragon figure on the left and a tiger on the right, formed by arranged clam shells.[32] Five thousand years later, together with the Dark Warrior (a turtle and snake intertwined) of the North and the Vermilion Bird of the South painted on the walls of the two famous tumuli of Takamatsuzuka and Kitora in Asuka, they reveal that this geocosmic iconography was still active during Tenmu's reign.[33] These figures also decorated huge banners at New Year ceremonies in a plaza in front of the Daigokuden in Fujiwara-kyō, starting at least in 701, to be discussed later in this chapter.

The *Wuxing dayi* offers a more complex picture, which includes not only space, but a dimension of time and process as well by linking the zodiac sign of the Tiger with the beginning of the season of weak yang, the early spring in the first month of the year governed by the spirit of (growing)

Wood as the first of the Five Phases (Gt 164, 168, 252a; Cd 380, 382, 383, 440). Wood is furthermore linked to the East and agriculture (Gt 113, 117; Cd 201, 216), having an affinity with the *zhen/shin* trigram of the *Yijing* (two divided lines over an undivided one) and the Dragon (Gt 184; Cd 433). This trigram stands for the origin of all things, the direction of the East, the source of life, regeneration, and thunder.[34] Thus, at the macrocosmic level, the following concatenation of signs and values ensues:

> Tiger = weak yang = brings forth Wood = 1st month = regeneration = East = *zhen*

At the human level, this is further expanded in two ways. Agriculture correlates with Wood and with the East (Gt 113; Cd 201).[35] Most important, powerful rulership is the hallmark of *zhen*, the third of the trigrams following those of Heaven and Earth. The heavenly ruler was born at the beginning of time (Gt 160; Cd 377) at *zhen*, in the East, appearing as Fu Xi (or Pao Xi), the first of the five Chinese mythological emperors, ruling through the virtue of benevolence, associated with Wood, the first of the Five Phases (Gt 240b, 241b; Cd 390–391, 394).[36] Thus, the associated meanings extend further:

> *zhen* = East = Wood = beginning = benevolence = agriculture
> = Fu Xi (first ruler)
> = powerful ruler

Another level of correspondences lies within the human body. Here, Xiao Ji, the *Wuxing dayi*'s author, relies exclusively on Daoist writings. The yang soul, recalled in the *zhaohun/shōkon* ritual, was believed to be lodged in the liver. This organ was also infused with the spirit of Wood and the virtue of benevolence (Gt 218–223 passim; Cd 286–305 passim). An important organ, it was thought to rule the body like a military commander (*shogun*) (Gt 221b, 222a; Cd 297, 298). If orders were followed, the liver had a benevolent life-giving (Wood) effect, providing the eyes with sight, the skin with a healthy complexion, hair and nails with color (Gt 219b, 221b; Cd 290, 296). With the spirit absent from the liver, the eyes would grow small and bluish around the eyelids and lose their luster — symptoms of impending death as we would diagnose today.

> liver = Wood = benevolence = rulership = life-giving

The links between values in these series may each seem arbitrary, far-fetched, meaningless, and anything but persuasive. However, they make up a family of meanings, made possible through the indeterminacy or polysemy of symbols. The overdetermination of these symbols, paradoxically, makes them indeterminate because the logical operation that creates them is one of aggregation, not of specification.[37] To conclude simply that Tenmu suffered from a bad liver would amount to diagnostic reductionism. Such aggregations are typical of a logic of accumulation that keeps signifieds continually, rather than reifying and eliminating them, thus constituting what Wittgenstein called a "family resemblance."[38] The value brought into operation by the trigram *zhen*, for instance, varies with the signified to which it is juxtaposed.

The semiotic and somatological cluster of signs associated with the Chinkon-sai foregrounded not only notions of rejuvenation, the yang soul, rulership, and benevolence, but also of Tenmu as heavenly ruler, for the *tennō* was born at the beginning of time, *zhen*, in the East, under the Wood sign, the first of the Five Phases (Gt 160, 240b, 241b; Cd 377, 390, 394). The ritual constituted a theatrical affirmation of the *tennō* nature of Yamato's first ruler to go by that title. That Daoist connotations were present as well becomes clear at the end of the illness (the beginning of which triggered the Shōkon-sai), when Tenmu received posthumously the new identity of perfected one, immortal. Moreover, the winter solstice, as the pivotal notion around which Tenmu had planned the location of the Daigokuden and his palace-city of Fujiwara-kyō, as analyzed earlier, played a crucial role in his conception of rulership.

The Shōkon-sai of 685/11/24 was one of the first of many measures taken to restore Tenmu's health. He eventually died within less than a year on 686/9/9 (Fire-Senior/Horse). As far as we know, the onset of his final illness dates from 685/9/24, two weeks before Tenmu dispatched two men to fetch the herb *okera* from Mino. These were followed by two others, ordered to make preparations for setting up a temporary residence (*karimiya*) in Shinano, probably for an eventual visit to hot springs as the chronicler surmises. On the first day of his illness, Tenmu also ordered Buddhist scriptures to be read for three days at three temples — undoubtedly magically significant numbers. At least two dozen similar activities for spiritual remedies were taken during Tenmu's final year. He had 180 men and women take Buddhist orders, bodhisattva statues set up, temples and pagodas cleaned, penitential services or great purification ceremonies held, and amnesties proclaimed. There is little doubt that the impending loss of the first *tennō* was experienced as a momentous, cosmic development and that (or because) it was orchestrated as such. Within this context, Tenmu took the *okera* infusion for prolonging life and, fearing that his soul was on the point of leaving his body, had it "called back" on 11/24.

It is possible that Hōzō, the monk in charge of this whole affair, had di-agnosed Tenmu as suffering from a liver disease. Sickness, especially the ruler's when suffering from a malfunctioning "ruling" organ, is obviously more than a physical ailment. The ontological and cosmological con-notations of synchronizing the cure with the winter solstice — the two men were dispatched to Mino on 10/8, six weeks ahead of the important date — were prominently present. Knowledge of the vast symbolic system of the *Wuxing dayi*, the source for the above reconstruction of the Shōkon-sai's fuller meaning separate from the later Chinkon-sai, came to Japan mainly through Buddhist monks. Hōzō, in charge of preparing the *okera* infusion, was one such monk from Paekche. Most likely he orchestrated the Shōkon-sai on behalf of Tenmu as well. Seven years later (692/2/11), Hōzō is mentioned in the *Nihon shoki* as drawing the stipend of doctor of yin-yang at the Yin-yang Bureau. There was only one such position. A number of other Buddhist monks were laicized later, as was most likely Hōzō, and afterwards appointed to the Yin-yang Bureau,[39] where the *Wuxing dayi* was probably already being used as a key text before being declared essential for students at the bureau in 757.

TO SUMMARIZE, a Buddhist monk from Paekche, soon appointed as the foremost official authority on matters of yin and yang, plausibly constructed for a Yamato sovereign, newly referred to as heavenly ruler, a Daoist ritual to prolong his life, a ritual that soon became one of the most important imperial ceremonies in the yearly cycle of "Shinto" events at the court, into which later a version of the Amaterasu epic was incorporated along with Buddhist spells.

The details of Tenmu's Shōkon-sai are unknown, and for good reason. The *Nihon shoki* was not meant as a documentary, a full reportage of events. It sufficed that the enchanted aura surrounding the *tennō*, even at the end of his mortal life, be communicated. The later accretions and modifications of the ceremony further increased the aspect of wonder tale by shifting registers from the cosmic and restorative to the mythological and celebra-tory. At least by the early ninth century, but possibly already around 700 if one accepts Bentley's dating of the *Sendai Kuji hongi*, the winter solstice was linked to Amaterasu's returning light to the world when enticed out of the cave where she had ensconced herself, accepting symbols of author-ity (mirror and jewels), restoring joy and order to the worlds of both *kami* and humans,[40] in a ceremony repeated yearly and held the day before the enthronement of new emperors.[41] The female *kami* Ame no Uzume played an important role in the *Kojiki* version of the episode by engaging in a strip-tease on an overturned tub.[42] In the *chinkon* ritual as described in the *Sendai Kuji hongi*, a Sarume female diviner claiming descent from Ame no Uzume reenacted Uzume's dance on top of an overturned tub, tapping it with a spear.[43]

In this ceremony, the Sarume "shamaness" also took an imperial garment and shook it. The head of the Office of Kami Affairs, representing officialdom, tied knots in a rope, and both rope and garment were put in a *tamabako* (spirit/life-force box), symbolically tying down and locking up the emperor's life force ("soul") in his body, thus preventing its flight. The box was perhaps shaken to generate more life, as is suggested by the alternative reading of *mitamafuri* for *chinkon*. Buddhist recitations were added as yet another source of life-generating benefit.

Rituals, like myths, are not fixed once and for all. The work of time does not allow that and makes them evolve and change. The consumption of *okera,* an herbal remedy, Daoist like almost all such remedies at the time, was linked with the *shōkon* ritual only on the one occasion of Tenmu's illness. The yin-yang connotation faded, except for the day of the Tiger and winter solstice. The Daoist term for spirit, *kon,* still in the name of the festival, is now often replaced by other characters or readings — *tama* or *rei,* older notions that resonate well with the concept covered by *kon* — dimming allusions to the dual *kon-haku* soul of Daoism. The symbolism of the ceremony became centered on Amaterasu's epic. Buddhism found a place as generator of surplus spiritual power through spells. The result was a new event for the court, where Daoism's horizon of meaning had receded.

The scholar Shinkawa Tokio attaches great symbolic value to Tenmu's institutionalization of the Shōkon-sai with its prominent Daoist features and its subsequent transmogrification whereby such elements disappeared from view.[44] For him, it illustrates the fate Daoism met in Japan, and he wonders why history took such a turn, a question we shall take up later. The Chinkon-sai's trajectory was not unique. A number of other symbols have a Daoist genealogy.

The Daigokuden, Swords, and Mirrors

Tenmu's design of his new capital was sino-mythical, as were many of the symbols that were put in operation in Fujiwara-kyō. These symbols pointed in two directions. They spoke of Tenmu's new authority, and they steered the mind to the heavens and the stars. Rulers now were Heaven's rulers who made their most solemn proclamations in the Daigokuden. This symbolic language of authority was taken from China, where astral and Daoist no-menclature had been adopted over time by the culture of the court — and vice versa, as Daoism had created its own imagery on the model of the state bureaucracy.

The earliest Daigokuden in China was probably built by Mingti, the second emperor of the Southern Wei, one of the post-Han Three Kingdoms, in the south palace of Luoyang in 235.[45] This was some twenty years after the general Cao Cao had dissolved the Eastern Han and forced the celestial masters to resettle in various parts of China. The first emperor of the Southern Wei, Cao Zhi, took on the identity of a Daoist perfected one. The Northern Wei, however, played a greater role as a model for Yamato. It had a similar audience hall, the Taiji Gong in the imperial "Purple Palace" at the capital Pingcheng.[46] A number of important Japanese names are Yamato pronunciations of Chinese terms from the Northern Wei: Daigokuden for Taiji Gong; Heijō (Nara) for Pingcheng. Also, Emperor Taiwu, whose father's name reads "Shōmu" in Japanese, created a "Genji" of demoted imperial offspring and turned them into a military family charged with the task of protecting the emperor.[47] (Moreover, the Wei Law Code was sufficiently known in Yamato as early as 569 to have influenced the creation of administrative and military units of "villages" in royal domains, modified later by the Tang, but kept as such in the Taihō Code.)[48]

The eighth century was Daoism's golden age in China. In 712, the reign title was changed to Taiji (Daigoku). Sima Chengzhen (647–735), "court Daoist extraordinaire"[49] in service of the Tang emperors Ruizong and Xuanzong (r. 710–756) presented to Emperor Ruizong a ceremonial sword and mirror, a set of magically potent emblems of imperial power that Chengzhen had forged with his own hands. This was not the first time that Daoist magical power was made available to Chinese emperors by the presentation of swords and mirrors. Tao Hongjing had made thirteen swords for Emperor Wuti (r. 502–550) of the Liang, and Emperor Taiwu (r. 424–452) of the Northern Wei had been offered one.[50] This constituted a reversal of their signification because both emblems had been used *against* imperial power in the early religious Daoism of the first three centuries CE.[51]

It was the weft texts around the first century CE that ascribed prognostic and ruling power to mirrors inscribed with Daoist cosmic signs, alleging that they had been proven to have the power to foretell the rise and fall of past dynasties.[52] (Subsequently, they were used in immortality techniques.)[53] Thus, it was only around the time that Daoism became appropriated by imperial power or, to put it another way, that it succeeded in capturing the status of official supplier of spiritual symbols of power, during the Northern Wei, that the set of mirror and sword became imperial emblems. That this was Daoist is clear from the fact that no Confucian texts ascribed any magical or spiritual power to swords or mirrors,[54] or to spirits, and neither do they speak of perfected ones.

Symbolic devices such as swords and mirrors, held to be magically potent, were meant to increase ruling power. Since *qi/ki* power is lodged in unusually dense concentration in swords as well as in emperors, the two were symbiotically connected. Ideally, the flow of vitality should be tapped and controlled by the emperor. However, imperial power could also be drained by a reversal of the flow.[55]

An attempt to divine (*uranau*) Tenmu's final sickness, one of several measures taken to diagnose and cure Tenmu, revealed that he had been cursed (*tatareri*) by the famous Kusanagi sacred sword, which was immediately removed from the palace and deposited far away in the Atsuta shrine of Owari (686/6/10). As mentioned earlier, the Kusanagi sword, via Susanoo, Amaterasu, Ninigi, the Ise priestess, and Yamato Takeru wound up in Owari, from where a monk succeeded in stealing it in 668 but failed to smuggle it out to Silla. It was retrieved, and that may have been why it was still in the palace during Tenmu's illness, although one wonders whether Tenmu might not have kept this potent source of power close by since his regime, like Keitai's probably, originating in warfare, may have needed some extra source of legitimacy.[56] The sword that was one of the three regalia possessed awesome power, which is why it was kept far away from the palace, as was the mirror, enshrined in Ise.

Duplicates of the original sword and mirror were used for the investiture of great kings and *tennō* in Japan.[57] Until Jitō's rule, these regalia were referred to as *jifu* or *ji'in* (imperial tokens/seals). From then on, however, they came to be regarded as *shinji* (sacred/spirit regalia) or *tenji* (Heaven's regalia).[58] As detailed earlier, the number of objects assigned regalia status was a matter of dispute among ritual houses. In the early ninth century, the Nakatomi succeeded in having their view of three regalia rather than two prevail over the Inbe. These regalia, nowadays often still thought of as essentially "Shinto," have their origins in Daoist worldviews, as has the term "Shinto" itself.

The "Shinto" Question

The combination of graphs for *kami* and "way" with the modern pronunciation of "Shinto," as a comprehensive term for practices and beliefs in Japan does not go back further than the fourteenth century. Before that time, especially from the seventh through the ninth centuries, worship of *jingi* (*kami* of Heaven and Earth) mentioned in law codes and historical annals was about ritual at official "state" shrines (*kansha*) and does not cover the wide variety of folk practices still too often called today "primitive" or "ancient" Shinto.[59] We have to go to Chinese texts to find the earliest use of the graphs that ultimately came to be read as "Shinto."

Since Han times, *shenmingdao* (Jp. *shinmeidō*) referred to the "way of the spirits of the dead." *Akitsukami*, "manifest god" of seventh- and eighth-century Japanese texts, is actually written with the same graphs as *shenming/shinmei*, but in reverse order. Later, the term *shendao/shintō* (the way of the gods/spirits) was used by Daoist masters Tao Hongjing in his *Zengao* and Ge Hong in his *Baopuzi* as a synonym for Daoism.[60]

The earliest relationship between what Chinese people knew about or observed in the archipelago and their own culture is found in the *Wei zhi*. This text uses *guidao/kidō* (way of the spirits [of the dead]), with the same meaning as *shendao*, in a report about Queen Himiko, most likely a shamaness who was said to have "practiced the *way of the spirits* and led her people astray through it."[61] This reference, however, constitutes no evidence of Daoism's presence or Shinto's in the islands, as used to be argued in the past.[62] *Guidao* appears again in the *Wei zhi*'s biography of Zhang Lu, organizer of one of the first Daoist religious movements, the Way of the Five Pecks of Rice.[63] Zhang Lu's mother, politically active with the governor of the province, contributed to the organization of the movement through her magical skills in *guidao*.[64] Elsewhere, she is referred to as "having been the first one to have used *guidao*." Thus, the *Wei zhi*, in reporting on the style of Himiko's regime, used the term *guidao* possibly because of resemblances with either the practice itself or female magicians. The Yamato referent for *guidao/kidō* in this Chinese text is a practice that one cannot label Daoism or Shinto. Similarly, the presence of bronze mirrors, especially the large ones, and ceremonial swords arguably is no more than an indicator of the status of the distributors, rulers like Himiko, and their recipients, local leaders.

Today, the view that the term "Shinto" was adopted during the last decades of the seventh century as the "Idealvorstellung des japanischen Gott-Kaisertums," as Nelly Naumann summarized the scholarly consensus thirty-five years ago, is being questioned.[65] As mentioned earlier, the term itself, absent from the *Kojiki*, appears only three times in the *Nihon shoki*. *Kami* worship was a much wider phenomenon than the state institutional ritual system organized around *jingi* by the *ritsuryō* state, mentioned in the Taihō Code's Jingi-ryō.[66] Only in the fourteenth century did "Shinto" come to function as an umbrella for a great diversity of practices and beliefs one could call *kami* worship.[67] The term refers to a belief in the action of gods, but not to an institution that one could call "Shinto," which emerged only in the nineteenth century when Buddhism and Shinto were forcefully separated by the Meiji state.[68]

At least by Tenmu's time, *kami* that were honored by attention from rulers constituted not a "pantheon," but "a quasi-society . . . whose members were given roof, regular food, and other types of offerings" and "were granted ranks."[69] Tenmu's promotion in rank of three *kami* whose oracles had benefited him during the war reflect not only their approval of his rebellion, but also Tenmu's power over them, a power he would use many times subsequently with his court as well.

In the seventh century, institutionally endowed and structurally organized Buddhist clerics stood out clearly in the field of religious practice. In addition, Daoist and Daoisant practices and beliefs were present in the fields of medicine and what might loosely be called the proto-sciences (astronomy, alchemy, the calendar, yin-yang, etc.), and a great variety of *kami* worship was practiced at all levels, although as a rule shrines seem to have lacked a permanent priesthood until very late in the tenth century.[70] Tenmu and Jitō ordered Buddhist temples and clergy to perform on behalf of the realm without closely identifying the state and Buddhism. They did not claim the title of *cakravartin* (Ch. *zhuanlun shengwang*; Jp. *tenrin shōō*) as the founder of the Sui or Empress Wu did, or later in Japan Emperor Gosanjō in 1068; neither did they become officially "servants of the Buddha," a title Emperor Shōmu and his consort adopted in 749, and Empress Shōtoku in 764.[71]

Elements from the other two "nontradition traditions" (Daoism and *kami* worship), however, were used to construe the image of the polity. The world of the *kami* was put in order, publicly and officially, to the extent that the state created that order. We have seen the role played in this development by *hafuri* and the disbursement of oblations (*hanpei*). In his appropriation of Daoist elements also, Tenmu had a free hand, unhampered by a "church." Emperor Wu of the Later Zhou had to eliminate institutional interference with a decree "abolishing" both Daoism and Buddhism in 570 before engaging in a task similar to Tenmu's. Using Daoist scriptures, Wu refashioned state ritual, mining Daoist ideology or at least reshaping and controlling it, free from the Daoist establishment. Tenmu also ordered the collection of all (Buddhist) sacred texts, and he and Jitō mobilized Daoist notions and values to represent their new polity as well.

In China, legitimization of the emperor in his position as supreme ruler was started by producing his cosmic counterpart in Heaven, Taiyi.[72] This took place during the Western Han. Inspired by the Daoist notion of Heaven and its center, the Pole Star was associated with Taiyi, the Great One. This concept was personified as the Celestial Emperor. His possible counterpart in the *Kojiki* is Ame no minakanushi (Lord of the August Center of Heaven). He is the first of the three creation deities from the opening line of the *Kojiki*. However, he is never mentioned again, leaving the actual creation to other *kami*, starting with his two companions, the *-musuhi* gods Takami- and Kami-. He is "the beginning of everything, and at the same time, as the first and highest of all gods, the heavenly counterpart and the symbol of the emperor," Nelly Naumann writes, detecting Daoist notions at play.[73]

Archeology has provided visual proof of the existence of his symbolization through the discovery of the astral representations on the ceiling of the Takamatsuzuka burial chamber in Asuka, which dates from the late seventh century. The cosmos, represented by the lunar lodging asterisms, revolves around the stars of the Northern Culmen forming the celestial court and its four attendants in the center of the ceiling (see figure 9). An almost identical mid-Tang burial chamber, however, lacks the Northern Culmen and its four attendants.[74] It is hard not to conclude from this comparison that political ideology was expressed in Asuka specifically also through astral Daoist symbols.

New Year 701

At the beginning of the *Shoku Nihongi* (covering the century between 697 and 791), we read about New Year's Day of 698: "Emperor Monmu proceeded to the Daigokuden and received the court. New Year's greetings from the civil and military officials and from Silla were presented. The ceremony was held as in the past." The first year of Taihō, 701, the New Year's audience was described in more detail, without indication, however, that this particular ceremony differed from previous ones:

> The emperor proceeded to the Daigokuden and received the court. At this ceremony, the standard in the shape of a bird was placed at the front gate. On its left were an effigy of the sun, and banners of the Blue Dragon and the Vermilion Sparrow; on its right, an effigy of the moon, and banners of the Black Warrior and the White Tiger. Envoys from border vassal states and barbarian countries (*ban'i*) [Silla on the one hand, and the Emishi and the Southern Islands on the other] were ranged [separately] in rows at the right and left. Matters civil and ceremonial (*bunbutsu no gi*) were arranged this way.[75]

The insignia lined up in front of the Daigokuden refer to seven nine-meter-high poles: three standards with figures on top and four poles holding banners 5.60 meters long. From colored drawings in an illustrated scroll from 1444 documenting an enthronement ceremony that took place in the thirteenth century we know what these insignia looked like.[76] (See plate 5.)

In the center, surrounded by the banners, stood a standard bearing at the top a yellow copper figure of a three-legged bird, wings spread. The standard on the left supported a gilded copper disk, representing the sun, with the three-legged vermilion bird or crow in the center. On the right was a standard with the silver copper disk of the moon. The red crow, essential yang, with three legs, a yang number, is a lucky bird, legendary for having delivered the scepter of rulership to the founder of the Zhou dynasty.[77] The moon disk bore three figures: a cinnamon tree in the center flanked by a standing toad and a hare preparing the elixir of life.

These three standards were flanked on each side by two banners, representing the four directional animals. At the left, the yang and sun side, banners with the Blue Dragon (east) and the Vermilion Sparrow (south) were held up high; at the right, the yin and moon side, banners with the Black Warrior (a turtle and entwined snake, the north) and the White Tiger (west). The significance of these symbols displayed at the New Year event of 701 changed over time.[78]

The four directional animals, like all symbols, are multivalent signs that can be put to different uses, even simultaneously. They can signify the cosmos, a political space, or the seasons; they even have military usage. Each animal could also stand for a group of seven of the twenty-eight lunar lodgings, and the whole assemblage for a cosmically ordered hierarchy.

The three-legged copper red bird occupied the center of the lineup at Fujiwara-kyō. It is unclear which way it faced. During Heian times, when this ceremony was limited to enthronement celebrations, the New Year occasion having been dropped, we know that the bird faced north, toward the newly enthroned emperor and, behind him, the Daigokuden. In 701, however, the bird probably faced south, namely toward the officials and the delegations from tribute-offering polities. A cluster of symbolic associations suggest that this bird may have sent a strong message of imperial(istic) power to those present.

Military strength — twice yang through the bird's color and its three legs — was probably further amplified by its association with the Yatagarasu crow from the *Nihon shoki* and *Kojiki*, works on the drafting board in 701. The Yatagarasu functioned as a messenger flying ahead, helping the founding ruler Jinmu in his campaign eastward to subdue barbarian tribes. Thus, at the New Year's ceremony, the bird with wings spread as if in flight or about to fly, the emperor behind him, would have faced the subdued (the Southern Islanders) and the presumably submissive (the Emishi and the messengers from Silla) — barbarians and "vassal states," indispensable components of a *tenka*, here essentially a staged one, more imaginary than real. When facing north later in Heian, that meaning would have been lost, not in the least because the foreign presence had disappeared by then. The three-legged bird, facing the new emperor at the beginning of his reign, would have been offered then as a major auspicious portent by the officials lined up behind it.[79]

Perceiving political relevance in wondrous phenomena such as three-legged animals was fairly new in Yamato around the end of the seventh century. When on 650/2/9, a governor presented Great King Kōtoku with a white pheasant, a long discussion among foreign experts was needed to inscribe the bird with its proper meaning. They concluded that, as sign, it was even more auspicious than a dead three-legged crow, which, a Buddhist priest from Koguryŏ explained, envoys to the Tang had brought back home.[80]

A few decades later, however, when a three-legged sparrow was offered as a positive omen to Tenmu at New Year's in 683, the symbolics were well in place. The figures in the moon, although older than Daoism, accrued Daoist connotations of longevity and immortality. Vermilion birds like the one that held center place in the lined up insignia were rare portents. Only five of them are listed in *Ruijūkokushi*, four of them between 699 and 739, apparently a period when investment in Daoist or Daoisant signs was high.[81]

Whether or not some or all of these meanings were "believed in" is a moot question since they were displayed by the authorities who, by officializing them, imposed a dominant meaning. An anecdote about Empress Wu (r. 690–705), contemporary of Jitō and Monmu, illustrates the point that the act of public display itself may have as much weight as, or even more than, the material support conveying the specific meaning. In 690, the year Empress Wu replaced the Tang dynasty with a restoration of the Zhou, a courtier eager to supply the new dynast with a potent sign of cosmic approval presented her with a three-legged crow. Unfortunately, one of the legs of the animal dropped off. The empress, however, unfazed, "merely laughed," Schafer writes, "and ordered the favorable prodigy entered in the official archives. 'Why need we examine into whether it is genuine or counterfeit?' she said."[82] Authority needs symbols, but it can also draw profit (even more, perhaps) from circumventing them without negating them (the event was entered in the archives).

Tenmu's and Jitō's mausoleum. Source: Nara bunkazai kenkyūjo sōritsu gojū shūnen kinen. *Asuka, Fujiwara-kyō ten*, 119.

Fujiwara Palace site. Facing north toward Miminashi yama; archeological site of palace with Daigokuden in the center. Source: Nara bunkazai kenkyūjo sōritsu gojū shūnen kinen. *Asuka, Fujiwara-kyō ten*, 137.

Imperial ceremonial coat worn by Emperor Kōmei (r. 1847–1866). (Imperial Household Agency Collection.) Source: *Kōmei Tennō:*

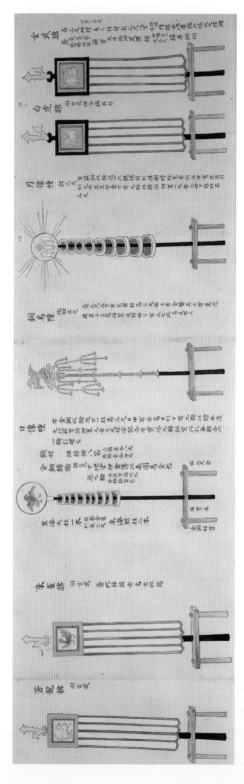

Standards and banners used at New Year's ceremony. Sketch drawn by Fujiwara Mitsutada in 1444, explaining specifics of paraphernalia used in the twelfth century (*Bun'an gosokui chōdo no zu* in the Ise Shrine Collection). Nara bunkazai kenkyūjo sōritsu gojū shūnen kinen. *Asuka, Fujiwara-kyō ten*, 119.

The New Year celebration as styled in 701 continued to be held through-out the eighth century, but not further. From the early Heian period down to the early sixteenth century (1501), it was held at enthronement ceremonies instead, the four directional animals depoliticized, symbolizing the time of the four seasons rather than universal dominion.[83] In the seventh and eighth centuries at Fujiwara-kyō and Nara's Heijō-kyō, however, the four directional animals symbolized space, the four cosmic directions implying a cosmic center.[84] The presence of delegations from Silla, referred to as a "border vassal state" (the *ban* of *ban'i*) and from the "barbarians" (*i*), the Southern Islands, and the Emishi from the north constituted the living reality of pretended reach of the Yamato *tenka*.[85] Their presence on this occasion was the crowning moment of a policy that had been pursued first under Tenmu, its pre-Tenmu history incorporated ten years later in the *Kojiki*'s inflated story of the Korean kingdoms' "tributary" relationship with Yamato.

Contacts with the Southern Islands are mentioned twice in the early seventh century (616, 629), but starting in 677, the number of visits by present-bearing delegations from the islands to the court increased markedly, possibly pulled by the new power of the Yamato center, but most probably pushed by emissaries from Tenmu, Jitō, and Monmu. On 698/4/13, eight men were dispatched from the court to the Southern Islands, literally "to claim these countries." Two months later (6/14), Emishi from Echigo brought regional products as gifts; a year later (699/4/25), 106 Emishi were given "court rank." (The Emishi, among Saimei's targets in a campaign to subjugate "the peoples beyond [the realm, civilization]" (*kegai no min*), had even earlier, in 581, participated in a ceremony of submission to Yamato.)[86] Later in 699 (on 7/19), Southern Islanders arrived ("following/obeying" court emissaries, possibly those sent to "claim these countries"), bearing gifts, which were forwarded to the Ise shrine; they also received court rank a few weeks later. Co-optation Chinese-style was in full swing around the turn of the century.

"From this time onward," the record tells us, "men from Tokamu [one of the islands] started to come to the Central Country." This is the first time that Yamato is referred to as the Central Kingdom, just when a delegation was being prepared to head for China, the one and only Central Kingdom. Actually, the *Kojiki*'s "Country in the Center of the Reed Plains" may very well be a camouflaged version of "Central Kingdom." That the policy of "claiming these countries" led to an armed rebellion on 700/6/3 gives a clear imperialistic sense to the delegation from the conquered Southern Islands at the grand event staged six months later at New Year's of 701. In the eighth century, at public functions such as the New Year's audience, Hayato from Satsuma functioned as guards, famous for "ululating like dogs."[87]

The four directional animals had in China also unmistakable military applications.[88] In the early-Han *Book of Rites* (*Liji*), together with the central banner bearing the Great Dipper, they were used by marching troops.[89] The military aspect of these New Year assemblies became emphasized very quickly. On 705/11/13, the delegations gathering for the New Year assembly two weeks later were met with mounted warriors mobilized from several provinces. On 709/10/26, a delegation of 188 Hayato heads of districts and lower entities from Satsuma were met by no fewer than 500 mounted warriors from the provinces. The show of force may be explained by their rebellion seven years earlier on 702/2/8, but it seems to have had little effect because they rose up again on 720/2/29. In 710, the Hayato and Emishi entered the plaza for the New Year lineup, led by mounted warriors.

The delegations from Silla were also met with greater displays of military force. On 714/11/11, a small group of twenty emissaries was welcomed when they landed by 990 horsemen, mobilized from the Home Provinces and beyond, in part granting greater pomp to the occasion, but certainly a formidable show of force and distrust. A month later, on 12/26, the foreign mission and delegations from the Southern Islands were welcomed at Mihashi outside the capital by 170 horsemen.

The description of the New Year's audience of 715 revealed a much expanded ceremony.[90] The newly installed crown prince, the future Shōmu, was present. Music was added (drums and bells being used for the first time), and pipers and drummers lined up with mounted warriors. Emishi from Mutsu and Dewa brought their regional products, as did men from the Southern Islands of Amami, Yaku, Tokamu, Shigaki, and Kumi.

It is important to note that the court's ritual posture as central kingdom vis-à-vis the Southern Islands, put together during the Tenmu-Monmu reigns, did not last long. Tribute from them is not mentioned after 727. About the same time, the relationship with Silla having soured over the connotation of submission in the offering of "tribute," Silla also is no longer mentioned as present at the New Year's audiences. By midcentury, relations with Silla were deteriorating quickly precisely around the issue of their status (parity or tribute?), and in the 760s, preparations for a full-scale invasion of Silla were under way, including the construction of some five hundred vessels and having forty young men learn the Silla language.[91] The New Year ceremonies ceased to be staged altogether by the early 800s.[92]

The foreign presence was central to the meaning of these New Year's events staged at Fujiwara-kyō and in early Nara, as illustrated by the one of

701. This was part of a feverish assemblage of things to impress the Tang. That same year the Taihō Code was finished, to be promulgated a year later when also the Confucian Festival (Sekiten) was held for the first time and, after a thirty-year lapse, a delegation was sent to the Chinese court. China was much in the forefront of the major changes that had come about recently, including the ideology of a Chinese-styled centrality and ambitions for military power. These meanings were prominent in the displayed symbols — meanings or connotations that did not escape the Silla delegation or the men from the islands who had just rebelled and who would do so again a year later and again in 720.

Astral Symbolism

The sky was an expansive canvas for a dazzling and live display of Daoist and imperial mythemes because Chinese astrological constructs, asterisms, were more than symbols. They were simulacra, counterparts (象 Ch. *xiang*; Jp. *shō, katadoru*) of earthly formations (Ch. *xing*; Jp. *kei, katachi*) and sources of supernatural power.[93] Daoist lore and weft writings contributed greatly to the creation of a heavenly duplicate of society. The Emperor of Heaven and his consort resided in a Purple Palace located in the Hooked Array, the asterism constituted by the four stars of our Little Dipper's handle.[94] Nara ruling empresses tapped into that source of heavenly rulership.

In the imperial edict regarding the decision to move the capital to Nara, Empress Genmei referred to herself as "occupying the exalted place of the Purple Palace." Empress Genshō expressed metaphorically both a social and geographic distance, and her way of bridging it, by stating "my body may be in the Purple Palace, but my heart is with the people." Empress Kōken declared that "the sun (日[emperor] and the moon (月)[empress], together shining bright (明), are the pattern (象 *katadoreri*) for everlasting rule from the Purple Palace."[95]

Tang ideology projected in great detail all manner of social, political, material components, institutions, activities, and objects of an entire empire onto the sky because asterisms had specific functions as *xing guan* (celestial officials).[96] The center of the northern sky was constructed around two key asterisms: the Northern Culmen (Ch. Beiji; Jp. Hokkyoku), also called North Pole Office, and the Hooked Array (Ch. Gouchen; Jp. Kōchin),[97] and not around the Pole Star proper or what we today consider its two main constellations, the Big and Little Dipper; the Little Dipper was not constellated into an asterism during the Tang.[98]

The Northern Culmen consisted of five stars. At the true mathematical pole was a star called the Pivot. Four stars were lined up from there, forming the celestial court: the Heir Giver's Palace and the reddish glowing Emperor (Di/Tei), also called Great Monad (Taiyi/Taiitsu), flanked on either side by the Prince(s) and the Grand Heir.[99] They were served by the asterism of the four attendants (Sifu/Shiho). The Northern Culmen was one of eleven asterisms that together constituted the Purple Court (see figure 9).[100]

Culmen (Ch. *ji*; Jp. *kyoku, goku*) meaning penultimate, a term occasionally applied to the Pivot, was mostly used for the Northern Culmen, also known as the Great or Extreme Culmen (Ch. Taiji; Jp. Daigoku). In Daoist cosmogonic terms, the Great Culmination constituted the sixth phase in the origin of things from a Primal Pneuma or Cosmic Breath (Ch. Yuanqi; Jp. Genki), whence yin and yang polarized, and ultimately everything under the sun materialized.[101]

Tenmu's Kiyomihara palace had a Daigokuden. At the New Year ceremony the emperor appeared in front of it, emerging symbolically from the Great Culmination, the center of the Heavens where time began and whence everything had generated. Around the same time, at the Tang court, "Great Culmen" served as reign name in 712, signaling a restoration following Empress Wu's usurpation, and as the name of the Hall of State (Ch. Taijidian; Jp. Daigokuden) as it had been during earlier dynasties.

The second major asterism is the Hooked Array. Its two middle stars constitute the Purple Palace, residence of Heaven's Illustrious Great Emperor (Tennō taitei), whose epiphanous soul is our Pole Star (which in turn is the secret embryo of the Great Monad from the Northern Culmen). The Great Dipper functioned as the Great Emperor's chariot that he rode around the Pivot of the sky, regulating and ordering the seasons, time's progress, and the layout of space. However important its function in the center of the sky may have been, the Great Dipper was but one of the twenty-eight lunar lodges and was lined up with them in drawings of the sky.

On the ceilings of the two burial chambers of the Takamatsuzuka and Kitora tombs in Asuka, the celestial court of the Northern Culmen, including its four attendants, is represented in midsky, centered on the Great Monad/Emperor (see figure 9). Taiyi is the divine name Daoism gave the emperor of this heavenly court. On the ceiling along each wall the directionally appropriate groups of seven lunar lodges are drawn. Each of the four walls is adorned with its proper directional animal. The presence of a specific asterism at the center of the tomb's ceiling must be an expression of a sacralizing and centralizing imperial ideology within the cosmic forces

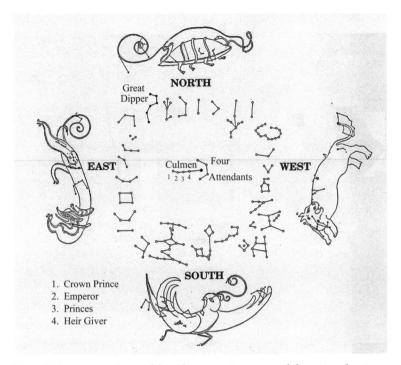

Fig. 9. Takamatsuzuka tomb's ceiling asterisms, mural directional animals (diagram). Source: *Takamatsuzuka kofun hekiga* (Asuka: Hekigakan, 2002), p. 10, modified.

at the beginning of the eighth century. This conclusion is strengthened by the fact that the oldest mid-Tang burial tomb with a design of the sky, discovered in Uighur Turfan (Sinkiang province), similarly has the lunar lodgings arranged, without, however, a heavenly court at the center (occupied instead by drawings of sun eclipses).[102]

On the two long walls of the Takamatsuzuka burial chamber, two groups each of men and women line up in a procession, some carrying what seem to be presents. The solemn occasion pictured here was probably not a New Year's audience but a funeral procession for the one buried there, perhaps an important member of the royal family inasmuch as the tomb is located in fairly close proximity to Tenmu and Jitō's tomb (see figure 7). Anyway, the stars above and the people below seem to be synchronized in an orderly arrangement of hierarchy and service to the heavenly ruler. Later, astral symbolism was also magnificently displayed on the red coat worn by the *tennō* on official occasions.

The Emperor's Clothes

We know what the emperor's official attire looked like in the early 800s (see plates 3 and 4). It is harder to figure out for certain what it was before then. On 685/7/26, Tenmu decided on the color coding for princes and officials when attending court, but ceremonial attire for part of officialdom is spelled out for the first time only in the Taihō Code. The emperor is not mentioned in this regard, but he is said to have appeared at the New Year's audience of 732 dressed Chinese-style (*benfuku*). Some scholars, however, are of the opinion that he may still have been wearing pure white then. The red Chinese-style ceremonial coat is explicitly mentioned in the early 800s but may have been in use earlier.[103]

This ceremonial attire of the Japanese *tennō* displays twelve embroidered insignia, eight on the coat and four on the skirt.[104] The vermilion red coat, at its center on its back and spread across the nape, displays the asterism of the Great Dipper, flanked on the shoulders by the symbols of the Sun and Moon. On the side of each sleeve, a large dragon climbs and coils across the space provided by the wide garment. Below the Great Dipper are five single rows of creatures, starting from the spine and moving left and right all the way to the front of the coat: dragons, mountains, pheasants, fires, and a row of alternating tigers and monkeys. Chinese and Daoist lore, familiar to the educated officials and members of the court, associate dragons with rain and water, essential for the welfare of the realm, and with immortals who commute on them. The mountains are marchmounts, connecting the Earth to the sky, and places where spirits dwell. Tigers and mountains are associated with the Queen Mother of the West, who associates with exemplary rulers.[105] Pheasants combine yin and yang elements (as do the Sun and Moon), signifying a balanced cosmic order.[106] The most important symbols, besides the Great Dipper, are the Sun and Moon, represented with their familiar inhabitants (the crow, the hare preparing an elixir of immortality under a cinnamon tree of everlasting substance, and a toad).[107]

This Japanese ceremonial coat is a variation of the Chinese emperor's as described in the *Book of Rites*. Some of the important symbols, however, are arranged differently. Most strikingly, the Great Dipper is not positioned in the center of the original.[108] The Sun, Moon, and stars of the lunar lodges and stations of Jupiter (Shafer: "starry chronograms")[109] decorate the shoulders while the seven-star constellation of the Great Dipper is found on the left sleeve, the counterpart of the Star of the Weaver Maiden (Vega) on the right sleeve. This symbolism conveys the message that the emperor is the mediator and supreme officiant who helps regulate and support agriculture and sericulture. Agriculture relied heavily on the regularity of the calendar and seasons, for which the Great Dipper functioned as the great clockwork in the sky. The Heavenly Weaver Maiden, the Heavenly Emperor's daughter, wove the sky patterns and was the protector of silkworm cultivation and textile work. The *Wuxing dayi* confirms the values represented on the emperor's coat as described in the *Book of Rites* when it states that the Son of Heaven performs the spring ceremony of cultivation of the soil, while his royal spouse opens the season to raise silkworms.[110]

I consider the difference in design between the Chinese and the Japanese ceremonial coat significant because the modified spatial arrangement directly identifies the emperor with the Great Dipper, or at the very least he is accorded its power and protection. Asterisms, Schafer writes, were believed to be "impersonal powers, the energetic equivalents on the fully numinous level of the political and social powers exercised by the earthly offices to which they correspond and with which they are in resonance."[111] The greatest of all celestial sources of power for the Daoists was the Great Dipper itself with its seven visible and two invisible stars.[112] Each of these stars was considered a visual epiphany of a true, invisible spiritual being.[113]

The Japanese emperor, wearing his coat, personified the power of the Great Dipper and the source of yin and yang, forming a triad with the Sun and the Moon. According to the *Baopuzi*, this triad constituted a source of powerful protection: "Merely by writing in red the words Great Dipper and Sun and Moon on one's own weapons, it was claimed that one need have no fear of bare blades."[114] Taiyi and the Great Dipper were also believed to possess apotropaic powers and to oversee military fortunes.[115] The Japanese emperor may also have been identified with Taiyi himself inasmuch as the Dipper, the carriage he rides in the sky and thus regulates time and space, is given the central position on the emperor's ceremonial coat.

Taiyi, according to texts of the fourth century BCE, was constructed politically as the single origin of the universe, above and beyond Heaven and yin-yang, and not controlled by them.[116] Emperor Wu (Wudi) built his cult in 113 BCE around Taiyi as his cosmic counterpart to sacralize his centralizing his rule. Wudi attempted to bring great local cults under central control while demoting the five traditionally original emperors, especially the most elevated one, the Yellow Emperor, and made them Taiyi's assistants while Tianhuang (Tennō) and Di (Tei) became the counterpart of Taiyi.[117] As the cosmogonic origin, Taiyi's vapor produced yin and yang, and ultimately all things. From near the polar center Taiyi rode his carriage, the Great Dipper, to bring about the regulation of the seasons and time.

Wudi's armies marched under a banner depicting the Sun, the Moon, the Big Dipper, and the ascending dragon, the four dominant figures of the Japanese emperor's coat. Wudi himself carried a standard of the Great Dipper; the Japanese emperor carried it on his back, evoking cosmic and state power of supreme rulership. This identification had already been made in works such as the *Huainanzi*, which states that "the Emperor embodies Taiyi." Moreover, Taiyi was also central to ritual. In the *Liyun* chapter of the *Liji* it is written that "Ritual necessarily has its roots in Taiyi."[118]

Taiyi's circuit in his carriage, as "pacing out time"[119] by riding and writing it in space, became the center of the important Shangqing Daoist practice of the Steps of Yu, the quintessence of all movements, heavenly, earthly, human, a ritual choreography that joins Heaven, Earth, and humanity."[120] Japanese emperors performed it, although we do not know since when, but it is mentioned in a Kamakura document.[121]

By traversing and measuring the world, step by step, and thus bringing back order to the world and the movement of time, the mythological Emperor Yu also effected "a transfer of the patterns of heaven to earth." The calendar, as issued by Chinese emperors, "does not merely describe the course of the year, it institutes that course." Similarly, the emperor's seasonal moves around the compartments of the Mingtang are more than a ritual following of Taiyi's cosmic clockwork. They constitute a performative act of coestablishing cosmic order and regularity.[122]

Toward the end of the Nara period and continuing in the Heian period, cults of the Pole Star became widespread. That is also, as far as we know, when the Great Dipper became prominently associated with the figure of the emperor, a symbolism displayed on the imperial coat used on all ceremonial occasions. As mentioned at the beginning of this chapter, Emperor Kanmu took some steps in the 780s to start sacrifices to Heaven, Chinese-style, a practice that, however, did not become institutionalized.

Invisibility and Tenmu's Daoist Trajectory

The manner in which Tenmu's person and special skills are described in the *Nihon shoki*'s two chapters devoted to him and in the *Kojiki*'s Preface, and the extent to which Tenmu and Jitō are surrounded by Chinese symbols and ideology point to an encyclopedic use of politically motivated Daoist, Buddhist, and *kami* worship symbols to reformat their personae as rulers of a new regimen. Tenmu's portrait, although perceptible only as a dim glimmer, suggests a super sorcerer mastering avant-garde techniques that were available to only a limited number of initiated. Foremost and chronologically the first in this overall representation is the mentioning of Tenmu's mastery of "the art of becoming invisible" (Ch. *dunjia*; Jp. *tonkō*), a technique brought over in 602 by the monk Kwallŭk. How should one understand this term?

There are several aspects to this art, including some created by popular imagination, that are relevant to understanding Tenmu's enchanted image.[123] Technically, *dunjia* is more accurately translated as "the technique of the hidden period," which refers to the hiding (*jia/kō*) of the *ki no e* calendrical mark "senior wood," one of the ten celestial stems.[124] It was a prevailing calendrical art during the Sui.[125] *Dunjia* divines angles of auspicious movement through a rather complicated computation based on the ten celestial stems and the twelve earthly branches to locate the hidden period, which one may enter and thus become invisible and be protected from any danger.[126] Its basic method consists of a ritual progress along the lines of the Steps of Yu on the pattern of the Great Dipper, "a procedure which is at the same time a form of divinatory computation and a performance of *bugang*" (Pacing the Mainstays [of Heaven]).[127] There is no way to corroborate the statement in the *Nihon shoki* that Tenmu was initiated in this calendrical-cum-ritual knowledge. He is said to have performed divination, however, which is part of the technique.

"Through their knowledge of that calendrical technique," Schipper writes, "the heroes of the past knew how to confound their enemies, to travel in a flash to distant places, and, best of all, to enter normally inaccessible realms of time and space and thus render themselves invisible to the outside world." Thus *dunjia* texts were also (and by the Song almost exclusively) manuals of military strategy.[128] Linking Tenmu with *dunjia* was a formula to create a cluster of associations including an aura of mysterious divinatory knowledge, the ability to perform heroic deeds, and mastery of spectacular military strategizing on the battlefield.

It is in Yoshino, where Tenmu sought refuge, that he practiced his divination in 672, Yoshino which by that time had already acquired a mystical aura. Spirits resided there. A detached palace built there by Saimei in 656, and possibly another one by Jitō, most likely had connections with Daoist practices as did Jitō's raised platform to observe, interpret, and venerate the stars. "In the southern mountains" of Yoshino Tenmu shed his former self "cicada-like" in response to Heaven, a metamorphosis described in the *Kojiki* that can be taken metaphorically or literally. He indeed became the first *tennō*, and was celebrated in poems, starting soon after his military victory as a god-in-the-present. When Tenmu and Jitō, looking ahead toward Tenmu's succession, called their sons together to extract from them pledges of harmony and mutual support, they did not hold this important meeting at the palace in Asuka, but chose to travel to Yoshino, one surmises at least partly in order to secure supernatural sanction.[129]

The most hallowed part of the palace Tenmu planned and Jitō built in Asuka, the state room, was called the Hall of the Great Culmination, the earthly counterpart of Taiyi's residence near the North Pole. Toward the end of his life, when reorganizing the court rank system, he not only elevated his immediate family to the highest levels, but also devised new rank names for them as dwellers of the pure realm of Daoist heavens above the rest of ennobled officialdom.

During his final illness, Tenmu mobilized all venues to the supernatural —shamanistic, Buddhist, Daoist. He ingested a concoction based on a Daoist medicinal formula and held a ritual of recalling the spirit that resonated with references to his status as a ruler tied into the flow of cosmic forces. Shortly thereafter, he gave his palace what he must have considered the more appropriate identity of Palace on the Pure Plain of Asuka. After he passed away, his own self became transformed in the public memory, locked into his posthumous name, as a Daoist perfected one.

Yoshino, the Land of the Immortals, became even more important for Jitō as her frequent visits indicate. Since that mountain retreat is always described in the literature of the time as a hallowed space particularly dense with supernatural presence, one may assume that Jitō's intense relation to Yoshino had also to do with a spiritual re-sourcing for her rulership, which experienced major crises. It was also during her reign that the Nakatomi clan was put in charge of drafting court rituals befitting a heavenly rulership.

Starting at least during Jitō's reign, the Chinese-Daoist astral symbolism displayed during New Year's audiences in front of the Hall of the Great Culmination spoke of empire and a cosmically ordained regime. The astral designs on the ceilings of the Takamatsuzuka and Kitora burial chambers make visual the point that the Yamato court's function of ordering the realm (tenka) was analogous to, and actually tied into, the operation of Taiyi's cosmic stewardship through his circuit of the Great Dipper, a performance that could be enacted in different modalities, large and small, through the Steps of Yu, which were essential in the ritual performance associated with dunjia, the occult art that allegedly launched Tenmu's career.

About a century later, the emperor's official garment was fixed, not to be changed fundamentally for a thousand years, until declared unsuitable by the Meiji government in 1909. On the most solemn occasions that spoke of his public status and authority when the ruler disappeared behind his official persona, the emperor donned a ceremonial garment embroidered with signs that amplified his position and power as coterminous with Taiyi, the supreme authority in Heaven.

The Great Exorcism

Great purifications (*ōharae*) were grand manifestations of the imagined expanse of the realm and the spiritual power centered in the *tennō*. In the beginning, and occasionally later as well, they were held as the need arose. At least since the time of the Taihō Code's promulgation, however, they took place twice a year, on the last day of the sixth and the twelfth months. The graphs for *ōharae* (great purification/exorcism), however, initially were not 大祓, *ōharae*, but 大解除, *daikaijo*, a term that was in common use in the Daoism of South China.[130]

The text of the exorcism (*Engishiki*, book 8), written in Chinese, was addressed to Daoist deities: the Supreme Thearch of the Exalted Heaven (Ch. Huangtian shangdi; Jp. Kōten jōtei); his three Great Advisers (the three stars south of the handle of the Great Dipper, rulers over the Three Pure Heavens); the Sun, the Moon, and the Starry Chronograms; the Gods of the Eight Directions, the Director of Human Destiny and the Director of Records (of the souls); the King Father of the East on the left; the Queen Mother of the West on the right; the Five Rulers of the Five Directions; and the Four Ethers of the Four Seasons. The emperor is presented with silver human effigies upon which he transfers all sources of impurities and calamities of the realm (by rubbing them or breathing over them before they are brought to the river and cast into the water) and with a gold-plated sword to prolong his reign. After this introductory invocation and brief ritual, the charm is pronounced: a triple "*banzai!*" to extend the pure rule for ten thousand years over a thousand towns and a hundred countries, "to the East as far as Fusang [Japan], to the West as far as Yuyan, to the south as far as [the land of] the burning light [of the tropics], to the north as far as [the land of] the weak waters [of the arctic]."[131]

The identities of the deities addressed, the presentation of the ceremonial sword as a source of concentrated efficacious cosmic energy transferable to the ruler, the use of human effigies as carriers of calamities to be removed, and the reference to Japan (Fusang; Jp. Fusō) as located in the "far east" — the topographical reference left untouched possibly because magical formulas, when altered, would lose their efficacy — clearly reveal this crucial Yamato court ceremony as unadulterated Chinese/Daoist. The allochthon *fuhito* who performed the ceremony in 702 were undoubtedly knowledgeable in yin-yang matters, but, given their identification in the text as Yamato and Kawachi *fuhito*, it is unlikely that they were yin-yang masters from the Yin-yang Bureau established by Tenmu. Yin-yang Masters from the Bureau were probably employed for prognostication and apotropaic purposes only.[132]

By the Heian period, the Nakatomi and the Urabe were the two houses in charge of ritual at the court, except for the Sarume, who played a role in the Chinkon-sai. Each had a different function in the regular great purification ceremonies, functions we know from a particular circumstance at the end of 702. That year, because of the mourning period for Retired Empress Jitō, who had died a week earlier, the Nakatomi part of the ceremony, consisting of the reading of the *norito* prayer for the *kami*, was canceled, but the exorcism rite was held as usual. The rationale for this distinction is not spelled out in the *Nihon shoki* entry. The spell used by the exorcists, an unalloyed Chinese formula invoking the powerful cosmic entities, must have constituted the core of the ceremony where the performative ritual power was lodged.

The term *urabe* refers to practitioners of divination. Some of them, however, adopted the title as their *uji* name. One such *uji*, the Urabe, functioned as diviners and exorcists at court ceremonies. They recited *norito* at festivals such as the Fire-pacifying Festival and the Road-Feast Festival listed in the *Engishiki*. The Jingi-ryō and the *Engishiki* list the Yamato Fuhito, assisted by the Kawachi Fuhito (allochthon "scribe" clans), as presenting the emperor with ceremonial swords, and *urabe* performing the exorcism at the great purification.[133] The 702 entry of the *Shoku Nihongi* mentions that these two clans were allowed to proceed with the exorcism that year. It must have been later in the Nara period that an Urabe *uji* succeeded in taking over the exorcism part.

Staffing the Yin-yang Bureau

Tenmu secured access to the special knowledge about the powers that governed the cosmos and its human replica, the state, through a special institution, the Onmyōryō or Yin-yang Bureau, which he established early in his reign. It is mentioned for the first time on New Year's Day of 675 when a number of students from the bureau received presents. The institution housed three kinds of specialists: one doctor of portent astrology (*tenmon hakase*); ten men in the Calendar Division; and a proper Yin-yang Division with seventeen specialists (one doctor, six masters, and ten students). To staff the bureau, Tenmu tapped into refugee talent, as he also did for the university and for drafting his law codes. Some of these specialists were practitioners and former officeholders from Paekche or were Buddhist monks, often connected to Silla.[134] It appears that around the end of the seventh century, the generation of refugee intellectuals needed to be replaced and that this was done by employing monks who were first laicized before being appointed as yin-yang masters in the bureau. Everyone, including monks, was prohibited from divulging yin-yang-related knowledge and speculation. Yin-yang specialists were public servants who handled classified information.

The contrast with Heian, 150 years later, is striking. Then, many of the so-called yin-yang masters were private entrepreneurs, working in an open market, enjoying the reputation of being able to perform magic, see spirits, and the like. Many of them were monks of a sort, or held to be such, as they were called "clerical yin-yang masters" (*sō-onmyōji, hōshi onmyōji*).[135]

The laicization of these monks was neither a voluntary move on their part nor a penal defrocking.[136] The record makes clear the purpose of the ordered laicization: utilizing the monks' skills and specialized knowledge. These laicizations were concentrated in the two decades that straddle the turn of the eighth century (692–714). The monk Hōzō, who served Tenmu his infusion of *okera* in 685 and "recalled the spirit" in the Shōkon-sai, received a stipend as yin-yang doctor-monk (*hakase hōshi*) in 692. He may have been one of ten monks laicized in those decades.[137] A total of fifteen names of people explicitly associated with yin-yang knowledge appears in all the written records, including the *Manyōshū* and the *Kaifūsō*, during the first three decades of the eighth century (in contrast to only four during the next three decades).[138] Four of them were monks, ten were allochthons, and two were closely involved in relations with the continent.

In the 720s, several attempts were made to seek out new talent and entice them, through rewards, to take up the study of various subjects, from medicine to law (721/1/27). A year later (on 2/27), stipend fields were distributed to twenty-three men of "learning and skills" (*gakujutsu*, a term used for the first time). An edict of 730/3/27, where the Council of State addresses the sorry state of schooling and training in various branches of learning, gives voice to the expertise crisis as follows: "Knowledge such as yin-yang, medicinal skills, and calendar making constitute the backbone of the state and can therefore not be left to deteriorate. However, it is clear that the holders of doctoral degrees are advanced in age and old. If they have no one to teach, their occupations will die out."

The council took the further step of ordering seven scholars in various branches of learning to seek students and teach them. At least three yin-yang specialists, three medicinal specialists, and four calendar-making specialists were needed. In addition, five Chinese state employees were ordered to each teach Chinese to two students. Material support on a par with students at the university was promised. These measures were aimed not at filling the ranks of university students, but at securing the transmission of institutional knowledge from one generation to the next.

Foreign knowledge was vital to the state and was mostly mastered by allochthons and foreigners, often monks. Yet ideally such knowledge ought to remain controlled by the state. This explains the prohibition of private use and perhaps, the relocation of immigrant communities in hinterlands. Language may also have been a barrier. All these factors played a role in the intelligentsia crisis, which was further aggravated by the suspicion under which "Daoist magic" had fallen with the Nagaya affair of 729, as will be analyzed in chapter 9. It is possible that the state was trying to train autochthonous talent. The laicization virtually stopped with Haguri no Tsubasa in 734. He was born in China of a Japanese father and a Chinese mother, and returned that year at age sixteen to become a Buddhist monk. His future, however, was decided for him. He became employed as a teacher of Chinese, was appointed secretary of a delegation to China in 777 and was ultimately put to work on the calendar.[139]

Yin-yang knowledge, referred to in 730 with other related fields as the "backbone of the state," included its use in matters of defense, which may explain the alarmist tone of this edict because relations with Silla were deteriorating seriously. When two years later measures were being taken to prepare for war by shoring up coastal defenses, yin-yang specialists were called upon. On 732/8/17, special emissaries, advisers to the Council of State, were dispatched to the coastal circuits, the Tōkaidō, Tōsandō, San'yōdō, and Saikaidō. Each of these circuits was provided with four operation supervisors (third-level bureaucrats), four fourth-level officers, one medicine man to treat the wounded in case of conflict, and a yin-yang master to interpret the possible maneuvers of the enemy. One yin-yang master was also permanently attached to the Dazaifu office; in the second half of the ninth century, others were placed in the frontier provinces of Dewa, Musashi, Shimōsa, Mutsu, and Hitachi.[140]

Era Names

Portentology, the interpretation of the political significance of anomalies, constituted the basis for the change of era names.[141] The purpose was to read Heaven's will in relation to political decisions taken or to be made. This practice, implemented by law after Taihō 1 (701),[142] when applied during the eighth century as a legitimating device for rulership through the ruler's exercise of his power to change era names, revealed a particularly strong predilection for Daoist motifs, not present in later times.

Eleven out of thirteen era name changes between 701 and 782 were prompted by positive auguries, some "coinciding" with enthronements of new rulers. Names referred to material such as gold or copper, or gifts presented to the court, or to the auspicious discovery of white turtles or the sighting of unusual cloud formations.[143] Starting with Kanmu in the late eighth century, however, only two kinds of era changes were practiced: those at the beginning of a new reign and those caused by calamitous events. There were only five exceptional positive omens prompting era changes between 848 and 877. In 923, the first midreign era change occasioned by natural disasters took place, and henceforward midreign era changes were always attempts to ward off or stop natural calamities.[144]

It is not that positive auguries are found only in Nara, plus a few in early Heian. They were dominant, accounting for seventeen out of twenty-four era changes. Moreover, six of these positive signs (between 715 and 851) have to do with turtles, the animal par excellence of longevity and immortality.[145] Turtles provide the occasion for era changes four times in the eighth century, and they figure in three era names. Three times, a turtle augury accompanies the starting of a new reign: Genshō, Shōmu, and Kōnin, respectively in 715, 724, and 770. In addition, there is the Yōrō name (717), which, as mentioned, has also Daoist connotations. It appears that the dynasty was in dire need of assurances that it would last, and Daoism presented symbols that promised overcoming the debilitating work of time.

We are still too accustomed to think of the Nara period (710–784) as the first time that Japan enjoyed the stability of a firmly based dynasty, buttressed by a legal system, ruling from its historically first real capital. A close look, however, modifies that picture drastically. Nara was not the first "real" capital. Fujiwara-kyō had preceded it, and barely thirty years after Nara was founded, Emperor Shōmu moved out, and built four new "capitals" (two of which were palaces, *miya*, rather than capitals, *kyō*) between 740 and 745. Then he returned to Nara, which Kanmu abandoned thirty-nine years later for Nagaoka. Thus Nara functioned as capital for only two generations, interrupted in the middle by a five-year hiatus. Nagaoka's life span was even shorter. Kanmu stayed there for ten years, and then settled in Heian.[146]

The Nara period was a time of incessant instability, when the dynasty was seriously threatened several times. Prince Nagaya, the top royal and bureaucrat of his day, though innocent, was accused of a plot and put to death in 729; Fujiwara Hirotsugu's rebellion of 740 was followed by Tachibana Naramaro's in 757 and Fujiwara Nakamaro's of 764, and finally the monk Dōkyō's rumored usurpation five years later. These were realm-shaking events. Tension at the top was generated by the fact that Tenmu's numerous sons (and grandsons) remained a threat to Jitō's line, which, via Kusakabe, produced six Nara sovereigns. The reign of Emperor Junnin (758–764), deposed and subsequently killed in exile, constituted a brief interlude before the Jitō-Tenmu line shifted to Kōnin, a change accompanied by murder within the royal family and achieved through an alleged edict of the deceased Shōtoku, forged by the Fujiwara.[147] Intrigues, murder, plots were in part due to the ambitions of the Fujiwara houses. A dozen or more members of the imperial family were most likely murdered during the short eighth century that Nara represents. Somewhat understandably, Heaven was seen as a much-needed active, positive, and indispensable partner in rulership during this turbulent period.

To make sure that Heaven was on their side, Tenmu and his successors relied heavily on yin-yang knowledge, which Tenmu had filtered out of the Chinese and Buddhist cultural material available to him, by establishing a Yin-yang Bureau. Tenmu mobilized Daoisant symbols for the creation of his political emblematics. However, yin-yang masters did not only provide support. They were also embroiled in a number of plots during the Nara period as consultants about strategies to follow and eventual outcomes to expect. After all, if we are to believe the *Nihon shoki*, Tenmu had used yin-yang prognostication for a rebellion.

Events in Chinese and Japanese history show that the precautions regarding this classified body of learning were necessary, even though often ineffective. The change of mandate theory, used by Tenmu in 672, was again being discussed toward the end of his life, this time by Prince Ōtsu's circles in 686. Ōtsu was swiftly executed. Six of the thirty conspirators whose names and careers are known were intellectuals, and the leader seems to have been the monk diviner Gyōshin from Silla, who was exiled to a temple in Hida and pardoned in 702; the other conspirators were not punished. Gyōshin's son was laicized and reemployed in 703 because of his knowledge in matters of divination. One of the aims of the Yin-yang Bureau must have been to catch and contain holders of potentially dangerous knowledge, but the record shows that success was mixed.[148]

8 PLOTTINGS

The Council of State issued a directive that, following a
curse by the Illustrious Kami, the Buddhist sites within
the boundaries of the Take and Watarai districts have to
be purified, cleansed, and made into *kami* sites.
—774/7/23. *Heian ibun*

The *ritsuryō* state was a new creation of the late seventh–early eighth
centuries, and so was the ritual that was meant to buttress its authority.
Monmu's anticipated succession, which took place in 697, seven years
after Jitō ascended the throne, provided an occasion for plotting the public
transmission of ruling power. The Fujiwara and the restored Nakatomi *uji*
played an important role in this process. The Fujiwara *uji* was created in 669
for Kamatari, known until just before he died as a Nakatomi, when Tenji
changed Kamatari's *uji* name from Nakatomi to Fujiwara. In 698, however,
a branch of this Fujiwara clan became Nakatomi again.

One year after Monmu's accession, possibly partly in recognition for service rendered in developing the ceremony, the Nakatomi name was restored
to Fujiwara Omimaro's house with the purpose of solidifying its ritualist
function separately from the bureaucratic one, reserved for Fuhito, Kamatari's son, who alone was to continue the Fujiwara line.[1] The Nakatomi
eventually wound up being put in charge, among other things, of the Ise
shrine as it gained a special place in the new state's ritual setup. The lineage
was upgraded to Ōnakatomi (Great Nakatomi) in 769.

Fuhito was a member of the committee that drafted the Taihō Code,
which gave final shape to the structure of the new bureaucratic state, where
he succeeded in launching the careers of his sons into high office (see figure 10). Through a number of marriages of his daughters, especially two
who became consorts to the *tennō* Monmu and Shōmu, and through other
schemes, the Fujiwara came to position themselves as protectors of the
throne.

Two of Fuhito's grandsons, however, fostered different designs for the
future of their house and the dynasty. Hirotsugu and Nakamaro plotted
armed rebellions that had to be put down by force. They were not alone.
Tachibana Naramaro led another revolt, backed by warrior power, and nu-

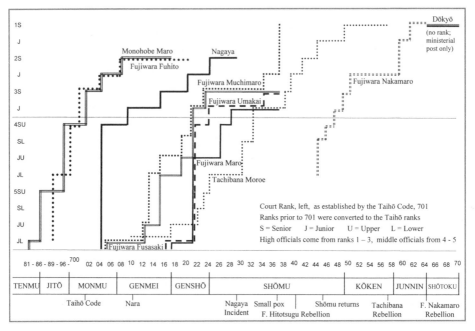

Fig. 10. Court rank promotions. Source: Sakaehara, "Heijō-kyō jūmin no seikatsu-shi," vol. 9: 217, fig. 1, modified.

merous other plots developed that were aborted early. Ritual designs and political plots, often intertwined through their aims and the lineages of their actors, will be examined in this chapter.

Ritual Centers: The Mingtang and Ise

Chinese state ritual, known in Yamato mainly indirectly through texts but also through eyewitness reports, may have prompted the need to construct a ritual supplement to state power without, however, serving as a close model the way the Tang law codes had. The Chinese emperor's main function as intermediary between Heaven and Earth consisted of keeping human affairs and the realm properly aligned with cosmic coordinates by enacting a yearly cycle of ritual performances. The most important rituals secured the regularity of the seasons, rains favorable to agriculture, and placating spirits and gods. Ideally, these rituals took place in the Mingtang. The emperor was supposed to move through the structure, each month to another hall, in perfect alignment with cosmic space marked by the twelve stages of the Jupiter cycle and synchronized with seasonal time through the twelve months of the year. The emperor also ideally reported to Heaven on the state of the realm through elaborate and costly *feng* and *shan* sacrifices. The origins of the Sacred Halls and the ritual were intertwined.

The first Mingtang was built by Emperor Wu of the Former Han in 109 or 106 BCE after performing the *feng* and *shan* sacrifices at Mount Tai. Mythologically, the sacrifices had been inaugurated by the Yellow Emperor; allegedly, they had been performed by the historical founder of the first empire; and they were probably established by Emperor Wu of the Western Han. Subsequently, very few dynasties had a Mingtang, however, and the *feng* and *shan* sacrifices were hardly ever held, in part, the story goes, because they were too awesome. They were repeated only a few times ever: once during the Later Han in 56 CE; twice during the Tang, in 666 and 725; and once by Empress Wu in 695.[2] The Mingtang's layout and its numerological formulae were matters of endless debate, and the sacrifices themselves highly secretive.

Both institutions had a far richer existence in scholarly discourse than in actuality, and it is as such that knowledge of them reached Japan by the sixth and seventh centuries. In an entry in the *Shinsen shōjiroku* of 815, it is claimed that a ground plan (*zu*) of a Mingtang reached Yamato under Kinmei (539–571). If true, it could have been a plan of the one built in Luoyang, the Northern Wei capital, in 526.[3] The building of a Mingtang in the Sui capital was hotly debated, as were its monthly rituals, the regulations of which were compiled in works such as the *Yuzhuo baodian* (Jp. *Gyokushoku hōten*) based on chapter 4 of the *Liji*.

This work was well known in Yamato, where it exerted a greater and longer influence than in China.[4] In one of Emperor Kōtoku's Taika edicts (issued on 646/2/15), various Chinese governing practices by China's mythological emperors were upheld as exemplars. In this context, the Mingtang was mentioned as the place where the Yellow Emperor held conferences. This was also the time in China when intense discussions developed about the need of building a Mingtang and what it should look like. In 689, Empress Wu built one and rebuilt it a few years later after the first one burned down.[5] The Mingtang is also briefly mentioned in the *Wuxing dayi* (Gt 240a; Cd 389) as the site where the emperor made offerings to the mythological emperors of China's past.

Yamato rulers never built a Mingtang, but knowledge of its existence must have impressed upon them the importance of a ritual center befitting a *tenka*. It is possible that the Yamato embassy that left for China in 665 witnessed the processions and pageantry accompanying the great sacrifices on Mount Tai the following year. Upon their return, the members of the delegation must have brought home tales of the grandeur of the Tang state ritual — the Tang, which by then, acting after Paekche's defeat as if the whole Korean peninsula were part of the empire, had developed into the region's superpower. Yamato's strengthening of its military defenses, begun under Saimei, was continued by Tenmu and accompanied by the introduction of realmwide liturgical events such as the four yearly harvest-related *hanpei* oblations and the great purification ceremonies. The Ise shrine's new importance was signaled by Tenmu's appointment of an Ise *saiō*, a virgin "consecrated princess" (literally, "the *sai* [abstinence] royal").

The *saiō* resided in the Saigū (the *sai* palace/shrine, *gū*)[6] where she presided over rituals to *kami* that were perfectly coordinated with the same rituals performed simultaneously at the imperial court, a principle of ritual synchronization analogous to the Mingtang's, which coordinated imperial ritual with the cosmic forces. The *saiō* and Saigū were governed by the strictest purity taboos. Unlike the Mingtang, the institution functioned uninterruptedly for over six hundred years until the mid-fourteenth century.

The Mingtang and Ise shrine are obviously different institutions, and some will judge it irresponsible to mention both in the same breath. Additional detail (spelled out in the *Huainanzi*)[7] besides the principle of ritual synchronicity, however, is intriguing. The Mingtang was supposed to be built of plain wood, be unadorned and not sculpted, and have a thatched roof (maintained even at one point when a tiled roof was built over it); sacrifices were to be offered there to the mythological emperors of the beginning of Chinese history. Its structure had to reflect yin-yang and other cosmic stipulations.

The layout of the Ise shrine was also structured along yin-yang coordinates.[8] Its distinctive requirement of architectural primitivism, still followed today, may have as much to do with Chinese (textual) models as with an autochthonous Yamato tradition. The main shrine of Yoshida Shinto, the Saijōsho Taigenkyū (Consecrated Site of the Shrine to the Great Origin), built by Yoshida Kanetomo in Kyoto in 1484, may owe even more to Chinese models. Its thatched roof, round, rests on an octagonal structure. Yoshida Shinto, established then, borrowed yin-yang and Daoist elements extensively.[9]

The Saigū in Ise

Tenmu's appointment of a *saiō* was not an innovation. At least that is what the *Nihon shoki* suggests. He is said to have resurrected the custom after a fifty-year lapse when at the beginning of his reign he sent Ōku, a daughter by a sister of Jitō, to Ise. The custom of appointing a female royal relative at the beginning of each reign is projected back into prehistoric times (Yamato's tenth ruler, Sujin, in the first century BCE). The record, however, provides no more than ten names of such princesses for the subsequent thirty rulers during the six centuries between Sujin and Tenmu, the last one being a daughter of Yōmei (r. 585–587) whose tenure, exceptionally, extended across the two following reigns of Sushun and Suiko. The *Nihon shoki*'s entry of 673/4/14, a month and a half after Tenmu's coronation, reads as follows: "With the intention of dispatching Princess Ōku to serve at the shrine of the Great Kami Amaterasu, she was made to dwell in the Abstinence Palace (Saigū or Itsuki no miya) of Hatsuse. This was so that she would purify her person before starting to approach the *kami*."

Book 5 of the *Engishiki*, the largest of fifty and devoted entirely to the institution of the Saigū, provides an extremely detailed description of the *saiō*'s preparations and the tasks expected of her. Since this account, compiled between 905 and 967, reflects prescriptions (and presumably practice, largely unverifiable) of the late ninth century, it is impossible to learn much about the institution as it was restored and undoubtedly restructured, perhaps even created, under Tenmu. One should keep this in mind when reading the description that follows.

After lengthy purifications, the new *saiō* left the capital, its culture, and its amenities for good, and undertook the five-day progress to remote Ise, where she remained, in principle, until the end of the reign of the ruler who had appointed her. (Sickness or death in the *saiō*'s immediate family in the capital or loss of virginity would terminate her tenure prematurely.) As a close relative of the reigning emperor, a somatic link bound her to the actual ruler on the throne.

In Ise she took up residence, accompanied by a large staff of attendants, diviners, and support personnel in a special compound some ten kilometers from the Outer Shrine and fifteen from the Inner Shrine. This, at least, was the situation in the Heian period. During most of the eighth century, however, she resided within the shrines' precinct.[10] The later large, rectangular compound, measuring two kilometers east-west and seven hundred meters north-south, constituted a miniature capital with the *saiō*'s quarters located in the north together with sanctuaries where the deities of the palace were venerated.[11]

Judging from the *Engishiki*'s description, a preoccupation with *sai* or purity that was nothing short of a paranoid ritual "puromania" must have created a tense and intense atmosphere of sacred awe, produced by multiple divinations, lustrations, and purifications, repeated again and again, effecting not so much a removal of impurities as their prevention, and an irresistible inculcation of the awesome sacrosanct character of an institution out of this world.

At various stages of the process, diviners from the Yin-yang Bureau were instrumental in selecting personnel, choosing an imperial virgin to start the process, and holding monthly divination sessions to select those from her attendants and helpers who would perform certain functions or, occasionally, who from among visiting officials would be allowed entrance in the Saigū. Yin-yang diviners also decided on dates and places for the innumerable ritual occasions, large and small, that accompanied the selection of residences, travel, and so forth.

After being selected by divination from among the emperor's close kin, the *saiō* moved into a special residence within the palace precincts, the Shosai'in (Initial *sai* Cloister), which was served by a staff of approximately eighty. She lived there for about a year, after which a site near the capital was divined and built, the Nonomiya (Country Villa) with a staff of 145.[12] Here, she spent another year in seclusion before finally setting out, accompanied by a large entourage of several hundred, for her compound in Ise. At each of the six rivers, and a couple of provincial borders that had to be crossed, an advance party of diviners conducted a preliminary purification in preparation for the lustration or other miniceremony that took place when the *saiō* herself arrived at the spot.

In the compound, surrounded by two walls and a moat, were also offices, storehouses, lodging quarters for the several hundred helpers, maids-in-waiting, assistants, all varieties of diviners and ritualists (Nakatomi, Inbe, and from the Yin-yang Bureau), chefs, medicinal specialists, accountants, housekeepers, and so forth. The number of each personnel category for each ritual, the ceremonial implements, and the supplies are all listed in great detail in the *Engishiki* chapter, which reads like a script, thirty-five pages in the English translation, of props needed for the mega-production of a pure enclave in time and space. Divinations were held at the beginning of the month to decide who would participate in various activities, and exorcisms on the last day of the month.

The ages of the *saiō* varied. The youngest was chosen at age two, which made her five at the start of her tenure in the Saigū; the oldest was twenty-eight.[13] A *saiō* was neither a shamaness nor a ritualist, a *miko* delivering oracles, or even a priestess. Her official schedule was filled mostly with presiding over rituals, one imagines, the way the emperor did in Nara or Heian, rituals that were synchronized duplications of court rituals. As a duly certified and guarded incarnation of purity, her role was perhaps to secure the efficacy of court rituals performed for the *kami*. Serving the imperial ancestral *kami* Amaterasu at the inner Ise shrine was also part of the *saiō*'s duties, although not the most preoccupying one.[14]

Three times a year she left the Saigū and undertook a three-day progress to the Ise shrines, representing her emperor: for the Tsukinami festivals of the sixth and twelfth months and for the Ise Kanname festival in the ninth month (the only divergence from the court's equivalent Niiname festival, which took place in the eleventh month). On these occasions, the *saiō* spent the two nights in yet another detached lodge located between the Saigū and the Ise shrines. Each day she purified herself at the river she had to cross.

A great purification marked the start of her career when she graduated from her three-year-long preparation in the capital, thoroughly steeped in the purified environment of her cloistered residences. It was held at the court the day she departed from the capital for the Saigū. Messengers announcing the event were dispatched, one to the left and right halves of the capital, one to the Home Provinces, and one to each of the seven circuits.

Any new Saiō proceeded from the capital to Ise in the ninth month. That whole month was decreed especially sacrosanct as a *sai* month (*saigetsu*). Mourning and reburials were prohibited during that month in the capital, the Home Provinces, Ise and Ōmi, and other nearby provinces to keep death pollution at bay. Neither were celebrations of the North Star allowed during that month (because of their tumultuous and orgiastic character).[15] Sixteen euphemisms (two more than at the Ise shrines proper) were devised to replace taboo terms that referred to sickness, death, or Buddhist items (temples, sutras, etc.).[16] These were de rigueur at all times.

Buddhism in and out of Ise and the Court

Judging from the *Engishiki*, by the ninth century the Saigū and Ise were clearly set up as non-Buddhist enclaves. Buddhist ceremonies that had become part of the court's ritual calendar were not performed at the Saigū. This institutional separation was a development of the late eighth century. It reveals not only changes in the ceremonial idiom at the ritual center of the realm, but also struggles among ritualists whose main recourse for pushing their ideas was the interpretation of signs, which actually meant the production of signs since an item got "signed" only through a hermeneutic gloss. The turning point came after Empress Shōtoku's reign in the 770s, when the Buddhist presence was removed from Ise.

In the early Nara period, *kami* shrine-temples (*jingūji*) were being built within the same precincts, fusing through juxtaposition sacred sites for

The Dōkyō-Shōtoku years

758/8/11	Empress Kōken retires; Emperor Junnin succeeds
762/4	Dōkyō cures Retired Empress Kōken
763	Dōkyō's clerical promotion to junior prelate (*shōsōzu*) at the Sōgō
764/9/18	Daijōdaijin Fujiwara Nakamaro's rebellion fails
764/9/20	Dōkyō's political promotion to Daijin zenshi
764/i10/2	Dōkyō's promotion to the highest political post of Daijōdaijin zenshi
764/10/9	Junnin deposed, then exiled; Kōken returns as Empress Shōtoku
765/11/22	Shōtoku's enthronement
765/10/23	Junnin killed
766/7/23	Buddhist statue erected at Ise shrine
766/10/20	Dōkyō receives title of *hōō* (Dharma king)
767/3/20	Dōkyō receives office in the palace
767/10/3	Ōkasedera becomes Ise's *jingūji* (*kami* shrine-temple)
769/5&6	Usa Hachiman's oracles
770/8/4	Shōtoku dies
772/4/7	Dōkyō dies
772/8	Ōkasedera moved away from Ise
776	Ōkasedera's status as Ise's *kami* shrine-temple withdrawn
778	Ōkasedera moved farther away

rituals addressing *kami* and Buddhist deities. Fujiwara Muchimaro appears to have been the first sponsor of this combination in 715; others were built the next several decades. The Ise shrines also were reconstituted in this way. Under Empress Shōtoku's enthusiastic support for Buddhism, the Ōkasedera in Ise was decreed in 767/9 to be the Ise shrines' shrine-temple.[17] A year earlier (766/7/23) a Buddhist statue, nearly five meters tall, had been erected in the shrine. After Shōtoku's rule, however (she died in 770), a reaction set in. In 772, the temple was moved; four years later, the combination shrine-temple for Ise was officially abolished; and in 780, the temple was moved again farther away.

Thus, the scrupulous preservation of ritual purity that permeates the institutional life at the Saigū was something that developed and increased over time. The Saigū as briefly sketched above constitutes the culmination of that development toward mid-Heian. There is no denying, however, that it was set in motion during Tenmu and Jitō's time. The intrusion of Buddhism in Ise during Shōtoku's rule in the 760s triggered a further articulation, and possibly a new application of the notion of purity.

A Change of Procedure

On the occasion of her reenthronement during the Daijō-sai ceremony in 765, Shōtoku issued a dramatic declaration of a policy change.[18] A secret ritual constituted the center of the enthronement ceremony. It took place from around sunset until sunrise, starting on the appropriate Tiger zodiac day of the eleventh month, which in 765 was the twenty-second day. The following morning, Shōtoku granted rank to the two officials from Mino and Echizen responsible for the two ceremonial Yuki and Suki temporary structures used during the ceremony, and she promoted Nakatomi Kiyomaro, the *jingihaku* (director of the Office of Kami Affairs) who had been in charge of the event, which had several untraditional aspects. During the second half of the ceremony, namely the reception/banquet (*naorai*) signaling the lifting of the *sai* sacred time, she explained in her enthronement edict to the gathered officialdom what had been unusual in the ceremony, and why:

> This time the *naorai* is different from the way it has always been conducted. The reason is that, as a disciple of Buddha, I have received the Bodhisattva's precepts. Accordingly, it is after first paying homage to the Three Treasures [of Buddhism], then venerating the *kami* of the Heavenly and Earthly [Country] shrines, that I re-ascend the throne in order to bestow compassion and grace upon the venerable princes, ministers. . . . And, even though some hold that *kami* matters should avoid the Three Treasures, and that they should not be in contact with each other ["not touch"], I also decree that the sutras make it clear that *kami* are protectors of the Buddhist Law. What used to be [kept apart by] taboo (*imi*) is no longer tabooed. There is no obstacle to monks being included in *kami* ceremonies. Therefore, this is the way we are holding this Daijō-sai.

Unprecedented was the presence of monks on this most solemn occasion of state, and specifically Dōkyō's, but so was, of course, the enthronement of a nun. After she met Dōkyō in 762, the then retired Kōken had taken Buddhist orders, which explains her reference to having received the Bodhisattva's precepts.[19] Dōkyō may even have functioned as the official witness to the secret ceremony the preceding night, taking the place of a high official (which at a later day would be the regent, *kanpaku*). He certainly must have led the procession of officials greeting the new empress.

The rise of Dōkyō constituted one of the most serious of many crises the Tenmu dynasty faced in the eighth century. It was one of several plots aimed at the highest seat of power, but it was unique in that the attempt showed signs of being directed at establishing a church-state to be led by Dōkyō. Under Emperor Shōmu, Buddhism had acquired the position of a state-church, with the establishment of an institutional Buddhist network in all the provincial capitals in the form of provincial temples, monasteries, and nunneries, eventually centered in Nara's enormous Tōdaiji temple. Although Shōmu, his principal consort Empress Kōmyō, and their daughter successor Empress Kōken had all declared themselves "servants of the Buddha," the clericalization of the throne went one step further when Kōken, after deposing Emperor Junnin, assumed imperial authority again, this time as a nun and childless, and moved in the direction of making the monk Dōkyō her coruler.

The Clericalized Court

The political map of factional positions and political position takings around the court was complicated in those years. Fujiwara Nakamaro, grandson of Fuhito, member of the Council of State since 743, and head of the new Household Agency of Empress Kōmyō, led the Fujiwara faction, which was encountering hostile moves from Shōtoku and Dōkyō.

After Nakamaro was killed in his rebellion of 764/9, in quick succession, Dōkyō was promoted, Junnin was deposed and sent into exile together with his mother, and Kōken replaced him as Empress Shōtoku before the year was over. One year later, also in quick succession toward the end of the year, Dōkyō was promoted again, Junnin was killed, and Kōken was enthroned in the unorthodox Daijō-sai.

Two promotions occasioned by this particular Daijō-sai have drawn the attention of historians: Dōkyō's, which made possible his presence as the top official at the enthronement, and Nakatomi Kiyomaro's, no doubt as a reward for modifying the ritual. Kiyomaro's promotion was as unprecedented as Dōkyō's because he was brought into the ranks of the court nobility by being granted third junior rank (from fourth senior lower, skipping one step). This opened up his career to further honors, promotions, and political appointments. In 768/2, he added the position of middle councilor on the Council of State to his directorship of the Kami Office. Unprecedented was the appointment of a Kami Office ritualist functionary to high political office. The following year, his lineage was honored with a new name, Ōnakatomi. Now he was a Great Nakatomi.

Dōkyō's promotion to the position of *daijōdaijin zenshi* (lit. prime min-

Fujiwara Court Intrigues: From Fuhito (d. 720) to Nakamaro (d. 764).

Fujiwara Fuhito's political gains from securing important administrative posts for his four sons, often against resistance by the imperial clan, were wiped out when all four died in the 737 smallpox epidemic. His daughter Miyako, who had become Emperor Mommu's consort in 697, bore him a son in 701, the future Emperor Shōmu, but she suffered from a debilitating depression for the next thirty-six years (Watanabe Akihiro, *Heijō-kyō*, 131, 207). His other daughter, Kōmyō, as the first nonroyal female to rise to the rank of empress (729–760) and mother of Kōken, was thus the Fujiwara clan's only trump card left, but a strong one.

In 738, the Fujiwara/Kōmyō succeeded in appointing a princess (Abe, unmarried, the future Kōken) as crown princess, an extraordinary event that was opposed by the Tachibana clan, which had grown stronger because of infighting among Fujiwara lineages that led to Hirotsugu's rebellion in Kyushu two years later. Shōmu then left Nara for five years even though his succession had enjoyed Fujiwara support against royal bilineal claimants who objected to his nonroyal ancestry on his mother Miyako's side. In 749, a year after his aunt, Retired Empress Genshō, died, Shōmu decided to take her place as retired monarch, and left the throne to his daughter Kōken.

Kōmyō and her nephew Fujiwara Nakamaro circumvented the Council of State, no longer able to do the Fujiwara's bidding, by operating out of Kōmyō's Household Agency while Shōmu retired to a temple and Kōken moved into Nakamaro's residence. After Shōmu's death in 756, the Tachibana faction succeeded in having Prince Funado (a Tenmu grandson) appointed crown prince. Fujiwara reaction was swift: they arrested over four hundred of their opponents, executed Funado, and appointed a new crown prince. The next year, they crushed a full-scale rebellion by Tachibana Naramaro. The Fujiwara candidate, another Tenmu grandson and married to the widow of Nakamaro's son, became Emperor Junnin (r. 758–764). Kōken retired and a few years later became an ordained nun.

As retired monarch, Kōken started in 762 to maneuver against Nakamaro, linked up with the monk Dōkyō, moved into a Buddhist temple, and proclaimed that she would be in charge of all important governmental matters. In 764/9 Nakamaro was killed in his own rebellion. The same month, Dōkyō was appointed *daijin zenshi* (minister prelate). A month later, Kōken deposed Junnin, banished him to Awaji Island where he was killed a year later, in 765/10, allegedly during an attempted escape. This elimination of Junnin coincided with the beginnings of the preparations for Kōken's reenthronement as Shōtoku, which took place two months later, and with Dōkyō's promotion to *daijōdaijin zenshi* (prime minister prelate), a title that justified his place of honor at the Daijō-sai.

ister prelate) in 765 put him as head of the Council of State on the top of the administrative ladder. *Daijōdaijin* was actually more a title than an office, and one that few had ever held. This most honorable title in the administration constituted its holder, part as a representative of officialdom, part as a "secretary of state." In the seventh century, when it did not have that meaning yet, Tenji had bestowed the title upon his son Prince Ōtomo, a clue perhaps that Ōtomo was the preferred heir. Jitō granted it to Prince Takechi with the same intention, but she stalled with the implementation of the succession until he died, when she enthroned Monmu. The Taihō Code defined the post differently as to be filled only exceptionally by individuals who would function as imperial advisers and preceptors, and it was thus expected to remain vacant most of the time.[20] In the eighth century, only two men enjoyed the honor, one after another: Nakamaro in 761 and Dōkyō in 765, a year after Nakamaro perished in his failed rebellion (see figure 10). Exceptional as the title was, it was certainly unprecedented to grant it to the Buddhist priest Dōkyō even though he had been promoted into the ranks of the nobility. This indicates how high the stakes in the political struggles were in the 760s when these two protagonists were catapulted to the top to secure their power with the additional symbolic profit of this title — ultimately, however, to no avail for either one.

Shōtoku went even further and, for all practical purposes, made Dōkyō the equivalent of an emperor, putting herself more and more in the background. This happened when on 766/10/20 she bestowed upon him the title of Buddhist King (*hōō*; literally, "king of the [Buddhist] law" or "Dharma King"), an event "in-augurated" by the necessary auguries signaling cosmic approval. These signs appeared in the form of divine *shari*, Buddhist relics preferably from the Buddha himself, discovered in a statue of Bishamon in Sumidera by the monk Kishin (and planted by him, as it turned out). Led by a procession of 23 nobles of fifth rank and above and 177 of sixth rank and below, the *shari* were transferred to the nearby Hokkeji temple and made available for the empress' devotion. Kishin and his student Enkō were promoted to ranks (with stipends) unprecedented for monks, equivalent to senior councilor (*dainagon*) and adviser (*sangi*) to the Council of State. Dōkyō's rank (and stipend) was equivalent to an emperor's.[21] Kishin obtained a *kabane* name (Mononobe Kiyoshi) and a guard of eight warriors, one more breach of precedent. Less than two years later, however, it was "discovered" that "Kishin had planted the *shari*," for which he was exiled on 768/12/4 to Hida (in today's Gifu prefecture, a not too far "exile"). Enkō was demoted much later. Dōkyō succeeded also to seat two monks on the Council of State.[22]

Five months after becoming "king" (on 767/3/20), Dōkyō was given a special residence and office commensurate with his new position. The office had a staff of eight, the same number as those serving the quarters of the empress and the crown prince (the *Chūgū* and the *Tōgū*), and was run by three allochthons.[23] On the third day of the New Year of 768, Dōkyō received in audience in his part of the palace, very much in the manner of an emperor, the officials whom Shōtoku had greeted the previous day in her quarters.

A note of caution is warranted regarding the *Shoku Nihongi*, the source for the information regarding these developments. It is possible that the text overemphasizes the degree of illegality or deviation from past practice. Kanmu, under whose rule this work was compiled, may have used this material to suggest a constitutional crisis, which was solved by shifting the dynasty from the Tenmu lineage to that of Tenji, Kanmu's great-grandfather. The temperature generated by the crisis may have been turned up in the official history. We have no alternative sources. The important events of this episode, however, should not be questioned.

Signs of Approval

It is clear that every step of Shōtoku's policy of integrating Buddhism into Ise and the court was in great need of supernatural sanction. Thus, in 767/8, one year after the Buddhist statue was erected at the Ise shrine, following the necessary nods from heaven, the era name was changed to Jingo-keiun (Kami Protection Auspicious Cloud). The signs were provided by multiple appearances of multicolored auspicious clouds (five and seven colors), interpreted as an endorsement of the new policy direction by the Three Treasures, the Heavens, and the *kamigami* of Heaven and Earth. On 767/8/8, on the occasion of the sighting of one of the unusual cloud formations that prompted the era name change, six hundred monks from state temples were invited into the yard attached to Shōtoku's private quarters for a meager feast (*sai*) following a Buddhist expounding of doctrine. The compiler of the *Shoku Nihongi* makes the explicit point that they then greeted Dōkyō with a "clapping of the hands just like laymen do," thus drawing attention to an uncanny scene. The scholar Takatori, in a lengthy discussion of this remark, has concluded that these monks, by not using the cleric's praying hands to greet a confrere, in the setting of the palace, positioned themselves as servant officials greeting their ruler.[24]

Political gain was to be garnered for reporting omens. The staff of the outer Ise shrine was promoted after reporting the nimbus over their sanctuary, a sketch of which was forwarded to the court. The large number of supernumerary appointments made during Dōkyō's time in power suggests that he was actively developing a dependent and loyal clientele.[25] In addition, Dōkyō filled a number of positions with members of his lineage who, before they could be appointed, had to be given court rank and promoted quickly. Militarily important posts also went to them. They were in control of two of the Palace Guard units and were appointed in strategically important provinces. Dōkyō's brother Kiyohito combined many of them. He commanded one of the guard units, became "emergency shogun" (*kenkōhyōgo shogun*) in charge of the arsenal in the palace,[26] and in 768/2 rose to the top when he became senior councilor on the Council of State, a position he combined with the governorship of the province of Kazusa and the headship of the newly created Office of the Pages.[27] In addition, in 768/11, he was appointed concurrently governor-general of Kyushu (*Dazai sochi*), whose jurisdiction included the Kyushu shrines, the most important of which was Usa Hachiman's. Around the same time, Nakatomi Asomaro, vice-governor of Buzen, was made head *kami* officiant of Kyushu (*Dazai kanzukasa*).[28] Everything was in place for Hachiman's oracle to request Dōkyō to ascend the throne, which came some six months later. It was Asomaro, whose office was overseen by Yuge Kiyohito, Dōkyō's brother and governor-general of Kyushu, who communicated the oracle.

Two other appointments were made in the field of yin-yang. These officials played a legitimizing role through their skills in cosmic hermeneutics that was needed to recognize and validate omens. The supernumerary yin-yang official, Ki Masumaro, who had reported the appearance of the numinous nimbus to the Yin-yang Bureau, was promoted to its directorship, and Yuge Satsuma (related to Dōkyō's Yuge lineage) was made vice-director. There is sufficient evidence for some historians to conclude that Masumaro had been a slave (serf) who had been freed on 764/7/12 on orders of Kōken during her retirement. (During the Dōkyō years, a number of temple slaves were set free and given court rank: five in 767, two in 769,[29] but there were many more, since on 773/7/17, after Shōtoku and Dōkyō had disappeared from the scene, seventy-five former slaves from Kidera temple who had been freed on 764/7/13 were returned to their slave status, except Masumaro, who was stripped of his court rank and became a commoner.) It is possible that Masumaro had put his divinatory skills in Fujiwara Nakamaro's service during the latter's rebellion that year. He may also have been involved in the request of Prince Wake, Prince Toneri's grandson, to his ancestors, called upon in a séance, to kill Shōtoku and Dōkyō and reinstall Junnin in 765, as we shall see later.[30] It should also be noted that the colored clouds were followed the next year by portents, all white, auspicious obviously: two pheasants, a turtle, and a crow, anything even remotely albino like a white-tailed gray horse. They were volunteered by various provinces, one of them being Musashi, where Dōkyō's nephew had been appointed second-in-command.[31]

Signs had come from everywhere. The Buddha had placed some relics. Heaven had released a plethora of portents. All these extraordinary phenomena coincided with the momentous changes that were taking place in the center. Everything was leading up to a change of the regime into a theocracy. But the *kami* had not spoken yet, and no sign could "in good faith" be interpreted that way. Then the *kami* spoke. This was the famous episode when an oracle from the Hachiman shrine from Usa in Kyushu, a shrine with strong syncretistic leanings (or with considerable political savvy or both), was brought to the court in 769, promising peace to the realm if Dōkyō became emperor. Once brought into the open, what many must have suspected or feared, the message had to be certified one more time. Probably someone (obfuscated in the narrative as "a dream") persuaded Shōtoku to double-check the veracity of the oracle, and it turned out that something had been lost in the transmission of the message from the medium (a nun shamaness in service at the Hachiman shrine) via Nakatomi Asomaro, the newly appointed head *kami* officiant of Kyushu whose superior was Dōkyō's brother Yuge Kiyohito, governor-general of Kyushu, also recently appointed.

It turned out that Hachiman had proclaimed the exact opposite: that only royal blood could flow in imperial veins. Shōtoku apologized to the court, and passed away less than a year later in 770/8, at age fifty-two. Dōkyō was discredited and removed to a temple outside Nara, where he outlived Shōtoku by two years.

Sign Reversals

Things changed quickly after Shōtoku left the scene. The day after she died, childless, on 770/8/4, the soon-to-be emperor Kōnin was made crown prince through a last will forged by the Fujiwara; he was installed on 10/1. The appropriate supernatural signs again appeared miraculously well-timed. That very day, and again on the seventeenth, an extremely auspicious white turtle was found in Higo province, prompting the era change to Hōki (Treasure Turtle). The reptile sanctioned a change of the guard not only at the court, but also in Ise. The head of the shrine, who had been appointed six months before the installation of the Buddhist statue, was dismissed and replaced by a Nakatomi (Ōnakatomi Kiyomaro's nephew), whose lineage henceforward remained in charge of the shrine. The next year, Kiyomaro's son was

202 PLOTTINGS

appointed second-rank official in Ise and eventually promoted until he succeeded Kiyomaro as director of the *kami* office in 777.

The *kami* also reversed course, for in 772 their *tatari* (curse; in this case,
storm damage to a shrine structure) prompted the removal of the Buddhist
temple from Ise, but not far enough because they took recourse to another
curse in 780, when the structure was moved even farther — all measures
taken by Kiyomaro's son. A 774/7/23 document of the Council of State refers to the need "to purify and cleanse (*harae-kiyomete*) a Buddhist site, following a curse of the Illustrious Kami, to make it a *kami* site."[32]

The Nakatomi

In 769, a year after Nakatomi Kiyomaro, as director of the Kami Office, was
given the extraordinary political appointment of middle councilor to the
Council of State, his lineage was honored with the new name of Ōnakatomi,
Great Nakatomi. He was sixty-eight when Kōnin, only seven years his junior, succeeded Shōtoku the following year. Kiyomaro's advanced age notwithstanding, during the Kōnin decade (770–781), he held the most powerful position on the Council of State after, in 771, as second-rank holder, he
became minister of the right, a post he held for ten years.[33] Thus, Kiyomaro
presided over both the Shōtoku-Dōkyō phase of inserting Buddhism at the
heart of court ceremonies in Nara and Ise and its undoing in both sites.
The struggle he became involved in was ostensibly about ceremonial prerogatives, the definition and composition of the ritual field where purity
was at stake, but it was also about the nature of the polity. The issue was
whether the Nara state, a liturgical state where ritualists functioned in the
realm and at a bureaucratic level, but separate from the officials in change
of administration, would transform into a hierocracy. During the second
phase of his career, Kiyomaro helped steer Buddhism away from the center
of the polity.

The Nakatomi lineage of ritualists eventually in charge of the Ise shrines
goes back to pre-Taika times. As mentioned, because of his role in the Taika
coup, Nakatomi Kamatari was given the new *uji* name of Fujiwara on his
deathbed in 669. Thirty years later (on 698/8/19), however, only one of his
sons, Fuhito, was allowed to pass the name on to the next generation. All
other Fujiwara houses, including Omimaro's, were ordered to change their
name back to Nakatomi in order to set his lineage aside for *kami* affairs,
and specifically for the immediate purpose of preparing the Daijō-sai inaugurating Monmu's reign, an assignment undoubtedly seen as an enviable

trophy by competing houses of ritualists. From then on, the Nakatomi were in charge of regulating and fixing the format of court ceremonies.

In 708, Omimaro became *jingihaku*. The splitting of the clan of (former Nakatomi) Fujiwara Fuhito, in charge of producing the Taihō Code, and (former Fujiwara) Nakatomi Omimaro, in charge of ceremonial matters, constituted a form of separation of administrative and ritual matters, formalized in the two central offices of the Council of State (Daijōkan) and the Office of Kami Affairs (Jingikan). The fourth rank attached to the *jingihaku* officeholder put him below the *kugyō* group of nobles, third-rank holders and higher, the pool for important administrative posts, especially those on the Council of State. The rank of the *jingihaku* was two or three rungs below that of the head of the Council of State. Thus it was precedent-breaking to promote Omimaro's son, the *jingihaku* Nakatomi Kiyomaro, into the *kugyō* ranks and seat him on the council, where he even functioned as its head. No doubt, this was a move to counter Shōtoku's elevation of Dōkyō to that same position and beyond and her appointment of monks on the council.

The scholar Takatori attaches great importance to the Fujiwara/Nakatomi split ordered by Jitō in the fall of 698 in the context of preparations for Monmu's enthronement ceremony, entrusted to Nakatomi Omimaro, a time when work on revising and shaping Yamato's mythology was under way, as well as the drafting of the Taihō Code, the latter entrusted to Fujiwara Fuhito. Takatori surmises that the separation of the administrative field, where "modernization" was pushed in the form of a Tang-style centralization of imperial power, from the ritual field, which provided a scenario for the change that incorporated elements from the past, was meant also to assuage the conservative *uji*, more attached to traditional forms; it was a signal that not everything was up for drastic change.[34]

As chancellor under five Yamato rulers, from Tenmu to Genshō, Fuhito was making history, codifying the state and shaping its power. His Fujiwara lineage became an office nobility, overshadowing other great *uji*. By 730, ten years after Fuhito's death, a daughter had become Empress Kōmyō to Emperor Shōmu; another daughter as consort to Emperor Monmu had been Shōmu's mother; and four of the ten seats on the Council of State were held by Fujiwara. In 769, they occupied seven out of the fifteen seats.[35]

Nakatomi Omimaro, the grandson of one of Kamatari's two uncles, was assigned the task to misrepresent the result of the historical change wrought by Kamatari and his son Fuhito, reencode it as nonhistory, and consecrate the ruling house's enhanced power as the enchanted work of cosmogonic *kami.* His lineage was in charge of ritual at the court, occupying the position of *jingihaku* starting in 708, passed on to two brothers consecutively, then to his son Kiyomaro, and later to his grandson. At the Ise shrines (since Monmu, the *Great* Ise shrines, Ise *daijingū*), Kiyomaro started a Nakatomi line of head priests in 770 through his nephew. The Ōnakatomi succeeded in encroaching upon the terrain of other ritual houses, as the Inbe complained a few decades later in their *Kogoshūi*.

It is plausible, as I have argued, that Tenmu started the process of the creation of a liturgical state, reaching for Daoisant signs while keeping Daoism at institutional arm's length, isolating yin-yang notions for monopolistic use by his house, hierarchizing the world of the *kami*, and giving Ise an enhanced ritual importance. Nakatomi Omimaro was put in charge of finalizing this project in 698.

As historians have often pointed out, under Shōmu and Kōken, from the 720s to the 750s, the Buddhist establishment put its rich and imposing arsenal of symbols, rituals, and institutional power at the service of the state and started to build first shrine-temples (*jingūji*), then provincial temples (*kokubunji*). However, as Shōtoku's remarks in her enthronement decree indicate, there were "things that some people considered taboo." This is how Shōtoku formulated the anticipated critique of her new policy. Even though borrowing from the Tang informed considerably the construction of *kami* ritual, the latter stood out by a more pronounced sense of taboo, particularly with regard to the imperial house, as reflected in the Taihō Code. However, contrary to what Shōtoku implies in her edict, none of these ritualist taboos were directed at Buddhism.

One Year, Three Eras

The year 749 was one of momentous events as indicated by two era name changes. It started as the twenty-first year of Tenpyō (Heavenly Peace), and it ended as Tenpyō-shōhō (Heavenly Peace Victorious Treasure), but not before another change to Tenpyō-kampō (Heavenly Peace Response to the Treasure) had been declared on 4/14, the "Treasure(s)" being the "Three Treasures of Buddhism," a reference to Buddhism in general. Retired Empress Genshō had passed away the previous year (on 748/4/21), and Emperor Shōmu who, after returning to Nara following a five-year absence (740–745), had shown far more interest in the Tōdaiji temple project than in governmental affairs, decided to retire himself, which he did with great fanfare. Two months after Genshō passed away, Shōmu ordered the copying of sutras, most likely to secure the Buddha's blessings in preparation for the eventual succession of his daughter, Crown Princess Abe, as Kōken a year later (749/7/2).³⁶

Two weeks before the prelate Gyōki died, he inducted Shōmu and his empress Kōmyō into the Buddhist order on 749/1/14. Gyōki was Japan's first popular Buddhist preacher and organizer of devotional works, initially censured by the government, then enrolled to garner contributions for the building of the Great Buddha of Tōdaiji; he was considered a bodhisattva while still alive and was made the first occupant of the new post of grand senior prelate (*daisōzu*) of the Clerical Office, the Sōgō.

Shōmu's intention of retirement was made clear in the Buddhist title he took, the first part of which read *daijōtennō* (retired emperor). Then, on 4/1, Shōmu, "Retired Emperor Monk," accompanied by his empress-nun Kōmyō, Crown Princess Abe, hundreds of officials, five thousand monks, and commoners progressed to Tōdaiji, offering thanks to the Buddha Rushana for the discovery of gold in Mutsu, just in time for the gilding of the colossus. On that solemn occasion, he posed as a "servant [slave?] of the Buddha," a terminology almost identical to the one his daughter would use fifteen years later when she resumed the throne. This was followed the same month by a general amnesty, a report to the Great Ise shrine of the auspicious discovery, promotions of the officials involved in the Tōdaiji project, and an era name change from Tenpyō to Tenpyō-kampō. Shortly thereafter, Shōmu took up residence in the *miya* of Yakushiji temple, and Kōken succeeded him on 7/2, the occasion for the new era name Tenpyō-shōhō.

At the end of the year, the *kami* Hachiman from the Usa *jingūji* in northern Kyūshū was enshrined near Tōdaiji. This followed a request by the *kami* himself; he, that is to say his officiants, seems to have been very opinionated, making clear what he wanted, as in the two famous oracles regarding Dōkyō and imperial succession. Hachiman intended to help bringing the construction of the Great Buddha, which had run into many difficulties (its casting had several times resulted in failure), to a successful end. Hachiman's ritualists, who had already developed Hachiman into a syncretistic *kami*, must have perceived the emergence of Buddhism at the center as a serious historical force and had wanted to be in on the action.

The Usa Hachiman shrine appears in the record of the early eighth century, first in relation to a local uprising of Hayato, then on 737/4/1, when a delegation from the court was sent to five shrines, including Hachiman, to seek protection for the country, prompted by rising friction with Silla. Fujiwara Hirotsugu tried in vain to flee from there to Silla when defeat loomed for his rebellion in 740. The link with the continent had been significant in other ways as well. Priests and shamanesses from the shrine were reputed to have particularly strong healing powers. The mixture of *kami* and Buddhism was probably pronounced at the shrine for a long time before, in 745, seven images of the Healing Buddha (Yakushi) were erected on the shrine precincts — twenty years before Ise received its Buddhist statue.

The head priest and his female assistant were dressed in Buddhist garb when they were accompanied in 749 by an elaborate procession to establish a Hachiman shrine next to Tōdaiji in Nara. Hachiman, in contrast certainly to Amaterasu in Ise, was a deity who spoke.[37] Through occasional oracular pronouncements, the deity let it be known what he wanted — for instance, that a certain appointment should be made, some shrine lands should be divested, and that his help with the Tōdaiji project could be counted on. A few years later, he uttered the couple of oracles regarding Dōkyō and the throne.

The orchestration of the establishment of a Hachiman franchise in Nara was on a par with the imperial visit to the Great Buddha of Tōdaiji earlier in the spring: the new empress and the freshly retired royals led a procession of hundreds of officials and, again, (probably the same) five thousand monks. Kōken, now a bodhisattva, duly thanked and promoted Hachiman as well as his ritualists for their successful efforts.[38] Hachiman had traveled for a month, accompanied by nobles from the capital and a hundred warriors (forbidden to consume meat or wine en route), on clean roads from which defilement had been removed ahead of the procession, through provinces where the killing of living things was prohibited — a parade functioning like an elaborate *chindonya*, a traditional ding-dong band of parading street musicians publicizing the opening of a new establishment in the neighborhood. Ōmiwa Morime, the nun-shamaness from the shrine was carried in a purple palanquin that resembled the emperor's.[39]

Thus the full use of institutional Buddhism by the court or state, in tandem with the development of *jingūji* at major shrines, was not perceived as problematic by *kami* officials or others, most likely because the ceremonial rapprochement of Buddha and *kami* was contained within the ritual field. Fifteen years later, however, *kugyō* circles of the service nobility, not in the least the Fujiwara and their Nakatomi cousins among the Ise *kami* personnel, must have felt seriously threatened when Shōtoku, not only a "servant of the Buddha" but a nun, and not when stepping down from the throne into retirement as Shōmu and Kōmyō had done but when stepping up to it to assume power, promoted a monk as prime minister, granting him the title, followed by the office, of Buddhist King, who as such entertained hundreds of monks in the interior of the palace, not as monks but seemingly as his servants.

The Hachiman ritualists perhaps sought again to draw symbolic and real profit as they had some twenty years earlier by joining what they perceived as the wave of the future when they were willing to be instrumental in giving Shōtoku, the nun empress, a monk emperor by sanctioning Dōkyō's access to the throne. They had a way out, however, since ritualists can hide behind the mysteriously changing voices of the *kami*. Hence, when the politics pursued proved unrealistic, an oracular reversal followed, which, Wake Kiyomaro communicated to the interested parties — at his own risk.

The second oracle, obviously supported by a strong political sentiment of an important fraction of the service nobility who may have seen their careers threatened by Dōkyō's appointees, blocked the establishment of a Buddhist hierocracy. Nationalists have celebrated this episode as the unambiguous establishment of the principle of imperial lineality, valid to this very day.[40] Lineality, however, although vertical, is not necessarily unambiguously monolineal: imperial blood can flow through several lines, as the wrangling after Shōtoku to get succession away from the Tenmu dynasty to a grandson of Tenji, married moreover to women with Paekche peerage, would show very soon. The question of for how many generations blood qualified as royal would start to be addressed a few decades later, when a solution was sought to the problem of the over-abundance of candidates for the throne. Emperor Heizei (r. 806–809) had two sons, only one of which, his successor, could pass on the bloodline to the next generation (similar to the Fujiwara name, which Fuhito could transmit to only one of his sons). The other son's children were declared nonroyals — in other words, reduced to commoner status, a process of "dynastic shedding" or the "secularization of surplus royals."[41] (This is the way the Minamoto house of later shogunal fame came into being.)

The other result of the Usa oracle episode, however, was that purity became the ground on which to stake out the defense of the throne and Ise. For sure, the enemy was Dōkyō as far as one can judge and not the "Buddhist establishment" as such, but as revealed in the document of 774 cited at the beginning of this chapter, impurity became activated as a "negative symbolic coefficient"[42] attached to Buddhism, one that would be fully deployed starting in mid-Heian, in far-away Ise certainly, but more significantly in the capital (where Buddhism was not the target, however). Yet the creators of this ideology, at least as far as the capital was concerned, were not *kami* officials but a new brand of yin-yang ritualists.

This may be surprising for two reasons. One, during the Tenmu dynasty, yin-yang specialists did not function as ritualists. They read portents and drew conclusions from them for the evolving course of events (including military developments), engaged in topographical divination, were ancillary to ceremonial moments, and at most, may have conducted apotropaic minirituals around the capital and in the Home Provinces — more about this later. Two, as the Nara period progressed, yin-yang masters are mentioned in the record less and less in their official capacities. Their numbers seem to have dwindled, but as specialists knowledgeable about the future, their services were sought by plotters and schemers eager to know their chance of changing the course of events.

Plots, rebellions, murder, often mixed with fortune prognostication and even sorcery, accompany many successions in the Tenmu dynasty through the eighth century. The miasma of sorcery, black magic, and fear of the spirits of condemned political figures that climaxes toward its demise in the 770s, however, may have constituted a remote cause for the revival and large expansion of yin-yang in the Heian period. Before approaching that story, however, one needs to understand what happened to the cosmic symbolics that Tenmu, through his elite spiritualists, had tried to contain in the Yin-yang Bureau, a symbolics where yin-yang portentologists operated in close proximity to adepts at curses and black magic.

Crossing Power Lines: Tenmu to Kanmu

Various lineages of the Yamato ruling house developed from Tenji and Tenmu throughout the eighth century. They produced real and would-be emperors, empresses, consorts, and other big players in the political conflicts, which usually revolved around succession issues. These royals had to contend with each other and with scions from a few important lines of nobility closely related to these Sun lines. The weapons used in these political wrangles spanned the whole spectrum from marriage alliances, which resulted in conflicts over who would be the emperor's main consort and who among his eventual offspring would succeed to the throne, to plots, murders, and full-scale rebellions with associated phenomena: plotters seeking credit for leaking subversive activity, accusations of black magic, questionable oracles, alleged threats by avenging spirits of some victims, all of this often followed sooner or later by well-timed restorations of titles, rank, and even amnesties of the accused or condemned. I shall outline a number of mininarratives that together present a complicated picture of an exceedingly turbulent dynasty (see figure 11). This will allow us to find our way through this maze of intrigues, alliances, and enmities and to perceive the role played by yin-yang specialists and other manipulators of supernatural symbolics.

Tenmu's successful sacralization of his position as *tennō* and immortal beyond all mortals, and that of his immediate family above other ennobled clans, established a symbolic "cordon sanitaire" that, he hoped, would protect his Sun line against rebellion, the very weapon he had successfully wielded against his brother Tenji's line when he vanquished the latter's son in 672. Exactly one century later, in 772, Emperor Kōnin, a grandson of Tenji who had ascended the throne only two years earlier and had made Inoue (Higami), a daughter of Emperor Shōmu, his official empress, thereby uniting both the Tenmu and Tenji lines, started severing his connection with the Tenmu line when he deposed both Inoue and their son, Crown Prince Osabe. He replaced Osabe with Prince Yamabe (the future Emperor Kanmu), his son by an allochthon of noble Paekche ancestry. Kōnin accused Inoue of resorting to black magic, locked her up with their son, and apparently eliminated both two years later when they reportedly died the same day while in custody. The Tenji line was thus embroiled in succession conflicts at both ends, in the beginning as loser in a civil war and a century later as victor through murder and the manipulation of accusations of black magic. These two events frame a century of dynastic turmoil among Tenmu's offspring.

Two Royal Camps

Tenmu's descendants fall into two groups. What became the main line, started via Kusakabe, Jitō's only son with Tenmu, produced all emperors (except Junnin) and reigning empresses until Inoue's brief tenure as non-reigning empress to Kōnin. Actually, Empresses Jitō and Genmei, although Tenji daughters, received their political identity from their spouses, Emperor Tenmu and Crown Prince Kusakabe respectively. Junnin belonged to a side line through his father Toneri, Kusakabe's half brother (see figure 1). He was enthroned by Empress Kōken in 758 but deposed six years later and exiled to Awaji Island in the Inland Sea. In an edict of 765/3/5, seven months before Junnin was eliminated during his alleged attempt to escape, Empress Shōtoku warned anyone against trying to reinstate "that man who lives in Awaji . . . who was sympathetic to the dirty Nakamaro [of the failed uprising the previous year] . . . but had not gained the approval of Heaven and Earth" — a dash of heavenly mandate theory thrown in for good measure. Between the time of the edict and Junnin's demise the same year, one of Junnin's nephews, Prince Wake, who had won praise for revealing Na-

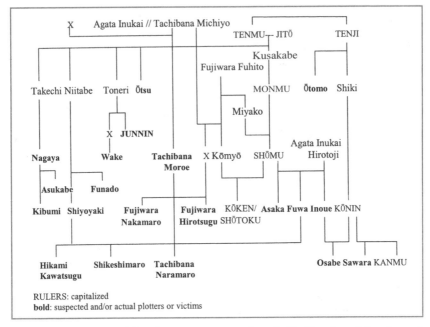

Fig. 11. Plots. A copy of this chart appears on a detachable "bookmark" at the end of this volume.

kamaro's plot, was now in turn suspected of plotting to reinstall Junnin. He had evoked his ancestors and begged them in writing — big mistake if true — to kill Dōkyō and Shōtoku, but it was he who got killed en route to exile in Iyo, Shikoku, after his written plea reached Shōtoku.[43] Junnin was henceforward known as *haitei* (abolished emperor).

It is quite possible that Junnin's murder (764/10/9) was precipitated by Prince Wake's plot of 8/1, which aimed at restoring Junnin to the throne. Kōken's reappearance as Empress Shōtoku, unmarried and without off-spring, had reopened the uncertainty of royal succession. Moreover, Wake himself had recently become qualified to succeed. In 755, as a great-grand-son of Tenmu, he had lost royal status and become a commoner, but in 759, one year after Junnin had become *tennō*, Junnin's close relatives were given royal rank: Prince Toneri, Junnin's father, was given posthumously a *tennō* title; Wake, now grandson of a *tennō*, became Prince Wake (fourth-rank holder) and was later promoted to junior third rank and held the post of adviser to the Council of State (*sangi*).[44] Junnin's disappearance thus solved two problems at once. No longer among the living, Junnin could not be reinstated. At the same time, his immediate relatives lost their royal titles and thus became disqualified to replace him. Nevertheless, they tried again and again (Shiyoyaki's children, Shikeshimaro and Higami Kawatsugu), as they had already in the past (Funado).

Three others were involved in Wake's plot. Kurita Michimaro died, locked up together with his wife. Ishikawa Nagatoshi, who had often been seen socializing ("drinking") at Wake's home, was sent to Oki, where he committed suicide several years later. Ōtsu Ōura was a yin-yang master and astronomer. He had been consulted by Fujiwara Nakamaro for making sure that the cosmic coordinates were lined up propitiously for the timing and execution of his plot because omens were believed to inscribe the future in the present. However, he reported Nakamaro's intentions and was handsomely rewarded with a promotion into the ranks of higher official-dom (rank four). Yet his association with Prince Wake cost him his post in Hyūga province (Kyushu), where he was ordered to remain in exile. His books on yin-yang and astronomy were confiscated because they had been misused. After Dōkyō's fall in 770, he was allowed to return to the capital, where he became head of the Yin-yang Bureau.[45]

Junnin was among the many victims of palace intrigues in which scions from Tenmu's sidelines were involved. His father, Toneri, was one of nine imperial princes (aside from Kusakabe and seven princesses) Tenmu had sired with nine consorts (aside from Jitō). One of Tenmu's sons, Prince Ōtsu, was possibly eliminated by Jitō; and a number of offspring (Princes Nagaya, Fune, Ikeda, and Shiyoyaki) from other sons — Takechi, Toneri, and Niitabe — in the next generation and in the one after that (Princes Wake, Hikami Kawatsugu, and Shikeshimaro and some of their consorts including Princess Fuwa, Inoue's sister) would be accused of plots or black magic or actually be involved in them, some of them repeatedly.

Three Outside Players

Three other lines of nobility produced important political actors during the Nara period. They are the Fujiwara, Nakatomi, and Tachibana, all inter-related. The Fujiwara was the Nakatomi's stem lineage, and the Tachibana were related by marriage to Fujiwara Fuhito, who served five sovereigns (from Tenmu to Genshō) in increasingly important capacities. After his four sons, all well placed in the bureaucracy, perished in the smallpox epidemic of 737, the clan's hope for fame and power rested on Fuhito's daughter Asukabe, who in 716 had become one of the first of five consorts to the future emperor Shōmu, who was fifteen then.[46] Shōmu, Monmu's son, had Asukabe's sister Miyako as his mother (ill most of her life after giving birth to Shōmu). Besides Asukabe, the Fujiwara had succeeded in providing

Shōmu with two additional consorts to hedge all their bets on a Fujiwara son as imperial successor. They were Asukabe's nieces. The Fujiwara thus positioned themselves strategically to become the major influence at the inner court.

As it turned out, through the vagaries of reproduction, they met one serious rival in Agata Inukai Hirotoji, who was the other consort who had been introduced around the same time as Asukabe, it being unclear who of the two was first. She must have been related, but it is unclear how, to the Agata Inukai lineage whence Fujiwara Fuhito took his main wife, the mother of his famous four sons and the two daughters (Miyako and Asukabe) who married into the Sun line. Another of Shōmu's wives was the niece of Tachibana Moroe, who, as we shall see, became the Fujiwara's main foe.

This Tachibana family is the third lineage besides the Fujiwara and Nakatomi families that played an important role in mid-Nara politics. It was linked to the Sun line through one of Shōmu's consorts; to the Agata Inukai line, which also provided Shōmu with a consort (Hirotoji); and to the Fujiwara via Fuhito's main wife (Agata Inukai Michiyo). Tachibana Moroe, once a prince, received his name in 736, when he lost his royal status. These entangled relationships made court politics a matter of complicated family intrigues.

Shōmu's Succession Conundrum

The mother of Fujiwara Fuhito's four sons and two daughters Asukabe and Miyako was a woman by the name of Agata Inukai Michiyo, initially married to a descendant of the late-sixth-century Great King Bidatsu. She changed her name to Tachibana, which was passed on to her two sons from her first marriage, one of whom was Tachibana Moroe. He acquired important positions and, after the demise of the Fujiwara Four, displaced their clan as the power behind the throne (see figure 10).

Rivals within Shōmu's household, the Tachibana and Fujiwara fought each other on the battlefield as well in 740, when Moroe crushed a rebellion by Fujiwara Hirotsugu, a grandson of Fuhito. Fujiwara Nakamaro, another of Fuhito's seventeen or more grandsons and Hirotsugu's half brother,[47] succeeded in gaining influence through his aunt Asukabe, who in 729 had become Empress Kōmyō — to the great dismay of the royals since Asukabe lacked royal pedigree. In 755, Nakamaro was able to force Moroe to retire, but the latter's son plotted a coup two years later. Another nine years later, Nakamaro was to be slain in turn, leading his own rebellion.

The rivalry over control of Shōmu's eventual successor between Asukabe and the Fujiwara on the one hand and Hirotoji and Inukai Tachibana on the other was fierce. The first round was a draw. Asukabe gave birth to a girl, Princess Abe (Empress Kōken-to-be) in 717; the next year, Hirotoji also produced a girl, Princess Inoue (eventually Emperor Kōnin's ill-fated and short-lived empress-to-be). The Fujiwara trumped their rivals when Asukabe produced a male child, Prince Motoi in 727/9, quickly made crown prince at the unprecedented age of one month. This Fujiwara triumph, however, ended when Motoi passed away a few days before turning one. Their situation was made worse that same year when Hirotoji bore a son, Prince Asaka, Shōmu's only male child, the obvious solution to the succession quandary.

Yet not only was Prince Asaka not made crown prince, but one year after his birth, on 729/8/10, his mother's line was made secondary to Fujiwara Asukabe's when the latter was promoted from consort to (nonreigning) Empress Kōmyō. Meanwhile, earlier that same year, Fujiwara strategists had succeeded in forcing Prince Nagaya to commit suicide on an apparently false accusation of plotting. Nagaya, a grandson of Tenmu and a "double royal," was a fierce defender of royals against intruders such as the Fujiwara. He may even have been a designated heir. It was literally over his dead body that a Fujiwara consort was made empress.[48] The last piece of the Fujiwara plan fell into place when in 738, a year after the loss of the Fujiwara Four to the smallpox epidemic, the clan succeeded in having Asaka passed over for the position of heir and in making Kōmyō's daughter Princess Abe crown princess.

Abe's appointment was highly unusual in that no empress in the past had received the title of crown princess before assuming power.[49] This turn of events was a political coup for the Fujiwara: Princess Abe was a Fujiwara through her father, Shōmu (son of Miyako, Fuhito's daughter), and her mother, Kōmyō (another daughter of Fuhito). In a sense, she was a "double Fujiwara." Kōmyō appears to have played a great role in Abe's appointment by mobilizing Buddhist scriptures, especially the *Konkōmyō-kyō* (Golden Light Sutra), and through lectures and transcriptions that provided Abe a new form of legitimacy as royal protector and transmitter of the Law of the Three Treasures. In one such event, organized by Kōmyō, Princess Abe is presented as sponsor of a lecture-cum-*sai-e* Buddhist vegetarian repast and referred to as "crown prince" twelve years before being appointed as such, at a time when a male "natural" successor, Prince Asaka, Abe's half brother, was alive. Thus, her male attributes were being constructed in part against a male competitor. A theory of turning women into males as bodhisattva transmitters of Buddhist teachings was spelled out in this sutra. Empress Wu in late-seventh-century China had used the same ploy.

Abe's new official status as crown princess did not have an immediate effect on palace politics. After all, Prince Asaka was still a potential successor. Power in the immediate future shifted to Kōmyō's half brother Tachibana Moroe, who benefited greatly from crushing Fujiwara Hirotsugu's rebellion in Kyushu in 740. This is when Emperor Shōmu decided that Nara politics had become intolerable, and left the capital, not to return for five years. In 744, toward the end of his absence, Prince Asaka fell ill suddenly and died at age sixteen — poisoned? Abe, childless, succeeded to the throne as Empress Kōken in 749 when Shōmu retired. Now the question of succession shifted down one generation and was more acute than ever because Kōken was still unmarried and childless.

When Shōmu died in 756, the Tachibana faction secured an edict elevating Prince Funado, a Tenmu grandson via Niitabe, as crown prince, a move undone the following year when Fujiwara Nakamaro demoted Funado and replaced him with his own son-in-law, Prince Ōi, yet another grandson of Tenmu via Toneri. Tachibana power received a more crushing blow, however, when Moroe's son Naramaro failed in his armed rebellion in 757/7.

Naramaro had plotted with some twenty men, including two sons of Nagaya (Kibumi and Asukabe) to depose both Empress Kōken and the heir designate, Ōi, and to choose a new emperor from among the two Nagaya sons and the two sons of Niitabe, Shioyaki and the former heir-designate, Funado. They planned to surround Nakamaro's compound with four hundred warriors. It should be noted that some of these plots were long in the making. Naramaro had been approaching candidates he sought to put on the throne for some twelve years, it turned out, and on 758/2/20, he forbade the drinking of sake at gatherings other than official ones, an attempt to prevent plotters from congregating.[50] Moreover, many plots leaked before they hatched. This was also the case with Naramaro's.

The Fujiwara retaliation was merciless. Princes Funado, Kibumi (whose father, Nagaya, had been forced to commit suicide in 729), and four others were caned to death under interrogation. Shioyaki, less involved this time, was pardoned. (In 742, he had been jailed with four ladies-in-waiting, banished to Mishima Island off Izu, allowed to return to Nara three years later, and restored to his rank in 746.) He was less lucky a third time, however, when Fujiwara Nakamaro took up arms in 764, declaring Shioyaki the new emperor (even giving him a name, Kinkō [current emperor]) in an uprising where both were slain.

During most of the Nara period, there must have been hundreds, possibly over a thousand people from the capital living in exile. Through an edict of amnesty issued on 770/7/23 during the last ten days of Shōtoku's final illness, in a penultimate attempt to accumulate credit to be cashed in post-mortem, thirteen years after Naramaro's coup, we learn that 443 people had been punished as conspirators of that coup; 262 among them having been lightly involved were pardoned then — but still were not allowed to set foot in the capital. The others, including accomplices in Nakamaro's rebellion, were pardoned a few months later, on 11/27, after Prince Ōi ascended the throne as Emperor Junnin. (The *Nihon kōki* on 799/2/21 reports that 375 had received the death penalty in that rebellion, but that all sentences were converted into exile.)[51]

After Tachibana Naramaro's failed coup of 757, the Fujiwara were again in control. The Tachibana, however, staged a brief comeback two genera-tions later when a granddaughter of Naramaro became empress to Emperor Saga (r. 809–823) and mother of Emperor Ninmyō (r. 833–850), only to be outflanked again by the Fujiwara, this time for good, when two of Ninmyō's sons by two different Fujiwara women became emperor (Montoku and Kōkō). This inaugurated the shadowy power of Fujiwara imperial in-laws for the next three centuries that was consolidated under the two child emperors, succeeding at ages eight and seven, between Montoku's reign (850–858) and Kōkō's (884–887).

The Endgame

Imperial Princesses Fuwa and Inoue (Higami), Shōmu's consort Hirotoji's two surviving daughters after her son Asaka died in 744, became the main players in the convoluted history of the end of Tenmu's line during and after Shōtoku's heirless rule (764–770). Fuwa tried to pull imperial succession to Hikami Kawatsugu and Shikeshimaro, her sons by Shiyoyaki (son of Niitabe). Inoue hoped to see her son Osabe eventually succeed his father, Emperor Kōnin, a battle she lost. The black magic she allegedly resorted to failed. The succession went to Kanmu, who in turn seems to have had his hand in the death of his younger brother Sawara in 785, made crown prince four years earlier, to make room for his own son as presumptive heir.

Princess Fuwa was involved in plots three times: in 764, 768, and 782. By descent through her mother Hirotoji, she was positioned against the Fujiwara camp of Kōmyō and Kōken/Shōtoku. When Fujiwara Nakamaro on 764/9/20 failed in his bloody rebellion to establish as emperor Shioyaki (elder brother of Funado, the crown prince killed under interrogation by Nakamaro only seven years earlier), an attempt costing the lives of both, Shioyaki's wife Fuwa was stripped of her status as imperial princess. So were Princes Fune and Ikeda (brothers of Junnin who had been promoted to imperial status when Junnin ascended the throne). Demotion from (or promotion to) the status of imperial prince (*shinnō*) or princess (*naishinnō*), a status reserved for siblings or children of imperial rulers — the next generation were simply princes (*ō*) or princesses (*joō*) — removed them from (or added them to) the pool of possible candidates for succession. Accused of having been part of the plot, the two princes were sent into exile, Fune to Oki, Ikeda to Tosa.

Four years later, in 768, in the midst of the Dōkyō affair (four months before the Usa Hachiman oracle, but after Dōkyō had been given the position and office of Dharma King), Fuwa, two princesses, and a certain Ineme, an Agata Inukai like Fuwa, tried to push Fuwa's son Shikeshimaro to the throne by putting a curse on Empress Shōtoku. They allegedly had stolen a lock of Shōtoku's hair — not difficult for princesses with access to the inner palace, one presumes, but no small feat since heirless Shōtoku was also hairless without any locks to speak of having had her head shaved seven years before on becoming a nun, unless hers was a partial tonsure.[52] They stuffed the hair into a skull picked up from the Saho River, brought it to the palace, and recited a curse, not once but three times. They were all banned from the capital. In addition, Fuwa was given an official stigmatized name (Kuriyame, "kitchen aide"), as was the apparent ringleader, Ineme, whose name was changed from Inukai ("raiser of canines," probably *fournisseur de la cour* for imperial hawking expeditions) to Inube ("dog menial").

However, in 771/8, a year after Kōnin had succeeded Shōtoku, the princesses were pardoned, as was the ringleader, Ineme, a year later because now it was argued that the whole affair had rested upon slanderous accusations of another lady, Tajiji Sukune Otome. (Fuwa was pardoned only after the Agata-Inukai link with the Tenmu line had been neutralized when in 772/3 Empress Inukai Inoue had been deposed, followed by the demotion of her crown prince son two months later.) On 769/5/25, it was stated that Shikeshimaro should have received the death penalty as accomplice to his father, Shioyaki, who had been executed when five years earlier the rebel Nakamaro had declared Shioyaki emperor, but Shikeshimaro had been spared then because of his mother. Too much was too much, however, so now he was exiled to Tosa.

THIS WAS NOT THE END of Fuwa's backstage political maneuvering even though it had cost her husband, Shioyaki, his life in 764 (and Shioyaki's brother Funado his in 757), and her son Shikeshimaro had been banished to Tosa in 769. In addition, her sister Empress Inoue and Inoue's son's lives had been snuffed out in 775. She had another son, Hikami Kawatsugu, whom she embroiled in 782 in a last effort to pull the imperial line away from Kanmu to him. Fuwa was fiercely loyal to her lineage, whose interests she promoted at any cost.

This incident took place in the beginning of the year (on the fourteenth of the intercalary first month, during the mourning period for former emperor Kōnin, who had been retired since 4/3 of the previous year and died on 12/23), only a couple of months after, following Kanmu's enthronement, Fuwa had been promoted to the second princely rank. The plot again was to start an armed rebellion, this time by taking over the palace and from there mobilize troops, but one of Kawatsugu's helpers was caught armed in an attempt to enter the palace.[53] Kawatsugu fled but was captured in Yamato province and received the death penalty. Some ten middle- and upper-rank officeholders and princes were also involved. We know of a total of thirty-five people exiled.[54] Because of the mourning period for Kōnin, Kawatsugu's death sentence was commuted to distant banishment, with his wife, to Mishima Island off Izu province. His mother, Fuwa, and sisters were banished to Awaji, the end of the line for a number of royals who, one suspects, must have formed a sizable island community of exiles.

Two months after this aborted armed coup, on 3/26, three of the conspirators were at it again, this time using black magic against the emperor. They were a princely couple and a certain Yamanoue Funanushi with a long career in divination and portent astrology that included the directorship of the Yin-yang Bureau. He was exiled to Oki, where he remained for twenty-three years until he was pardoned together with Kawatsugu and a few others in 805/3. A year later, on 806/3/16, the day before Kanmu died, their rank was restored. The next day, when Kanmu passed away, in a gesture to purchase extra insurance for Kanmu's spirit and his offspring against harm by the avenging spirits of past enemies, all those involved in the Ōtomo plot and Tsunetsugu's murder of 785 including Ōtomo Yakamochi, whether dead or alive, had their ranks restored. Sawara, Kanmu's younger brother and one-time successor who died under bizarre circumstances related to this plot and murder, received special treatment since monks in all provincial temples were ordered henceforward to recite the *Kongō hannya-kyō* (Diamond Sutra) on his behalf twice a year every spring and fall.[55]

The transitions from Shōtoku to Kōnin and from the latter to Kanmu were beset with a number of irregularities, including several accusations of witchcraft. When Shōtoku passed away in 770, two Shōmu daughters, Fuwa and Inoue (half sisters to Shōtoku), were alive. We have followed Fuwa's failed efforts to put her husband Shioyaki on the throne in 764, then her son Shikeshimaro in 769, her two attempts to displace Shōtoku, and in 782 her last plot to dislodge Kanmu with her son Hikami Kawatsugu.

FUWA'S SISTER INOUE was engaged in a different battle. She was born in 717, and at age four selected for a *saiō* career of consecrated princess in Ise, where she served for eighteen years, starting in 727. Her tenure was terminated because of a death in the family when her sixteen-year-old brother, Prince Asaka, suddenly passed away in 744.[56] Death of a close relative to the *saiō* terminated her term, which would otherwise run until the end of the reigning sovereign who had appointed her. She returned to Nara, became Kōnin's consort, and was made empress on 770/11/6 within three months after Kōnin succeeded Shōtoku. Their son Osabe, nine then, was made crown prince two months later, on 771/1/23.

Four years later, on 775/4/27 they both died, locked up in a confiscated residence of theirs in the Uchi district of Yamato province, most likely eliminated to make sure they would not claim the throne from Prince Yamabe (Kanmu-to-be), who had been designated heir to the throne on New Year's day of 773. This was after Inoue had been deposed on 772/3/2 and Osabe demoted on 5/29. The harassment of mother and son continued even after Yamabe had replaced Osabe as crown prince. On 773/10/19, five days after Kōnin's sister Naniwa no hime had died, they were accused of having cursed the princess. That is when they were locked up until their simultaneous death a year and a half later. A former *saiō* princess of Ise, also formerly an imperial consort, died violently, accused of witchcraft. (There is some circumstantial evidence that another *saiō*, Tenmu's daughter Ōku, may have been closely associated with her brother Prince Ōtsu, who was executed, accused of a plot around the time of Tenmu's funeral.)[57]

Kanmu's crisis, aside from Fuwa/Kawatsugu's plot at the beginning of his reign, developed also around the issue of succession. When he succeeded Kōnin in 781/4, he made his younger brother Prince Sawara crown prince, hoping thereby to cut short eventual succession problems right away. Complications arose four years later, however, with opposition to his decision to move the capital to Nagaoka. In 785/6, he put Fujiwara Tanetsugu in charge of supervising construction of the new capital. Tanetsugu was one of Kanmu's many fathers-in-law — Kanmu kept twenty-two consorts we know of, eight of them Fujiwara who gave birth to twelve of his thirty-six children.[58] Three months later, on 9/23, Tanetsugu was murdered in a plot by long-time Fujiwara foes from the Ōtomo clan. Sawara, Kanmu's brother, may have been involved given that the Fujiwara were apparently scheming to replace him as crown prince with Kanmu's first son (by a Fujiwara mother), Prince Ate, the future Emperor Heizei.

Sawara should have been suspicious inasmuch as, at age thirty-five, no Fujiwara had deemed him, the crown prince, worthy of one of their women. He was locked up in a temple on 9/28. The official chronicle states that during the ten days before his transfer to Awaji (where else?) he started to starve himself to death, and succeeded in doing so while in transit, which did not stop his exile, however; his corpse continued the trip to Awaji. With his own brother out of the way, Kanmu appointed Ate heir to the throne two months later.

Circles of the Accused Plotters

Plots were often a long time in the making — was there ever a moment during the eighth century when no plot was being hatched? — and the initiators or accused were figures close to the center of power. Scores of servants, dependants, and other associates had to be involved as well, and it is often from their ranks that informants emerged, usually well rewarded with gifts or promotions or both. Such are, for instance, Nuribe Kimitari, Nuribe Komano-osa, and Nakatomi Azumahito in the Nagaya affair of 729, to be discussed later, and a certain Mokuhi Tarushima in the Inoue affair in 772, all of them honored by having their name recorded in the *Shoku Nihongi*, a seeming veracity created by the inclusion of the identities of the witnesses.[59] Most of the protagonists, however, were members of royal lineages or affines of royals (the Tachibana, for instance). They often surrounded themselves with two kinds of adepts at the supernatural: yin-yang specialists to secure the right outcome for their plots (always men) and manipulators of black magic to work with curses (often women).

A number of plots are known to us only through a single line in the official histories, when the accused were punished. For instance, while Shōmu was in Kuni, Shioyaki, whom we have discussed earlier as participant in more than one plot, was arrested in Nara out of the blue on 741/10/12 and banished together with five lady servants from the women's quarters (*kōkyū*), which makes one suspect that some sorcery was involved. On 754/11/24, Ōmiwa Morime, the *kami* medium/Buddhist nun (*negi-ama*) (who in 749 had arrived in grand style in Nara from Kyushu, carried with great pomp in an imperial palanquin, to open the Usa Hachiman *kami*/Bosatsu franchise near Tōdaiji) was one of three accused of having engaged in sorcery, and was exiled. The others were Ōmiwa Tamaro, the *kami* officiant of Usa who was at Morime's side in 749, and Gyōshin from Yakushiji temple, who may have held the post of *daisōzu* in the Sōgō. Princess Fuwa, accused like Empress-consort Inoue of engaging "repeatedly" in black magic, was assisted by three women when trying to bewitch Empress Shōtoku with a lock of her hair stuffed into a skull on 769/5/29; they were a certain Agata Inukai no Ineme (probably a relative) and two princesses, Oshisaka and Iwata. Three years later (772/3/2), Empress-consort Inoue was allegedly assisted in her sorcery by two women also: Awata Hirokami and Ato Katashihame. In Fuwa's attempt of 782 to put her son Kawatsugu on the throne, she relied on Prince Mikata and his wife Princess Yuge for spells, as well as on the yin-yang master and portent astrologer Yamanoue Funanushi. Ki Masumaro, at one time director of the Yin-yang Bureau, is suspected of having been at Fujiwara Nakamaro's side during the latter's rebellion.

Meanwhile, harmful ghosts, mostly anonymous ones, began to make their appearance, and on occasion mountebanks started drawing crowds. On 730/9/29, we learn from an edict that

> people from Aki and Suhō are getting together in great numbers and wantonly rail about auspicious happenings and misfortunes, conjuring up the ghosts of the dead. Large groups of people are congregating in the mountains left [east] of the capital, several thousand, sometimes up to ten thousand, illegally spouting forth wildly about [impending] happenings, auspicious or otherwise.[60]

In 746, popular belief ascribed the monk Genbō's death to Fujiwara Hirotsugu's ghost.[61] On 752/8/17, seventeen shamans (*fugeki*) were sent away from the capital in exile to distant places. On 757/7/8, during Tachibana Naramaro's uprising, people were again enthralled by oracles from ghosts of the dead. On 780/12/14, the record reports an edict, followed by a comment:

> "Recently, simpleminded people have congregated around shamans, male and female, seeking fortune from their oracles. They have recklessly conducted unauthorized rituals, practiced magic with straw dogs, spells, and the like, and engaged in all manner of absurd and outrageous things, filling and clogging streets and roads. Pretending to seek fortune, they instead have crossed the line into black magic (*enmi*)." Not only have they shown no fear of the law, they actually have persistently nourished the weird and the magical. This will be strictly forbidden henceforward.[62]

On 779/6/23, a private slave of a certain Ōshi Atai Ashihara (who had purchased senior outer fifth rank in 772) scared the people in Suō (Yamaguchi prefecture) by claiming that he was Crown Prince Osabe who had been killed with his mother, imperial consort Inoue, four years earlier. He was promptly banished to Izu. These entries in the official record, including one about a crazy slave in a far-away province, show that the government was very nervous about the political connotations of "popular hysteria," whether in large groups or of an individual nature. Moreover, these incidents remained hot for years — witness the symbolic rehabilitation process — in remote locations as well as in the capital. One more incident illustrates the latter.

On 738/7/10, nine years after Prince Nagaya met his tragic end, a lower guard of the Left Arsenal at the palace, a certain Ōtomo Komushi, drew his sword and cut down a certain Nakatomi Azumahito, the head of the Right Arsenal. They were comrades of sorts, engaged that day in a game of Go when the conversation turned to the subject of Nagaya, whom Komushi had served and who had treated him well. When Azumahito started slandering Nagaya, Komushi drew his sword and cut him down. Azumahito, it turns out, was one of two men whose false accusation had resulted in Nagaya's death — and in Azumahito's being granted rank for the first time.

The presence of women in the realm of magic should not surprise. In many cultures, the fields of symbolic production are gendered in such a way as to relegate the darker side of manipulating supernatural forces to women. On the other hand, some men, like Prince Nagaya, were also accused of black magic. Yin-yang masters, during the Nara period, were state employees whose main concern was to gauge various courses of action suggested by their reading of signs and understanding of the conjunctures of invisible cosmic *ki* energies. Black magic was irredeemably condemned, but some use of spells was officially sanctioned; after all, there were spell masters within the Bureau of Medicine.

THE FIRST MENTION of mantic arts in the record reports En no Gyōja at the turn of the eighth century as one who taught the art to Karakuni no Hirotari. Although En no Gyōja was exiled because of his (mis)use of magical power, Hirotari later was appointed spell master in the Bureau of Medicine. The knowledge En no Gyōja and Prince Nagaya, accused of having caused the death of an infant prince, relied upon was continental knowledge. Let us cast our net wide and take a look at the social environment where other "incidents" developed.

In the seventh century there were two such incidents: the killing of Prince Arima in 658 at age eighteen and of Prince Ōtsu in 686 at age twenty-three. Prince Arima was the son of Great King Kōtoku, who had died when Arima was fourteen and had been succeeded by Kōtoku's sister, who took the throne as Great Sovereign Saimei. Real power, however, was in the hands of Senior Prince Naka no Ōe (later Tenji), Saimei's son — as his title indicates, a strongly favored candidate for succession. During an absence of Saimei, the caretaker, Soga Akae, initiated talks about plotting with Arima, who suddenly had second thoughts and withdrew from the plan. Akae, however, double-crossed him and delivered Arima to Saimei. Naka no Ōe's "investigation" resulted in Arima's execution on 658/11/11 and, incidentally, the elimination of a potential rival for the throne.

The plot took place on top of a tower (for Daoist star-gazing?) where Arima divined the future of the plot, using short paper slips from a box. The historian Shinkawa Tokio, bringing his vast knowledge of Chinese history to bear on the details of the scene (divining with paper slips, a small box, the accident of a broken table, and an obscure denial of the accusation with the rather cryptic words "Heaven and Akae know. I do not understand at all"), has concluded that the scenario is presented as ominous and evil. Moreover, Shinkawa surmises, the post-Taika "modernizers," led by Naka no Ōe, may have feared that left-hand occultism and appeals to Heaven might destabi- lize their plans for establishing a "rational," law-based state structure that, as posthumous names of rulers at the time indicate, also invoked Heaven as a source of legitimacy.[63] Two were executed, and two were sent into exile. One among them later became a judicial officer. In Ōtsu's case, many more judicial officers were involved and pardoned.

Ōtsu had Tenmu as father and Jitō's sister as mother. Widely read and well trained in the art of warfare and in belles lettres, and surrounded by a circle of educated men as is clear from *Manyōshū* and *Kaifūsō* entries,[64] he was best suited to be Tenmu's successor, though a year younger than Prince Kusakabe. On 686/10/2, one week after the official mourning (*mogari*) for Tenmu had started — it would last two years — Ōtsu was accused of a plot against Kusakabe and summarily executed the following day, which meant that someone else (Kusakabe) would be Tenmu's main mourner and thereby position himself as successor. (Kusakabe, however, died on 689/4/13 at age twenty-seven, leaving Jitō to ascend the throne the following year.)

None of the more than thirty arrested conspirators in the Ōtsu plot was executed, and only two were sent into exile. The names and careers of six conspirators are known.[65] They were "intellectuals" such as Hakatoko, an envoy to China, in charge of foreign relations in the Dazaifu, eventually envoy to Silla and member of the drafting committee of the Taihō Code; Nakatomi Omimaro, who became a judge and later headed the Office of

Kami Affairs (708); Kose Tayasu, who became a judge, then was in charge of administrative nomenclature adopted by Silla from China in 686 and introduced to Yamato a mere three years later and who was responsible for ceremonies and also second in command in Dazaifu. Tayasu and Omimaro became judges two years after the affair, when there were only nine judges in the Penal Office, Fujiwara Fuhito being one of them. The leader of the conspiracy seems to have been the monk-diviner Gyōshin from Silla, who was one of the two who were exiled, but he and his son were pardoned in 702 and 703.[66]

Ōtsu's circle consisted thus of intellectuals steeped in continental culture, specifically ceremonial issues, which often were legal questions, or *kami* affairs or divination questions. They were not scions from powerful *uji*. Some of them were allochthons.

Chronologically, the next incident revolved around Prince Nagaya. His case constitutes a turning point in the way victims of false accusations who paid with their life were transformed in the public mind. They were believed to seek revenge that had been denied them in this world. In addition, his case also led to a modification of the laws regulating the use of spells and magic, Buddhist and Daoist alike. All this will be examined in the next chapter.

9 SPIRITS

Prince Nagaya is selfishly studying the Left Way for private
gain, and seeks to overthrow the state.
—729/2/10. *Shoku Nihongi*

A dry moat shall be dug around Prince Sawara's tomb, so
that there shall be no overflow of pollution.
—792/7/17. *Nihon kiryaku*

Ōtomo Yakamochi, poet and compiler of the *Manyōshū* and one-
time general in campaigns against the Emishi, died just before Fujiwara
Tanetsugu's murder on 785/9/23 at the hands of some Ōtomo, an *uji* with
a long-standing enmity against the Fujiwara. The record suggests that he
may have been involved, although marginally, in both Nakamaro's and
Naramaro's rebellions — accusations that cannot be verified. As an Ōtomo,
Yakamochi was considered to have been in cahoots with the plotters. He
was posthumously reduced to commoner status, and his children were banished. Worse, his corpse was left to rot for over twenty days before receiving
a burial — a sure formula to produce a disgruntled spirit. Yet Yakamochi
did not have an afterlife as a vengeful spirit, probably because "people" did
not judge him to fit the role. Others, however, did become vengeful spirits.
Most famous among them was Crown Prince Sawara, not a Fujiwara favor-
ite either, whose "suicide" followed Ōtomo's death within days.

The killings in the royal circles that accompanied the shift away from
Tenmu's line (Emperor Junnin, Emperor Kōnin's empress-consort Inoue
and their son Crown Prince Osabe, and Crown Prince Sawara, Kanmu's
brother) continued to make history after the victims were buried or cre-
mated. They kept haunting Kanmu personally for a long time, especially
Sawara's suicide/murder.

Revenge of the Living Dead

Immediately after Sawara's death, Kanmu sent messengers to the tombs of
Tenji, Tenmu, and Shōmu to announce that Sawara had been deposed. This
preventive strike to ward off rebuke from the political spiritual world, done

in an official, public manner, had precedents in his own life. On 777/12/28, after Kanmu (then Crown Prince Yamabe and forty years old) had been ill for three days, it was decided to upgrade his stepmother Empress-consort Inoue's grave by assigning a guard to it, more a measure of protection, however, than a promotion. Inoue, it will be recalled, had been eliminated by Kanmu's father, Emperor Kōnin, two years earlier.

On 778/3/20, Yamabe was sick again, and once more three days later it was decided that this time the ghost of deposed and killed Emperor Junnin might have been behind the illness. Junnin's grave was upgraded to the rank of imperial tomb and provided with a permanent guard. On 790/i3/10 Kanmu's empress died, a mere three months after his mother had passed away, prompting him to proclaim a general amnesty a week later. The same year he also assigned a permanent guard to Sawara's tumulus in Awaji who, however, must have been negligent in his duty, as it turned out two years later. At least that was the message from a divination of 792/6/10 after Crown Prince Ate had been sick for a long time. Sawara had cursed the one who had taken his place.

One may wonder how the supernatural sources of these earthly misfortunes came to be identified. The answer to this question is twofold. On the one hand, as sometimes mentioned in passing in the record, yin-yang specialists were instrumental in diagnosing causes and prescribing solutions. On the other hand, as to be discussed later in more detail, general public discontent and critique of court policies or economic distress may have guided the diviners, like shamans taking their clues from their audience, toward famous innocent victims of murderous court imbroglios.

After the finger was pointed at Sawara, the prince official in charge of imperial tombs was dispatched to Awaji to make amends to Sawara's spirit for the tomb guard's negligence. The idea behind posting a permanent guard was not only to provide an honor guard, but also and perhaps mainly in this case to keep Sawara's spirit in his tomb. Some spirits of the dead were dangerous and had to be contained, it was believed. Thus, to prevent curses from recurring and to remedy the human fallibility of guards, a dry moat was dug at the foot of the tumulus, so that "there shall be no overflow of pollution."[1] Pollution, as became overwhelmingly clear throughout the Heian period, was not believed to cross fabricated boundaries.[2]

Yet wronged spirits cannot be trusted to forget the past that easily. On 797/5/20, two monks were dispatched to recite sutras at the grave as repentance for sins and atonement (*sha*) to Sawara's spirit (*rei*).[3] Offerings were sent again on 799/2/15 for the same purpose.[4] On 800/7/23, a more drastic measure of rehabilitation was taken. Sawara was given the title Emperor

Sudō, while Kōnin's consort Inoue had her title restored as well. Their tumuli were declared imperial tombs. The past was erased; history was being rewritten. The junior commandant (shōsho) of the Imperial Guards was to protect Sawara's grave with assistance from yin-yang masters and many monks for making amends.[5]

The object of all this attention was a spirit who remained sequestered in exile. Thus, on 805/4/11 it was decided to remove that possible source of discontent, lift the banishment on Awaji, and proceed with a reburial in Yamato province.[6] The culmination of Sawara's career came two generations later, on 863/5/20. In a brand-new court ritual, the Goryō-e festival for malevolent spirits of the dead, the spirit of Sawara, alias Sudō Tennō, held pride of place among six vengeful spirits honored with great fanfare.[7] Whence this escalating attention to the living dead?

It had not always been the case that unhappy dead had an active afterlife as avenging spirits, at least as far as we can judge from the *official* record. (Legends that survive in other writings, however, reveal glimpses of alternate narratives.) Plenty of people lost their lives in the power struggles of the seventh century, often involving the Soga in one way or another. The lives of a number of prominent personalities came to a sudden, unexplained end, leading historians to suspect foul play: Tenmu's sons Ōtsu and Kusakabe, not to mention his nephew, Prince Ōtomo; Emperor Monmu. Could it be that Toneri, the *Nihon shoki*'s compiler, was not about to put the historical spotlight on unsavory episodes of his ancestry by allowing readers to think that avenging spirits had suffered grave injustices while still on earth and therefore were causing trouble in the realm? Or was it that Buddhism's influence was not as prominent in the early 700s, when the *Nihon shoki* was compiled, as compared to a century later when the sequel, the *Shoku Nihongi*, was put together and Buddhist services for these dead were taking place? Or, as Japanese historians now think is the case, was there pressure from below, an expression of public sentiment or resentment, an attempt to re-right and rewrite history?

Rewriting the Record

The historical annals were the work of committees whose members often had some connection to the tragic events recorded. Prince Toneri, for instance, devoted a whole chapter to his father's Jinshin campaign. Parts of the *Shoku Nihongi* were composed at two different times; there were revisions and controversies.[8] We know of one concerning precisely the treatment of Sawara's "suicide" and exile, and the related murder of Fujiwara Tanetsugu and its aftermath.

An entry of 810/9/10 from the *Nihon kōki* (the *Shoku Nihongi*'s sequel, covering the years 792–833), reads as follows:[9]

> In the *Shoku Nihongi*, all the unpleasant things about Sawara and Fujiwara Tanetsugu were destroyed. On the other hand, to restore the original version according to what people said would, again, be improper. So we shall now correct [again] the [amended] record and return it to what it was before.

The background for this terse statement is complicated, and can be summarized as follows. Out of fear of Sawara's avenging spirit, perhaps, or for political reasons or both, the record was purged of most matter related to the incident toward the end of Kanmu's reign. Under his successor, Emperor Heizei (r. 806–809), the full record may have been restored under pressure from Fujiwara Tanetsugu's son Nakanari and daughter Kuzuko, the mother of one of Heizei's consorts. Heizei was under the sway of both and had a liaison with Kuzuko that went back to the time when that he was still Crown Prince Ate. Under Emperor Saga (r. 809–823), however, the restored version was replaced with the original official one. Surprisingly, some of that elided material found its way into the eleventh-century *Nihon kiryaku* anthology of Japanese history, where more details regarding Sawara resurfaced, including the Goryō-e celebration.

Tanetsugu belonged to the Ceremonials House of the Fujiwara, and his two children Nakanari and Kuzuko appear to have used their influence with Heizei to instigate a purge of Fujiwara officials from the Southern House. Was this a revenge for their father's murder? The purge was framed with the accusation of an alleged plot against the government that would have been led by Prince Iyo, Heizei's half brother, closely related to the Southern House faction. Iyo and his mother, Fujiwara Yoshiko, were imprisoned and forced to take poison in 807, a year after Heizei succeeded Kanmu.[10] (The allegation of the plot, as it turned out, was fabricated.) However, the two Tanetsugu siblings followed Heizei to the old capital of Nara, where he retired two years later. In 810, Heizei started making moves to reascend the throne, declaring Nara the capital. His failure to raise an army in the east sealed the trio's faith: Heizei took Buddhist orders, Kuzuko committed suicide, and Nakanari was executed.

Therefore, Fujiwara Tanetsugu's two children may have prompted Heizei to restore the full record of their father's murder, and it may have been Emperor Saga, Heizei's brother and successor, who ordered the revision to be eliminated as "improper." The entry of the *Nihon kōki* is dated 810/9/10, the day before the retired Heizei hastened to the east to raise his army, unseat Saga, and reinstall himself as emperor. It reveals struggles about how to handle a hot episode of the recent past.

In 843, Funya Miyatamaro, governor of Chikuzen (who was embroiled in an extortion of merchants from Silla, which came to light in 842), was accused of plotting.[11] A search of his house and that of an accomplice produced a detailed array of weapons (a total of 25 bows, 160 arrows, 14 swords, 2 helmets, and so forth). He was given the death sentence, commuted into exile (to Izu) as was so often the case. His assistants were dispersed in exile to Sado, Tosa, Echigo, and Izumo. It is not clear what the real issue behind this affair was. Miyatamaro may have been related to Funya Akitsu, who had been demoted as a suspect in yet another plot, the one of 842/7/17, when, two days after Retired Emperor Saga passed away, an attempt was made to raise an army in the east to unseat Emperor Ninmyō (r. 833–850). Or he may have been "the man who knew too much" about the illegal traffic of goods with Silla.[12] Or, in all likelihood, all the detailed evidence and sentencing notwithstanding, the accusation may have been false. Why? Because twenty years later Miyatamaro figured as one of the six spirits of innocent victims venerated in the first official Goryō-e of 863.

Spirits, Honorable but Vengeful

Goryō-e literally means "[Buddhist] service (*e*) for venerable (*go*) spirits (*ryō*)." *Goryō* constitute a special class of spirits, namely those of famous individuals, wronged in life and in the way they died, especially powerful spirits and therefore the subject of intensely focused fear and veneration. Although the term can also refer to a multitude of such beings, it is most commonly used for strongly individualized spirits. To preserve this sense of individuation and respect (*go*), the romanized term deserves capitalization, as Anne Bouchy suggests.[13]

Goryō rank above ordinary spirits and belong to the higher numinous realm, close to *kami*. They are spirits "with a past," actually a double past: one relating to their existence in human form, the other pointing to the transformation they, it is hoped, will undergo as spirits. Originally, they were famous personalities, well-known nobles or officials who met a tragic end, judged by many to have been cruel and unjust. This explains why they did not simply become *rei* (written with the same character as *ryō*), but *onryō*, spirits with a chip on their shoulder: dangerous, "rancorous, vindictive spirits." Goryō, then, are *onryō* who are the object of unusual veneration in order to "convert" them — after all, the first official Goryō-e was a Buddhist ceremony — into powerful benevolent forces. They can be understood as representing the two sides of what anthropologists used to call "mana" power.

The graph *ryō* can have other readings and associated meanings. Like *rei*, it refers to various aspects of the numinous and allows for combinations with other graphs such as *kami/shin*. *Rei* (read *mitama*) can function as a synonym for *kami*, or something the *kami* send down, the spirit of the *kami* (*shinrei*); they protect the ruling house during rebellions.[14] "*Rei* things" (*reibutsu*) or "*rei* signs" (*reiken*) are omens.[15] When the famous Buddhist prelate Gyōki died on 749/2/2, many "miraculous (*ryōi*) numinous signs (*shinken*)" appeared.[16] In reference to the spirits of *kami* or emperors the graph is usually read *mitama*.[17]

Actually the two graphs with which *mitama* (imperial spirits) can be written are the same as those for Goryō. Only pronunciation differentiates the two meanings. They are thus signified as equally important (signaled by the honorific *mi* and *go*); both relate to the survival of the realm, the former positively, the latter ambiguously. The six Goryō addressees of the Buddhist service on the imperial palace grounds in 863 had all been accused of having threatened the state, which cost them their lives; the accusations, however, turned out to have been false, or to have been believed by sufficiently many to have been false. This circumstance changed them into real public enemies, suspected of having unleashed epidemics against the realm, which in turn triggered gestures of appeasement and rehabilitation. In other words, they were a special category of *onryō* that, like the Goryō, have not always existed. *Onryō*, often and more so than Goryō, direct their wrath at very specific targets: individuals who did them wrong.

Given the tumultuous history of the ruling house in the seventh century (and earlier), we might expect to find vengeful spirits sprinkled throughout the record. Yet this is not the case. The *Nihon shoki* does not mention them at all, although there is the curse by the Kusanagi sword during Tenmu's final illness — to be returned to later. Only the compilers of its sequel, the *Shoku Nihongi*, introduced the concept, but not the term. That appears in the sequel to the sequel, the *Nihon kōki*, in an entry of the year 805.

Yet tales of some dangerous spirits had been circulating. Prince Nagaya, most likely falsely accused of plotting and witchcraft, met a different fate in the *Shoku Nihongi* and in the *Nihon ryoiki*. In the former (729/2/12–13), after Nagaya, surrounded by imperial guards, committed compulsory suicide, and was followed in death by one of his four wives and four of his thirteen sons (he also had four daughters), his corpse and his wife's were buried in

Ikoma Mountain, although without the honors due to their rank—Nagaya because he was a grandson of Tenmu, she because of her innocence. "His corpse should not be vilified," an edict read—an admonition not to do anything that would bring retaliation, which is exactly what happened in a legend collected in the *Nihon ryōiki*.

Here, Prince Nagaya had been slandered and, when encircled by the guards, poisoned himself and his family. Then, "The emperor ordered their corpses thrown out of the castle, burned to ashes, and cast into the waters. Only the prince's bones were exiled to Tosa province, where many people died."[18] The people blamed the prince's spirit (*ki*) for numerous dead (from a contagious disease?). The emperor responded by moving the bones to an island closer to the capital.

PRINCE NAGAYA may have been the first to have been honored and feared in the popular imagination because of postmortem vengeful intentions. The *Fudoki* (provincial gazetteers compiled by court order in 713) report plenty of cases of angry gods, but *onryō* vengeful spirits of humans are not mentioned. If one is allowed to generalize, Prince Nagaya's case may constitute a shift from blaming *kami* to blaming humans for a supernatural curse (*tatari*). One should keep in mind, though, that Tenmu had considerably reduced the distance between the ruling family and the numinous world, so ascribing *tatari* action to famous dead courtiers may not have required a great leap of the imagination.[19]

The idea of a particular spirit targeting a particular individual appeared first in a rumor about the cause of the court prelate Genbō's death in 746/6/18.[20] Genbō's removal from the palace had been one of Fujiwara Hirotsugu's demands when he raised a rebel army in 740. Genbō, together with Kibi Makibi (two long-time China residents), had been the focus of wide discontent, and Genbō had actually been demoted from his post at the Sōgō and from his function at the Naidōjō five years later, in 745/11.

The Naidōjō (the Hall in the Palace), a permanent Buddhist ceremonial site within the palace, was abolished in the Heian period, in part as a reaction against the Shōtoku-Dōkyō regime.[21] Through it, monks acquired close access to the court. Using magical formulae, on 736/8/12 Genbō had been able to cure Fujiwara Miyako, suffering a lifelong depression after Shōmu's birth in 701. Genbō was replaced by Gyōki, a charismatic populist figure initially distrusted by the government. Dōkyō's entry into court circles was also through the Naidōjō, after he cured the retired Kōken with methods similar to Genbō's. Buddhist monks, dealing with spiritual forces as yin-yang masters did, were also at home with "magic" and spells, a skill that played a role in their rise to prominence and fall from royal favor. In 754, a famous nun-medium and the officiant of Usa who had brought Hachiman from Usa to Nara in 749 were both accused of sorcery and banished, together with Gyōshin, the grand senior prelate from the Sōgō, as mentioned in chapter 8.

Demoted, Genbō had been sent away to a temple in Dazaifu — ironically, the center of Hirotsugu's rebellion whence Hirotsugu issued his demand for Genbō's removal from Nara. After Genbō's death, the rumor circulated (*yo ni aitsutaete iwaku*) that he had received his just deserts: that he "had been harmed by Hirotsugu's *ryō*." This is the first mention of a postmortem targeted revenge by a dead spirit. Implicit in this rumor is widespread support (probably limited to Nara and environs) for someone who critiqued the government (Hirotsugu) and suffered the consequences.

Although the term *urami* (deep-rooted rancor), the *on* of *onryō*, is not used in this passage of the *Shoku Nihongi*, it is obvious that rancor, resentment, is what allegedly motivated Hirotsugu's ghost. In the *Nihon shoki*, "rancor" was mostly something the living directed at Silla, long-standing enemy of Paekche and hence of Yamato, the beginnings of which would go back to King Suinin (28 BCE). On 727/2/21, the rather outspoken Prince Nagaya reported, in a context of critiquing bureaucratic officials, that he had heard people "resentful" of governmental abuses say that Heaven and Earth would punish the culprits and that extraordinary spirit *kami* (*kijin'i*) would appear. On 757/7/3, Kōken lectured Naramaro's accomplices that they had no reason to harbor "rancor" against her.[22]

Urami is preeminently a passionate, righteous, political sentiment, at least as we encounter it in the official histories. Silla was its first target. The *ifu* (subjected Emishi) were said to harbor it (758/6/11). Prince Wake, on 765/8/1, in a supplication to his ancestral spirits apparently wrote, "There are two people [Shōtoku and Dōkyō] I *hate*; please kill them." Request denied. Instead, it was he who was killed, beheaded. A few months after Kanmu succeeded to the throne, on 781/7/5, admitting that yin and yang were not in unison, acknowledging the widespread existence of resentment in the country, he proclaimed that he accepted this as a punishment of spirits — Kanmu was well versed in Chinese learning and must have been aware of the mandate theory of government — and therefore declared a general amnesty.[23]

An entry from 799/2/21 in the *Nihon kōki* adds further detail to the Hachiman oracle of thirty years earlier, an episode that had already been treated in the *Shoku Nihongi*.[24] It describes Wake Kiyomaro losing control of his senses and fainting when in 769 he received the second oracle reversing the first one (which had urged Dōkyō to become emperor). This second oracle told him also that Hachiman was angry (*ikari*), but that there was no reason to fear Dōkyō's *urami*, perhaps because only people treated unjustly, which Dōkyō had not been, could or should harbor *urami*.

It was during the last year of Kanmu's life that the *onryō* appear on the scene. On 805/2/6, we learn that

> 150 monks are appointed to recite the *Mahā prajñā pāramitā* sutra in the palace of the emperor and that of the crown prince; a small granary is to be erected at the Ryōanji temple, and thirty sheaves of rice will be stored there . . . to appease the rancorous souls of the dead (*shinrei no onki*, "the rancorous souls of the *kami* spirits").[25]

The temple, the name of which means "pacifying the *ryō*," had been built by Kanmu on the spot where Inoue and Crown Prince Osabe had died together (on 775/4/27), imprisoned and accused of plotting and witchcraft. (They had been rehabilitated by Inoue's Emperor Kōnin in 777.)

Two months later (on 805/4/5), a similar directive was addressed to all the provinces to honor Sawara (by then Emperor Sudō): they had to build small granaries and store rice there (food for angry or hungry ghosts, one presumes). In addition, he received treatment reserved for deceased emperors.[26] A memorial day (*koki*) was established for him throughout the realm, and arrangements made for bringing offerings (*nosaki*, put together in the twelfth month from the first tribute of the year) to appease the *onryō*. Two other measures were taken the same year to keep this spirit under control: on 1/14, Sawara received his own Ryōanji in Awaji; on 4/11, he was reburied in Yamato.

Goryō-e

A long entry in the *Sandai jitsuroku* (Factual Record of Three Reigns [858–887])[27] describes how six Goryō were honored at the first court-sponsored Goryō-e of 863/5/20 in the Shinsen'en, a parklike garden in the imperial palace.[28]

First of all, the Goryō in question are identified. They formed a sextet, headed by Emperor Sudō, alias Crown Prince Sawara, Emperor Kanmu's nemesis. Next was Imperial Prince Iyo, a son of Kanmu, who together with his mother, Fujiwara Yoshiko, had been forced to take poison in 807 following false accusations of plotting. That year, and into the summer of 808, the first large epidemic in the new capital of Heian broke out. (On 808/5/10, Em-

peror Heizei took the blame, publicly admitting to a lack of virtue.)²⁹ Iyo's
and Yoshiko's ranks were restored in 818. The fourth Goryō was Fujiwara
Nakanari, Tanetsugu's son, executed in 810 after a failed attempt to put the
former emperor Heizei back on the throne. A large epidemic broke out in
843, the year following the accusation of Tachibana Hayanari (Naramaro's
grandson, one-time ambassador to China, literatus) by the Fujiwara of having attempted to dethrone Emperor Ninmyō. He died on the way to exile
in Izu, and was rehabilitated in 850. Finally, there was Funya Miyatamaro,
former governor of Chikuzen, also accused of plotting in 843 and banished
to Izu although he never admitted guilt. That same year, and again in 861,
new epidemics developed. All of these Goryō, the text notes,

> are spirits who had been falsely charged and received the death penalty for
> being accomplices in plots [and now] were spreading contagious diseases. In
> recent years, there have been many outbreaks of contagious diseases, causing
> masses of people to die. It is the Goryō who cause these disasters to the realm.
> . . . In the beginning of this spring, an epidemic of influenza took the lives of
> many. It is thanks to the court that prayers are offered and this celebration is
> held. Hereby a long-harbored wish is being fulfilled.

For each of the six Goryō, an altar was set up in the Shinsen'en, with a
tray and a mat for offerings of flowers and fruit. A monk lectured on sections of the *Konkōmyō-kyō* and the *Hanyashin-kyō*.

It is further acknowledged that this was not the first Goryō-e. Many had
been held before throughout the country. The custom had spread far and
wide beyond the Home Provinces. These ceremonies were usually held
in summer and fall, we are told. On such occasions, often Buddhist ceremonies were conducted or sutras read; there was singing and dancing;
mounted archery competitions were held, comic plays performed, sumo
wrestling matches took place. "It soon became the custom that onlookers
streamed in from far and near, jostling, shoving, and milling about." At this
Goryō-e, however, the court provided the entertainment:

> The princes and nobles were all there. . . . Palace musicians performed *gagaku*
> music; children of the emperor's attendants and of the aristocratic houses
> joined dancer entertainers; professional dancers from China and Korea dis-
> played their skills, a variety of performers and entertainers competed with
> each other. The court ordered to open the four gates of the Shinsen'en gar-
> den³⁰ park to give the commoners free entrance.

The presence of rowdy crowds at previous Goryō-e may explain why the
event was managed by the two (Fujiwara) middle commandants (*chūshō*)

of the Left and Right Guard units of the palace (each constituting a detail of three hundred troops).[31]

The Goryō-e is where the rehabilitation of prominent victims of accusations of plots followed by violent deaths wound up. This process was in good part driven by the expression of popular discontent with the government.[32] In 863, the court co-opted and neutralized a movement by containing its cathartic function literally within walls and enlisting the Buddhist establishment to provide a solution, which entailed a silent acknowledgment of past wrongs and posturing as a victimized state that needed as much protection against these unleashed supernatural forces as the masses did.

The scenario associating realm-shaking natural disasters with gross injustices suffered by famous personalities, now seeking commensurate vengeance and signaling that past restitutions had fallen short, played itself out in numerous mass gatherings. These disorderly celebrations unleashed impressive social power, serious enough for the government to take note and co-opt it. In a manner, the ritual statement of each such gathering enacted a recasting (in both senses of the term: a remolding, and a changing of actors' roles) of the past without the use of words and ultimately forced the hand of official history, which, although always scripted *post festum*, was unable to completely overwrite that modified past.

Kanmu tried to control the history of his own reign in an unprecedented way by having the first decade (781–791) of his rule included in the *Shoku Nihongi*, published during his reign in 796. A few years after he died, however, he was criticized for having elided "unpleasant things" regarding Sawara from the record. There are other indications that in the early ninth century attempts were made to formulate one official history. The *Kojiki* was judged irrelevant, its presentation to the court in 712 passed over in silence in the *Shoku Nihongi*. Court lecture-seminars to clarify, streamline, and unify the mythology of the first two chapters of the *Nihon shoki*, saddled with numerous variants, were started in 812. Two works claiming that foreign rulers in Silla, Koguryŏ, and several Chinese dynasties descended from Yamato ancestral deities were ordered returned or burned — obviously unacceptable variants.[33] Yet through the numerous Goryō-e that eventually forced the court to sponsor an official one, the people trumped Kanmu.

WHAT IS THE HISTORY of associating natural calamities of a magnitude that threatens the realm with the action of supernatural entities, either as their cause or solution? Discounting an epidemic that allegedly took place in the fifth year of King Sujin, which would correspond to the year 93 BCE, the *Nihon shoki* does not mention epidemics, except for an alleged pestilence, linked in 585 to the suppression of Buddhism.[34] They make their appearance in the first years of the *Shoku Nihongi*. The years 698 and 699 mention two in different months for each year, a few years after Yamato's first palace-city was built (perhaps in part the result of the large concentration of people). I computed these as four outbreaks. Counting as a single occurrence each month an outbreak is mentioned, even if multiple days or locales are given, between 698 and 863 (the year of the first court-sponsored Goryō-e) or a span of 165 years, I found ninety-seven entries spread over 57 years. In some of these years, droughts and famines overlapped with epidemics. (In an additional 63 years, droughts, sometimes combined with starvation, were mentioned by themselves.)[35]

In most cases, the dispatch of physicians and medicine or other assistance and relief (*shingō, shinjutsu*) are mentioned. Before the devastating smallpox epidemic of 735 and 737, which killed an estimated one-third to one-fourth of the population,[36] twenty-nine cases are recorded of which only four make reference to extraterrestrial entities: prayers to the deities of Heaven and Earth for an epidemic in "the realm" (*tenka*) on 706/1/20, and the same year "for the first time, a great exorcism (*taina*) using clay oxen"; on 707/2/6, a "great purification (*ōharae*)"; and on 4/29 of the same year, because the epidemic was particularly violent in three provinces, offerings (*mitegura*) at a number of shrines and sutra readings at temples in the Kinai provinces.

From this one should not conclude that prayers and the like were not resorted to in the other instances: the record is most likely incomplete and may be erratic. It is striking, however, how few entries of this kind are found in the first third of the eighth century, but the whole arsenal of potential supernatural forces (*kami*, Buddhas, and spirits, the latter in the exorcism) is being put to use. The exorcism, undoubtedly of Chinese (Daoist) provenance, does not make another appearance in this context.

In the 735 and 737 smallpox (possibly mixed with measles) epidemics, general amnesties were granted, the *kami* appealed to, and the temples of Kyushu where the epidemic had started resonated with the chanting of the *Kongō hannya-kyō*.[37] As the disease traveled eastward on the Saikai road from Nagato (Kawaguchi) toward the capital, the main officials of each province were ordered to observe abstinence (*saikai*) and entertain the *kami* of the roads and boundaries, seeking their protection by holding "road banquet" celebrations (*michiae matsuri*) (735/8/12).

In the *Engishiki*, this festival is described as occurring regularly twice a year (in the sixth and twelfth months) at the four corners of the Heian capital.[38] It is closely related to the Festival for the Kami of Epidemics, which was held at the four corners of the palace and ten boundary sites of the Kinai provinces. These rituals were undeniably Daoist in origin (or had become Daoist over time): the *Baopuzi neipian* advises using charms and spells to control ghosts and spirits and protect one against epidemics and placing amulets on the paths leading to the house and at its four corners.[39]

During the Heian period, these festivals were all taken care of by yin-yang masters. This was probably also the case in the eighth century and specifically in 735, when the *michiae* festival is mentioned for the first time. Apotropaic like the Goryō-e of 863, the two differ nevertheless. Exorcisms, road festivals, and ceremonies to halt epidemic diseases seem to have been predominantly the domain of yin-yang cognoscenti (often overlapping with Buddhist monks who also may have been called upon on their own), while the court's Goryō-e and some local ones preceding it were clearly managed by Buddhist clerics.

The thirty-five years between 735 and 770 were rather uneventful without need to bother *kami* or spirits for the five recorded outbreaks of contagious diseases that occurred during that period. This changed during the decade of the 770s, when there are thirteen incidents, ten of them accompanied by prayers, offerings, and "festivals."[40] In the realm of symbolic action, it needs to be noted that the focus of attention is now given a more precise identity: *ekishin* (*kami*/spirits of epidemics). Twice (774/2/3 and 4/11) the Daoist term *ki* (ether/spirit) is used (*ekiki, shitsu'ekireiki*).[41]

The evidence is scant, but the brief survey of the history of Goryō out of *rei* and *onryō* presented above suggests that spirits, souls, and supernatural entities referred to as *rei, ryō,* and *mitama* have had a longer existence than vengeful spirits, *onryō,* who, in turn, needed to be conceived before Goryō could be born. Furthermore, it was the outrageous and bloody politics at the court (news of which was no doubt spread by commoners who worked in the palace and the nobles' estates) together with a series of epidemics that generated widespread discontent. Victims of momentous events, political and natural, joined in a disparate movement of critiquing the government, a movement the court succeeded in neutralizing. In doing so, however, it only gave further sanction to a worldview where active spiritual agents were held to wield great influence.

Aside from vengeful spirits, *kami* also were said to be actors in politically volatile situations by stoking "*kami* fires" (*shinka*), predominantly in the eastern part of Honshū. A number of fires, concentrated mostly in the years 767–775 (the end of Shōtoku's rule and the beginning of Kōnin's) and the 810s (under Emperor Saga), ascribed to action by the *kami*, destroyed state property, mainly public granaries and some provincial temples.[42] On 773/2/6, fourteen granaries were set on fire in the province of Shimotsuke (today's Tochigi), causing a loss of some 23,400 *koku* (the eighth-century *koku* equaled twenty-four or seventy-two liters) of grain.[43] Four months later arson destroyed eight granaries and 334,000 sheaves of grain (one sheaf produced about three kilos of rice) in a single district of Kōzuke province (Gumma), followed the next year (on 7/20) by a loss of over 25,400 *koku* of grain in a single district of Mutsu province (Aomori). In one district of Kazusa (Chiba), 570,900 sheaves went up in flames in 816/8.

A directive of 786/8/8 revealed three possible kinds of arsonists: disgruntled "members of [registered] lineages" (*fudai no tomogara*) of local petty gentry families competing with each other for lucrative positions of tax collection, actual tax collectors at the district level who were hiding shortfalls in tribute by destroying the granaries, and the *kami*. The directive declared that "no matter what the source of the fires, whether human or divine," provincial and district magistrates were to provide relief and restore the lost amounts; otherwise, they would be released from their office and their house lose its *fudai* status, which qualified its head for office holding.[44]

The Case of Prince Nagaya

The major case of alleged conspiracy combined with black magic, left unanalyzed in the previous chapter, is Prince Nagaya's. On 729/2/10, a minor official (junior seventh rank lower) and a certain Nakatomi Azumahito (without rank) falsely informed Emperor Shōmu that the prince was plotting a rebellion: "He is secretly studying the Left Way and seeks to overthrow the state."[45] That evening, Fujiwara Umakai, minister of the Department of Ceremonial, had palace guards surround Nagaya's large estate (four city blocks, some 250 by 250 meters), which was adjacent to the southeast corner of the palace. The next morning two of Nagaya's uncles and sons of Tenmu, Princes Toneri and Niitabe, accompanied by four high officials, went to the site to investigate. A day later, 2/12, Nagaya, forty-five, was forced to commit suicide. His wife and four of his children voluntarily followed him in death. The speedy unfolding of the events is reminiscent of the Ōtsu incident.

Given that the accusation was high treason, the subsequent conclusion of the case was unusually swift, and virtually without any further victims. No other lives were lost. The court did everything to bring quick closure to the incident. Within a week, seven people were exiled, but ninety were pardoned, as were Nagaya's brothers, sisters, and grandchildren; all suspected officials were cleansed in a Great Purification ceremony. On 2/28, the stipends of Nagaya's siblings were restored. Nagaya's disappearance from the political scene seems to have been the whole and sole point of this affair.

Prince Nagaya, who had received his first court rank in 704, reached the top of his career in the 720s (see figure 10).[46] In 721, he became minister of the right after Fujiwara Fuhito passed away. When Shōmu ascended the throne three years later, he was further promoted to minister of the left, the highest position ever held by a prince.[47] Two uncles, Princes Toneri and Niitabe, who eventually were to preside over the investigation of his case, also received posts: the former became acting chancellor; the latter was put in charge of the Imperial Guards. Princely members from Tenmu's sidelines were thus being positioned in important posts in the 720s, outpacing Fujiwara scions.

Nagaya, married to a daughter of Kusakabe, was a double royal: as a grandson of Tenmu through his father, Takechi, and of Tenji through his mother. As such, he was in competition not only with Fujiwara officials in the administration, but also with Fujiwara cognates at the court. He was strongly opposed to nonroyals infiltrating the court, especially Fujiwara daughters becoming empress-consorts. Starting in 724/3/22, when Nagaya criticized the use of the title *kōtaibunin* (imperial consort, connoting imperial ties and prerogatives with the emperor as referent) for Asukabe, instead of *taibunin* (great consort, which implies hierarchy in the emperor's household, with other consorts as referents), he continued to object to making her empress (*kōgō*). Six months after Nagaya's death (on 729/8/10), Asukabe became Kōmyō kōgō. This also opened the door for the four Fujiwara brothers to the highest offices.

The political temperature surrounding this question of rank and succession — of eminent concern to someone like Nagaya, who had been head of the Department of Ceremonial, the Shikibushō — had been raised considerably the previous year, when Asukabe's only son, made crown prince only thirty-three days after he was born, died suddenly on 728/9/13 before he was even a year old. The victim of black magic?

This event provides an opportunity to ponder about many accusations of subversive activities — probably the majority — that turned out to be false. How had they been made to stick in the first place? I can think of two answers: power and plausibility (the two ingredients still needed today to start wars). Those in power hold a virtual monopoly over the conversion of data into facts (and eventually subsequent alterations of them) and therefore can have them accepted through some appeal to a form of plausibility that works sufficiently at the moment to produce the intended result — never mind later questioning of the "facts." Plausibility is a historically contingent, *social* criterion that makes something acceptable as "truth." In Nagaya's case, we have only the terse accusation (black magic and fomenting rebellion) by two men as recorded in the *Shoku Nihongi*. Is there any way we can reconstruct the social environment that made this accusation of magic sufficiently plausible to produce not Nagaya's murder, but his death sentence? The allusion to Nagaya's familiarity with the dark arts is contained in the reference to the "Left Way" by the accusers.

SHINKAWA TOKIO, upon whom I have relied often in this study, presents a detailed analysis of that accusation of black magic and its companion, the intention to overthrow the state. Concerning the latter, a postscript to the *Dai hannya haramitta-kyō* (Great Wisdom Sutra), copied under Nagaya's sponsorship, shows that Nagaya's commitment to Monmu's imperial line as it had reached Shōmu was strong. The enormous sutra transcription project (some six hundred fascicles, edited and copied), started in 712, was dedicated to the memory of Emperor Monmu, Nagaya's brother-in-law. The emphasis on loyalty is to be found in the phrase "Earth-bound ethical order" (*chi wa tenrin o kiwameru*) of the postscript, which refers to maintaining the normative link between brothers.[48]

This sutra project was undertaken while Nagaya was minister of the Department of Ceremonial, formerly named the Law Office, which evaluated the quality of officials, a perfect fit for Nagaya's ambition and his righteous sense of right and wrong. The Department of Ceremonial controlled promotions, dealt with omens and era name changes, and took the initiative in investigations and punishments. In a decree of 727/2/21, as minister of the left, Nagaya blamed the conduct of ministers and officials for the problems the government was facing. This is the first time we encounter in the record blame for the state of the realm being put squarely on officials. The fact that the natural disasters could not be stopped or the government conducted properly and that the people harbored resentment, he stated, were warning signs from Heaven, which was producing *kijin'i*.

During Nagaya's tenure in the Department of Ceremonial (710–717), hardly any natural disasters were recorded, but bad omens were suddenly emphasized around 720, when Fujiwara Fuhito died.[49] By 727, the upright officialdom Nagaya had hoped to establish was faltering in his eyes. Ultimately, his political critique was directed at the system Fuhito had helped constitute through the Taihō Code and which ideally would have been a polity that had been signified as pure during the Tenmu-Jitō regime. It is worth noting in this respect that one can interpret the two edicts of 716 and 725 regarding the cleanliness to be kept in temples and shrines (as they became more incorporated in the state's ambit, the shrines through *hanpei* ceremonies) as an indication of Nagaya's effort to implement Tenmu's ideals.

The decree of 727 was preceded five days earlier by a dramatic attempt to emphasize the seriousness of the situation and the extraordinary supernatural remedy needed to counter the problems of the polity by having six hundred monks and three hundred nuns address the cosmic powers through a highly theatrical recitation of sections from the *Kongō hannya haramitsukyō* in the inner court. It was also around this time that Asukabe's pregnancy must have been known, so that an additional purpose for this momentous gesture may have been safe gestation for a (hopefully, male) successor. That is also when Asukabe sponsored her own sutra-copying project. Obviously everyone was looking for help in the same direction. And so was Nagaya.

ON 728/5/15, NAGAYA ORDERED a new copy made of the *Dai hannya-kyō*. As should be clear by now, copying was not a matter of simply duplicating a text. Transcribing a sacred text was one of the most potent magico-spiritual exercises: it would activate and increase the power of its words, akin to a greatly multiplied power of spells. In the eighth month, however, the baby crown prince was showing alarming symptoms of weakness. He died on 9/13 and was buried on 9/19 before the transcription was completed (which happened on 9/23) and its full power put into effect. Could it be that the healing power of the sutra had been reversed into a curse? Given the tense environment for these developments, such thought does not seem far-fetched.

For his two transcription projects Nagaya relied on a variety of talent besides that of Buddhist monks, many of whom had multiple identities anyway (monk, spell master, healer, portentologist). This was an official undertakings, involving not only officials from the Department of Ceremonial with which Nagaya was well acquainted, but also a number of allochthons from Paekche and Silla. Yin-yang masters and adepts at Daoist arts, medicinal and other, were habitués in Nagaya's compound, where the transcription took place. There also stood a towerlike structure, a detail that recalls Prince Arima's "plot."[50]

Undoubtedly, there was an exotic flavor to the social and intellectual atmosphere in Prince Nagaya's estate. He was part of the literary circles we know of through the *Manyōshū* and the *Kaifūsō*. Half of the poems produced at his estate were occasioned when entertaining envoys from Silla.[51]

Although the *Shoku Nihongi* makes no mention of any other than Buddhist media in this critical situation, there is little doubt that every possible venue to save the precarious life of the precious inheritor was explored. An entry in the *Ruiju sandaikyaku* (Ordinances of the Three Time Periods, arranged by topic in the early eleventh century), regarding a regulation dated 9/6, a week before the crown prince's premature death, leads to that conclusion.[52]

On that day, the Bureau of Books and Drawing (Zushoryō) demanded that henceforward no more than one item at a time be borrowed by anyone, whether imperial princes or commoners, from among Buddhist icons, exoteric and esoteric classics and writings, law books, folding screens, paper doors, and drawings of various kinds. There seems to have been a run on such items at the time. It is more than likely that medico-magical material, prognostication manuals, and the like may have been used in attempts to save the princeling — or, given the atmosphere of intense fear and the negative outcome, may have been said to have been used to curse him.

That black magic was made the central issue becomes apparent in an edict issued on 4/3, barely one month after the case had been closed with the series of the pardons for all and the restoration of stipends for Nagaya's siblings mentioned above:

> Those, whether officials, warriors, or the people of the realm, here or elsewhere, who acquaint themselves with heterodox material, collect techniques of blinding people, engage in black magic, lay curses and thus harm others will be penalized: the principals involved will receive the death penalty; accomplices will be exiled [which is what happened in the Nagaya case]. Those who, dwelling and living in mountains and forests, fraudulently perorate on the Buddha's precepts, contrive their own teachings, expound on karma, make amulets and talismans, mix poisonous concoctions, create fear among the people, and do not observe prohibitions concerning these matters issued in the past will be punished according to their degree of guilt as spelled out above. The possession of prognostication books must be declared within fifty days of the date of this edict. If left undeclared within this time span, and this is reported later, those guilty, principals and accomplices alike, will be banished. Those who report the misdeed will be awarded thirty rolls of silk, to be levied from the guilty party's house.[53]

Magic, Legitimate and Illegitimate

It will be recalled that the Yōrō Code's first article of the Regulations for Monks and Nuns warned clerics not to "falsely expound on the nature of omens . . . bewitch and mislead the people."[54] In the second article, the following distinction was made between legitimate and illegitimate use of spells: "Monks and nuns who engage in portent hermeneutics or cure illnesses by relying on the Small Way or magical techniques (*fujutsu*) shall be defrocked; however, this shall not apply to the use of Buddhist spells for healing purposes."

The *Ryō no shūge* (Collected Interpretations of the Administrative Laws, a private compilation made in the 860s and 870s) explains: "By 'Small Way' is meant magic amulets and the like."[55] Article 17 of the Taihō Penal Codes on Violence and Robbery expands upon methods of magic:

> There are many methods of magic and summoning spirits, so that they cannot all be described. Magic entails the carving of human effigies, binding their feet, tying their hands, and in this way bewitching people. Spirit summoning refers to oracles by them or to wantonly engaging in practices of the Left Way; some use curses or spells to kill people.[56]

The *Anaki* commentary as quoted in the *Ryō no shūge* clarifies the meaning of healing through medicinal methods: "In the old law [i.e., Taihō Code], it meant healing through techniques of the Way (*dōjutsu*), spells (*fukin*), infusions (*tōyaku*), but now the item of infusions is left out." Thus, in the Yōrō Code, clerics practicing healing through "small way magic" and "techniques of the way," spells, and infusions, would be defrocked. This article assumes that Buddhist monks must have been knowledgeable about non-Buddhist formulae, which, if such a distinction holds up, would be a reference to Daoist and other know-how on charms, magic, and the like. This restriction and exception with regard to the field of magic was legislated in 757; but judging from quotations of earlier legal commentaries included in the *Ryō no shūge*, it constituted a change in the law.[57]

One of the sources for the *Ryō no shūge* is called the *Koki* (Old Comments), written during the period 737–740. It was thus based on the now lost Taihō Code of 701. When compared to the almost completely reconstituted code of 757 (the Yōrō Code), one can catch glimpses of some differences between the two. This is how we know that there were two additional items besides Buddhist spells that monks and nuns were allowed to use earlier: Daoist techniques and spells or talismans: " 'Spells' means Buddhist *dhāraṇī*; 'techniques of the Way' and 'talismans' refer to the method of masters of the Dao; today Karakuni Muraji practices it." Karakuni Muraji is Karakuni Hirotari (En no Gyōja's student) who, at the time the *Koki* was written, was a spell master in the Bureau of Medicine, where he became director in 732. Allowed in 701, why were "Daoist" techniques dropped by 757?

Spells and talismans were means to control spirits and cosmic forces (*shinki*) or the all-pervasive "cosmic stuff" (*ki*). In a tale where En no Gyōja is depicted with all the characteristics of a Daoist immortal, he is reputed, among other things, to have summoned and ordered spirits and *kami* (*kishin*) around — and, incidentally, in yet another innuendo linking Daoism and political subversion, he is accused of having had plans to usurp the throne![58]

One of the sources for Daoist spells in early Nara was undoubtedly the *Baopuzi*. Many wooden amulets have been found with spells from this and other Daoist works, which were probably introduced in Yamato in the second half of the seventh century.[59] The first mention of spell doctors (*jukon no hakase*) appears in an entry of 691/12/2 when two are named as recipients of twenty *ryō* of silver each;[60] the Taihō Code stipulated one medical doctor with ten students and one spell doctor with six students as posts in the Bureau of Medicine of the Ministry of the Imperial Household.

Tang law did not differentiate between Buddhist and Daoist spell masters. The same was most likely the case in Yamato as well. In the En no Gyōja story just mentioned, the *Hoke-kyō* (Lotus Sutra) is associated with spells, and he is also said to have acquired extraordinary powers from the "formula of the Peacock," which refers to the *Sutra of the Peacock Spell* (*Mahāmāyūrīvidhārajñī* sutra),[61] a work Michael Strickmann calls the "first in date and influence . . . [a]mong authentically Indian prototypes of specialized demonology and spellbinding . . . a principal source for the powerful *nomina barbara* that were essential to any effective manual of demonquelling"[62] — a sutra that was further expanded through Tantric Buddhist additions. In 692/2/11 mention is made of two "yin-yang *hōshi/shamon*" (yin-yang doctor-priests).

A decree from 717/4/23 aimed at straightening out outlandish practices that took cover under clerical garb, particularly perhaps those of crowds following the populist monk Gyōki, at that point deeply mistrusted by the government. In such a document, one might expect abuses of spells or charms to be mentioned, but they are not, most likely because they were not seen as a problem. In the 720s, Buddhists freely used spells, but a decade later, they were limited to "sutra-based spells." Buddhist practice, as standardized by the government, increasingly emphasized group lecturing on sutras or collective chanting.[63] On the other hand, in all incidents of magic following the Nagaya incident we surveyed earlier, the accusation of engaging in black magic was always linked to politically subversive intentions vis-à-vis the state.[64]

The Buddhists were allowed to use sutra-based spells. Yin-yang and Daoist spells were supposed to be monopolized by the state through its laicization of monks with the specialized knowledge and their relocation in the bureaucracy as yin-yang masters and spell specialists. Whence this link between magic and counterpolitics?

On 719/11/1, the monk Dōji returned from China after a stay of sixteen years. He brought with him Yijing's new translation of the *Konkō-kyō-saishōō-kyō*, which in 728 was distributed to all the provinces and became the standard version for official occasions throughout the realm. Dōji, concerned with correcting previous versions of the sutra, must have found a kindred spirit in Nagaya, who was preoccupied with straightening out the bureaucracy. Nagaya made him supervisor of his second sutra project.[65] On 722/4/21 Empress Genshō was presented by a Chinese (Ōgen Chū) with the first (recorded) cinnabar concoction made in Japan. These arrivals from China must have brought many of the volumes and paraphernalia that wound up in the Bureau of Books and Drawings. In addition they probably had tales to tell about Ye Fashan (631–720?), the Chinese emperor's thaumaturge, portentologist, Daoist master, and reputed immortal who in the Daoist center (*guan*, "monastery") in Changan engaged in spectacular displays of his power to control ghosts and spirits. He had cornered the market for spells, having devised ways both to curse and to kill people with voodoolike wooden dolls, and remedies to defend oneself against them.[66]

Archeological research has discovered 35,000 wooden tags from Nagaya's compound. Some 37 of them had magical spells written on them. At least one of them, possibly dating from the 720s or 730s, is a dragon spell to protect against contagious diseases. The text is extremely close to a spell from a Daoist manual published in China by Sun Simiao in 682 as a complement to his *Prescriptions Worth a Thousand Gold Pieces* (*Qianjin yifang*; Jp. *Senkin yokubō*).[67] In this work can be found "proscribed sutras" (*kinkyō*), amalgams of Buddhist and Daoist spells, Five Agents theories, Great Dipper worship, the four directional animals, et cetera.[68]

Such new information from China must have further charged the atmosphere in Nara with more tangible, yet invisible, dreadful creatures and forces. The embassy that went to China in 717 was the first one after that of 702, and the first one since the capital's move to Nara. In China Emperor Xuanzong had succeeded to the throne in 712, inheriting the legacy of murder, sorcery, and poisonings at the court that had surrounded Empress Wu's regime.[69] The embassy of 702 must have brought back tales about these events, and the one from 717 must have been well informed about the heated political discourse at the capital about orthodoxy and Left Way practices in Buddhism and Daoism, which was in part a response to those previous events, a discourse that developed in the years following Xuan-zong's accession to the throne.[70]

In Japan, Buddhists eventually succeeded in taking center stage for providing the means to defend oneself and the state against threats of dark cosmic forces, a development that started, on a macro political scale, with choruses of monks chanting sutras for the welfare of the realm in early Nara (for instance on 725/7/17)[71] and wound up in the Goryō-e of early Heian. (In the seventh century, sutra chanting or expounding seems to have been used mainly to extend life or to alter damaging weather conditions.)[72]

The Case of the Missing Daoism

In early 754, two years after the completion of the Great Buddha of Tōdaiji, a sixty-six-year-old blind Buddhist monk from China arrived in Nara, accompanied by some twenty-four disciples (among whom were a number of monks, a few nuns, a man from Malaysia, one from Nepal, and one from Central Asia).[73] This constituted the successful end of his sixth attempt to cross the sea to Japan, a most perilous undertaking. Ganjin had lost his eyesight during the shipwreck of his fifth attempt four years earlier. He had risked his life to lend his authority to the performance in Japan, for the first time, of proper ordinations whereby the rules and precepts governing monastic life would be officially accepted by monks and nuns. This solemn officialization of religious discipline on the part of the clergy helped the court organize and control institutional Buddhism, a process that on the state's side had been initiated through the Taihō Code. Actually, it had been Prince Toneri who, as acting chancellor in charge of the government, had sent two monks to China in 733 to bring back the precepts and a certified authority to introduce them in Japan.[74]

The first bestowing of the precepts took place in 754/4 on an ordination platform in front of Tōdaiji. Retired Emperor Shōmu and his daughter Empress Kōken were the first of more than four hundred others (mostly monks who had renounced their former faulty ordinations) to submit to the ceremony.[75] Shōmu's and Kōken's status, it should be understood, did not change through this ceremony. Their participation was rather an expression of intention to support the teaching of the Buddha and a public ratification of the promulgation of clerical rules and regulations.

Ganjin's voyage to Japan had been eventful in more ways than one. Some of his earlier attempts had ended in shipwrecks, and one of the four ships that sailed to Japan in his final crossing eventually wound up in Annam.[76] The Tang emperor Xuanzong had set conditions for the delegation from Nara to take Ganjin to Japan that its members were unwilling to fully meet. They therefore had to whisk blind Ganjin to a port, secure a boat, and smuggle him and his followers out of the country. They hid him as a stowaway part of the voyage, seriously concerned that if he was detected, his escape would jeopardize future relations between the two countries. Why was the Japanese delegation willing to risk so much?

Xuanzong was an enthusiastic supporter of Daoism. He had insisted that the Buddhist prelate could leave China only if he could take along Daoist priests. The Japanese refused, offering as excuse that "the ruler of Japan does not venerate Daoism." As an expression of good will, or as a cover-up for their scheme, they decided to leave four members of the mission behind to engage in the study of Daoism.

The delegation's response was correct to the extent that the Nara court had never sponsored institutional Daoism. There was no Daoist establishment on a par with Buddhism, which in the 750s, under Kōken and Retired Emperor Shōmu, reached a peak of governmental support. But why, on the part of the delegation, risk international tension?

An earlier mission is on record as having shown an active interest in Daoist matters. In 735/iii, Vice-ambassador Nakatomi Nashiro, having had to abort his return trip to Japan, requested that Emperor Xuanzong allow him to take Daoist scriptures and icons with him to promote "the sacred teachings" in Japan.[77] On the surface of it, this shows an eagerness on the part of an official delegation to spread Daoism in Japan. The circumstances of this request, however, make such an interpretation questionable.

Xuanzong's reign eventually developed into what historians call "the high-water mark of Taoist influence on Chinese political life."[78] Starting in 720, the state seriously sponsored the development of Daoist ritual, lectures at court, and scholarship of the *Daode jing*, its text engraved on stone steles in three different sites, once in 721, and again twice in 732. The next year, the emperor wanted every household to have a copy of this canon, and a number of examination questions on some of the Confucian classics were replaced with questions on the *Daode jing*. In 735, a priest had approached Xuanzong with the idea that a stele with the emperor's commentary on the text be placed wherever Daoist state rituals took place. That is the year when Nakatomi Nashiro approached the emperor with his request.[79]

Perhaps the delegation, which had been shipwrecked earlier, knew precisely how to get the emperor's ear when they were in a hurry for a permit to return to Japan. Moreover, one of that delegation's tasks was to bring the precepts for the regulation of Buddhist monastic life back to Japan, since Japan was entering what one could call equally well the high-water mark of Buddhist influence on Japanese political life. It is significant in this respect that the ambassador asked for Daoist paraphernalia, but does not mention Daoist teachers, even though they brought back a variety of cultural talent: five Chinese, one Persian physician, and two Indians (one of them a Brahman).[80] Daoist teachers were not on the list of desiderata in 735, and they were emphatically avoided in 753. Perhaps the rulers in Japan were aware that the fall of Koguryŏ had in part been blamed on Daoism. As mentioned, Yŏn Kaesomun's coup of 642 was followed by a persecution of Buddhism and active support for Daoism. His strengthening program failed, however, and Koguryŏ disappeared from the map in 668.

What happened to the four Japanese who were left behind in 753 to study Daoism? They may have returned later to Japan — not as Daoist priests, however, but as medical specialists, some even receiving court rank.[81] In the record, there is reference to a certain Ōkasuga Kiyotari and his Chinese wife, whom he brought over as a member of a delegation in the past. Both he and his wife received court rank on 792/5/10. Their promotion may have had to do with alleviating Crown Prince Ate's "long illness," recorded four entries later, on 6/10, as having been caused by Sawara's spirit.[82] Whatever the case may be, there is no historical trace of Daoist officiants.

Yin-yang, in and out of the Shadows

By establishing a Yin-yang Bureau, Tenmu intended to filter out of the body of continental knowledge the techniques indispensable for keeping his rule aligned properly with cosmic forces. This necessitated the creation of a corps of specialists, which he secured mainly from among allochthon circles that included laicized monks. Yin-yang learning, essential in the field of prognostication and divination, could not be freely available. Later, in the early Nara period, the state made an attempt at getting another area of supernatural power under control, namely magic, by outlawing non-Buddhist spells, specifically Daoist ones. Thus, yin-yang masters and the Buddhist clergy were supposed to use their spiritual techniques in the service of the court.

The powerful knowledge in the hands of these two groups of public servants was allegedly often put to use by schemers and plotters. Among those involved in Ōtsu's plot a week after Tenmu died, the only one sent into exile was a monk from Silla whose son, however, was later laicized and hired into the bureau. Yin-yang masters were known or suspected to have been moving in the circles of plotters, the most famous one being Yamanoue Funanushi, involved in an anti-Kanmu plot in 782. Another one most likely functioned as a consultant in Fujiwara Naramaro's rebellion. Such involvement followed from the fact that yin-yang knowledge was also essential in military and strategic planning.

It may have been because of the political dangers involved for the practitioners of mantic arts that by the 730s, the government had a problem filling the posts at the Yin-yang Bureau with new talent. The reading of portents and interpretation of signs was a risky undertaking because it entailed taking a stance in the treacherous field of politics, more often than not court intrigue. Around the ruling partnership of Empress Shōtoku and Dōkyō, the producers of portents were kept busy, sighting colored clouds or conveying oracles. Buddhist monks could rise in status and prestige through magical healing. Thus, Genbō gained access to the inner court by curing Shōmu's mother, Dōkyō by ministering to Kōken's health problems.

The interventions by all of these figures were always conditioned by unspoken political sanctioning. Five years after a famous nun-medium and the officiant of Usa brought Hachiman to Nara, they were both accused of sorcery and banished, together with Gyōshin. The fall of Dōkyō and his clerical associates is well known.

I WOULD LIKE TO illustrate this ultimate political sanction of supernatural events through two examples. They were not generated by yin-yang masters, but since they resulted in court decisions, the sanction of such masters, no doubt based on their sense of the balance of power at the court, must have allowed these events to have an actual effect. Both cases were curses that came from weapons, and both took place toward the end of the lives of Tenmu and Kanmu.

The first one is the Kusanagi curse, which was identified as the possible cause of Tenmu's final illness shortly before he died. Although the sword was immediately taken away to the Atsuta shrine in Owari, where it belonged, the prognosis of a curse on the first *tennō* toward the end of his rule must have constituted a serious critique of his regime. Whoever made that diagnosis, undoubtedly (with the help of) a yin-yang specialist, must have felt secure enough with certain factions at the court to come forth with it. That there was trouble brewing became obvious the week after Tenmu died, when his son Ōtsu was accused of plotting and promptly executed. Was this curse at the end of Tenmu's rule a critique of the way he had come to power?

Historical sleuthing by Ōtsuka Yasujirō has related this incident to a top bureaucrat's name change precisely around that time.[83] On the second of several days (686/9/28) when numerous eulogies were delivered during Tenmu's wake, Isonokami Maro pronounced one representing the corps of judicial officers. Until then, he had been known as a Mononobe Maro. According to one version of the *Nihon shoki*, Mononobe Maro had been the only important ministerial figure (*muraji*) from Prince Ōtomo's inner circle who had remained loyal to the prince to the end. He was by his side, "together with one or two attendants (*toneri*)" until Ōtomo's last moments, when, abandoned by all his generals, he had fled to the mountains where he "committed suicide." Yet, under Tenmu, this loyal servant of his enemy continued having a rising career (see figure 10).

The speculation is that Maro actually may have killed Prince Ōtomo and revealed his hideout (rather than hide the body from Tenmu's army as one might expect), with the prince's head winding up being offered to Tenmu. By the time Maro delivered Tenmu's eulogy fourteen years later, he had risen nine steps to fifth junior lower rank. He died in 717, as minister of the left, at that juncture the highest administrative post in the bureaucracy, holder of senior second rank. Why the name change from Mononobe to Isonokami?

By changing names, the hypothesis goes, Maro may have hoped to escape the curse of the sword, which he might have had reason to believe could be targeting him as well, if indeed this was interpreted — not too far-fetched a supposition — as a critique, at the end of Tenmu's life, of the way he had come to power (with Maro's indispensable help). Changing one's name gave one a different identity, in the strongest sense of that term. Only the ruler, himself beyond ordinary mortals' identity and therefore without a last name, could bestow names.

John Bentley presents several tentative reasons for the *Sendai kuji hongi*'s pro-Mononobe slant and for why this work, which he dates about one or two decades before the *Kojiki*, might have been commissioned by Mononobe Maro.[84] If this is correct, it would be plausible that Maro, a loyal follower of Prince Ōtomo almost to the very end but cursed because he ultimately betrayed his master, had plenty of reasons to emphasize a particularly close relationship as dynastic protector his house had with the Sun line since mythological time.

Isonokami, Maro's new name, linked him to the Isonokami shrine, which had always functioned also as an arsenal and been associated with the Mononobe, a military *uji*. The name change did not apply to the whole lineage, but just to Maro's branch — and it was not the end of name changes for this sublineage.

A grandson of Maro, Yakatsugu (729–781), had as illustrious a career as his grandfather. In 770, following Empress Shōtoku's death, he helped Fujiwara Nagate fabricate her last will, which designated Kōnin, Tenji's grandson, as her successor. In 775/12, eight months after Empress Inoue and her son Prince Osabe had died while under house arrest, Yakatsugu was allowed to change his name back to Mononobe. It seems as if now that, with these two royals out of the way, the Tenmu line had reached its irreversible end, Yakatsugu may have felt that the curse had lost its raison d'être. Needing no further protection, he reverted to his original family name of Mononobe.

Why then, four years later, in 779/11, yet another shift, back to Isonokami? In 777 and 778, Kanmu, then still Kōnin's Crown Prince Yamabe, had fallen ill twice. Divination pointed to former imperial consort Inoue (whose grave was promptly upgraded), and Emperor Junnin, two imperial members of Tenmu's line who had died a violent death. These spirits, who seemed busy trying to eliminate the assigned crown prince of the new Tenji line, might conceivably also direct their anger at the person who in 770 had assisted in drawing up the document that shifted the dynasty to Tenji's line. It would make sense that Yakatsugu sought protection for himself and his lineage under the Isonokami umbrella again. Obviously, yin-yang officials must have steered the political interpretation of these events. Sometimes, however, the pronouncements of "amateurs" had greater weight, or at least were allowed to have decisive power. Otherwise, why rely on them in another case involving the Isonokami shrine?

WHEN POWERFUL RULERS like Tenmu see the end approaching, much is at stake. Such was also the case with Kanmu.[85] In 804/2, Kanmu at age sixty-seven moved the weapons stored since ancient time in the Isonokami shrine in Yamato province closer to the new capital of Heian, "as a precaution against emergencies" (*hijō o tsutsushimu beshi*). A year later, however, an order was issued to mobilize 157,000 men — undoubtedly a seriously inflated figure — to return the weaponry to the shrine. This whole affair, having to do with a shrine where swords were venerated, most importantly the one used by the first emperor Jinmu in his eastward campaign, was surrounded by prognostications and oracular pronouncements.

After the first of these two moves, sounds of whining arrows were heard by houses attached to the shrine, but the interpretation of a divination searching for the meaning of this omen, forwarded to the throne, supported the fait accompli. Then other strange things happened. The storehouse that now held the weapons collapsed without apparent cause (*yue naku*), so that an actual arsenal had to be constructed. Then Kanmu fell ill. Next, by happenstance, Takerube Chitsugu, a woman from the women's quarters sent as a court representative to attend a ceremony at the Kasuga shrine, heard that there was a new *kami* in the Nara area making utterances through a shamaness (*jofu*). Questioned by Takerube about the identity and the will of this *kami*, the shamaness refused to be specific except that it concerned no ordinary human being. Then she mentioned Kanmu's illness in connection with the "treasures that had defiled the court," but added that simply returning them would not do. First the emperor had to be beseeched by all the *kami* of the realm to order the return of the weapons.

Takerube secretly informed Kanmu, who ordered elaborate ceremonial measures to honor this *kami*. Subsequently, Takerube was sent back to tell the shamaness to appease this *kami*. After a whole night of ranting and raving that the message of the *kami* had not changed, the shamaness calmed down in the morning. Kanmu had sixty-nine monks (the number corresponding to his age, by Japanese reckoning) chant sutras in the Isonokami shrine. He also ordered the weapons returned to the shrine because, during his illness, he had been inspired in a great dream to follow the *kami*'s will and restore the weapons to the shrine.

Behind the twists and turns of this unusually detailed episode (possibly because a member of the shrine family was on the editorial board of the *Nihon kōki*), one suspects a tug-of-war between different interested parties attempting to have their policies prevail through recourse to different sources of the supernatural. The report about the whining arrows came from a student of (Chinese) literature and history (*monjōshō*) who happened to belong to the family of the Isonokami shrine's priest officials.[86] Yet the omen was interpreted in favor of the move that had already taken place. One may suspect that this was the opinion of yin-yang masters. Then two ominous events were reported, first as unrelated: the collapse of the warehouse, and the emperor's sickness. Enter the women who provided different avenues of information and solution. Still, whoever succeeded in mobilizing the shamaness into linking the two events was not able to reverse the policy. Finally, pretending not to side with any party, the emperor decided on his own accord, under divine inspiration, to solve both problems by restoring the traditional role of the Isonokami shrine and involving its powers as well to help him continue living (for one more year) "without fear or punishment, in peace and quiet."

THAT ORACULAR OR divinatory interpretations often hide hermeneutic and therefore political struggles should come as no surprise. The sources do not reveal them because the state was in control of yin-yang operations as well as the historical record. During the Heian period, however, when this episode was recorded, this changed.

We have seen how dissident voices concerning the Sawara affair left their traces in the record. This is even more evident once yin-yang knowledge spread through private operators beyond the confines of state institutions. Different schools of yin-yang specialists even developed. People consulted them for managing the quotidian affairs of their daily lives. They could even get a second opinion if they did not like the first one. Fujiwara Michinaga (966–1027) was in the habit of checking both the Abe and Kamo line of yin-yang specialists. He did so, for instance, after hearing about a ghost that appeared at Tōnomine. Abe Yoshihira told him to take precautionary measures, while Kamo Mitsuyoshi told him not to worry because the appearance concerned people born in a different year from Michinaga. Nevertheless, he locked the western entrance to his estate.[87] Yin-yang had stepped out of the shadows.

10 PURITY

The titles of the official ranks were modified. . . . There were
two Bright and four Pure ranks. . . . These were the ranks
for princes.
— 685/1/21 *Nihon shoki*

Kami should be revered and Buddhas honored by cultivat-
ing purity above anything else, but it is reported that on
the grounds of many *kami* shrines, filth accumulates and
animals are allowed to graze. A concerted effort has to be
made to increase cleanliness.
— 725/7/17 *Shoku Nihongi*

Even though some hold that *kami* matters should avoid the
Three Treasures . . . what used to be taboo, no longer is.
— 765/11/23 *Shoku Nihongi*

Purity as a distinct politico-religious value emerges in the *Nihon shoki*'s historically reliable part toward the end of Tenmu's rule — he died on
686/9/9 — when he brought the notion of a heavenly court into focus.[1] In
his reorganization of the official hierarchy (685/1/21), Tenmu set two ranks
for princes apart from and above the rest of officialdom, titling them *myō* 明
(bright/sacred) and *jō* 浄 (*kiyoi*; pure). A year and a half later, on 686/7/22,
he renamed his royal quarters Asuka *Kiyomi*hara no miya (Palace on the
Pure Plain of Asuka), and ordered scores of men of pure conduct to retire
from the world, the event celebrated by a meager feast. At the same time,
pagodas and shrines were to be cleaned.

"Men of pure conduct" (*jōgyōja*) refers to men who have undergone some
purification or ascetic practice, most likely consisting of sexual abstinence.[2]
Later entries in the *Shoku Nihongi* refer to men having been pure "for a
while" before being assigned tasks such as reciting sutras. This was the case
on 772/8/18, when such a ritual was ordered for the grave of Emperor Junnin, reburied because he had died a violent death. Monks were not ipso
facto pure, however, since some particularly pure ones were selected for
certain tasks such as praying for rain (705/6/27) or reciting sutras as protec-

tion against lightning (737/4/8). Others had to be pure "for a period of three years" before entering Buddhism (734/11/21).

Restoration of health could also be achieved, it was believed, through a "conversion" to Buddhism, even by surrogates. On 721/5/6 Empress Genmei, like her father-in-law Tenmu suffering from a bad liver (very ominous for rulers), similarly ordered "one hundred men and women selected for their pure conduct to enter the Way and apply themselves."[3]

Symbolics, however, had been part of Tenmu's political practice from the very beginning of his rule and even earlier. During his Jinshin campaign, or at least in the record of his campaign, he saluted (from quite some distance) Amaterasu in Ise and promoted *kami* the day after his victory (which he promptly reported to Jinmu's grave). Shortly after his coronation, he sent one of his daughters as *saiō* to Ise. Each of these pure princess-officiants because of their somatic link with their ruler presumably kept him pure. Great purifications were staged as pan-realm politico-liturgical events suggestive of a *tennō* at the center as the universal officiant with extraordinary purgatory power. Yoshino, with which Tenmu and especially Jitō had a strong bond, was a hallowed space of pristine beauty for experiencing the sacred. Purity stood out on Tenmu's and Jitō's ideological horizon.

Prototypes: Zhou Kings, Daoist Masters, Buddhist Meager F(e)asts

The pure as rulership's quintessential quality was not Tenmu's and Jitō's invention, although it was new in the archipelago. They reenacted their version of it when they fashioned a new polity of scale. This notion had been introduced in China's first great dynasty, the Zhou. Purity achieved by fasting, abstinence, ablutions, and bathing was deemed essential for signifying the royal court as special. The sacred character (*ming*) of Zhou-dynasty kings was tangibly expressed by the requirement that lords, before being received in audience, had to purify themselves in a special domain near the capital specifically designed for that purpose, the "domain for bathing and washing."[4]

Before the third century BCE, as Henri Maspero has shown in a magnificent essay, *ming* 明 did not have today's meaning of "light."[5] Instead, it marked what was separated from the mundane and profane: the king and the dead. In writings about the way of the Zhou dynasty, the graph *ming*, when combined with objects related to the dead, including offerings to their spirits, or with funeral attire, signaled them as "set aside" and separate from human communities.[6] This graph was also used for kings, whom one could not approach without undergoing prior purification.[7] The common meaning across this usage is a state of "passive taboo" for sacred objects reserved for the dead or subjected to temporary or permanent taboos with regard to royalty.[8]

This quality of "being apart," providing social and political distance with an existential foundation, was staged, and in the process made tangible and proven real, through temporary active taboos in matters of doing 禁, speaking 諱, and eating 忌 (fasting, mourning), or permanent passive ones regarding something that had been constituted as sacred in essence, such as the ruler.[9] Closely related to *ming* was the value of the "pure" (*jie* 潔; Jp. *ketsu, isagiyoi*), which could refer to the state of offerings, either being naturally unblemished or having been purified (usually through washing or by fire).[10]

Used alone, *ming* (*akitsu* of *akitsukami*, "manifest god") had the same meaning as *ling* 霊: sacred, royal majesty.[11] Originally, in Chinese high antiquity, it combined the notions of sacred and kingship, and in late-seventh-century Yamato it was used in the same manner in the *Nihon shoki* and *Ritsuryō. Shenming* 神明 (*akitsukami* reversed) thus also meant "the divine and the sacred (person or thing), and literally to be divine and sacred."[12]

One of the oldest philosophical texts from China (the *Guanzi*, fourth century BCE) makes purity or cleansing the necessary condition for the indwelling of spirits: "If you do not cleanse, the spirit will not remain."[13] Similarly, in Daoism, without cleansing oneself, one could not get in touch with the spirits within; they would leave. A Chinese Daoist master from the early eighth century put it succinctly by stating that "Daoist masters consider the virtue of the Way as their father, spirits [*shenming/shinmei*] as their mother, purity [*qingjing/shōjō*] as their teacher, and great harmony [*taihe/taiwa*] as their friend."[14] This is a line from the *Chuxue ji* (Record of Initial Learning), Xu Jian's collection of poems and miscellaneous literary works intended for Emperor Xuanzong.

Names of Daoist schools and texts often denote notions of purity, clarity, brightness, light, using characters such as *ming* 明, *qing* 清, or *jing* 浄.[15] It should be noted, however, that, although central to Daoism's view of the spiritual world, Daoism had no monopoly on the value of purity. For Buddhists, all forms of suffering, ignorance, and vice are impurities, hence the need to purify the six senses. In Buddhism, also, *qingjing/seijō* and *qingjing/shōsei* 清浄 are necessary qualities.[16] In the *Wuxing dayi* synthesis of yin-yang and Five Agents knowledge, these terms redundantly describe the pure realm of the East.[17]

When Daoist movements became institutionalized as religious groups in

China in the second century, their theocracies adopted and adapted court rituals and were structured with administrative titles borrowed from the Han polity.[18] In addition, the celestial masters were purists. The *Scripture on Great Peace (Taiping jing)* of the late second century CE encouraged its followers to confess their sins in "purity chambers."[19] They were also puritanical, being critical of the Han state's use of diviners on the one hand and of popular religious practices on the other, especially bloody sacrifices.[20] Daoists co-opted the practice of communal rural feasts honoring the god of the soil, removed the sacrifice component, and called them "kitchen" or "merit meals."[21]

Around the time that merit meals developed, Buddhists brought to China a similar practice called "meager feasts," vegetarian feasts. These may have originated in India as a Vedic practice. In Buddhism, they functioned as confessional assemblies. Entertaining monks with meager feasts was also a meritorious deed. In 584/9, the first meager meal in Yamato is mentioned. Tenmu sponsored a great meager meal on 681/17/15 and two more; the last one, held on 686/6/19 during his final illness, was accompanied by a "repentance of sins."

Trying to differentiate between the various mainland practices — statist, Daoist, and Buddhist — to identify the cultural flow into Yamato or their reenactment there may ultimately be a futile exercise. Nevertheless, some suggestive points can be made. Early Daoism's rejection of blood sacrifices in China did not hold up against the pressure of folk traditions. Buddhism's aversion to the consumption of meat, however, had greater staying power as the meager meals (Ch. *zhai*; Jp. *sai*), among other things, show. This term, however, came to have a broad meaning, referring to a variety of abstention practices in Buddhism and Daoism. The *Baopuzi* reports that, in preparing medicines and elixirs, rites of purification had to be observed, including ablutions or bathing.[22] For Lu Xiujing, the great fifth-century Daoist codifier of *zhai* ritual, consuming and offering meat and the "five strong-smelling vegetables" were proscribed and, as the *Baopuzi* states, were an obstacle to ascending to heaven.[23]

Abstinence

At the Chinese and Yamato courts, a period set apart for abstention practices preceded all major and most other rituals, the important distinction being between partial abstinence (Ch. *sanzhai*; Jp. *sanzai* or *ara-imi*) and full or rigorous abstinence (Ch. *zhizhai*; Jp. *chisai* or *ma-imi*). In Yamato, the Taihō Code included a meat taboo as part of such abstinence, but this proscription was absent in the Tang Code. It should be noted, however, that animal sacrifices, tabooed in early Daoism but subsequently tolerated, were also widely practiced in the archipelago. They included the sacrifice of horses, often for rainmaking purposes (recorded to have taken place as late as 1501).[24] One wonders whether the Taihō meat taboo for officials was instituted with one eye directed at local practices, not to change them, however, as was the case in Daoist theocracies, but as yet one more device to set the court apart from the world of commoners.

A comparison of stipulations regarding rituals and purity taboos as they relate to the emperor in the Taihō Code and the Tang Penal Code shows the degree to which the Yamato ruler was surrounded by stricter taboos than his Tang counterpart.[25] Although lapses in various aspects of the preparation for rituals were penalized less in Yamato than in China, with taboo rules it was the opposite.[26]

Prescriptions varied for great, middle, and small festivals. In China, great festivals were important sacrifices that were the emperor's responsibility; as the principal ritual intermediary between the realm and Heaven, he had to be able to perform his function properly. In Yamato, only one festival belonged to that category, namely the Daijō-sai, the Great New Food Festival, held at the enthronement of a new emperor. Yamato's one and only great festival was centered on the persona of the emperor as such. The periods of full abstention (*chisai*) for this rank of festival were identical in both countries (three days), but there was an enormous difference in the period of partial abstention (*sanzai*): only four days in China, but thirty in Japan.[27]

Sanzai taboos in both countries included refraining from offering condolences, inquiring after the sick, issuing verdicts on punishments or death penalties, or administering them. Japan counted one additional taboo, namely, the consumption of meat.[28] Punishments for breaking any of these taboos were the same in Japan and China: fifty blows of the light stick. However, the purity of the Japanese ruler was guarded more strictly. Anyone memorializing the emperor about any of the taboo topics would receive seventy blows of the heavy stick, ten more than in China. For infringements during the period of full abstention, the penalties were increased by two degrees in Japan, one degree in China.

If purity was the condition for spirits to be present and the state to function, this liturgical logic extended to the sanctuaries of the spirits as the Yamato court increasingly called upon established religious institutions on various occasions. Cleaning and cleansing the body and sacred sites constituted a religious practice. In 686/5, during his final illness, Tenmu ordered that the "halls and pagodas of all the temples be swept and cleansed (*haki-*

kiyomeshimu)," followed less than two months later, on 7/3, by a great purification in all the provinces. In the early eighth century, keeping sanctuaries clean (清浄 *seijō*) on a regular basis was legislated first for Buddhist temples in 716/5/15 in a decree that drew a dismal picture of neglected temples, worship halls, and their shabby grounds; and again in 725/7/17, this time also for *kami* sanctuaries. "Filth [droppings] from grazing animals," the decree specified, "ought to be removed from the precincts." Cleanliness was, so to speak, upheld as a condition for holiness, or perhaps it was "stateliness" that was targeted in the structures servicing the state.

When the first of these two decrees was issued, Prince Nagaya was in charge of the Department of Personnel (or Ceremonial), and by 725 he had been promoted to the post of minister of the right. Nagaya was known for his rigor and his demanding efforts to improve the quality of public service. It would have been in character for him to have taken the initiative in this matter. At least, he must have given these measures his full support. This was also the time that *hafuri* from several thousand sanctuaries across the country became enrolled as servants of the Office of the Kami. Thus, the decrees regarding the physical appearance of temples and shrines were most likely related to the increased use of religious sites by the government for official purposes. In other words, these decrees may have been meant precisely for such sanctuaries and most likely for them only.

Purity as a Weapon

Purity in Tenmu's time was used primarily, as far as one can judge, to set the ruler and his close kin apart from common humanity and give them cosmic significance. Under Shōtoku, however, we discover that a notion developed, probably in limited ritualist circles, especially in Ise perhaps, that *kami* and Buddha "should not touch."

Ise may well have been a rare ritual center where the stakes of control were particularly high, resulting first in the establishment of a Buddhist presence within its precincts, then its removal — certainly the polar opposite of the thoroughly syncretistic Usa Hachiman shrine in Kyushu. Thus for Ise ritualists, "impurity" became a stigmatizing marker for Buddhist sites; taboos on terms for Buddhist items were established; and "filth" and "pollution" became weapons in ritualist turf battles. From its physical meaning of "dirt out of place" (to use Mary Douglas' famous definition of pollution) in precincts of temples and *kami* sanctuaries alike, where filth had to be removed by imperial decree, impurity came to be used in the controversy against Buddhism. Some people also were stigmatized in that way for the first time as far we know.

When Wake Kiyomaro, the captain (*shōken*) of the guard who had been sent to Usa to check the oracle's accuracy came back with bad news for Shōtoku and Dōkyō, he was demoted and banished to Kyushu; his sister nun, who had been assigned the mission in the first place, was laicised and banished to Bingo. Kiyomaro's name was mud, and was accordingly changed from "Pure (*kiyo*) Maro" to Kitanamaro, "Dirty Maro," but reinstituted with his name restored within one year of Kōnin's accession. After his uprising, Nakamaro was spoken of by Kōken as "that filthy fellow." Impurity came to be used as a public stigma.

Protecting the Realm against Impurity

The great purification ceremony, instituted under Tenmu, was the ultimate occasion when state power and spiritual efficacy were orchestrated. A twice yearly great purification was eventually legislated in the Taihō codes, to be held on the last days of the sixth and the twelfth months. In the beginning, it took place when needed, and it continued to be ordered on special occasions for safeguarding the realm against natural disasters and other calamities.[29] The regular yearly rituals most probably became institutionalized under Jitō toward the end of the seventh century.[30]

The allochthons' interpretive skill in matters of signs must have resulted in a marked increase in the population of the unseen world. On 637/2/23, Min, the allochthon monk who had returned from China after two dozen years of study, was arguing with people about a shooting star streaking through the sky that night. He was trying to enlighten them that what had passed over their heads was not a shooting star, but a *tengu*, a kind of benevolent devil. Several years later, on 650/2/9, foreign experts explained to the gathered court the meaning of a three-legged crow and its degree of auspiciousness as compared to that of a white pheasant. As mentioned earlier, allochthon *fuhito* from Yamato and Kawachi performed the exorcism part of the great purification ceremonies, using an unadulterated Daoist spell.

Exorcists were called upon regularly to remove evil spiritual matter that seemed to be generated with the passing of time, as inevitably as the succession of the seasons. They performed the great purification ritual at the gate of the imperial palace in the presence of all high officials. When evil was removed from the center, it was cast out from the realm.

Another type of allochthon talent was housed in the Yin-yang Bureau.

Through prognostications, yin-yang masters were able to track the presence and movement of cosmic forces and to devise rituals accordingly to prevent evil from spreading and causing harm. Of the thirteen yearly ceremonies held at the court of the *ritsuryō* state (some held twice, which explains the total of nineteen performances) three (each performed twice) were conducted by them: one to protect the capital against spirits, another one against fire, and a third one against contagious diseases (see table 2). In 737, the *michiae* roadside festival to feed the hungry spirit carriers of contagious diseases was held along the highway that led from the northern end of Kyushu to Nara, the path followed by the smallpox disease that year. Such festivals were held regularly at the corners of the palace, of the capital, and at several sites along rivers in the Home Provinces.

To keep evil spirits and pollution away was the purpose of these protective rituals. During Kanmu's reign, however, a new and particularly dangerous type of spirit appeared, the Goryō, honorable spirits of unjustly condemned famous personalities, avenging themselves as vengeful spirits, *onryō*, by unleashing contagious diseases. Although Kanmu had taken precautionary measures against some of them for personal reasons, it was commoners who linked the spirits to natural calamities and thus made a big issue out of a number of political scandals, in the process raising the stakes of spirit protection. These spirits could not be kept out, and neither was it easy to appease them. Protection against them was no longer a matter of casting them out. They did not come from the outside; they were inside and there to stay, or if they were not, they were actually invited in to appease them. They were structurally part of the realm, and specifically linked to administrative issues of justice, while evil *ki* were primarily cosmically defined. The most powerful of these spirits, Prince Sawara's, had thwarted efforts to contain it in its grave on Awaji Island where the corpse had been sent in exile and was brought in when given an abode in a new grave in Yamato province. Sanctuaries were built for them, and they were celebrated in grand style at the Goyō-e in 863.

Goryō aside, the capital, the palace, and the emperor himself above anything else needed to be preserved in a state of purity. During the Heian period, a full-fledged casuistry developed, legal as well as ritual, overdetermining the daily life and routines of officials and commoners living in the capital. In the tenth century, cases where the degree of pollution and corresponding level of purification could not be determined first by the metropolitan police (*kebiishi*), then by legal experts (*myōhō hakase*), or the highest authorities such as the regent were brought before the emperor to decide.[31] As this obsession spread, yin-yang masters offered their services

to commoners for their private use. As mentioned, several houses of specialists were available, allowing a choice if one was not pleased with a particular
brand of prognostication.

By then, yin-yang specialists were no longer employed only by the state.
Many of them were free entrepreneurs eliciting awe and building reputa-
tions as masters in the world of magic. In the *Shin sarugaku-ki*, Fujiwara
Akihira conjures up such a popular image when he describes powers of the
yin-yang master Dosei from the Kamo house:

> He can divine hidden items as clearly as if he saw them with his eyes. He can
> conjure auguries from weird phenomena as if he were showing you the palm
> of his hand. He orders the Twelve Spirit Generals around, and lines up the
> Thirty-Six Birds. He serves the Spirit of the Divination Board, makes the laws
> that govern talismans, opens and closes the eyes of spirits, interacts with male
> and female spirits.... The reason is that he has only the physical shape of a
> human, but his mind gets through to the spirits. His body resides among us,
> but he controls Heaven and Earth.[32]

This work dates from 1052, when purity and pollution had become central cultural concerns in the capital. Contemporaries linked it even with
what one could call Japanese identity. Minister of the Right Fujiwara Sanesuke reflected in his diary entry (the *Shōyūki*) of 1027/8/25 that this attention paid to pollution (*kegare*) was distinctly Japanese because pollution
taboos did not exist in China.[33]

Toward the end of the Heian period, notions of purity and pollution
were marshaled full force to produce social stigma that would increase over
time and eventually get further strengthened through legislation during
the Tokugawa period.[34] The Tenmu dynasty witnessed the beginnings of
a social application of the purity-impurity pair without, however, reaching
the level of intensity it acquired centuries later.

Senmin, Base People

The contrast between pure and impure, although not explicitly legislated
for social groups, probably started to become implicitly associated with the
legal classifications of free and unfree as "good people" (*ryōmin*) and "base
people" (*senmin*) formulated in the Taihō Code of 702. This official distinction between two tiers of subjects itself developed gradually in the last
decades of the seventh century.

We do not know much about the first population register, drawn up toward the end of Tenji's reign in 670, but there is no doubt that social catego-

ries were scrambled five years later. In a center-strengthening move, Tenmu abolished the *be* then, the dependent, subordinate groups of workers owned by the *uji* lineage groups; they were allowed, however, to keep their slaves. The aim was to broaden central authority and widen the state's tribute base. This "liberated" population was given a public status as "official servants" with the term *ame no shita no ōontakara* (meaning "great treasure under heaven," written with the graphs *kōmin*, "public people").[35] Removed from lineage control and appropriated by the state, they became tribute payers.

In Jitō's new population register of 690, and in an edict of 691/3/22, the *ryōmin/senmin* dyad of good/base people was introduced.[36] The status became hereditary, intermarriage between the two was prohibited, and slaves were not allowed to have (probably meaning "officially use") family names. Ultimately, the Taihō and Yōrō codes specified a number of social occupations besides slaves as being "base."

The good people were free, full members of tribute-paying households, which included commoners as well as the nobility (but not royals). Male and female slaves (*nuhi*), either privately owned or government property, constituted the core of the base people. This class consisted of "five base (occupational) groups" or *go* (*shiki no*) *sen* and seems to have included most of those who performed menial labor, some of them, such as the tomb guards, holding jobs that initially were probably not considered defiling. These five groups were the guards of the imperial tombs, government menials and servants in the royal and noble houses (*tomobe*), manual and skilled laborers (*zakko*), prebend or sustenance households (*fuko*), and slaves.[37]

In Sui and Tang China also, free and unfree people had been demarcated, the latter category including, besides slaves, a number of groups barred from the ritual order. Like criminals or people in mourning, they were considered unclean and hence kept away from religious celebrations.[38] On the peninsula, Silla had plenty of slaves, but the Chinese *ryōmin/senmin* status labels were introduced only in the tenth century under the Koryŏ dynasty.[39]

Compared to the Tang, in the Yamato hierarchy the distance between the two poles, the emperor and the slaves, was magnified, not only through an emphasis on ritual purity surrounding the emperor as mentioned above, but also by modifying the sartorial color coding of distinctions that signified what people were by what they wore. In Yamato, slaves were not assigned yellow, the color they shared with commoners in Tang China, but black. This color had been the stigmatizing mark for particularly despised groups of skinners, butchers, and merchants under the previous Sui dynasty.

In other words, Jitō used black to resuscitate a difference that had been dropped in the Tang. This color set slaves apart from commoners, who had to wear yellow. Jitō did this in a decree of 693/1/2, when the other end of the social spectrum was also highlighted. On that day, Jitō granted *jō* court rank to Prince Takechi (the presumed heir) and two other princes (Naga and Yuge) and made the "official servants" (*ōmitakara*, basically the free people) wear yellow and the slaves (*yatsuko*) black, the color that in the late seventh century became also the color for mourning. The contrast, however, was not only between black and pure, but also between black, the color for slaves, and white, presumably reserved for the emperor.[40]

The emperor was not marked by any official sign that allocated a hierarchical slot for lineages and nobles through names, ranks, rank-specific colors, official attire, or positions. He clearly stood above them, the source and origin of all signs. This included official attire, which the officials themselves did not procure but received from the emperor at the time of their appointments. Unmarked, the emperor was meant to be the unsignified signifier.

It is estimated that during the Nara period, before the *senmin* legal category was abolished in 787, when the offspring of mixed marriages were no longer considered *senmin*, between 4 and 10 percent of the total population were slaves.[41] Were they, perhaps, seen as polluted?

The question of pollution is complex, but has undoubtedly a strong social component.[42] Death and birth pollution developed as an issue only around matters related to the court and its rituals, matters that, I should add, go back to Tenmu's use of purity to mark his court. Guards posted at the mausolea of rulers (*hakamori*), not listed among *senmin* in the Taihō Code of 702, were so listed sixteen years later in the draft of the Yōrō Code, when they became hereditary houses attached to the mausolea (*ryōko*). Until then, tombs were sacred sites rather than sources of pollution.

The slaves owned by temples in China, Korea, and Japan had criminal backgrounds. They performed odd jobs, principally cleaning the buildings and grounds, a task that constituted also a punishment for monks. Thus, the demeaning connotation associated with purifying tasks had an old association with criminality, discipline, and punishment.[43]

Scholars have tentatively concluded that the status assigned to slaves in Buddhism differed from that in Daoism. Although, as I have emphasized, purity was a value central to Daoism, it played no role in the perception of slaves. In early Daoism, slaves were one of nine categories of believers and could become immortals.[44] Their place in Chinese Buddhism is unclear. Some unorthodox sutras allowed them to become monks; others put as a condition that their masters set them free first. In Nara Japan, they could not enter orders. This, however, changed in the Heian period, when, once set free, they could join a monastery. Saichō, the founder of Tendai, is believed to have been the first one to allow this.[45]

The Impure, Foreground and Background

When, in 764, Empress Kōken acceded to the throne a second time as Shōtoku Tennō and a nun, she declared that "what used to be kept apart by taboo was no longer tabooed." In 774, however, the ritualists in charge of Ise reinstated the taboo, as far as Ise was concerned, with the consent of the *kami*. A curse (*tatari*) had signaled that the Buddhist temple that had been joined to the Ise shrine had to be moved away and again even further in 780, in response to continued *kami* dissatisfaction. This was referred to as the need "to purify and cleanse" (*harae-kiyomete*) a Buddhist site, following a curse of the Illustrious Kami, to make it a *kami* site."[46]

Thus, purity and pollution became foregrounded as weapons by ritualists in a competition for the control of a major ritual center. In this controversy, it was no longer a matter of removing filth from sanctuaries in service of the government for ritual reasons. Pollution was used to stigmatize publicly a rival, Buddhism. Wake Kiyomaro's identity was changed to "Dirty Maro," Nakamaro was a "dirty fellow."

Undoubtedly, these terms — "polluted," "dirty," "filthy"— had a colloquial currency. While in ritualistic settings their use follows a predetermined course of meaning, in the above examples they jump to the fore as colloquial averments of contempt, explicitly targeting groups or individuals; at first sight, they seem to be isolated examples of an arbitrary assignment of meaning.

Yet as Pierre Bourdieu has argued with regard to gender differences, in any particular setting an opposition such as purity/pollution, "arbitrary when taken in isolation, receives its objective and subjective necessity from its insertion into a system of homologous oppositions." Bourdieu spells out the complex interplay of such visions of division as follows:

> Being similar in difference, these oppositions are sufficiently concordant to support one another, in and through the inexhaustible play of practical transfers and metaphors, and sufficiently divergent to give each of them a kind of semantic thickness, resulting from over determination by harmonics, connotations and correspondences.[47]

Such correspondences did exist in ancient Japan. They could even be packed into the small space of a short poem (*tanka*), which could, even though limited to a realistic description, trigger a chain of oppositions stored in "common sense" contrasts without recourse to explicit metaphoric transfer, an operation the reader or listener performs unknowingly. A *Manyōshū* poem by Naga no Okimaro, a courtier of the late seventh–early eighth centuries, reveals such doxa of the time (of all time?).

The explicit thematics of the title of the poem, highly significant in themselves, were conceived as a challenge to fit the conceptual pieces together in an original manner, meaningful culturally in the widest sense. The poetic result of the assignment "a poem about incense, a pagoda, a privy, a crucian carp, and a slave" was a play with oppositions hiding behind contrasts:

> Don't come near the pagoda —
> It's been rubbed with fragrant oil —
> You filthy slave girl
> Mouth reeking of the shit-carp caught
> In this stinking river bend![48]

The poem dips into commonsensical oppositions, interweaving and mutually reinforcing a number of binaries, forced to be seen in their unity in a mere five short lines: social (free/unfree), sexual (male/female), age and gender ("girl"), religious (sacred/sacrilegious; Buddhist/secular), spatial and cultural distanciation (pagoda/outhouse over the river; "don't come near"), all colored by the fundamental opposition between pure and impure, somatized and naturalized by the physical one (fragrant oil/shit); in the end, a cognitive structure nothing more complicated than a vision of the division of reality "based on an accentuation of certain differences and the scotomization of certain similarities."[49]

These oppositions define social universes that should spatially be kept separate, and are set up as negatively marked differences ultimately based on the undisputable reality of the senses, specifically olfactory repulsion, a kind of somatic doxa. The sense of smell impregnates one's entire being, collapsing instantaneously the felt into the known, producing in this way a most natural metaphor, unnoticed as such. Thus, the pure/impure binary metaphor can present itself as the fundamental opposition that defines the others.

It would be foolish to attempt a history of each of these oppositions, how they came to relate among themselves and to the one I interpret as fundamental. From the historical record, however, we know that purity and cleansing were particularly valued in Daoism and that Buddhism posited a Pure Land over and against this world; that purity was singled out as a politico-religious emblem by Tenmu and concentrated in the *tennō*, the center sacralized through taboos of realmwide expiatory offerings when great purification ceremonies were held; that, on the other hand, "baseness" was a legal stigma attached to the socially unfree under Jitō's rule; that cleaning and sweeping were legislated, first for temples and then for shrines in early Nara, as appropriate, obligatory, and even as a form of clerical punishment as defined in the codes; and finally, that Shōtoku brushed aside taboo notions whereby *kami* and buddhas should be kept apart, but without succeeding in preventing the Nakatomi high *kami* ritualists from arguing that *kami* sites had to be pure of Buddha presence and that the two had to be separated spatially in Ise.

The pair pure/impure was put to a variety of uses during the short Tenmu dynasty. This was only the beginning of a long career spanning more than twelve centuries. Its lingering effects still reverberate today.

ABBREVIATIONS

Cd   *Cosmologie et divination dans la Chine ancienne: Le compendium des cinq agents (Wuxing dayi, VIᵉ siècle)*, by Marc Kalinowski. Paris: École française d'Extrême-Orient, 1991

CdEA   *Cahiers d'Extrême-Asie*

CHC   *The Cambridge History of China.* 15 vols. Cambridge: Cambridge University Press, 1987–2002

CHJ   *The Cambridge History of Japan.* 6 vols. Cambridge: Cambridge University Press, 1988–1999

DH   *Daoism Handbook.* Edited by Livia Kohn. Leiden: Brill, 2000

Gt   *Gogyō taigi.* By Nakamura Shohachi. Chūgoku koten shinsho. Tokyo: Meitoku shuppansha, 1973

HAKB   *Higashi Ajia no kodai bunka*

JAS   *Journal of Asian Studies*

JJRS   *Japanese Journal of Religious Studies*

JJS   *Journal of Japanese Studies*

KBKK   *Kokubungaku kaishaku to kaishō*

KDJ   *Kokushi daijiten.* 15 vols. Tokyo: Yoshikawa kōbunkan, 1979–1994

KST   *(Shintei zōhō) kokushi taikei.* 66 vols. Tokyo: Yoshikawa kōbunkan, 1929–1967

LL   *Légitimités, légitimations: La construction de l'authorité au Japon.* Edited by Anne Bouchy et al. Paris: École française d'Extrême-Orient, 2005

MN   *Monumenta Nipponica*

NKBT   *Nihon koten bungaku taikei.* 102 vols. Tokyo: Iwanami shoten, 1958–1969

NSK   *Nihon shoki.* 2 vols. NKBT 67, 68

NST   Nihon shisō taikei. 67 vols. Tokyo: Iwanami shoten, 1970–1982

OMS   *Onmyōdō sōsho.* Edited by Murakami Shūichi. 4 vols. Tokyo: Meicho shuppan, 1991–1993

SNG   *Shoku Nihongi.* 6 vols. SNKBT 12–16

SNKBT   *Shin Nihon koten bungaku taikei.* 99 vols. Tokyo: Iwanami shoten, 1989–

TASJ   *Transactions of the Asiatic Society of Japan*

Chapter 1: Bricolage

Epigraphs: *Kaifūsō*, 81; SNG 1: 121.

1. In Chinese records, the archipelago is referred to as the land of Wo (Japanese pronunciation, Wa), written with one of the graphs adopted by the islanders themselves to refer to Yamato (today's Nara prefecture), the site of the first Yamato kingdom in the fourth century. The earliest reference to the land of Wo (meaning "dwarfs," although arguably the graph had only a phonetic and no semantic value) is found in *Shanhai jing* (The Classic of Mountains and Seas; compiled between 300 BCE and 250 CE). Wo is listed there among "mountains, deities, mythical creatures and foreign peoples and lands," which include "the cosmic Kunlun Mountains and the Queen Mother of the West," two Daoist icons that predate Daoism; see Nakagawa, "The *Shan-hai ching* and Wo," 46, 48. It is debated to what extent the Kyushu chiefdoms mentioned in the third-century *Wei zhi* (Annals of the Kingdom of Wei, 220–265) shared cultural traits with counterparts in the coastal regions of south China, especially the states of Wu and Yue. Over time, the term Wa became limited to the archipelago, and by the seventh century it referred to Japan as a whole; see Hudson, "Ethnicity in East Asian Archaeology," 46–63, esp. 54, 58. For information regarding Japan in the early Chinese dynastic histories, see de Bary et al., *Sources of Japanese Tradition* (2nd ed.), 1: 6–13. For a discussion of Chinese records in the light of archeological findings, see Farris, *Sacred Texts*, chap. 1. Zhenping Wang treats many of these issues in his *Ambassadors*.

2. For the recent view that the early eighth century considered Tenji rather than Tenmu as the founder of the lineage, see Kimoto, *Nara-chō seiji to kōi keishō*, chap. 1; Inoue Wataru, *Nihon kodai no tennō to saigi*, 46–48; Fujidō, "Ritsuryō kokka no koki," 17, 24; Mizubayashi, "Ritsuryō tennōsei (1)," 150–158.

3. Yoshie Akiko has demonstrated that before the end of the seventh century, a sovereign's consorts enjoyed an independent status in a society that was bilateral; they often maintained their own residence, as did Jitō before she succeeded Tenmu. See Yoshie, "Gender in Early Classical Japan," 438 (status), 439 (bilateral), 467 (Jitō); see also Farris, *Sacred Texts*, 227–228.

4. On the historiographical controversy surrounding the Taika Reform, see Farris, *Sacred Texts*, 203–209.

5. The titles for rulers changed over time. Even *tennō* fell in disuse between 1200 and 1840 (Watanabe Hiroshi, *Higashi Ajia no ōken*, 7). Ancient Japan's rulers were *kimi*, kings among other kings (*uji* leaders), until the second half of the fifth century, when Yūryaku (456–479), the twenty-first in the Sun line, seemingly adopted the title of *ōkimi* (great king) to signal preeminence over other warrior kings (Kumagai, *Ōkimi*, 13, 123; Piggott, *Emergence*, 54. Under Tenmu, *tennō* (heavenly sovereign) replaced "great king." I shall translate *tennō* as heavenly sov-

ereign for the beginning of the Tenmu dynasty when the connotation of heavenly rulership was new. Otherwise, when referring to particular rulers, I shall adopt the conventional "emperor" or omit the title altogether.

6. The Taihō Code is no longer extant, but its slightly modified version, the Yōrō Code, compiled two decades later (promulgated in 757), has been reconstructed almost completely from a number of later legal commentaries, which also remark on differences between the Taihō and Yōrō codes. Hence, we have a fairly trustworthy understanding of the minor differences between the two codes. References to the Taihō Code in this study, in the narrow documentary sense, are thus to the Yōrō Code. Chronologically, the year 701, when its draft was completed, is meant, or 702, the year of its promulgation.

7. The Yamato basin consists of a few provinces around Yamato province, later called the Kinai or Home Provinces, an area that includes Asuka, Nara, and the Osaka-Kyoto regions.

8. "Nonroyal" here means non-Yamato royal, because Kanmu's mother hailed from the Paekche (Korea) royal family, which had sought refuge in Japan in the late seventh century.

9. Mizubayashi Takeshi has calculated that the comparative number of pages per year for each of the last thirteen rulers (539–697) minus Tenmu in the *Nihon shoki* (in a modern edition) varies between 0.4 and 2.67 (1 being the value given to Tenji's yearly average), compared to Tenmu, whose average was 9.33. In this computation, the chapter on the Jinshin War, which lasted only one month, was counted as one year. See Mizubayashi, "Ritsuryō tennōsei (2)," 107.

10. The *Rikkokushi* (Six National Histories) covers Japanese history up to 887 in six volumes, starting with the *Nihon shoki* and *Shoku Nihongi*. For an in-depth analysis of the historiographical aspects of these chronicles, see Sakamoto, *Six National Histories*. On the Sawara question, see 116–117.

11. Some ten pages of exclusively genealogical data for the rulers after Kenzō bring the information, but not the narrative, down to 628.

12. John Bentley notes that "[t]he 'Age of the Gods' section of the *Nihon shoki* contains 49 quotations from variant sources — none of which are named" (*Authenticity*, 48).

13. For a discussion of plausibility as a standard between objectivity and subjectivity in historical writing, see my *Tokugawa Ideology*, 10.

14. Several Japanese editions of the *Kojiki* exist. Unless indicated otherwise, I shall refer to NST 1 (p. 15 for this reference). For Philippi's English translation, I shall refer simply to Philippi (p. 41 in question). Unless otherwise noted, dates before 697 refer to entries in the *Nihon shoki*, and those between 697 and 791 to its sequel, the *Shoku Nihongi*. I use the NKBT edition of the former (vols. 67, 68) and Aston's English translation (Aston) and the standard six-volume critical edition of the latter (SNG). A prewar English translation for the early years (697–715) of the *Shoku Nihongi* by J. B. Snellen can be found in TASJ 11 and 14. Bruno Lewin made an excellent and very useful German translation (*Die Regierungsannalen*) abundantly annotated, of Kanmu's reign (781–806), culled from the last five chapters of the *Shoku Nihongi*, the *Nihon kōki*, and passages from the *Nihon kiryaku*.

15. The consensus is that penal codes (*ritsu*) were not part of the Kiyomihara Code. A much later document from the early Heian period refers to an "Ōmi Code," of questionable historicity, an administrative code allegedly issued by Tenji in 668.

16. Mizubayashi Takeshi (*Kiki shinwa*, 331) interprets an entry of 689/8/2 in the *Nihon shoki* in that way. It reads, "All official functionaries assembled in the Jingikan [the Kami Office, mentioned here by its *ritsuryō* title for the first time] for a proclamation by the sovereign [Jitō as regent] concerning matters of the Kami of Heaven and Earth."

17. See *uji/kabane* in *Rekishigaku jiten*, 10: 43–44.

18. Umezawa, *Kiki hihan*, 371–373.

19. Mizubayashi, *Kiki shinwa*, 208–210.

20. For a study and new translation of the *Kogoshūi* text (2002), see Bentley, *Historiographical Trends*, chaps. 2, 3. Bentley has also produced a thorough linguistic study with translation of the *Sendai kuji hongi*, a royal genealogy with the middle chapters devoted to the two *uji* (*Authenticity*). The text argues (82n45, 156–162) that Ninigi, when sent down by Amaterasu to rule the land, was given a far greater escort than reported in the *Kojiki*: thirty-two *kami* and an additional twenty-five *kami* from the Mononobe lineage as military protectors.

21. The lawsuit was initiated and resolved in 716, reopened in 775, and received a different settlement in 792. Bentley, *Historiographical Trends*, 39–42, 93–102.

22. Brownlee, "Ideological Control," 131–132.

23. For the *Kaifūsō*, I use *Kaifūsō, Bunka shūreishū, Honchō monzui* (NKBT 69); for the *Manyōshū*, Edwin Cranston's superb partial translation in his *Waka Anthology*, henceforward referred to as Cranston.

24. Mauclaire, "Que transmettre par l'adoption?" 174.

25. Kouchi, *Kodai seijishi*, 22. The three transitions during the Heian period were those from Emperors Montoku through Seiwa to Yōzei (850–884), Kōkō through Uda to Daigo (884–930), and Shirakawa to Tōba (1072–1123). Tenmu's successors will be dealt with in detail later.

26. Sakaue, *Ritsuryō kokka no tenkan*, 72–76; *Ritsuryō*, NST 3: 281–282.

27. The decision to give Tenji a tumulus was made on 699/10/13. On Tenji's resurrection as founder, displacing Tenmu, see Fujidō, "Tenji misasagi," 4–5.

28. This happened on 760/12/12, six months after the death of Shōmu's empress Kōmyo (Mizubayashi, *Kiki shinwa*, 340–342; and SNG 1: 346n161). By Kanmu's time, sixteen *koki* had been established; he reduced these to seven, arguing that they were too numerous, and redrawing the ancestral line in the process (KDJ 5: 597–598, "*koki*").

29. The early Meiji government filled the gap in the "unbroken line" by restoring Junnin's nodal position when it reintroduced him, fully vested, as Emperor Junnin.

30. *Ritsuryō*, NST 3: 281–282; KDJ 2: 442, "*ō*"; Ishi, *Nihon sozoku hōshi*, 24–30. For commoners, inheritance was partible among all children, main heirs and others, including those of concubines, and regardless of sex (*Ritsuryō*, NST 3: 232). Primogeniture was recognized for commoners in a procedure (*shiki*) of 721 and

added to the Yōro Code whereby the eldest son received half of the heritage, a rule that also applied to the nobility's material estates. Yet partible inheritance continued to be practiced (KDJ 9: 452, "*chakushi*").

31. *Ritsuryō*, NST 3: 228. See Mauclaire, "La construction du rôle du père," 29–33.

32. Kouchi lists some of these points (*Kodai seijishi*, 29).

33. The first three female monarchs on record, Suiko and Kōgyoku (the latter, according to the official record, ruling a second time as Saimei), appear in the first half of the seventh century, and chronologically the last two took the throne a thousand years later, during the Tokugawa period, in 1629 (Empress Meishō) and 1762 (Empress Gosakuramachi). In between, female rulers occupied the throne only in the Tenmu dynasty. The last one, Shōtoku, had ruled a first time under the name of Kōken. The historicity of the reign (642–645) of female "Great King" Kōgyoku and her abdication, which is the first one reported in the *Nihon shoki*, is questioned by Kouchi, *Kodai seijishi*, 57–60.

34. Portal, *Korea: Art and Archeology*, 59.

35. *Kisaki* was only one of the titles for the main consort, and in some cases it may have been added by the editors of the *Nihon shoki* to enhance the legitimacy of the progeny of some consorts.

36. Piggott, "Chieftain Pairs," 17–52. Wondering about this loss of variation in the gene pool, I inquired with a geneticist, who explained that the probability of a child's inheriting recessive genes because his or her father and mother were related did not increase beyond a one-in-four chance, even after several generations.

37. On the complicated matters of Bidatsu's successors and Tenji's own succession, see Kouchi, "Ōi keishōhō shikiron," 74–81; idem, *Kodai seijishi*, 47–60.

38. For the construction of the myths surrounding Shōtoku Taishi, see Michael Como, *Shōtoku: Ethnicity, Ritual and Violence in the Japanese Buddhist Tradition* (Oxford: Oxford University Press, 2008); and Shinkawa Tokio, *Shōtoku Taishi no rekishigaku: kioku to sōzō no 1400 nen* (Tokyo: Kodansha, 2007).

39. Kouchi, *Kodai seijishi*, 58, 60.

40. After his father became Great King Jomei in 629, Tenji was called Naka no Ōe, "middle senior prince," indicating him as the preferred candidate for the throne. Only fifteen years old at Jomei's death, he was probably considered too young to take over, but in 645 he was officially being referred to as crown prince, a title he sustained for twenty-three years (645–668).

41. Kouchi, *Kodai seijishi*, 61–62; idem, "Ōi keishōhō," 80–83.

42. It is only after the Tenmu dynasty, when on 806/3/17 the regalia or symbols of imperial authority were handed over by the dying Kanmu to his successor, that succession acquired the air of being automatic; see *Nihon kōki*, 339. The late date for his transmission of supreme authority to develop points to the shaky nature of dynastic mechanics, especially inasmuch as Chinese practice must have been known. Even as far back as the Western Han, accession occurred preferably the day following the death of the emperor, while the Eastern Han moved it up to the same day (Goodman, *Ts'ao P'i*, 34).

43. Less than thirty years later Tenmu used Furuhito's tactic successfully when he also retired to Yoshino, from where to start his rebellion.

44. Prince Ōtsu, accused of plotting by Jitō a few days after his father Tenmu's death and promptly executed, had another daughter of Ishikawa and Tenji as his mother; see figure 4.

45. Ebersole, *Ritual Poetry*, 229.

46. Inoue Mitsusada, "The Century of Reform," 203–204. He reappears at court during Tenji's reign and was appointed minister of the left by Tenmu.

47. Saimei engaged in massive public works, especially those of national defense, related to the wars on the Korean peninsula. She sought the expansion of the Yamato imperium by attempting to reconquer Paekche and reestablish its exiled king and by launching an expedition against the Emishi (Kumagai, *Ōkimi*, 292, 302).

48. For other genealogical diagrams, see Saigō, *Jinshinki o yomu*, 16–17; Terasaki, *Nagaya-ō*, 9, 28; and especially Inoue Wataru, *Nihon kodai no tennō to saigi*, 32.

49. Bidatsu's son received the title imperial ancestor senior [crown] prince; the grandmother and mother (Saimei) were imperial ancestral mother (Kouchi, "Ōi keishōhō," 83). These were cumbersome titles, their pronunciation remaining an open question. Motoori Norinaga reads them as *ōmi*; others suggest *sumemi* (*Nihon shoki*, NKBT 68: 567n2).

50. On the succession question surrounding the Jinshin civil war, see M. Inoue, "Reform," 216–219.

51. In the opening paragraph of the first of Tenmu's two chapters in the *Nihon shoki*, one reads that Tenji made Tenmu heir apparent when Tenji assumed the throne in 668/1. Yet the preceding Tenji chapter does not record this event. Tenmu is represented several times as the heir, on 669/10/15 and 671/1/16 and 5/5, while Prince Ōtomo was made *daijōdaijin* (chancellor, 671/1), this title from the later *ritsuryō* legal codes appearing here for the first time, possibly a sign that Ōtomo should take charge after Tenji (who died on 12/3 that same year).

52. Naoki Kōjirō in Mori and Kadowaki, *Jinshin no ran*, 212–215.

53. The practice of giving rulers, even retrospectively, the two-graph sinicized names still used today started in the late eighth century.

54. *Ritsuryō*, NST 3: 281.

55. Mizubayashi, *Kiki shinwa*, 343–344.

56. For the text, see Piggott, *Emergence*, 156.

57. Someone like Prince Nagaya had impressive credentials as a candidate for the throne: he was a grandson of Tenmu through Tenmu's oldest son Takechi and was married to a daughter of Kusakabe (Tenmu and Jitō's son) and Genmei (Tenji's daughter). He became the fiercest opponent of the Fujiwara, marrying another daughter to Shōmu and seeking to make her empress. They eventually succeeded, but not before eliminating Prince Nagaya in 729, when he was accused of witchcraft and forced to commit suicide.

58. In the *ritsuryō* system, consorts (*kisaki*) came from the ranks of the court nobility; spouses (*bunin*; also read *fujin*), were to be of third-rank stock and above;

274 | NOTES TO PAGES 24–28

concubines (*hin*) of fifth rank and above. At Shōmu's accession to the throne in 724, his mother Miyako was made great royal spouse (*daifujin*), immediately followed by imperial great royal spouse (*kōtaifujin*), and in 749, at Kōken's succession, she first received the title of principal empress (*kōgō*), then great principal empress (*taikōgō*).

59. This is a figure for Heian (McCullough, "The Capital and Its Society," 131).

60. On the mutual political interests of Jitō and Fuhito, see Kasahara, "Kōi keichō to kanryōsei," 217–237; and Mayuzumi, *Ritsuryō kokka seiritsu-shi*, 633–660.

61. Joan Piggott offers a cultural explanation for the unusual number of female rulers in this period, writing that "an indigenous tradition of rule by gender-complementary chieftain pairs during the Yayoi and Kofun [pre- and proto-historic] periods [200 BC to 500 AD] . . . provided the sociocultural context from which later female sovereigns emerged," and that this practice did "replicate the archaic pattern" ("Chieftain Pairs," 17).

62. Saigō, *Jinshinki*, 29; Piggott provides a translation of the key section from Genmei's accession edict (*Emergence*, 228). Herbert Zachert offers a full German translation, amply annotated, of all sixty-two edicts of the *Shoku Nihongi* spanning the period from Monmu's accession in 697 into Kanmu's rule (until 789) in his *Semmyō*. Partial translations or summaries of fifty-eight of them are available in Sansom, "Imperial Edicts." For a summary of the historiographical debate, see Abe Takeshi, "Fukai jōten," 60–61. Delmer Brown ("Introduction," CHJ: 40–43) surmises that the principle of succession by the eldest son may have been accompanied by the building of a new capital for him: Fujiwara-kyō by Tenmu and Jitō for Kusakabe, Nara for Monmu's son Shōmu, whose building and moving to four new capitals, three of which were actually royal residences, constituted a "desperate attempt to obtain a larger measure of divine assistance for [his] troubled imperium" (43).

63. Jitō also received a National Memorial Day, but we are not told when (KDJ 5: 597–598, "*koki*").

64. SNG 1: 429n23.

65. Saigō, *Jinshinki*, 29. The *Kaifūsō* poets are introduced with short biographical sketches, which is where the meeting is described. See *Kaifūsō*, NKBT 69: 81–82.

66. Joan Piggott (*Emergence*, 161) makes Kadono Tenmu's grandson via Prince Ōtsu, rather than through his mother; he was also Tenji's grandson through his father.

67. Kusakabe was born in 662, eleven years before Tenmu took the throne.

Chapter 2: Mythemes

Epigraph: *Manyōshū*, Book II, poem 167; Cranston, 209, modified.

1. Dagron, *Empereur et prêtre*, 17. Roman and Byzantine emperors were associated with the Sun; see Sergio Bertelli, *The King's Body: Sacred Rituals of Power in Medieval and Early Modern Europe* (University Park: Pennsylvania State University Press, 2001), 10, 12.

2. Takeda Yukio, *Kōkuri shi to Higashi Ajia: "Kōkaido-ō hi" kenkyū josetsu* (Tokyo: Iwanami shoten, 1989), 341–343; reference from Lee, "Koguryŏ no taiwa gaikō," 11–12.

3. Heine-Geldern, "Conceptions of State," 22.

4. Dagron, *Empereur et prêtre*, 20.

5. Kōnishi's main publications are as follows: *Kojiki no sekaikan*; "Kodai shinwa no porifoni"; *Kojiki to Nihon shoki*. See also *Kojiki no tassei: sono ronri to hōhō* (Tokyo: Tokyo Daigaku shuppankai, 1983); and "Kodai ōken to Nihon shinwa," in Ishigami Ei'ichi et al., eds., *Tennō kenryoku no kōzō*, 7–37; he presents a clear summary of his interpretations in his "Constructing Imperial Mythology."

6. For the six variants regarding Ninigi's descent, see chart 61 in Mayuzumi, *Ritsuryō kokka seiritsu-shi*, 618.

7. On Amaterasu's role in the *Nihon shoki* regarding Ninigi's descent, see the beginning paragraphs of chapter 2 (Aston 1: 64–70). For the transmission of the regalia in the *Kojiki*, see Philippi, 139; compare with the *Nihon shoki*, where it is mentioned only as an alternate version to the main text (Aston 1: 76, 83).

8. Aston 1: 115–116 (Jinmu); 237 (Jingū); Philippi, 238, and Aston 1: 205 (Takeru) (Kōnoshi, *Kojiki to Nihon shoki*, 126, 128).

9. For the record, it should be noted that during the reigns of the mythological rulers numbers 10 to 12 (Sujin, Suinin, Keikō), Amaterasu is mentioned in connection with her move from the royal residence to Ise, where also a *saiō* (royal princess) is sent in permanent attendance (Aston 1: 151, 176, 200).

10. The institution of the *saiō* whereby each ruler sent a relative as virgin princess to reside in Ise, to be studied in chapter 8, functioned until the Muromachi period. Neither Jitō nor Genmei, two female monarchs, sent *saiō* princesses to Ise. Some scholars surmise that, as female rulers, they personally may have embodied the *saiō* function. Genshō and Kōken, the other two female rulers, although virgins themselves, sent a virgin representative to Ise.

11. *Manyōshū*, Book II, poem 199; Cranston 221.

12. *Manyōshū*, Book II, poem 162 (not in Cranston).

13. He sent the delegation from Seki no miya (some fifty km from the Ise shrines), where he spent ten days on falconry outings without, however, sparing any time for proceeding himself to Ise. Watanabe Akihiro, *Heijō-kyō to mokkan*, 216.

14. We do not know for sure whether Takechimaro's resignation was accepted. He was probably reinstated to an official post when, on 702/1/17 (three weeks before Jitō died), as holder of junior fourth lower rank, he became governor of Nagato (in today's Yamaguchi prefecture). His resignation under protest must have been much talked about, since the incident is mentioned in a tale of the early-ninth-century *Nihon ryōiki*; see K. Nakamura, *Miraculous Stories*, Part I, Tale 25. His reinstatement is the subject of two poems in the *Manyōshū* (poems 1770, 1772). Assuming that the Ise Sun cult was already closely associated with the ruling house since the time of Keitai (early sixth century), scholars including Kawamura ("Miwa no kami," 147–148) surmise that the shift from Miwa to Ise may already have taken place then.

15. Philippi, 81. This role of guarantor of political order is emphasized by

Kōnoshi (*Kojiki to Nihon shoki*, 98; "Imperial Mythology," 53). Mizubayashi, on the other hand, foregrounds the hidden, creative energy of Takamimusuhi, who is positioned one step above Amaterasu (*Kiki shinwa*, 125–126, 134–135).

16. Kōnoshi, *Kojiki to Nihon shoki*, 128–130.

17. Philippi, 74–75. Mizubayashi, *Kiki shinwa*, 271.

18. Aston 1: 33; *Nihon shoki*, NKBT 67: 102.

19. Compare Philippi, 80 (NST 1: 50), and Aston 1: 41 (NKBT 67: 112).

20. Kōnoshi, *Kojiki no sekaikan*, 23.

21. Kōnoshi, *Kojiki to Nihon shoki*, 87–97. Ōkuninushi appears only in the *Kojiki*, where he plays the important role of completing the pacification of the land in preparation for Ninigi's descent (Philippi, 93–136).

22. In the first lines of the *Kojiki*'s Chinese-style preface, Yasumaro alludes to the creative activity of Izanagi and Izanami as yin and yang. In the body of the text, however, no further reference to this Chinese worldview is made when the two *kami* proceed with the creation of the archipelago. For Mizubayashi's rather one-sided critique of Kōnoshi's assertion that the *Kojiki* has no tale of the creation of the world, see Mizubayashi, *Kiki shinwa*, 23. The two opening lines of the Preface (as well as the style of the whole Preface) stand separate from the work as such.

23. The term shows up four times in variants noted in the *Nihon shoki* (Kōnoshi, *Kojiki no sekaikan*, 4).

24. This was Jitō's second posthumous name. The issue of the name change for her and Monmu is taken up later in the chapter.

25. Philippi, 163.

26. Kōnoshi, *Kojiki to Nihon shoki*, chaps. 1, 2, 7; "*Nihon*" *to wa nanika*, chap. 4.

27. Kōnishi, "Kodai shinwa no porifonii," 49.

28. Kōnoshi, "Kodai shinwa no porifonii," 50.

29. Mizubayashi, *Kiki shinwa*, 338.

30. On the two scholars' contrasting methodologies of literature and history, see their discussion in Kōnoshi and Mizubayashi, "Tairon," 101–151, esp. 129, 133, and 140–141. Mizubayashi, less text-bound than Kōnoshi, the literary critic, more willingly ventures into the realm of the plausible, without abandoning the requirements of rigorous scholarship.

31. Mizubayashi, *Kiki shinwa*, 330–331.

32. This is the theme that runs through Mizubayashi, *Kiki shinwa*.

33. Already in 569, the Wei legal definition of village composition (fifty households rather than the Tang's one hundred) was applied in some Yamato royal domains and remained used afterward. Allochthons under the direction of the Soga introduced it (Shinkawa, "Rettō Nihon," 104).

34. All but 6 of the 281 *kami* are crammed into the *Kojiki*'s first chapter (*Shinto jiten*, 716–732). The *Kojiki* edited by Nishimiya Kazutami lists 321 *kami* names in its Appendix; a number of *kami* have several names.

35. The methodological remarks of this paragraph paraphrase Jean Pouillon's *Le cru et le su*, 48–49. They express succinctly Mizubayashi's approach to the Yamato mythology, which I follow in this chapter.

36. For Mizubayashi, the *Kojiki* functions like a "constitution" for the *ritsuryō* state (*Kiki shinwa*, 367).

37. *Manyōshū*, Book II, poem 167; Cranston, 209, lines 23–30, modified.

38. Ebersole, *Ritual Poetry*, 201, 217.

39. Kōnoshi, *Kojiki no sekaikan*, 2.

40. The degree to which a tributary relationship with Korean kingdoms (about which more later) was established is a matter of debate (great in Japan, intense in Korea). Nevertheless, it is clear that both texts present Japan's relationship with the peninsula in that way.

41. On these points, see Kōnoshi, "*Nihon*" *to wa nanika*, 30–31, 45–46, 50.

42. Kōnoshi, *Kojiki no sekaikan*, 186, 189.

43. Barnes, *State Formation in Korea*, 189.

44. Zhenping Wang, "Chinese Titles," 7–8; idem, "Speaking with a Forked Tongue," 23–32; idem, *Ambassadors*, chap. 2.

45. Himiko sent four missions to Luoyang during the Wei dynasty and received the title Pro-Wei Queen [of Wa], which was granted only twice, the other recipient being the chief of the Dayuezhi, an Indo-Scythian tribe. From Chinese sources, we know of ten missions to the court of the Southern Sung in the fifth century, none of them mentioned in the *Nihon shoki* (Zhenping Wang, *Ambassadors*, chap. 2, esp. 18–20, 24–27; idem, "Speaking with a Forked Tongue," 27; idem, "Chinese Titles," 16–20; also CHJ 1: 140–143).

46. Zhenping Wang, "Chinese Titles," 23; idem, *Ambassadors*, 29. These titles were of crucial importance as a source of legitimacy for Korean kings. In the second half of the sixth century, Koguryŏ's king, who had received investiture from the Northern Qi, approached the Zhou after the Qi disappeared. When the Zhou in turn were defeated, Koguryŏ approached Yamato under Suiko. Yamato gained its reputation as a "Great Country" in good part because its great kings no longer sought titles from Chinese courts (Lee, "Koguryŏ no taiwa gaikō," 3).

47. Rulers of "tribute states" were supposed to refer to themselves as "king [name] of [country's name]." On this question, see Kumagai, *Ōkimi*, 236–238. For the new interpretation of the misreading of the title as a personal name, see Zhenping Wang, "Speaking with a Forked Tongue," 28–31; idem, *Ambassadors*, 147.

48. *Tenka* appears in a text engraved on a sword under Yūryaku's rule (456–479). See Kumagai, *Ōkimi*, 112–115; Piggott, *Emergence*, 54.

49. Saimei died in 661/7 while getting a fleet ready to assist Paekche.

50. Aston 2: 275, 277; Ishigami, "Ritsuryō kokka to tennō," 52.

51. Philippi, 260. In the *Nihon shoki* story (Aston 1:115–116), Amaterasu plays a far lesser role during one of Jingū's subsequent domestic campaigns, but she is the one who sends the crow. Coincidentally, the crow-in-the-sun is found in China since ancient times.

52. Succession problems are mentioned in the first part of the chapter (Nintoku to Kenzō, 394–487) while the second part (Ninken to Suiko, 487–628) only reports names of rulers, their consorts and offspring, and the year they died.

53. On this complicated issue, see a lucid exposition by Cornelius Kiley, in his "State and Dynasty," 25, 31, 40. For a list of rulers to 715 that clearly differenti-

ated between the various dynastic regimes, see Barnes, *State Formation in Japan*, 22–24.

54. Bentley, *Authenticity*, 75.

55. See note 2, this chapter.

56. In the episode where Amaterasu is enticed out of the cave to which she had withdrawn, Ame no koyane played an important role. The *Kojiki* mentions this *kami* as the ancestor of the Nakatomi; the *Kogoshūi* notes that this *kami* is offspring of Kamumusuhi (Inbe, *Kogoshūi* [Kato] 17; [*Gunsho*] 1).

57. Philippi, 78; NST 1: 49; Mizubayashi, "Heijō-gū dokukai," 157–158.

58. Mizubayashi, *Kiki shinwa*, 78, 146, 125. The distinction was highlighted by Motoori Norinaga and picked up by Mizubayashi. The text seems to fully justify such a reading.

59. Philippi, 148–158.

60. Philippi, 61–67.

61. See, for instance, Mizubayashi, *Kiki shinwa*, 24–25, 37, 66. This is one of several points of dispute between Kōnoshi and Mizubayashi; see also their debate: "Tairon," 101–151.

62. For the long story of Ōkuninushi, see Philippi, 93–136.

63. Philippi, 102, and additional note 11, pp. 408–409.

64. Philippi, 148–157.

65. See Mizubayashi, *Kiki shinwa*, 248, table 18b.

66. Mizubayashi, *Kiki shinwa*, 85, 175, 245, 356–357.

67. Abe, "Jinshin no ran," 38.

68. Grayson, *Myths and Legends from Korea*, 135.

69. Bruce Batten uses *ethnie* to refer to the late-seventh-century communal identity of the Yamato elite vis-à-vis other political entities. This term, however, applies less well to internal "others" that were part of Yamato without constituting another political entity; see his *To the Ends of Japan*, 91, 93. For the allochthons' contributions, see Como, "Ethnicity," 61–84. By the mid-ninth century, reference to them as *kikajin* ceases although their status as such became recorded in the *Shinsen shōjiroku* (Newly Compiled Record of Surnames) compiled between 799 and 815.

70. Como, "Ethnicity," 76–81.

71. Farris, *Sacred Texts*, 87. "Bell-shaped," like the *dōtaku* ceremonial bells, signs of ritual authority, may be a more appropriate description.

72. On these octagonal tombs and their significance, see Aboshi, "Hakkaku hōfun, 181–226; and Shiraishi, "Kinai kofun no shūmatsu," 107–109, 112, 118–120.

73. Aboshi, "Hakkaku hōfun," 205–206. Kōtoku's palace in Naniwa had two octagonal small structures, but the only State Hall referred to as a Daigokuden before Kiyomihara's (694) was in Saimei's palace, in 645.

74. Buddhist influence, moreover, apparently had not extended to the area of funeral practices during this time. A good number of Buddhist monks were active during the last months of Tenmu's life, but as Aboshi has pointed out ("Hakkaku hōfun," 210–212), they were not formal participants or wailers at his funeral.

Hence, Tenmu was not the first emperor to have received a Buddhist funeral as is sometimes thought.

75. Aboshi, "Hakkaku hōfun," 191.

76. Aboshi, "Hakkaku hōfun," 219.

77. Schafer, *Pacing the Void*, 16–19. This symbolism was still used in the twentieth century. A monument in Miyazaki, erected in 1940 to celebrate the 2600th anniversary of the founding of the Japanese empire by Jinmu, refers through four characters — *hakkō ichiu*, "the whole world under one roof" — to imperial Japan's ambition to unite the entire world under its leadership. *Hakkō*, "eight corners," is a variant of *hakkaku* (Edwards, "Forging Tradition," 291–292).

78. Aboshi, "Hakkaku hōfun," 197.

79. For example, see the first lines of poems 3, 38, 45, 50 in Book I.

80. Aston, 178. This cost the life of Soga father and son in 646. In Book 3 of the *Analects* ("The Eight Rows"), on the subject of usurpation of royal rites, chapter 1 refers to the royal privilege of conducting the eight-row dance in the king's ancestral temple.

81. Edwards, "Contested Access," 374–375.

82. Mizubayashi, *Kiki shinwa*, 316–317.

83. Mizubayashi interprets the contrast between *ten* and *neko* as one between authoritarian leadership, exercised during the post-Taika state building, and a subsequent emphasis that the *tennō* was also "from the soil" that had produced the local magnates, partners, or confederates of a leader at the center whose authority they acknowledged but who signaled that his power was less than absolute. Even Amaterasu, having been born on earth, was a fitting *neko* ancestor for a ruler seeking to portray him- or herself also as a primus inter pares. Mizubayashi, *Kiki shinwa*, 239, 304, 336, 361. According to some scholars, the posthumous titles that appear in the *Nihon shoki* starting with Ankan, who died in 535, may have been composed under Jitō (see KDJ 6: 728, "shigō").

84. Mizubayashi, *Kiki shinwa*, 359; SNG 1: 3, 240n3.

85. Jitō's initial posthumous title was *Ōyamato 'neko ame' no hirono no hime* (princess [or daughter of the sun] of the wide field of heaven, root child of Great Yamato); Monmu's, *Yamato 'neko' toyo ōji no sumera mikoto* (heavenly ruler of venerable ancestry, Yamato root child). Genmei and Genshō were still alive during the time of the name changes; thus their posthumous titles that contain the *neko* component could not have been at issue.

86. Mizubayashi, *Kiki shinwa*, 363, 365.

87. Junnin's reign (758–764) was an interregnum that was overshadowed by the two reigns of Shōmu's daughter, who ruled first as Empress Kōken (749–758), installed Junnin, and then deposed him, ascending the throne a second time as Shōtoku (764–770).

88. Kōnoshi, *Kojiki to Nihon shoki*, 173–182; "Imperial Mythology," 56–59.

Chapter 3: Alibis

Epigraphs: NSK 2: 493; *Manyōshū*, Book I, poem 52; Cranston, 643–644, modified.

1. The first twenty lines of the Preface summarize the narrative before Tenmu, followed by twenty-seven lines of ecstatic praise for Tenmu, while the last twenty-two address Empress Genmei, who had requested the *Kojiki*'s completion only four months earlier (Philippi, 37–44).

2. Doe, *A Warbler's Song*, 7–8.

3. This absence has led to some wild speculation that Tenmu was not of royal blood, or not even from Yamato; on this controversial topic, see Ōwa Iwao, *Tennō shusshō no nazo* (Kyoto: Rinsen shoten, 1993). A thirteenth-century genealogical list of rulers, the *Ichidai yōki* (Essential Record of Reigns) mentions that Tenmu lived to the age of sixty-four. Counting back from the year of his death, he would have been born in 622, making him older, however, than Tenji, supposedly the older of the two brothers. On this question, see Shirosaki Shōichirō, "Tenmu tennō nenrei kō," HAKB 29 (1981): 116–125.

4. For the most extensive discussion of Tenmu's rule in English, see Piggot, *Emergence*, chap. 5.

5. Fujiwara Nakamaro compiled the *Tōshi kaden*, a brief two-part family history of the Fujiwara, between 761 and 763, when he was at the height of his power after putting down Tachibana Naramaro's rebellion in 757. At the time, a projection of the Fujiwara clan's founder as savior of the dynasty functioned also to cover up his own imminent rebellion of 764, which he had been contemplating for some twelve years (see chapter 8). Part 1 of the *Tōshi kaden* is about Kamatari and Fuhito, part 2 about Nakamaro's father, Muchimaro. See *Gunsho ruijū* 78; for part 2, see also NST 8: 26–38. For the incident at Tenji's coronation banquet, see *Gunsho*, 350. Bentley's translation of part 1 (*Historiographical Trends*, 133–150) should be used with caution, for he misidentified the crown prince of the incident as Prince Ōtomo as the one (146). Hermann Bohner's German translation is reliable: "Kamatari-den. Kaden, Oberer Band," MN 4 (1941): 207–245.

6. This episode has also led some historians to speculate that the tension between the two brothers may explain Tenji's extremely long tenure as crown prince. For this hypothesis, see Ōwa Iwao, "Tenji tennō wa naze nijū-shichi nenkan mo 'kōtaishi' ka," HAKB 104 (2000): 168–195. When, on 766/1/8, two years after Fujiwara Nakamaro's rebellion, Empress Shōtoku appointed his cousin Fujiwara Nagate to the high post of minister of the right, she needed to remind officialdom of the long-standing loyal service of the lineage since Tenji's reign, recent events notwithstanding. In her edict of that day, she quoted from the royal obituaries (*shinobi no koto*) for Nagate's grandfather Fuhito and great-grandfather Kamatari, which justified her trust in the Fujiwara: "Those of your descendants who serve the court with a pure and clear heart (*kiyoku akaki kokoro*), we shall honor [with rank, office, stipends]. We shall never terminate this [bestowal of honors] for your descendants" (SNG 4: 109). The rehabilitation of the Fujwara as "pure and clean"

was necessary, since less than a year earlier, on 765/3/5, the empress had referred in another edict to Nagate's cousin Nakamaro, the rebel, as "evil" (*ashiki Nakamaro*) (SNG 4: 79).

7. This is the first time this *ritsuryō* post is mentioned in the record, possibly anachronistically.

8. Bruno Lewin reports that respectively thirteen Aya and two Hata *uji* sided with Tenmu, versus three and one with Ōtomo (*Aya*, 153). On the military aspect of the Jinshin War, see Farris, *Heavenly Warriors*, 41–45; on Tenmu's carefully planned timing, see Tamaki, "Jinshin no ran," 20–30.

9. For a detailed analysis of the relation between the foreign threat and domestic reform during the reigns of Tenji and Tenmu, see Batten, "Foreign Threat," 199–219.

10. Under Tenji (664–671), five embassies arrived from China, four from Silla, while respectively three and two missions were dispatched from Yamato. Between the years 672 and 707, however, Yamato received twenty-four embassies from Silla, and sent twelve (Suzuki, *Kodai taigai kankeishi*, 611–618).

11. Suzuki, *Kodai taigai kankeishi*, 16–17, 21–26.

12. Kuramoto Kazuhiro (" 'Jinshin-nen kōshin' tachi") has culled the data on the postwar careers of men who distinguished themselves in the armed conflict. He found ninety-one names of "meritorious servants" from during the Jinshin War. Their number breaks down as follows: ten royals, eighteen *maetsukimi*, forty-nine *tomo no miyatsuko* (local vassals of great kings), and fourteen local *uji*. Too little, however, is known of their careers to come to significant conclusions about the degree to which they received preferential treatment.

13. Jinno, "Tenmu jūnen-ki no tenka," 54.

14. Philippi, 259–260.

15. See Yoko Williams' exhaustive but ahistorical study of sins, offenses, and retribution in pre-Nara Japan (*Tsumi*, 145).

16. Williams, *Tsumi*, 133–141. In Heian and later, such physical carriers of pollution used in purification and exorcism rituals were called *nademono* (rubbing object) or, if shaped as a human figure, *hitogata* (human figure/shape). In certain ceremonies described in the *Engishiki*, the use of the number eight is very striking. It may refer to occasions that express universal rule, like the octagonal tombs for rulers Kōtoku to Tenmu. Eight horses and eight slaves are among twenty-eight offerings (out of thirty-one) that have to be presented in groups of eight, eighty, or eight hundred in the Thank Offerings in the Outer Quarter (Rajō), held once during each reign; see *Engishiki* (Bock) 1: 104 (Book 3). In the case of 469/3, retribution consisted of eight horses and eight swords.

17. These items were later fixed in the Jingi-ryō of the Taihō and Yōrō codes and may already have been part of Tenmu's Kiyomihara Code. Hemp in great quantities figures in the yearly *hanpei* ceremonies of distributed oblations by the Jingikan, to be discussed in chapter 5.

18. Wada, "Nanzan no kyūtōryū," 307, 317 (*mokkan* no. 467-83-7-032). The *Mahāmāyūrī vidyārājñī* (Sutra of the Great Peacock Spell), known to En no Gyōja,

was a Tantric text of demonology about Buddhist magic spells with heavy doses of Daoist and yin-yang philosophy. For En no Gyōja, see Nakamura, *Miraculous Stories*, Part I, Tale 28, p. 141.

19. *Engishiki* (Bock) 2: 84–89 (Book 8); *Engishiki* (Torao) 1: 477–481.

20. Jinno Kiyokazu (*Ritsuryō kokka to senmin*, 59) uses the image of local governors as holders of ritual power linked to Tenmu as the great king ritualist.

21. Ueda, "Dōkyō no ryūden," 8.

22. Kuroda, "Shinto in History"; see Teeuwen, "*Jindō* to Shinto," 233–263, for a variation on this theory.

23. Mizubayashi, *Kiki shinwa*, 369–371.

24. For a detailed study of the enthronement ceremony, see Ellwood, *Feast of Kingship*.

25. At the end of the eighth century, further changes took place. With Kanmu's enthronement in 781, the succession ceremony was integrated into the Daijō-sai, while at the same time the ceremony for the *kami* was degraded to a preliminary event. Mizubayashi's arguments regarding these ceremonies are dispersed throughout wide swaths of his *Kiki shinwa*, esp. 178–206, 321, 369, 386–387.

26. Mizubayashi, *Kiki shinwa*, 184, 386.

27. Mizubayashi, *Kiki shinwa*, 228–230, 329.

28. Dagron, *Empereur et prêtre*, 20. Pierre Bourdieu (*The Logic of Practice*, 262) contrasts "aggregation" and "specification," a terminology borrowed from Kant's *Appendix to the Transcendental Dialectic*.

29. Goodman similarly mentions interchangeability, multiplicity, and overlap (*Ts'ao P'i*, 141, 168).

30. Philippi (40) identifies King Wen as the "king of Chou" of line 34. I am following Yamaguchi and Kōnoshi, who see in this line and line 31 references to King Wu (*Kojiki*, 20n10, n16).

31. NSK 2: 493. Aston (2: 389) does not translate the remark on "Sun succession." Mizubayashi Takeshi has drawn attention to this brief line in his "Heijō-gū-*Kojiki* shinwa," 140–141.

32. For a list with the dates of the death, burial, and length of temporary interment for all Yamato rulers before Jitō, see Ebersole, *Ritual Poetry*, 130, table 1.

33. For the discussion that follows, see Mizubayashi, "Ritsuryō tennōsei," 153–156.

34. Philippi, 390–391.

35. It is unclear whether Tenji married Furuhito's daughter before or after he slaughtered Furuhito and his family shortly after the Taika coup. She may have been involved in the question of the succession following Tenji's death (KDJ 14: 193, "Yamato hime no mikoto").

36. Fujidō, "Ritsuryō kokka no koki," 14, 17, 24.

37. *Kaifūsō*, 60.

38. Denecke, "Chinese Antiquity," 104–105.

39. Fujidō, "Tenji misasagi," 1, 11; Mizubayashi, "Ritsuryō tennōsei," 150–151.

40. *Nihon shoki* 2 (NKBT 68): 352, headnote 1.

41. The event is recorded in the *Nihon shoki* (672/6/24) and alluded to in the

Kojiki's Preface, line 23 of Philippi's translation. The two quotations in this paragraph are lines 36 and 24 (Philippi's translation modified).

42. Goodman uses this phrase to describe the last Eastern Han's explanation of why the Han fell (*Ts'ao P'i*, 123).

43. Goodman, *Ts'ao P'i*, 23.

44. Puett, *Become a God*, 160–162. Robinet, *Taoism*, 12, 135. Li Ling ("Taiyi Worship," 25) shows that in pre-Qin times already Taiyi was "a concept that included the senses of astral body, spirit, and ultimate thing." Ling also mentions that Wudi's sacrifices to Taiyi, Lord Earth, and the Five Emperors required him to travel within a radius of some two hundred kilometers from the capital Changan (6).

45. Puett, *Become a God*, 301–311; Ling, "Taiyi Worship," 10, 11. In religious Daoism, the Yellow Emperor took center stage again, instead of Taiyi (Cammann, "Magic Square," 63).

46. "The Emperor embodies Taiyi" (quoted by Poul Andersen, *"Bugang,"* 29n28; Xiong Lihui, *Xin yi Huainanzi*, 363).

47. In drawing attention to these Daoist connotations, I am following Japanese historians such as Fukunaga Mitsuji ("Taoizumu," 5–46) rather than heeding others who caution against such emphasis; Kumagai (*Ōkimi*, 339) expresses reservations.

48. Posthumous names for Yamato rulers are lengthy, poetically belabored titles, originally given most probably in elegies during *mogari* mourning rituals, a practice that started in the mid-fifth century. Earlier posthumous names are obviously later inventions. They form the titles of the *Nihon shoki* chapters, each devoted to a ruler. The Chinese-style posthumous names consisting of only two graphs were introduced in the second half of the Nara period (*Iwanami Nihonshi jiten*: "shigō," "kanfūshigō," "shinobigoto").

49. Fukunaga, "Taoizumu," 23. *Mahito* is sometimes translated as "true man."

50. The Eastern Sea is the Bay of Bohai of the Yellow Sea, between the Liaodong peninsula and Shantung province.

51. Charlotte von Verschuer mentions that, around 753, Chinese poems dedicated to the Japanese envoy Abe Nakamaro referred to Japan as Penglai, the Island of the Immortals, a posture adopted in 804 by another envoy, Fujiwara Kadonomaro, in his letter of introduction to the Tang court, actually composed by Kūkai ("Le Japon, contrée du Penglai?"), 440, 452. For translations of the 804 document, see von Verschuer, *Les relations officielles*, 12–15; Zhenping Wang, *Ambassadors*, 233–235.

52. Wada, *Nihon kodai no girei* 3: 228; Fukunaga, "Taoizumu," 22–23.

53. I was led to most of the poems by Ōwa, *Tenmu tennō ron*, 2: 9–60.

54. *Manyōshū*, Book XIX, poem 4260; Cranston, 531.

55. Poetic license, in this case, may have included dating the poem. Ozawa Tsuyoshi has pointed out that the rural setting (stallions, paddy fields, marshes) of this and the following poem as the place for the new palace was not likely the Asuka site where already three residences had been built by three former great kings, but the fields just north of it, where Fujiwara-kyō would rise in 694 — which, according to Ozawa (*Nihon kodai kyūto*, 239–240), is the subject of the poem.

56. The lament for Kusakabe is in Book II, poem 167 (Cranston, 209). *Sumeroki* is on line 31. For these remarks on the variation in writing *ōkimi* in the *Manyōshū*, see Fukunaga, *Dōkyō to kodai Nihon*, 19–26. The line of the poem in question is cited on p. 24.

57. Saigō, *Jinshinki*, 231.

58. The epithet *kami ni shi maseba* is used for Tenmu in *Manyōshū*, Book XIX, poems 4260 and 4261; Jitō in III: 235, Princes Naga (III: 241) and Yuge (II: 205), possibly Prince Osakabe in III: 236, while Princes Takechi (II: 199–202), Niitabe (III: 261) and Kusakabe (II: 167–169) are praised in other godly or solar terms (sun prince, peer of the sun).

59. *Manyōshū*, Book I, poem 38; Cranston, 194.

60. *Manyōshū*, Book II, poem 161; Cranston, 188. For a detailed exegesis of this poem, see Bialock, *Eccentric Spaces*, 20–22.

61. *Manyōshū*, Book II, poem 167, lines 24–25, 35–36; Cranston, 207–210) (modified following a suggestion by Torquil Duthie). According to Kōnoshi, this variance with Yasumaro's *Kojiki* indicates that, while there certainly was a plurality of mythological material available at the time, the poet Hitomaro created his vision by using it one way, and Yasumaro later organized it differently (*Kakinomoto Hitomaro kenkyū*), 182, 188, 190; Kōnoshi "Tairon," 108. Ebersole thinks that in this episode of the mythology, we have to do with a "retrospective 'rewriting' of the myth" (*Ritual Poetry*, 217). This would presuppose that there was a single myth to rewrite. Kōnoshi's position is that various mythopoetic versions developed simultaneously.

62. Cranston, 208.

63. *Manyōshū*, Book II, poem 199; Cranston, 219–223 (217 for the quotation); see lines 11–12 (*kamusabu*) and 89 (*kamunagara*).

64. Lines 79–86 of the same poem. Cranston remarks that a much earlier poem in the *Kojiki* already had used *kamukaze* as a pillow word for Ise; for a translation, see Cranston, 16. The *saiō* princess of the Ise shrine (a daughter of Tenmu) uses the same expression in a poem (*Manyōshū*, Book II, poem 163; not in Cranston). For the *Nihon shoki*, see Aston 2: 306.

65. *Manyōshū*, Book III, poem 261; Cranston (196) transliterates *takaterasu*.

66. *Manyōshū*, Book VI, poems 907–912, 920–922; Cranston, 295–297.

67. Puett, *Become a God*, 239.

68. Today the graphs for the latter are read *myōshin*, "illustrious god(s)," and refer only to *kami*, not to emperors.

69. Ōwa, *Tenmu tennō ron*, 2: 18; Fukunaga, *Dōkyō to kodai Nihon*, 45–46. The formula reads "*akitsu mikami to ame no shita shirasu yamato no sumera mikoto no ōmikotorama*," which Aston translates as "This is the mandate of the emperor of Japan who rules the world as a god incarnate" (Aston 2: 198). "God incarnate" might be a better translation for *arahitokami* than for *akitsu kami*. Herbert Zachert (*Semmyō*, 17–18) translates *akitsu mikami* as "Gegenwärtiger Gott" (a present god). The term was probably anachronistically inserted in several of Emperor Kōtoku's Taika Reforms edicts such as the one quoted above, which dates from 645/7/10; see Naumann, "Einige Bermerkungen," 12.

70. Saigō, *Jinshinki*, 230.

71. *Manyōshū*, Book VI, poem 1050. Saigō, *Jinshinki*, 230.

72. Ōwa, *Tenmu tennō ron*, 2: 11; Fukunaga, "Tennō to shikyū," 966−968. Ōwa rehearses the various theories on *akitsukami*, etc., on pp. 9−20, 49−52.

73. These explanations were apparently the work of Pei Xuanren, a transcendental from the Highest Purity, and were quoted in Tao Hongjing's *Zhengao* (Declarations of the Perfected) (Fukunaga, "Tennō to shikyū," 962−963). On Tao Hongjing, his work, and their relationship to the *Baopuzi*, see p. 150.

74. See *Ritsuryō*, NST 3: 476 (*Zōryō*, art. 8), as commented on in the *Ryō no gige* (KST 22: 334); reference from Saeki, *Nihon kodai no seiji*, 147, 165.

75. *Ton* means "to seclude, evade," and *kō*, "shell, carapace." See Morohashi, *Dai kanwa jiten* 5: 5301, and 11: 11645; see also under *jutsusū* (10: 10596). For *hōjutsu*, see *fangshi* and *shushi* in Csikszentmihàlyi, "Han Cosmology," 56. For a modern handbook to *tonkō* divination, see Hayashi Kosei, *Hachimon tonkō hōijutsu* (Tokyo: Aoyama-sha, 2000). On *tonkō*, see also Schipper and Wang, "Progressive and Regressive Time Cycles," 185−205.

76. Hsiao, *A History of Chinese Political Thought*, 521.

77. On the positions taken by various scholars, see Ōwa, *Tenmu tennō ron*, 2: 421−436.

78. Tamura, "Onmyōryō seiritsu izen," in OMS 1: 53.

79. Tamura, "Onmyōryō seiritsu izen," in OMS 1: 50−52.

80. Yoshino, *Jitō*, 84−85. A Chinese work compiled by Lu Buwei (241 BCE), the *Lushi Qun Qiu* (Spring and Autumn of Lu Buwei), revealed a theory of the cycles and transmutations of the Five Agents as related to the first Chinese emperors; see Fung, *A History of Chinese Philosophy*, 1: 161−162. For instance, King Wen, founder of the Zhou dynasty, ruled under the Fire sign emblematized by a vermilion bird. Fire came after the sign Metal (the Shang) and was followed by Water "which was utilized by the First Emperor [of the Qin dynasty] to serve as a theoretical basis for his political power" (Hsiao, *Chinese Political Thought*, 1: 568). On the color symbolism applied to various early Chinese dynasties, see Loewe, *Divination, Mythology and Monarchy in Han China*, chap. 2: "Water, Earth and Fire: The Symbols of the Han Dynasty."

81. Wada Atsumu reports the discovery of wooden tags in Fujiwara-kyō, Jitō's capital, with references to the *Wuxing dayi*. See his "Nanzan no kyūtōryū," 307. The full original Chinese text and transcription into Japanese of a selective number of the chapters is available in Nakamura Shohachi, *Gogyō taigi* (henceforth Gt in the text). For a complete French translation, see Kalinowski, *Cosmologie et divination dans la Chine ancienne* (henceforth Cd in the text). For a reference to the interpretations of Han and pre-Han dynastic successions according to the sequence of the Five Phases and the colors associated with them, see Gt 229, Cd 327−328. Aside from the *Wuxing dayi*, this theory can be found in several other works, some of which were certainly available by the end of the seventh century: the *Zuozhuan* (sections of which are quoted in Shōtoku Taishi's "Seventeen-Article Constitution" of 604; see Spae, *Itō Jinsai*, 19) and the *Lushi Qun Qiu*. For the specific passages of the former, see Legge, trans., *The Chinese Classics*, Vol. 5: *The Ch'un Ts'ew*

with The Tso Chuen, 667–668; for the latter, see Richard Wilhelm, trans., *Frühling und Herbst des Lü Bu We*, 160–161. In the *Zuozhuan*, a ruler of Tan reports that each of his predecessors was associated with what amounts to a particular totem (cloud, fire, water, dragon, phoenix, etc.), which functioned as a genus, while species belonging to the genus were used as names for officers. This, it was reported, was a custom learned from "the wild tribes all round about."

82. Yoshino, *Jitō*, 86–109.

83. Thus, for instance, the dates of Emperor Tenji's move to Ōtsu, his coronation, the installation of his main consort and senior prince, and the appointment of Prince Ōtomo as prime minister are related to the Wood sign through the zodiac symbols of Tiger, Hare, and Dragon (Yoshino, *Jitō*, 91). Dates of days and months in the *Nihon shoki*, starting with Jinmu, are given using the sexagesimal cycles of roots and branches and lend themselves to symbolic readings. Years are indicated as year N of Jinmu, Jitō, etc. Era names to mark reigns were introduced in 701, which is Taihō 1, although two are mentioned earlier in the record, without having been used as year markers following their one-time appearance: White Pheasant in 650 and Vermilion Bird shortly before Tenmu's death.

84. Yoshino, *Jitō*, 113–114.

85. Yoshino surmises that the sudden increase of Buddhist ritualist performance (seventy persons of pure conduct ordered to retire from the world, the holding of meager feasts, the making of images of Kannon, expounding the Kannon sutra, ordination first of eighty monks and nuns, then an additional hundred, etc.) following the era name change may have taken place during the intense forty-nine days of purification and mourning that follow death, a period that indeed would have ended on or around 9/9. The era name change would have assured, through the mobilization of cosmic forces, the continuity beyond death of Tenmu's achievements. Thus, Tenmu would actually have died around 7/20. It should be kept in mind, however, as Aboshi Yoshinori has pointed out ("Hakkaku hōfun," 210–212), that Tenmu's was not a Buddhist funeral, and monks did not officiate then in an official capacity.

86. This activity started when Tenmu fell ill in 5/24 with the expounding of the *Yakushi-kyō* (Sutra of the Healing Buddha) and the start of a Buddhist retreat within the palace. This was followed by a general amnesty, the request to the high priests of Buddhism (members of the governmental body for the oversight of Buddhism) to offer prayers, repentance made for sins, penitential services, the reading of the *Konkōmyō-kyō* (Golden Light Sutra) at the palace, and a cancellation of debts for the poor. The search for a "Daoist" herb of long life during Tenmu's final illness will be discussed later.

87. Hon'iden, "Kakumeikan to saii shisō (1)," 24–26. For an extensive treatment of the pervasive millenarian prognostications at the end of the Former Han, see Hsiao, *Chinese Political Thought*, 503–523. Some scholars have also discovered, less successfully in my view, references to Liu Pang in other graphs of Tenmu's posthumous name (Ōwa, *Tenmu tennō ron*, 2: 425–426).

88. Fukunaga Mitsuji, in Mori and Kadowaki, *Jinshin no ran*, 255.

89. "If we look back to antiquity, to the Great Beginning, man was there born

out of Non-Being. Having form, he was regulated by things. But he who is able to revert to that state out of which he was born, so as to be as if he had never had physical form, is called the True Man. The True Man is he who is as if he had not yet separated from the Great Oneness" (Fung, *History of Chinese Philosophy*, 1: 399). For the transference of the attributes of the mystic to the sage ruler, see Le Blanc, *Huai-nan Tzu*, 195–196. A number of scholars have independently translated seventeen of the twenty-one chapters of the *Huainanzi*. For a bibliography of these translations until 1985, see Le Blanc, *Huai-nan Tzu*, 15–16; since then, additional chapters have been translated in Major, *Heaven and Earth*, and Larre, Robinet, and de la Vallée, trans., *Les grands traités du Huainanzi*. The first four emperors of the Han dynasty had an intense interest in Daoism, which became the unofficial doctrine of the state according to Le Blanc (*Huani-nan Tzu*, 5). See also Griet Vankeerberghen, *The Huainanzi and Liu An's Claim to Moral Authority* (Albany: State University of New York Press, 2001).

90. On the *Huainanzi*'s anti-Confucianism (in chap. 2), see Evan Morgan, *Tao: The Great Luminant: Essays from Huai Nan Tzu* (Shanghai: Kelly and Walsh, 1933), 43; for the endorsement of regicide (in chap. 15), see 184.

91. On *mahito* discourse as a savior around the time of the restoration of the Han dynasty and its use by Tenmu, see Hon'iden, "Kakumeikan," 208: 24, 27. On *mahito* in Daoism, see Fukunaga, "Tennō to shikyū," 958–959, 962–963; in English, Le Blanc, *Huai-nan Tzu*, 141, 150, 195.

92. The Jinmu myth, scholars agree, was fabricated in the early sixth century around the time of the reign of Great King Keitai, who, most likely, started a new dynastic line (see Kiley, "State and Dynasty," 31, 40). Edwards refers to this scholarship in his "Contested Access," 374n9.

93. Puett, *Become a God*, 239 (quotation modified); Sima Qian, *Records of the Grand Historian: Qin Dynasty*, 57.

94. In descending order, they were Princes Kusakabe, Ōtsu, Takechi, Kawashima, and Osakabe.

95. It is very unlikely that any era names were given officially in Yamato before 701. For a discussion concerning the era names of Taika (645), Hakuchi (650), Hakuhō (672), and Shuchō (686), see Tokoro Isao, *Nengō no rekishi*, chap. 3.

96. For vermilion birds as belonging to the same species as phoenixes, see Gt 180–189 passim, 237b, 253; Cd 368, 430–435 passim, 444.

97. Farris, *Sacred Texts*, 157, 161. For layouts of Fujiwara-kyō, see Ozawa, *Nihon kodai kyūto*, frontispiece and 214, 243; and Nara bunkazai kenkyūjo soritsu gojū shūnen kinen, *Asuka, Fujiwara-kyō ten*, 180. Fujiwara-kyō was larger than Luoyang, the capital of the Northern Wei, and about half the size of Changan, the Tang capital. For a comparison of these three capitals, see *Nihon no rekishi: Shūkan asahi hyakka*, vol. 2 (Tokyo: Asahi shinbunsha, 1987), 107, which, however, shows the small scale of Fujiwara-kyō before the recent excavations.

98. Ozawa, *Nihon kodai kyūto*, 220.

99. Steinhardt, *Chinese Imperial City Planning*, 33; for a sketch of the imaginary Zhou capital, see 35; note that the discussion of Fujiwara-kyō, on 110, is based on the old, small version.

100. Wheatley, *Pivot of the Four Quarters*, 425.

101. Palmer," Land of the Rising Sun," 75–76, 87.

102. For the move to Nara, see SNG 1:131 (708/2/15).

103. Steinhardt, *Chinese Imperial City Planning*, 30, 32.

104. Tatsumi, "Yama to kyoseki," 57–71; "Hyūga to Hitachi," 104–115, esp. 113–114; Yamada Yasuhiko, *Kodai no hōi*, 163–166.

105. *Manyōshū*, Book I, poem 52; Cranston, 643. For the interpretation of the link between Fujiwara-kyō and the immortals' Everland, see Senda, "Tokoyo," 46–47.

106. The story of Ninigi landing in Hyūga is found not only in the *Kojiki* and *Nihon shoki*, but also in the *Sendai kuji hongi* (Bentley, *Authenticity*, 229) and the *Hitachi Fudoki*. For the latter, see Aoki, *Records of Wind*, 70.

107. Leonardo Benitez, who has researched astro-geological sites in South America, has kindly verified the astronomical measurements for the location of the three mountains and found the Unebi yama line the most precise. For the Ama no kagu yama, there was a variation of 4 degrees. Miminashi yama was due north of the Daigokuden with a declination of 3 degrees east.

108. *Manyōshū*, Book I, poem 50; Cranston, 642.

109. Farris, *Sacred Texts*, 160 (building finished only by 715), 168 (Daigokuden dismantled and abandoned); for the numerous theories concerning the date and reason for reconstruction of the palace and administrative center during the Nara period, see 165–173. Mizubayashi's theory, which I present in the pages that follow, was published several years after Farris's study.

110. Mizubayashi, "Heijō-gū dokukai," 105–188.

111. NST 1: 119, 135; Philippi, 167, 186; Mizubayashi, "Heijō-gū dokukai," 154.

112. Mizubayashi, "Heijō-gū dokukai," 112–113.

113. Mizubayashi, "Heijō-gū dokukai," 128–129, 132.

114. Mizubayashi, "Heijō-gū dokukai," 141–142.

115. The information for the following paragraph comes from Katsuura, "Kōken to Bukkyō," 98–104.

116. For Emperor Wu, see Janousch, "The emperor as Bodhisattva," 113.

117. Katsuura, "Kōken to Bukkyō," 104. For the texts of edicts 19 and 43, see SNG 3: 217 and 4: 241.

118. I have checked Mizubayashi's argument by measuring the approximate surface of the Jingikan's courtyard, based on maps of archeological excavations. The available space in the courtyard, no more than perhaps 2,200 square meters, could have accommodated comfortably the some seven or eight hundred delegates (and all of officialdom) expected to be present when their numbers were reduced in the last years of the eighth century, but not the large numbers early in the century.

119. Mizubayashi, "Heijō-gū dokukai," 136; *Kiki shinwa*, 178–179, 195, 284–285, 288.

120. Mizubayashi, *Kiki shinwa*, 383.

Chapter 4: Allochthons

Epigraph: Tanaka Takashi, *Shinsen shōjiroku no kenkyū*, 264.

1. On the complicated question of language affinities in this region, see Marshall Unger, "Layers of Words and Volcanic Ash in Japan and Korea," JJS 27 (2001): 81–111.

2. On ancient Japan's Korean connection mainly regarding material culture as revealed through comparing archeological findings with historical records, see chapter 2 by that name in Farris, *Sacred Texts*.

3. The *Nihon shoki*, however, reports also that Wang-in, the legendary Paekche ancestor of the Fumi no Obito lineage of scribes, arrived at King Ōjin's court in 285 CE (Aston 1: 262).

4. The official year for the "introduction" of Buddhism in Yamato is 553, although some scholars put the date fifteen years earlier (Kumagai, *Ōkimi*, 198).

5. After four centuries of division, the Sui reunited China in 589 and were replaced by the Tang in 618. Charlotte von Verschuer's exhaustive study of these and later embassies (*Les relations officielles*) includes the biographies of the main envoys and full translations of the relevant Japanese sources; for a list of the embassies, see 517. See also Zhenping Wang, *Ambassadors*.

6. Zhenping Wang, "Manuscript Copies," 59n9; idem, *Ambassadors*, 307n32. On foreigners in Changan, see Iwami Kiyohiro, "Tōdai chōan no gaikokujin: Kokushikan to ryūgakusei," HAKB, 123 (2005): 37–50.

7. Lewin, *Aya*, 51–61.

8. NSK: 540/8 (Aston 2: 38–39).

9. Watanabe Akihiro, *Heijō-kyō to mokkan*, 16.

10. These institutions are mentioned in a *Nihon shoki* entry of the first month of 675.

11. Queen Sŏndŏk from Silla (634–647) had already built a nine-meter-high astronomical platform that is still standing today as the oldest extant observatory in East Asia; see Portal, *Korea*, 70–71. In a poem from 808, titled "The Observation Tower," the Tang poet Bo Juyi describes the function of these platforms: "From the observation tower, looking up they observe, looking down they examine, linking [signs in] heaven with [events] on earth. . . . The signs in the sky, the changes in the times, in both cases it is the same. The Son of Heaven within the palace of neither is informed. So for what use is it for that tower to be hundred feet in height?" (South, "Po Chü-i's 'Tower,'" 3). On the historiographical debate regarding the nature and function of these towers in seventh-century Japan, see Bialock, *Eccentric Spaces*, 68–73.

12. Aihe Wang, *Cosmology*, 2. This system is a Chinese adaptation of macroand microcosmic correspondences between the universe and the human world, and a companion portent astrology that probably originated in Babylonia in the fourth millennium BCE and spread to Europe, India, and Southeast Asia as well (Heine-Geldern, "Conceptions of State," 15–16). In China, combined with theoretical elaborations of the Five Phases and their transformations and configurations,

this system came to provide the most widely used framework for all branches of learning (Hellmut Wilhelm, *Eight Lectures*, 81).

13. Kumagai, *Ōkimi*, 144–145, 184, 254; Hesselink, "Mounted Archery," 47.

14. According to the *Nihon shoki*, two years earlier the Mononobe, blaming Buddhism for an outbreak of pestilence, had received permission to destroy Soga temples, ransack the images, and arrest and flog nuns. On Soga patronage of Buddhism, see M. Inoue, "Reform," 61, 171–174; and Sonoda, "Early Buddha Worship," CHJ 1: 359–371.

15. Murayama, "Kodai Onmyōdō," OMS 1: 19; idem, ed., *Nihon onmyōdō-shi sōsetsu*, 26–27.

16. Tamura, "Onmyōryō seiritsu izen," OMS 1: 40–41. This was also a time of murderous politics. Suiko assumed the throne after Soga Umako, an uncle, had arranged the assassination of Emperor Sushun, her half brother. Her succession by Emperor Jomei was accompanied by another assassination: her coruler Shōtoku's son, Yamashiro Ōe, was eliminated by Soga Emishi (Umako's son), with Emishi's son, Iruka, finishing the job by exterminating the Yamashiro clan.

17. Tamura, "Onmyōryō seiritsu izen," OMS 1: 38. For a table of various categories of portents for each year between 513 and 685, see the fold-out page between 38 and 39. The information that follows is taken from Tamura's chapter.

18. In China, oxen were sacrificed by the emperor when worshipping Heaven; human sacrifices took place even in the Tang. See Schaefer, *Pacing the Void*, 93, 221. Although sacrifices are often considered alien to Japan and "Shinto," prohibitions against sacrificing horses were issued in the ninth century, and even as late as 1501 the bones and head of deer were used in rainmaking ceremonies. Emperor Kanmu made animal sacrifices to Heaven in 785 and 787. See Hereto, *Rekishi no kome to niku*, 72, 74. The *Nihon Ryōiki* has a story about oxen being sacrificed during Emperor Shōmu's reign (724–749) (K. Nakamura, *Miraculous Stories*, Part II, Tale 5, p. 164). On 791/9/16, prohibitions were issued in seven provinces against sacrificing oxen to Han gods. The *Hachiman gūdōkun*, around the turn of the fourteenth century, reports that it was customary in the Niukawakami shrine (Yamato) to sacrifice white horses to make rains stop and black ones in times of drought; see Matsumae, *Matsumae chosakushū*, 7: 133. Ueda Masa'aki documents in detail how widespread the practice was in ancient Japan down through the Heian period ("Satsugyūba shinkō," in Ueda, ed. *Kamigami no saishi*, 19–34).

19. Wada ("Nanzan no kyūtōryū," 316) argues that it was this rainmaking sutra that was chanted, rather than "Mahayana sutras" as the text says.

20. NSK 2: 424 (676/8/16). The term was common in South China, where it referred to magical expulsion formulae (Confucian, Buddhist, and especially Daoist) used for healing purposes. See Fukunaga Mitsuji in Mori and Kadowaki, *Jinshin no ran*, 29.

21. The Kinai region includes the five Home Provinces of Yamato, Kawachi, Izumi, Yamashiro, and Settsu. They are located in an arc around the inner end of Osaka Bay, roughly a hundred kilometers inland, with Kyoto to the north and the foothills of the Yoshino Mountains to the south.

22. For the figures of the temples, see Piggott, *Emergence*, 95, 147.

23. For details, see De Visser, *Ancient Buddhism in Japan*, 1: chap. 1.

24. Hayami, "Ritsuryō kokka," 5–8. On the Sōgō in English, see K. Nakamura, *Miraculous Stories*, Introduction, 18–19; and Abé, *Weaving of the Mantra*, 30–33.

25. The Yōrō Code of 718 had a special section for the worship of the gods and a twenty-seven-article section for monks and nuns (*Sōni-ryō*). Scholars agree that these sections were basically no different from those of the now lost Taihō Code of 701, and it is probable that Tenmu's Kiyomihara Code of the 680s contained similar provisions. See *Ritsuryō*, NST 3: 541.

26. The first omen in the record dates from 599, under Suiko, whose rule started in 592. For these figures, see Tamura, "Onmyōryō seiritsu," table, 37–38; and Murayama, *Nihon onmyōdō-shi*, 51–52.

27. Matsumoto, "Ritsuryō kokka sai-i shisō," 147 (Northern and Southern dynasties; book burning); CHC 3, Part 1: 178 (Sui prohibition), 384, 429 (respectively an accusation of astrology in 726, and one of fortune-telling in 752).

28. I have followed Wallace Johnson's translation of the Tang Code (*T'ang Code* 2: 78–79) rather than relying on the headnotes of *Ritsuryō*, NST 3: 68–69. The Confucian apocrypha will be discussed later.

29. SNG 4: 181 (767/9/16); 345 (771/7/23). For details of the plot, see chapter 8.

30. *Ritsuryō*, NST 3: 476.

31. *Ritsuryō*, NST 3: 99–100; Johnson, *T'ang Code* 2: 275.

32. *Ritsuryō*, NST 3: 216.

33. *Nihon kōki* (810/9/28): 533; see Frank, *Kata-imi*, 43.

34. Lewin, *Aya*, 5–10.

35. Hesselink, "Mounted Archery," 30–33.

36. Hesselink, "Mounted Archery," 43.

37. The number of "Chinese" *uji* is taken from Lewin, *Aya*, 192; the other figures have been slightly revised recently (Seki, *Kikajin*, 6–7).

38. Seki, *Kikajin*, 24. Kakubayashi ("Reconstruction," 13) places the beginnings of *kabane*-like titles early: in the third and fourth centuries with the rise of the Yamato state.

39. Seki, *Kikajin*, 91.

40. For a detailed narrative of these developments, see K. Lee, *A New History of Korea*, 19–24; for the Three Kingdoms up to the unification under Silla, see chaps. 3 and 4, the source for the information that follows. See also pertinent sections in CHJ 1.

41. A much debated theory that horse riders invaded Yamato in the fourth century (and possibly established the Yamato Sun line of rulers) has been seriously criticized, although recent archeological evidence of armor found at Kaya sites may have reopened the question (Portal, *Korea*, 55). For the earlier debate, see Gari Ledyard, "Galloping along with the Horseriders: Looking for the Founders of Japan," JJS 1 (1975): 217–254; Walter Edwards, "Event and Process in the Founding of Japan: The Horserider Theory in Archeological Perspective," JJS 9 (1983): 265–295; Kakubayashi, "Reconstruction"; Hesselink, "Mounted Archery."

42. Lewin, *Aya*, 5.

43. Brown, "Yamato Kingdom," CHJ 1: 142.

44. Recent scholarship has concluded that the year was not 631 (the *Nihon shoki* date), the date also adopted by M. Inoue ("Reform," 205); see Kumagai, *Ōkimi*, 299–300.

45. K. Lee, *History of Korea*, 69.

46. Ōwa, *Tenmu tennō ron* 2: 75.

47. K. Lee, *History of Korea*, 48; see also Naoki in Mori and Kadowaki, *Jinshin no ran*, 209–210.

48. Wechsler, "Founding of the T'ang dynasty," CHC 3, Part 1: 185–186.

49. K. Lee, *History of Korea*, 74.

50. Naoki Kōjirō surmises that these ships may have been returning Japanese war captives, which would explain the large number of people aboard (Naoki and Kuroiwa, "Tenmu," 5).

51. For the naval defeat's consequences and aftermath, see Batten, "Foreign Threat," 208–216.

52. The *Nihon shoki* mentions delegations from Paekche in 667 and 668 (without specifying that they came from the Chinese commandery after the defeat of 663). Chejudo (Tamna in Aston) sent two embassies under Tenji, three under Tenmu, and two under Jitō.

53. SNG 1: 81 (704/7/1). For an English rendering, see Snellen, "Shoku Nihongi," 216. For a more accurate French translation, see von Verschuer, *Relations*, 262.

54. Ōtsu Tōru has gathered the data on the refugees between 661 and 833 in a table (*Ritsuryō kokka shihai kōzō*, 97).

55. Seki, *Kikajin*, 100; see also NSK 2: 376, headnotes 16–19.

56. Seki, *Kikajin*, 119, 121, 128; on Kanmu, see SNG 5: 453 (790/1/15).

57. Seki, *Kikajin*, 6–7; *Shinsen shōjiroku* text related to the *kikajin*, 263–385. Lewin (*Aya*, 192) has a statistical table that breaks down the numbers of the *Shinsen shōjiroku* by province and declared country of origin; his figures differ slightly from Seki's, which are based on more recent scholarship.

58. Kiley, "A Note on Surnames," 178.

59. Kiley, "A Note on Surnames," 177.

60. SNG 3: 185 and 184n14.

61. Lewin, *Aya*, 155.

62. Seki, *Kikajin*, 104, 124–125.

63. For detailed maps of Aya and Hata settlements throughout the archipelago, see Lewin, *Aya*, 50–100 passim, esp. 49, 80.

64. There are two aspects to the term "Nihon." In the *Nihon shoki*, where it occurs twenty-nine times, its connotation expresses the "vassal" status of Paekche and Silla vis-à-vis Yamato (Kōnoshi, "Nihon" to wa, 30–42) and was used as an honorific term by the peninsular kingdoms. It is absent from the *Kojiki*, where the two kingdoms are treated as extensions of Yamato (45–46). Instead, the *Kojiki* uses Yamato (sixty-four times) as a neutral term without international implications (62). "Nihon" (where the sun rises) as a term without specific reference to a country may have been used in China already around the turn of the fourth century (65, 82). It was on the occasion of the 702 embassy to the China of Empress Wu that "Yamato" was officially replaced with "Nihon" (12–17).

Chapter 5: Liturgies

Epigraphs: NSK 2: 414; Philippi, 139, modified; Inbe, *Kogoshūi* (Katō), 27 (*Gunsho*), 5; *Ruijū sandaikyaku*, 321.

1. Miyoshi, *Iken jūnikajō*, 119. For a variant partial translation of this passage and its sequels that follow, see *Engishiki* (Bock) 1: 13–14; for a German translation, see Kluge, *Miyoshi Kiyoyuki*, 40–70. According to Kluge (46n10), the first line is a quotation from the *Hanshu*'s biography of Li Shichi.

2. Six of the thirteen festivals were held twice yearly. The five harvest-related ones were Toshigoi, Tsukinami (twice), Kanname, Daijō/Niiname, and Ainame (Jingi-ryō, art. 2–9, in *Ritsuryō*, NST 3: 212–213; for a translation with brief comments, see George Sansom, "Early Japanese Law ([Part II]," TASJ, 2nd ser., 11 (1934): 122–127). For the list and a brief description of their characteristics, including the great purification ceremony held twice yearly, see Nishimiya, *Jingi saishi seido*, 17, table 1.

3. For a concise introduction to these ancient festivals, see Naumann, "State Cult," 52–63. For the detailed procedures regarding these festivals, see *Engishiki* (Bock) 1: Books 1, 2, 3 for the Middle Festivals; 2: Book 7 for the Daijō-sai, and Book 8 for prayers. On the Daijō-sai and the Toshigoi festivals, see respectively Ellwood, *Feast of Kingship*, and idem, "Spring Prayer."

4. Ōtsu, *Kodai no tennōsei*, 89–90; Maruyama Yumiko, "Sai'in niiname-sai," 81–86. The earliest group of shrines was already closely connected with the Tenmu court since they were sent offerings during Tenmu's illness (686/7/5). For a map of the geographical distribution of these shrines in Yamato, see Nishimiya, *Jingi saishi seido*, 82.

5. *Kojiki*, NST 1: 170, 208; *Manyōshū*, Book I, poem 50, and Book VI, poem 956; SNG 1: 5 (697/8/17) (Monmu's enthronement), 2: 139 (724/2/4) (Shōmu's enthronement). On this subject, see Ōtsu, *Kodai no tennōsei*, 62–63; Nakamura Ikuo, "'Osukuni' no shisō," 315–337.

6. Examples are local products brought to the court by the Emishi from Echigo on 698/6/14 or entertainment on the occasion of Genshō's visit to Mino (717/9/12 and 18).

7. Nishimiya, *Jingi saishi seido*, 21.

8. Ōtsu, *Kodai no tennōsei*, 87–89. Maruyama Yumiko ("Sai'in niiname-sai," 77) points out Chinese precedents for this practice.

9. The entry of 673/12/5 is about an Ōnie (first fruits) festival (later called Niiname/Daijō-sai) held by Tenmu, but from various elements mentioned here and at Jitō's coronation (690/1/1) it is clear that this was held on the occasion of Tenmu's enthronement. Tenmu: "Emoluments were given to all those who offered their service (*tsukaematsureru*) at the Ōnie: the Nakatomi and Inbe, the officials from the Kami Office (*kamutsukasa*) and the district governors of the two provinces of Harima and Tanba." Jitō: "... Nakatomi Ōshima, head of the Kami Office, recited the prayer to the *kami* of Heaven, Inbe Shikobuchi presented the sacred emblems of sword and mirror to the empress-consort, who thereby assumed the throne." The selection by divination of two provinces for the First Fruits Festival

is mentioned explicitly on 676/9/21 and continued through the Nara period for the yearly Niiname festival; afterward it became reserved for the Daijō-sai only at the beginning of each reign. Ōnie literally means "great offering."

10. They were the Toshigoi festival, the two Tsukinami festivals, and the Niiname and Kanname festivals. In the early ninth century, the Kamo festival was added.

11. *Hanpei* is the technical term (literally meaning "distributed [*han*] offerings [*hei, mitegura*]") for the royal oblations distributed in the Jingikan. *Mitegura* is used for royal offerings to the *kami*, while the same character is read *nusa* for offerings to the *kami* by others than the monarch. On this terminology, see Nishimiya, *Jingi saishi seido*, 341, 352.

12. *Mitegura* were also distributed for a variety of reasons: yearly to Ise; to all government shrines at the time of enthronement; to specific shrines for protection against spreading contagious diseases; for rainmaking purposes; for victory in war; and so forth (Nishimiya, *Jingi saishi seido*, 380–397). On these occasions, however, emissaries were sent out by the Jingikan to deliver the oblations, rather than by representatives from shrines having traveled to the capital to receive them.

13. Weber, *Economy and Society* 2: 1022–23 (italics in original).

14. Farris, *Sacred Texts*, 218.

15. The first instance of this practice takes place on 692/12/24 when Jitō had Silla tribute articles brought to five shrines, including Ise (to which she had paid an exceptional visit earlier that year), followed on 698/1/19 with a similar ceremony at Tenmu's tomb. (By then Tenji had not received an official tomb yet.) For eleven such cases between 692 and 839, see Ōtsu, *Kodai no tennōsei*, 96–97.

16. Farris, *Sacred Texts*, 160.

17. Maruyama Masao, "The Structure of *Matsurigoto*," 32–34, 38; Ōtsu, *Kodai no tennōsei*, 81, 82, 90 on *mitsugi*.

18. Maruyama Masao, "*Matsurigoto*," 272n7.

19. The Emishi were already subjected to rites of submission in 581 (Kumagai, *Ōkimi*, 292).

20. On Jitō's first posthumous name, see chapter 2; on the issue of interdependency, see Mizubayashi, *Kiki shinwa*, 78, 125, 301, 336, 356–357; Ōtsu, *Kodai no tennōsei*, 60. A comparison with Korean founding myths leads to the same conclusion that in Yamato greater acknowledgment of local powers was incorporated into the myth; see Grayson, *Myths and Legends, from Korea*, 135.

21. *Engishiki* (Bock) 2: 66 (Book 8: Norito of the Toshigoi Festival); *Engishiki* (Torao) 1: 445.

22. See entries in the *Nihon shoki* for 404/9/18, 554/2, and 672/7/23; Hayashi, "Jōdai shinshoku seido," 12.

23. Nishimiya, *Jingi saishi seido*, 150.

24. Nishimiya, *Jingi saishi seido*, 114.

25. Sasada, "Ritsuryō," 3, 11.

26. The discussion of the ritual aspect of Tenmu and Jitō's rule follows Sasada, "Kenkyū nōto," 37–62.

27. Ellwood, *Feast of Kingship*, 152.

28. Kanō, *Nihon kodai no kokka to tojō*, 85–86.

29. Grapard, "Shrines Registered," 219–222.

30. Four edicts (Monmu, Kōken twice, Saga) mention no religious groups; one is unclear, and two (Genmei and Shōmu) refer only to monks (Nishimiya, *Ritsuryō kokka saishi*, 148–150).

31. In the early Nara period, we know that the *kami* tribute was registered separately. After being reported to the Council of State and the Ministry of Popular Affairs, it was transmitted to the Jingikan when requested: *Ritsuryō*, NST 3: 540n20a, n20b. The Code for the Office of Kami Affairs stipulated that this *kami* tax was earmarked for the building of shrines and as offerings for the *kami* and could not be used as loan seed rice: *Ritsuryō*, NST 3: 215 (Jingi-ryō, art. 12).

32. *Engishiki* (Torao) 1: 793–794n2.

33. *Ritsuryō*, NST 3: 540n20a.

34. Sasada, "Ritsuryō," 11.

35. *Engishiki* (Torao) 1: 794.

36. Computation for the four festivals mentioned earlier is based on table 2 of Nishimiya, *Jingi saishi seido*, 18–21; it includes another minor harvest festival, the Ainame festival for seventy-one shrines in Yamato province. Conversion into metric values is based on the table of weights and measures in KDJ 10: 481, "*doryōkō*"; and Dettmer, "Die Maßeinheiten der Nara-Zeit," 10. For more figures in English, see also *Engishiki* (Bock) 1: Books 1, 2; 2: Book 9; and Grapard, "The Economics of Ritual Power," 81–84. Caution, however, is necessary since Bock's Table of Measurements in *Engishiki* (Bock) 2: 173, and Bock, "Enthronement Rites," 308–309, apparently used by Grapard, gives Tokugawa values for measurements, some of which are substantially different from eighth-century ones. Thus one *koku* is not the equivalent of 180 liters, but only 24 (or 73); I chose the 24-liter (*shō*) equivalent over the 73-liter one (*daishō*), which is sometimes used.

37. Ōtsu, *Ritsuryō kokka shihai kōzō*, 197, 256–258. For the important role played by minor capital and provincial officials in trade through the conversion of tribute rice, see Farris, "Trade, Money and Merchants," 321–323.

38. Three days of partial abstinence and one day of total abstinence. See the *Engishiki*'s prescriptions for the Toshigoi festival (Bock 1: 64).

39. Naumann, "State Cult," 62.

40. See *Engishiki* (Torao) 1: 31. In Bock's translation (1: 64) of the Toshigoi festival, the line about using the regular tribute is dropped, although Ellwood translates it ("Spring Prayer," 11). See also the stipulation, "the things of each province," *atari kuni no mono* in *Ruijū kokushi* 1 (KST 5), Book 10: 85. For the practice toward the end of the first half of the eighth century, see *Engishiki* (Torao) 1: 744n1, n2.

41. Nishimiya, *Ritsuryō*, 35, 37.

42. Nishimiya, *Ritsuryō*, 97, 99.

43. Sasada, "Kenkyū nōto," 40. Actually, one earlier entry of 670/3/9 mentions that Tenji had "mats (*za; mimashi*) for various *kami* laid out near Mount Mii to make offerings," which, however, were not *hanpei*.

44. The *Engishiki*, (Bock) 1: 74–75 offers details of the preparations for the festivals. The stipulation for the official delegation to each shrine is a prince of fifth rank or above and a member of the Office of Kami Affairs of sixth rank or above, aside from diviners and a deputy governor of the province; the cost was to be shouldered in part by regular taxes.

45. The data for this chronology come from Nishimiya, *Ritsuryō*, 32–34.

46. Sasada, "Kenkyū nōto," 47–49 (map on 48); see also Hayakawa, *Kodai kanryōsei*, 14, 15.

47. Maruyama Yumiko, "Sai'in niiname-sai," 85.

48. For the dates in this paragraph, see Aston 2: 396, 398 (690); SNG 1: 51–55 (701, 702).

49. Gt 103; Cd 158.

50. For the illustration of the set used in 758, see Nara kokuritsu hakubutsukan, ed., *Dai gojikkai Shōsōin ten*, plates 35, 39.

51. *Manyōshū*, Book XX, poem 4493; Cranston, 480–81.

52. For the dates in the paragraph, see Aston 2: 296 (671); SNG 2: 403 (742), 419–425 (743).

53. Andreas Janousch has counted only thirty-eight performances during the eight centuries of pre-Sui imperial times, eleven of them by Emperor Wu (502–549) of the Liang dynasty. For Emperor Wu (265–290), founder of the Jin dynasty, the ceremony was clearly linked to establishing legitimacy for his rule ("Rhapsodies on the Sacred Field"; paper delivered at the Forty-fifth Annual Meeting for the Association for Asian Studies, Los Angeles, California, March 26, 1993). It seems to have had a similar function for Empress Shōtoku.

54. I discovered that Yoshie Akiko agrees with this interpretation when she writes that the ritual of 758, "cannot be taken as evidence of even an abortive attempt to adopt the Chinese-style farming and silkworm-raising ritual" (Yoshie, "Gender," 459). She also notes that only in modern times (1875) did it become "customary for the empress to conduct a ritual sweeping of the silkworm-rearing room" (460n77).

55. Nishimiya, *Ritsuryō*, 36.

56. The coat was called *konpen jūnishō* (ceremonial coat with twelve embroidered insignia); it is mentioned on 820/2/2 in the *Nihon kiryaku* (KST 10: 310) and was probably introduced toward the end of the eighth century; it is doubtful, as some argue, that Emperor Shōmu already wore it in 732 (Takeda, "Tennō no kan to ifuku," 75–78).

57. This argument is spelled out in Hayakawa, *Nihon kodai kanryōsei*, chap. 1.

58. Nishimiya, *Ritsuryō*, 54–56.

59. Wada, "Shinpinron," 61–82.

60. Philippi, 90, 238.

61. Philippi, 246–249; Aston 1: 209–210.

62. Personal communication from Kamata Jun'ichi, chamberlain at the Imperial Household Agency, July 2, 2005.

63. For the specific changes in the enthronement procedures up to and includ-

ing the Heian period, see Hashimoto, *Girei*, 1–32 (introductory chapter). Three great kings received symbols in 412, 480, 484; after Keitai and before Jitō, three received a sword and jewel in 535, 592, 629; five times a platform ceremony is mentioned, the last time in 645 (Hashimoto, *Girei*, 8–11).

64. Wada, "Shinpinron," 64–66.

65. Ōtsu, *Kodai no tennōsei*, 56–57.

66. See note 9 of this chapter.

67. Mayuzumi, *Kokka seiritsu-shi*, 634, 646, 659. For the text in the catalogue, see Tokyo Daigaku Shiryōhensanjo, *Dai Nihon komonjo*, Hennen monjo 4, 25: 138–139.

68. Mayuzumi, *Kokka seiritsu-shi*, 650.

69. Mayuzumi, *Kokka seiritsu-shi*, 618.

70. Bentley, *Authenticity*, 81–83, 156–162.

71. Mayuzumi, *Kokka seiritsu-shi*, 603, 620.

72. *Kogoshūi* (Katō), 27; (*Gunsho*), 5.

73. Philippi, 140; Hashimoto, *Girei*, 21–22.

74. Grayson, *Myths and Legends from Korea*, 31, 135.

75. Mayuzumi, *Kokka seiritsu-shi*, 626.

76. *Nihon kōki*, 806/3/17 (339; see notes pp. 5 and 1195).

77. *Ritsuryō*, NST 3: 198 (*Gokū shiki'in ryō*, art. 5); 101 (*Zokutō ritsu*, art. 24).

78. Mayuzumi, *Kokka seiritsu-shi*, 624.

79. Fujiwara influence in the Rear Palace began when Fuhito's daughter Miyako married Monmu *tennō* in 697, three weeks after his enthronement; her sister then became Shōmu's main consort. *Shōzō* included Fujiwara women and wives: daughters of three of Fuhito's four sons (Muchimaro, Fusasaki, Maro); wives of the next Fujiwara generation (Yoshitsugu, Nagate, and Fuyutsugu among others). Mayuzumi, *Kokka seiritsu-shi*, 628, table 62.

80. Kamikawa, "Chūsei no sokui," 130.

81. Kamikawa, "Ondoiement," 179–181; Bouchy, "Du légitime et de l'illégitime," 147–153; on the *cakravartin*, see Abe, *Weaving of the Mantra*, 330–332, 352–353.

82. Kamikawa, "Ondoiement," 179; idem, "Chūsei no sokui," 127–128.

83. Taira, "La légitimation de la violence," 80–82.

84. Moerman, *Localizing Paradise*, 6-7, 139–148 passim, 238.

Chapter 6: Deposits

Epigraph: NSK 1: 310; Aston 1: 210, modified.

1. Shinkawa, *Dōkyō*, 31, 43; also see Pradel, "Tenjukoku Shūchō Mandara," 257–289.

2. Seidel, "Chronicle of Taoist Studies," 301.

3. On the relationship between Daoism, Confucianism, and Buddhism (as a foreign religion) in China during these centuries, see Schipper, "Purity and Strangers," 61–80.

4. Zhenping Wang, *Ambassadors*, 210.

5. Barrett, *Taoism under the T'ang*, 22; for India, see Kohn and Kirkland, "Daoism in the Tang (618–907)," 343; for Koguryŏ, see Jung, "Daoism in Korea," 795; Shinkawa, *Dōkyō*, 244–245.

6. For an overview of the Japanese scholarship, see Masuo, "Nihon kodai no shūkyō bunka to dōkyō," 256–258. The iconoclastic group, represented by Fukunaga Mitsuji, is maximalist; the traditional cohort (Shimode Sekiyo, Naba Toshisada), minimalist. Positions on the place of Daoism at the beginnings of Japanese and Korean history are overdetermined by political issues. Japanese scholars are eager to deconstruct the homogeneous view of Japanese culture through highlighting the indispensable role played by continental elements, even in the formation of Shinto. In Korea, the trend is the reverse. Over the last fifteen years Korean scholars have emphasized a primordial autochthonous Korean Daoism to which China's version would have been a later addition. See Jung ("Kankoku dōkyō no kigen," 206–222) for a more detailed critique of Korean scholarship than in his slightly earlier English article "Daoism in Korea." For highly informative, slightly older, but still valuable overviews of Japanese scholarship on Nara and pre-Nara Daoism in Japan, see Seidel, "Chronicle of Taoist Studies,"299–304; Kohn, "Taoism in Japan," 389–412. See also Bialock, *Eccentric Spaces*, 24–30. My own introduction to the why of institutional Daoism's absence in Japan came through reading Shinkawa, *Dōkyō*.

7. The Law codes organized a network of shrines for official sponsorship and state service, but these covered only a fraction of *kami* worship practices. On the problems caused by the application of the term "Shinto" and the preference for "*kami* worship," and the *ritsuryō* role in formatting some of these practices, see in JJRS 29, no. 3/4 (2002), articles by Teeuwen and Scheid, "Tracing Shinto" (195–207); Grapard, "Shrines Registered" (209–232); and Teeuwen, "*Jindō* to Shinto" (233–263).

8. Seidel, "Tokens of Immortality," 87, 110.

9. Chan, "*Daode jing*," 4. The *Daode jing* is a small, randomly arranged collection of paradoxical insights into the condition of humans as part of cosmic nature, the unfathomable Way, with which they should seek to become one, and thus reach immortality. The *Zhuangzi* is a more elaborate work containing treatises, stories, amusing anecdotes, and occasional poetry on the same theme. Mair writes that although both texts "have been intimately linked since the Han period" the linkage "became especially prevalent in the Six Dynasties period" (principally the third and fourth centuries CE) ("*Zhuangzi*," 44, 33–34).

10. These were the texts of the Profound Learning (Xuanxue) movement of Daoist metaphysics of the third century (Mair, "*Zhuangzi*," 34, 44).

11. *Muchimaro den*, NST 8: 26.

12. The discussion that follows benefited greatly from Smith, "Sima Tan," 129–156, and Puett, *Become a God*.

13. Puett, *Become a God*, 173, 293, 297, 319. Csikszentmihàlyi provides an excellent overview of Han mantic practices in his "Han Cosmology."

14. Csikszentmihàlyi distinguishes between theories of homologies and the use

of yin-yang terms "independently as descriptions of natural phenomena" ("Han Cosmology," 66).

15. Tan was grand astrologer at the Western Han court and father of the famous astrologer and historian Sima Qian (?–ca. 85 BCE). Tan's essay "Yaozhi" (Essential Points) was preserved in Sima Qian's *Shiji* (Records of the Grand Historian) (Smith, "Sima Tan," 129).

16. Puett, *Become a God*, 304. *Fangshi* is variously translated as masters of the directions or of formulas, or witchcraft, recipe masters, magicians, mountebanks. Their overwhelming presence at the Western Han court becomes evident from a quick perusal of chapter 28 of Sima Qian's *Shiji* (Sima Qian, *Records of the Grand Historian: Han Dynasty*, 2: 3–52). Shamans eventually claimed as their ancestor Laozi's servant boy who stayed behind when Laozi retired in the West from the world of men. See Schipper, "Taoism," 54n7.

17. Seidel, "Taoist Messianism," 166.

18. Puett, *Become a God*, 243–244, 269, 303. Puett also notes (202) that since there are no references in the Chinese record of journeys by spirits or ascensions before the fourth century BCE, these phenomena cannot be explained by reference to shamanism, which obviously is far older.

19. Smith, "Sima Tan," 146–147.

20. Smith, "Sima Tan," 137–138.

21. Smith, "Sima Tan," 149.

22. Smith, "Sima Tan," 130. The rivalry included magic, if one is to believe an Eastern Han account, which reports that "Emperor Wu hired a shaman to curse Dong Zhongshu, but by chanting the classics Dong was able to avoid injury and cause the shaman to die suddenly" (Csikszentmihàlyi, "Han Cosmology," 69).

23. Puett points out that one commentary of the *Yijing*, the *Xici zhuan*, may be understood as supportive of a correlative cosmology based on an assumption of definable forces of change rather than one ruled by willful spirits (which the *fangshi* claimed to be able to direct). Thus sagehood and rulership ought to submit to textual authority, rather than to the visionary power of charlatans (*Become a God*, 189, 256).

24. Csikszentmihàlyi, "Han Cosmology," 55–56.

25. Hendrichke, "Early Daoist Movements." Seidel casts doubt upon the supposition that *fangshi* started the genre. See her "Imperial Treasures," 291–292.

26. Victor Xiong, *Sui-Tang Chang'an*, appendix 1.

27. Seidel, "Taoist Messianism," 162, 164–165.

28. Goodman, *Ts'ao P'i*, 6, 98, 134.

29. Mather, "K'ou Ch'ien-chih," 103–122. Mather (104n1) lists Taoist-led rebellions in various regions of China in 324, 335, 341, 345, 356, 370, 402–411, 407–417, 424–427. The rebellion between 407 and 417 took place in the Changan area, the southern part of the Wei empire.

30. On the political ideology of pre-Tang Daoism, see Seidel, "Imperial Treasures," and "Image of the Perfect Ruler"; and for the connection between the Li clan and the Han and Tang houses, see "Image," 219, 244. For the prophesies sur-

rounding the founding of the Tang, see Bokenkamp, "Time after Time"; for the Tang dynasty itself, see Barrett, *Taoism under the T'ang*.

31. Seidel, "Imperial Treasures," 306. This is a subgenre of "weft books" (*wei-shu*), which, according to Schafer (*Pacing the Void*, 54–55), were "[f]reely accessible to the lettered classes . . . in the Han dynasty. These passed under the deceptive guise of scholia on the old Chou dynasty classics (the *ching*, or canonical "warp threads"), and enjoyed a certain modest respectability without official approval . . . and were even consulted by the high court astrologers."

32. Seidel, "Image," 219, 226. Puett (*Become a God*, 225) refers to a carved inscription of 218 BCE where the First Emperor titled himself *huangdi*, which literally means "august god."

33. Seidel ("Taoist Messianism," 164–165) sees "Taoist mysticism [as] . . . complementary and congenial to Confucian rationality. The difference was not so much between the two systems of thought, but it was social. Not Taoist philosophy but a popular Taoist religion became the alternative, not to Confucian teachings, but to the literati regime that subscribed to it."

34. Csikszentmihàlyi, "Han Cosmology," 57–60, 68–69.

35. Seidel, "Taoist Messianism," 163.

36. Kleeman, "Ethnic Identity," 25; Nylan, "Afterword," 313. Similar texts by recipe masters were meant to argue the legitimacy of Wang Mang or his successor, the Eastern Han, and in 56 CE six such prophecies were quoted in an official inscription. This brought them into the orbit of official discourse by elevating them as commentaries on the Confucian classics, some of them even allegedly written by Confucius, but relativized them at the same time as the classics' esoteric counterparts ("weft" apocrypha) (Seidel, "Imperial Treasures," 306–307).

37. Seidel, "Imperial Treasures," 291, 294.

38. Schipper, "Purity and Strangers," 63, 67, 73.

39. The first time, before 217, they were proscribed together with books on warfare. The other occasions were 267, 336, 369–379 (the two Jin dynasties), 457–464, 486, 502–519 (Northern Wei), 589, 605 (Sui), and 767 (Tang) (Dull, "Historical Introduction," 404–406).

40. Thus, the founder of the Song dynasty of the house of Liu (420–479), on the one hand claimed descent from the Han house, which, however, although reestablished with Laozi's help, had failed to hold on to the Mandate. Accordingly, the celestial master had given the Mandate to the people. On the other hand, the Liu were now judged worthy by the current celestial master to receive the Dao.

41. At the same time, his regime sought to purify Daoism from "practices which tended to make Taoist communities into a sort of sub-government, potentially dangerous as pockets of rebellion" (Mather, "K'ou Ch'ien-chu," 109).

42. Cui Hao, a trusted adviser of three emperors of the Northern Wei who was using his ministerial power to purify society along Confucian lines for Emperor Taiwu, teamed up with Celestial Master Kou Qianzhi, who in 424 had arrived at court with revelations from Mount Song and was seeking to purify Daoism to establish a Daoist utopia. The culmination of this joint cleansing impulse was the declaration of Daoism as state religion in 440 and a purge of Buddhism, labeled

a "religion of foreign gods." Because Buddhism was predominantly embraced by Xianbei allochthons, the establishment of Daoism contra Buddhism was a move against Xianbei aristocrats (Mather, "K'ou Ch'ien-chu"). For the ethnic conflict interpretation, see David Yu, *History of Chinese Daoism*, 389; and esp. Orzech, "A Buddhist Image of (Im)Perfect Rule," 147–148; see also Ch'en, *Buddhism in China*, 145–158.

43. For the next two paragraphs, see Seidel, "Imperial Treasures," 356–366.

44. Pearce, "Form and Matter: Archaizing Reform in Sixth-Century China," 150, 156–157, 172.

45. Janousch, 'The Emperor as Bodhisattva," 113.

46. These archaic and awe-inspiring rituals had nothing to do with organized Daoism. They were said to have been inaugurated by the Yellow Emperor and were rarely performed: before Taizong arranged for them to be held in 666 and Xuanzong repeated them in 725, it was said that they had taken place only six times, the last time in 56 CE. On the *feng* and *shan* rituals and the Mingtang, see Loewe, *Chinese Ideas of Life and Death*, 130–140. On the history of the Mingtang, see Maspero, "Le Ming-t'ang," 1–71; see also Forte, *Mingtang and Buddhist Utopias*.

47. Twitchett, "Kao-tsung," 259–260; "Hsüan-tsung," 387–388.

48. The founder of the Sui liked to be referred to as the *cakravartin*, the universal ruler of the Buddhist scriptures and a surrogate buddha (Wright, "Sui Dynasty," 75–76). Anything expressing the idea of supernatural supremeness would do. The Empress Wu constructed a Mingtang in 689 and rebuilt it in 696 after it burned down. The latter had a third floor in the form of a pagoda for Buddhist ceremonies (Seidel, "Imperial Treasures," 356). For a fairly detailed description of Empress Wu's planning and building of her Mingtang, see Schafer, *Pacing the Void*, 16–19. See also Fracasso, "The Nine Tripods," 85n1; and Forte, *Political Propaganda*. Empress Wu, styled as "a Cakravartin and a Bodhisattva . . . celebrated Buddhist rites in the Ming-t'ang" (Forte, *Political Propaganda*, 164). The *cakravartin* ideal goes back beyond Buddhism as it is found in Vedic texts; see Tambiah, *Universal King*, 3.

49. Livia Kohn, "The Northern Celestial Masters," in DH, 287–289.

50. Wechsler, "T'ai-tsung," 218.

51. For the full story of Tang Daoism, see Barrett, *Taoism*, esp. 53 (the 721 turning point), 60 (canon copied), 36 (princess nuns).

52. For Ganjin's story, see Zhenping Wang, *Ambassadors*, 207–215, which, however, leaves out the detail regarding Daoism. The story is based on a disciple's memoirs, which have been fully translated by Takusu, "Le voyage de Kanshin."

53. Fukunaga, "Dōkyō ni okeru kagami to ken," 76, 89 (Northern Wei); Fukunaga, *Dōkyō to Nihon bunka*, 14 (apocrypha).

54. Zhenping Wang, *Ambassadors*, 144–145. Goodrich, ed., *Japan in the Chinese Dynastic Histories*, 15. For an authoritative discussion of these mirrors, their significance and use, see Barnes, *State Formation in Japan*, 99–103, 149–151, and 162–170.

55. Kakubayashi, "Reconstruction," 9.

56. Ware, trans., *Alchemy*, 255–256.

57. Ōwa, "Himiko," 88–89.

58. Loewe, *Ways to Paradise*, 88; and idem, *Chinese Ideas of Life and Death*, 82. For a picture of a mirror portraying the royal pair, see Barnes, *State Formation in Japan*, 102. Barnes writes (178–179) that according to the *Xunzi*, this mythological pair symbolized power and legitimate authority and that "the *Xunzi* specifies she [the Queen Mother of the West] is able to confer the right to rule, and symbolizes power and longevity." Yet the *Xunzi* makes no mention anywhere of the Queen Mother of the West. The *Zhuangzi* simply states that she possessed the Dao; see Burton Watson, trans., *The Complete Works of Zhuang Zi* (New York: Columbia University Press, 1968), 82. Loewe is silent about the queen's conveying legitimacy; she maintains cosmic order, and once met with the legendary ruler Yu, and with Emperor Wu from the Early Han (*Ways to Paradise*, 93–95, 115–119).

59. Aston 2: 144–145; K. Nakamura, *Miraculous Stories*, Part I, Tale 4, pp. 108–110.

60. Nishimura Key ("The Prince and the Pauper," 307–308) also suggests a Daoist influence.

61. NSK 2: 200n2.

62. On this subject, see Seidel, "Post-mortem Immortality."

63. Aston 1: 210–211.

64. The "art of invisibility" and "corpse deliverance" share the character *dun/ ton*. For tales of invisibility, see Christoph Kleine and Livia Kohn, "Daoist Immortality and Buddhist Holiness: A Study and Translation of the *Honchō shinsen-den*," *Japanese Religions* 24 (1999): 119–196; for the Paekche monk, see K. Nakamura, *Miraculous Stories*, Part 1, Tale 14, pp. 125–126). The Dunjia calendrical calculations using yin-yang methods were prevalent during the Sui and Tang. Many were related to the name of Ge Hong (283–343), who refers to a number of them in his *Baopuzi* (esp. chapter 19). The techniques center on calendrical precautions to be taken when entering mountains to avoid evil forces, and eventually also include magical claims to invisibility, although this does not seem to have been the most central part of these texts (Sakade, "Divination as Daoist Practice," 547–548, 557). For a complete but misleadingly theistic translation of the *Baopuzi neipian*, see Ware, *Alchemy*; for a more accurate but partial translation, see Ge Hong, *La voie des divins immortels*.

65. Isabelle Robinet, "Metamorphosis and Deliverance from the Corpse in Taoism," *History of Religions* 19 (1979): 57–58; Strickmann, "On Alchemy," 181–184.

66. Saigō Nobutsuna (*Jinshinki o yomu*, 42) finds this interpretation for "shedding" in Sima Qian's *Shiji* of the Former Han. In the *Manyōshū*, Cranston remarks (394), *utsusomi no hito* (the mortal race of man; Book II, poem 165) is close to *utsusemi* (the cast-off husk of cicada, an image for the empty husk of the world of the living) of Book III, poem 482; elsewhere, in Book III, poem 466, our locust-husk bodies are said to be but borrowed flesh (*utsusemi no kareru mi*). My colleague Torquil Duthie, however, suggested that the connotations of "ephemeral" may be Heian rather than Nara.

67. Kohn, "Taoism in Japan," 398–400. Such references can be found as early

as the reign of Yamato's eleventh king (71/3/12). See the end of his reign in Aston, 1: 186–187.

68. Aston 2: 189n4.

69. Cranston, 117–120, 464.

70. This sect, also called Maoshan Daoism, constituted a new synthesis between the teachings of the celestial masters, who had moved south, and southern pre-Daoist spiritist and shamanistic techniques. Robinet, "Shangqing — Highest Clarity," 196; see Strickmann, *Chinese Magical Medicine*, 49.

71. Shinkawa, *Dōkyō*, 69. On the important contribution to the understanding of late-seventh- and eighth-century Japan by the discovery of a total of nearly 200,000 *mokkan*, see Farris, *Sacred Texts*, chap. 4.

72. Wada, *Nihon kodai no girei to saishi* 2: 24; Shinkawa, *Dōkyō*, 68–73. Wada relates (138–139) that the Daoist annotations disappeared from Japanese herbalogical texts in the tenth century. Longevity techniques were already part of general "physical" practices during the Qin and Western Han dynasties, before Daoism.

73. Ware, *Alchemy*, chap. 5. Emperor Junna, Kanmu's son, is believed to have ingested an elixir (without fatal consequences); Fukunaga, *Uma no bunka*, 148.

74. Wada, *Nihon kodai no girei to saishi* 3: 140, 172, 227–228; Pregadio, "Elixirs," 190. Charlotte von Verschuer reports that the exceptionally superior quality of liquid mercury found in Japan was used predominantly for gilding and for export to Tang China, and that longevity solutions were mostly herbal in Japan ("Le Japon, contrée du Penglai?" 439–452).

75. For a poem by a wandering beggar-minstrel (*hokai*) who served in such *kusurigari* and reports a long lamentation by a deer about to be caught, see *Manyōshū*, Book XVI, poem 3885; Cranston, 758.

76. Wada, *Nihon kodai no girei to saishi* 2: 25, 99–115, esp. 101–103, 115, 122; see also idem, "*Kusakari to 'Honzōshūchū,'*" 3–50. Masuo Shin'ichirō (*Manyō kajin*, 17–20, 23–24), however, contra Wada, has underplayed the medicinal aspect of this yearly ritual, arguing it to be merely an elaborate ceremonial occasion to display and confirm publicly the hierarchical structure of the court and to convey wishes for a long life.

77. On 610/5/5, for instance, herbs were collected in Uda, east of Nara.

78. For details, see Piggott, *Emergence*, 239–241.

79. The discussion that follows is based upon Wada, *Nihon kodai no girei to saishi* 2: 245–264.

80. Wada (*Nihon kodai no girei to saishi* 1: 257), based on references in *Manyōshū* Book VI, poems 1034–1035, makes a plausible case for the fact that the spring was known before Genshō's progress.

81. *Manyōshū*, Book I, poems 36–39 (Cranston, 193–195).

82. Philippi, 282–283; Aston 1: 264.

83. Takagi, *Yoshino no ayu*, 358–359. Eleven of the sixty poets in the *Kaifūsō* wrote about Yoshino.

84. The Urashima Tarō story of *Manyōshū*, Book IX, poems 1740 and 1741, fuses the Everworld Tokoyo with P'eng-lai, the Isle of the Immortals (Cranston, 323–

326); the Tanabata myth of the two lover stars (Cranston, 246) is a theme in thirty-eight poems of Book X (Cranston, 822); Book V, poems 847 and 848, refer to drinking elixirs to make you fly: "It is not drinking Quintessence of cloud-flying . . ." (*kumo ni tobu kusuri hamu*) (Cranston, 548).

85. For instance, in poems 48, 80, 99, 108.

86. For a Tang poem on sky rafts, see Schafer, *Pacing the Void*, 262–263.

87. Jitō took twenty-nine of these trips during her ten-year reign as empress, one before it as Tenmu's consort, and two after she abdicated. Ebersole (*Ritual Poetry*, 283) lists the dates of all royal visits to Yoshino. In contrast, Tenmu went only once, Monmu twice, Genshō once, and Shōmu three times. Shōmu's visits had most likely to do with seeking magical protection against outbreaks of smallpox (Wada, "Nanzan no kyūtōryū," 304).

88. Wada, *Nihon kodai no girei to saishi* 3: 150–151. For a discussion of the presence of Daoist belvederes in the second half of the seventh century in Yamato, see Bialock, *Eccentric Spaces*, 70–75.

89. *Manyōshū*, Book I, poem 38. Princes Arima (640–658), Kōtoku's son, and Nagaya (684–729), Tenmu's grandson, had a towerlike structure in their compounds. They were both killed, accused of plotting and using black magic (Nagaya) or conducting prognostications in a tower (Arima) as part of their schemes (Shinkawa, *Dōkyō*, 133, 197). Emperor Wu of the Former Han may have been the first one to have built such a tower (Tanaka Tan, "Appearance and Background of the *Lou*," 286–287).

90. The information on En no Gyōja is taken from Miyake, *En no Gyōja*, 19–26.

91. The story is to be found in the *Nihon ryōiki* (K. Nakamura, *Miraculous Stories*, Part I, Tale 28, pp. 140–142).

92. See also Bialock, *Eccentric Spaces*, 92–94.

93. In an insightful chapter, Anne Bouchy has discussed the ambivalent institutional legitimacy of Shugendō, based on the ambiguous emblematic figure of En no Gyōja, servant of the court, yet accused of plotting against the state (Bouchy, "Du légitime et de l'illégitime," 127–132).

94. Masuo, "Daoism in Japan," 830.

95. Von Verschuer, *Relations*, 217.

96. I wonder whether it is purely accidental that *katsura* of Katsuragi is written with the same graph as Ge.

97. On these not uncontroversial interpretations, see Ōwa, *Tenmu tennō-ron* 2: 45–46; Wada, *Nihon kodai no girei to saishi* 2: 143; Shinkawa, *Dōkyō*, 133. Sakashita Keihachi was the first scholar to suggest in 1978 a possible link between Tenmu's zodiacal timing and the *Baopuzi* (Saigō, *Jinshinki*, 36).

98. Pierre Bourdieu's terminology ("aggregation" rather than "specification") in his *Logic of Practice*, 262, is borrowed from Kant's *Appendix to the Transcendental Dialectic*.

99. For the following paragraphs on Korean Daoism, see Jung, "Daoism in Korea," 795–796.

100. For the dates of the introduction of Buddhism to each of the Three Kingdoms, see K. Lee, *New History of Korea*, 37, 38, 43, 59.

101. For a Western audience, Jung Jaeseo (or Chong Chaeso) writes "around the sixth century" ("Daoism in Korea," 795), while he puts it much earlier for Japanese readers: "plausibly before the early fourth century" ("Kankoku dōkyō," 213).

102. For a photo of the mirror, see Wontack Hong, *Relationship between Korea and Japan in Early Period Paekche and Yamato Wa* (Seoul: Ilsimsa, 1988), fig. 11, p. 59.

103. The early Tang Chinese sources are the *Beishi* (The Northern History — from the Northern Wei to the Sui dynasty [242–618]), the *Zhoushu* (History of the Northern Zhou [557–589]), and the *Suishu* (History of the Sui [589–618]); the additional line is missing from the *Suishu* (Masuo, "Nihon kodai no shūkyō," 258; idem, *Manyō kajin*, 287). It should be noted that none of the contemporary histories of Paekche, such as the fourth-century *Sōgi* (Documentary Records) survive, although their material may have been worked into the twelfth-century *Samguk sagi* (History of the Three Kingdoms). Even though the Sui dynasty (581–618) was a strong supporter of Buddhism and feared the subversive potential of Daoism, their first calendar was made by Daoists (Wright, "The Sui Dynasty," 76–78).

104. Smith, "Sima Tan," 130.

105. Nylan, *Canon of Supreme Mystery*, 8 (quoted by Smith, "Sima Tan," 150n56).

106. As some poets under Jitō's rule phrased it after describing the splendid royal entertainment they were part of, "We live in the realm of the immortals" and "have no intention of becoming immortals." They are poems 20 and 28, *Kaifūsō*, NKBT 69: 90, 98. I owe these references to Jason Webb.

Chapter 7: Articulations

Epigraph: NSK 2: 382; Aston 2: 301, modified.

1. SNG 5: 293 (785/11/10), 353 (787/11/5). A third sacrifice took place on 856/11/25 under Emperor Montoku (*Montoku jitsuroku*, KST 3: 85–86). The site for all three known sacrifices was Katano, outside Nagaoka (between Nara and Heian), the capital for ten years (784–794). On the second and third of these occasions, Emperor Kōnin, who had restored the Tenji line, was venerated together with Heaven. These rituals, therefore, appear to have added a new emphasis to the sacral character of a new dynasty.

2. Sima Qian in chapter 27 (on astronomy) of his *Shiji*: Tsukamoto Tetsuzō, ed., *Shiki*, 6 vols. Kanbun sōsho (Tokyo: Yūhōdō shoten, 1920), 2: 123–124; see also Chavannes, *Les mémoires historiques de Se-ma Ts'ien*, vol. 3, part 2, p. 342.

3. The Little Dipper as such was not observed as an asterism by the Chinese during the first millennium (Schafer, *Pacing the Void*, 47). The celestial circumpolar region, however, was very important in Chinese astrology, astronomy, and even more so for Daoists (49). The actual pole (Pivot of Heaven) was located at some distance from the North Pole (44, 46). The Purple Palace was located in some of the stars of the Little Dipper. The Heavenly Ruler Great Emperor/God (Tianhuang dadi; Jp. Tennō taitei) was identified as the invisible god whose visible

epiphany was Polaris of the Little Dipper, resided in the Hooked Array (the arm of the Little Dipper), and rode his chariot, the Great Dipper, around the Pivot of Heaven, also called the Knot, the actual polar center.

4. Puett (*Become a God,* 174–175, 160–166 passim) emphasizes that the imperial cult of the Great One, started by Emperor Wu, paralleled Wu's casting himself as a religious autocrat surrounded by *fangshi*, a development of which Sima Qian was critical (306).

5. Fukunaga, "Kōten jōtei," 13–14.

6. Huangdi (Supreme Deity of the Pole Star) was the title through which the first emperor, Qin Shihuangdi (r. 221–206 BCE), "attempted to present himself as a divine immortal" (Schipper, "Taoism," 38).

7. In Yamato, the title change for the emperor's main consort from *ōkisaki* (*taikō*) to *kōgō* took place under Tenji.

8. Fukunaga, "Kōten jōtei," 12.

9. Masuo, "Nihon kodai shūkyō," 264–265.

10. *Ritsuryō,* NST 3: 157 (*Shokuin-ryō*).

11. Aston (2: 373) omits the day of the month, and hence "on this day" erroneously links the ceremony to the date of the previous entry, which is 11/6.

12. Watanabe Katsuyoshi, *Chinkon-sai,* 168.

13. Watanabe Katsuyoshi (*Chinkon-sai,* 168–169) refers to the *Yunji qiqian* (The Seven Lots from a Satchel), a compilation of older texts, made in the 1020s.

14. *Shaku Nihongi,* KST 8: 205–206, 282; Watanabe Katsuyoshi, *Chinkon-sai,* 202.

15. Bentley, *Authenticity,* 81.

16. Bentley, *Authenticity,* 209; *Kuji hongi,* KST 7: 59. The ceremony is also partially described in the *Engishiki,* compiled approximately between 870 and 950; see *Engishiki* (Bock) 1: 94–97. For a traditional "Shinto-historical" and folklore interpretation, see Matsumae, "The Heavenly Rock-Grotto Myth; see also Ellwood, *Feast of Kingship,* 124–130.

17. Inbe, *Kogoshūi* (Katō), 49–50; (*Gunsho*) 11.

18. The first Daijō-sai, the Chinkon-sai's twin, seems to have been Jitō's, which took place the first day of the year 690. It is generally accepted that the ceremony was given final form under Tenmu and Jitō, mainly by the Nakatomi.

19. Watanabe *Katsuyoshi, Chinkon-sai,* 139–151.

20. For the discussion in this paragraph, see Watanabe Katsuyoshi, *Chinkon-sai,* 18, 20, 144–145, 152n11.

21. I am following here Shinkawa's argument (*Dōkyō,* 88–99).

22. The dates are as follows: four under Shōmu (725/11/10; 728/11/13; 731/11/5; 732/11/27), one under Shōtoku (769/11/28), two under Kanmu (784/11/1; 803/11/1), and one under Ninmyō (841/11/1) (Yamada, *Kodai no hōi,* 172).

23. H. Wilhelm, trans., *Change,* 97.

24. For Watanabe's discussion of the winter solstice and its meaning, see *Chinkon-sai,* 172–184. I continue following mainly Shinkawa's discussion.

25. This is the explanation given in the *Ryō no gige* (Legal Commentary; KST 22: 29) in 833, which Watanabe Katsuyoshi (*Chinkon-sai,* 225–126, 230) cites as an

example of undue Chinese influence that obfuscates the Chinkon-sai's original meaning.

26. Yü Ying-Shih, "'Oh Soul,'" 365.

27. Andersen, "Bugang," 20; see also Watanabe Katsuyoshi, Chinkon-sai, 204–205.

28. Ware, Alchemy, 49–50, 87, and 102: "recalling a man's ethereal breaths."

29. Masuo, "Daoism in Japan," 834. The work was well known in the Nara period, when it was copied several times (Masuo, "Nihon kodai no dōkyō juyō," 308).

30. Wada ("Nanzan no kyūtōryū," 307) reports the discovery of wooden tags in Fujiwara-kyō, Jitō's capital, with references to the Wuxing dayi (Cd 37, 48).

31. Shinkawa, Dōkyō, 89–90. Shinkawa Tokio encouraged me personally to look in the Wuxing dayi for clues regarding the specific mantic correlations involved in the Chinkon-sai.

32. Sun and Kistemaker, The Chinese Sky, 116. For a photograph of the grave, see CHC 1: 51. On the tiger in Chinese lore, see Naumann, "Der Tiger," 117–120.

33. On the Takamatsuzuka mound, opened in 1972, see Kidder, "The Newly Discovered Takamatsuzuka Tomb," 245–251; for the Kitora mound, photographed in 1986, see Nara bunkazai kenkyūjo, Kitora kofun.

34. Its meaning is clarified in the fifty-first hexagram, built from two zhen trigrams on top of each other.

35. It is worth noting that the winds from the east and southeast are described as of pristine clarity and purity, prominent Daoist values: qingming/seimei 清明, mingjing/meijō 明浄, qingliang/seiryō 清涼 (Gt 236b; Cd 356).

36. This theory of the first five mythological emperors following one another in a natural cosmic sequence the way the five virtues associated with the Five Phases lined up was applied as the natural cycle to explain the succession of dynasties. It was formalized by Dong Zhongshu during the Former Han and further expanded in the apocrypha toward the end of that dynasty. See chapter 6.

37. Bourdieu, Logic of Practice, 261, 264.

38. In such a series, neighboring items (A and B; B and C) are homologous or similar in certain respects, but nonneighboring items (A and C) are less consonant.

39. Tamura, "Onmyōryō seiritsu," 56–57.

40. Kojiki, Book 1, chap. 17 (Philippi), one of the longest chapters of Book 1.

41. The two ceremonies were not yet linked when Jitō acceded to the throne on 690/1/1.

42. For an original interpretation of this episode and ritual, from which I borrow, see Naumann, Einheimlische Religion Japans, 1: 83–88. Naumann points out that it was ultimately laughter by the myriad gods at Uzume's lascivious dance that resulted in Amaterasu's return, and not the divinatory and ceremonial attempts by the ancestral kami of the Nakatomi and Inbe. It is suggestive to note that the fifty-first hexagram of the Yijing, the hexagram that symbolizes the beginning of things in the east, the light moving up from below, and thunder making itself heard again in the spring, includes laughter. A loud laugh was also the first act of

Buddha when he was born. See Lamotte, *Traité de la Grande Vertu*, 7 (reference from Roger, *Mythe et souveraineté*, 92n4).

43. Naumann, "State Cult," 55.

44. Shinkawa, *Dōkyō*, 99.

45. Watanabe Akihiro, *Heijō-kyō*, 34.

46. Steinhardt ("Taoist Architecture," 61, 62, 74n21) mentions that Taiji Gong were also built in the Eastern Jin capital and both Tang capitals and that during the Sui and Tang, Daoist buildings were found inside the walls of the enclosed imperial palaces.

47. Fukunaga, *Uma no bunka*, 15, 150–151. The *den* of Daigokuden and the *gong* of Taiji Gong are different graphs, the former meaning "hall," the latter meaning "palace."

48. Shinkawa, "Rettō Nihon," 104.

49. Penny, "Immortality and Transcendence," 116.

50. Fukunaga, "Kagami to ken," 60, 91.

51. Fukunaga, *Uma no bunka*, 152.

52. Fukunaga, "Kagami to ken," 77.

53. Fukunaga, "Kagami to ken," 83; see, for instance, Ware, *Alchemy*, 255–257, 281, 306.

54. Fukunaga, "Kagami to ken," 76, 89. Swords and mirrors had already been described as symbols of heavenly rulers in apocrypha of the second and third century (Fukunaga, *Dōkyō to Nihon bunka*, 14).

55. This dual nature of *ki* (including ceremonial swords as its support) is also at work in the Izanagiryū ritual tradition, heavily influenced by yin-yang and Daoist notions, Simone Mauclaire reports in her study of a Muromachi village ("Histoire et événement rituel," 71, 75, 76, 77).

56. See chaps 19, 39, 82, 85 of the *Kojiki* (Philippi), and Aston 1: 53, 79, 211. See also *Shinto jiten*, 385, "*sanshu no shingi.*" For Keitai, see chapter 5 under "Enthronement Implements."

57. Only the curved jewel was kept in the palace. In China, jewels became used as a symbol of authority in Confucian contexts during the fourth century (Fukunaga, in Mori and Kadowaki, *Jinshin no ran*, 19).

58. Okada, "Ōkimi jūnin gishiki," 22.

59. See chap. 6, note 7.

60. Fukunaga, "Tennō to shikyū," 965–968. What Ware translates as "five divine processes [for vanishing]" in the *Baopuzi* (*Alchemy*, 251) are five *shendao* (Jp. *shintō*), five ways of manipulating spirits to become invisible.

61. De Bary et al., *Sources*, 1: 7, renders the sentence as follows: "She occupied herself with magic and sorcery, bewitching the people."

62. The argument that follows comes from Ōwa, "Himiko," 84–86.

63. Later, Zhang Lu's organization became the movement of the celestial masters. Lu was the grandson of his organization's legendary founder, Zhang Daoling. He established a theocracy in remote Sichuan in the latter half of the second century. Zhang Lu's mother was married to Daoling's son.

64. See a brief reference to this in Hendrichke, "Early Daoist Movements," 140.

65. Naumann, "Einige Bemerkungen," 13; Teeuwen, "*Jindō* to Shinto."

66. Grapard, "Shrines Registered," 229.

67. Teeuwen and Scheid, "Tracing Shinto," 199; Teeuwen, "*Jindō* to Shinto," 242, 259.

68. Kuroda, "Shinto in History," 1–21.

69. Grapard, "Shrines Registered," 222; on the ranking of *kami*, see 219–222.

70. Teeuwen, "*Jindō* to Shinto," 250.

71. It is unlikely that Suiko or Tenmu would have adopted the mantle of *cakravartin*, as suggested by Piggott (*Emergence*, 96, 215). For Shōmu, see Piggott, *Emergence*, 267; for Gosanjō, see Abé, *Weaving of the Mantra*, 359.

72. On Taiyi and the cult of Heaven in the Western Han, see Bujard, *Le sacrifice au ciel*, 11–12 and 146.

73. Naumann, "Taoist Thought," 166, 167, 172. The second and fourth graphs of Takamimusuhi's name are the same as one of the names for the heavenly ruler of the sky in Chinese; see Hirohata, *Bansei ikkei*, 8–9.

74. Schafer, *Pacing the Void*, 79–81.

75. See SNG 1: 7–8 (698/1/1); 1: 33 (701/1/1).

76. See *Kan'yaku chūshaku Shoku Nihongi*, 1: 18n1–n5. The document in question is the *Bun'an go sokui chōdo no zu*. For a reconstruction of the scene in 701, see the catalogue of the exhibit: Nara bunkazai kenkyūjo sōritsu gojū shūnen kinen, *Asuka, Fujiwarakyō-ten*, 166–167. The sun bird crow is specified in the text as having three legs, but for unknown reasons, it has only two in the original illustration. Recent archeological excavations have uncovered the holes in which these poles were placed.

77. Schafer, *Pacing the Void*, 165.

78. I follow Shinkawa's detailed analysis of these symbols (*Nihon kodai no girei*, 128–176). For the Chinese cultural interpretation (including the original texts) of the symbolism of the four directional animals on the banners, see Schlegel, *Uranographie chinoise*, 59–72.

79. The opening section of Book 21 of the *Engishiki* lists three-legged birds among the major portents.

80. Aston 2: 236–239.

81. The *Ruijūkokushi* (Classified Supplement to the Six Imperial Histories or Japan's Annals up to 887) was compiled in 892 in two hundred volumes, sixty-one of which are extant. It lists a total of 165 portents, five of which, in the years 699, 705, 721, 739, and 784, are red birds (Shinkawa, *Nihon kodai no girei*, 158).

82. Schafer, *Pacing the Void*, 165; Shinkawa, *Nihon kodai no girei*, 151–152.

83. Shinkawa, *Nihon kodai no girei*, 129, 130, 136, 146. A large woodblock print in three sheets by Yoshitsuna, probably dating from 1847, represents Taira no Masakado, the rebel who declared himself emperor in 940, with all the Daoisant paraphernalia necessary to identify him visually as emperor: the four directional animals, several banners with the Sun and Moon, others with the Big

Dipper — emblems that are repeated on his coat as well. His stare is so powerful that it kills two ducks in midflight. The popular image of what identifies an emperor is shaped by the ceremonial setting established around 700. The print was brought to my attention by Christine Schoppe. See Ozaki Hotsuki, Kata Kōji, and Tokinoya Masaru, *Kamigami to Yoshitsune no jidai*, Nishiki-e Nihon no rekishi 1 (Tokyo: Nihon Hōsō shuppankai kyōkai, 1981), 44–45.

84. Another spatial use of the directional animals was in geomancy. They are mentioned in choosing the site for the new capital of Nara (708/2/15).

85. The delegation from Silla, having arrived on 700/10/8, was most likely present, as they had been in 698. The Southern Islands refer to Tanegashima and other islands, including the Ryūkyū Islands.

86. Kumagai, *Ōkimi*, 292, 302.

87. On the Hayato in the literature and in the study by Ban Nobutomo, see Macé, "Notes sur les *Hayato*."

88. For this paragraph, see Shinkawa, *Nihon kodai no girei*, 141–142.

89. Couvreur, *Mémoires sur les bienséances*, vol. 1, part 1, art. 5, p. 55. From the time of the Three Kingdoms through the Sui and Tang, banners were displayed on oxen in military parades and on special occasions (Shinkawa, *Nihon kodai no girei*, 136).

90. Shinkawa, *Nihon kodai no girei*, 165.

91. Watanabe Akihiro, *Heijō-kyō*, 245–246, 296–297.

92. Shinkawa, *Nihon kodai no girei*, 146.

93. Schafer, *Pacing the Void*, 55. Schafer cites the *Yiching*: "In the sky are formed counterparts (*hsiang*); On the earth are formed contours (*hsing*)." (H. Wilhem, *Change*, 280: "In the heavens, phenomena take form; on earth shapes take form.")

94. Schafer, *Pacing the Void*, 46–47.

95. The respective dates for the entries of these items in the *Nihon shoki* are 708/2/15 (Genmei), 721/2/16 (Genshō), 757/8/18 (Kōken) (Shinkawa, *Nihon kodai no girei*, 163).

96. The empire in the heavens provided for everything as it included even a celestial outhouse and the pit of manure. There were 283 asterisms, comprising 1,464 stars (about half of all stars visible to the naked eye), compared to 48 in the Greek sky of Ptolemy (Sun and Kistemaker, *Chinese Sky*, xiv, 1, 95–96).

97. The information that follows is culled from Schafer, *Pacing the Void*, 44–46; and Sun and Kistemaker, *Chinese Sky*, 134, figure 6.7 (the Ziwei Yuan, the central celestial court).

98. Based on what I could gather from Schafer's and Sun and Kistemaker's books, and correspondence with Nancy Shatzman Steinhardt, and indirectly Nathan Sivin, it appears that the Han and post-Tang skies configured a Little Dipper, but that it was missing during the Tang.

99. The Theocrat and the Grand Heir are the outer two stars of the cup of the Little Dipper.

100. Sun and Kistemaker, *Chinese Sky*, 82.

101. Schafer, *Pacing the Void*, 25, 29.

102. Schafer, *Pacing the Void*, 79–81.

103. Takeda, "Kan to ifuku," 79 ff.

104. Yoshino, *Inyōgogyō to tennō*, 161–162. The model here was a statement in the *Book of Documents* where Emperor Shun specified to Yu the desired design for his ceremonial dress. See Legge, *The Shoo King*, 80.

105. See chap. 6, note 58.

106. The *Wuxing dayi* explains these elements in terms of cosmic balance (Cd 545n5). The black crow, a Yin bird with three Yang legs combines with the Yang of the sun (Cd 332, 445). On three as a Yang number ("Yang is realized in three"), see Cd 332, and Schafer, *Pacing the Void*, 164–165. Schafer also mentions that actual portentous three-legged crows were found in 559, 608, 762, and 790, and a vermilion crow in 776. Pheasants are yang birds that, when they sing, elicit a response from the female, and if done at the right moment, the response represents order (Cd 445).

107. The toad and hare are both yang within the yin substance of the Moon (Cd 333). Others see the hare as yang and the toad as yin (Schafer, *Pacing the Void*, 185, 189, 195).

108. Yoshino, *Inyōgogyō to tennō*, 167–169. Takeda ("Kan to ifuku," 94) has argued that it is difficult to pin down the Chinese model, because it was modified frequently through the Sui and Tang; nevertheless, the red color seems to have been modeled on the Sui founder. The difference discussed here is with the model of the *Book of Rites* and the *Shang shu*.

109. Schafer, *Pacing the Void*, 5.

110. Gt, 103; Cd, 158.

111. Schafer, *Pacing the Void*, 44.

112. Schafer, *Pacing the Void*, 44, 49, 215.

113. Schafer, *Pacing the Void*, 50, 230. As mentioned, directional animals date from the fourth millennium BCE, while Dipper worship antedates Daoism by many centuries. From oracle bones we know that offerings to the Dipper were already made during the Shang period (before the first millennium BCE) (Stephenson, "Chinese and Korean Star Maps," 514). The Great Dipper and the twenty-eight lunar mansions are already represented during the Warring States period, and the texts referred to in the *Baopuzi* appear to be related to worship of the Great Dipper; see Yamada Toshiaki, "The Lingbao School," 228, 242; Little, "Taoism and the Arts of China," 712.

114. Ware, *Alchemy*, 249–250.

115. Wang Mang, the usurper emperor, tried in his last hour (in vain) to "use the Dipper as a cosmic weapon to protect himself against his approaching enemies." Andersen, "Bugang," 19; Robinet, *Taoism*, 144.

116. Puett, *Become a God*, 160–162. Robinet, *Taoism*, 12, 135.

117. Puett, *Become a God*, 301–311; Ling, "Taiyi Worship," 10, 11. For a brief history of Taiyi worship, see Cammann, "Magic Square," 60–64).

118. The two quotations are taken from Andersen, "Bugang," 29n28.

119. Robinet, *Taoism*, 144; Harper, "Warring States," 156.

120. Robinet, *Taoism*, 144; Schafer, *Pacing the Void*, 238–240; Unschuld, *Medi-*

cine in China, 44. Originally, the Steps of Yu constituted an exorcistic dance already mentioned in documents of the third century BCE (Harper, "Warring States,"157). The Steps of Yu along the stars of the Great Dipper, also called Pacing the Mainstays of Heaven (*bugang*), is described in the Shangqing revelations of the 360s, which "rely heavily on religious practices already current in South China, giving these a new and more meditational shape and conceiving the revelations as the 'true' versions of already circulating texts on which these practices were based" (Andersen, "*Bugang,*" 18).

121. Itō Kiyoshi, *Chūsei ōken no seiritsu,* 144; Kyoto bunka hakubutsukan, *Abe no Seimei to onmyōdō ten,* 66. The ritual is also practiced in Shugendō (Masuo, "Daoism," 830). In 2003, I witnessed a Dance to Lengthen the Years (Ennen no mai) in the Motsuji Tendai temple of Hiraizumi, usually performed on the night of the twentieth of January and said to go back over eight hundred years. I have little doubt that this dance was an adaptation of the Steps of Yu, where the dancer slinks along with a particular gait, imitating the semiparalyzed Yu, or, another (shamanistic) interpretation, a wounded bear.

122. Andersen, "*Bugang,*" 22. See also Schipper and Wang, "Progressive Time Cycles," 199.

123. Hokusai in the early nineteenth century poked fun at the term by sketching, on a page of *manga* peopled with magicians, one who had made himself half disappear. See Katsushika Hokusai, *The Hokusai Sketchbooks: Selections from the Manga,* edited by Kames A. Michener (Ruthland, Vt.: 1958), plate 139, p. 208.

124. Schipper and Wang, "Progressive Time Cycles," 198.

125. Sakade, "Divination," 547–548. Ge Hong, in his *Baopuzi* in the early fourth century, writes that he knew sixty different *dunjia* writings (Andersen, "*Bugang,*" 33; Ware, *Alchemy,* 284).

126. Sakade, "Divination," 547–548. On the complex calculation of the "hidden period" in the calendrical system, see Andersen, "*Bugang,*" 33–37; and Schipper and Ware, "Progressive Time Cycles," 201.

127. Andersen, "*Bugang,*" 34.

128. Schipper and Wang, "Progressive Time Cycles," 198–199; Andersen, "*Bugang,*" 34, 37.

129. NSK 2: 434–436 (679/5/6); Aston 2: 341–342.

130. Fukunaga, "Taoizumu," 29.

131. For alternative translations, see *Engishiki* (Bock) 2: 88–89; Philippi, *Norito,* 50.

132. For a similar argument, see Bialock, *Eccentric Spaces,* 103.

133. *Engishiki* (Bock) 2: 84.

134. The creation of the Yin-yang Bureau was part of the urgent effort to provide Yamato with state institutions during the period that Yamato had broken off relations with Tang China (669–702) but maintained intense, almost yearly relations with Silla. In contrast to earlier missions, the emissaries were mainly monks.

135. See Noda, "Onmyōdō no seiritsu," 63.

136. Defrocking was the most severe punishment for clerics. Penalties for monks and nuns were calibrated on a milder scale than for commoners. The lower end

of the range of penalties for laymen ran from ten blows with the light stick to one hundred blows with the heavy stick; heavier penalties ranged from one year's imprisonment to the death penalty. For monks, this scale of the number of blows was converted into an equivalent number of days of a specifically monastic form of "hardship service" (kushi), which actually was no more than manual devotional labor: cleaning the premises, painting Buddhist statues, decorating altars, copying sutras. If the offense called for more than the lay equivalent of one hundred blows with the heavy stick, the offender was defrocked and subject to the unmodified scale of penalties for commoners beyond the one hundred blows (Sōni-ryō, art. 21). On these laicizations, see Seki, Kikajin, 106–107, 237–254; see also Tamura, "Onmyōryō seiritsu," 56–57.

137. Seven of the ten laicizations were clustered in the years 700–703; the one laicized in 714 was made head of the bureau.

138. Noda, "Onmyōdō no seiritsu," 75–77.

139. Von Verschuer, Relations, 26, 76, 216, 410.

140. SNG 2: 554n30.

141. On era names in Japan and East Asia, see Ōi, "Les nom d'ères (nengō)."

142. See the Law on Ceremonial, Ritsuryō, NST 3: 350 (Gisei-ryō, art. 26).

143. See the table in Tokoro Isao, Nengō, 279–281. A couple of era changes were made on the day of succession of a new ruler, always accompanied by positive auguries. When Empress Kōken took power, first as Kōken in 749, then as Shōtoku in 764, she dispensed with them, possibly because of her involvement with Buddhism.

144. Actually, Miyoshi Kiyoyuki (847–918), in a convoluted argument based on two little-known apocrypha and buttressed by a manipulation of Chinese and Japanese historical calendrical calculations, introduced a dual sixty-year cycle for era change, starting with Engi 1 (901), which continued until the end of the Tokugawa period. Although a man of literature, his calendrical innovation was accepted, its rationale being that, unless era changes took place in those years (901, 961, 1021 and 1024, 1081 and 1084, . . . 1861 and 1864) political upheaval (kakumei, "a change of the mandate") would ensue, as almost happened with the Sugawara Michizane affair in 901 (Tokoro Isao, Nengō, chap. 4).

145. Two of these changes took place in the Heian period, in 848 and 851. In China, too, many era names reveal a Daoist influence (Ōi, "Les noms d'ères," 44).

146. On Shōmu's erratic moves to Kuni, Shigaraki, Naniwa, and back to Nara, see Brown, "Introduction," 42–44; Naoki, "Nara State," 252–253; Watanabe Akihiro, Heijō-kyō, 216–221, 228–241.

147. Naoki, "Nara State," 265.

148. Hon'iden, "Kakumeikan," 208: 32–33.

Chapter 8: Plottings

Epigraph: Heian ibun 1: doc. 233, p. 343.

1. Omimaro was the grandson of one of Kamatari's two uncles, and of the same generation as Fuhito. Omimaro died in 711, Fuhito in 720.

2. Chavannes, *Le T'ai chan*, 16–20; Loewe, *Chinese Ideas of Life*, 130–140.

3. The *Shinsen shōjiroku* (815) mentions that a map or sketch of the Mingtang was among 164 fascicles brought over. See Saeki, *Shinsen shōjiroku no kenkyū*, 285.

4. Cd 34, 124n144.

5. Seidel, "Imperial Treasures," 356.

6. "Saigū" is a multireferential term that can mean the institution, the residential compound, or the princess herself. The discussion of the institution that follows is based on *Engishiki* (Bock) 1: Introduction, 51–56, and Book 5; Ellwood, "The Saigū," 35–60.

7. I have culled these details from Maspero, "Le Ming-t'ang," 5, 9, 10 (thatched roof), 45 (plain wood), 16 (cosmic dimensions); and Soothill, *The Hall of Light*, 85, 87 (plain wood, *Huainanzi*).

8. Yoshino, *Inyōgogyō shisō*.

9. For a ground plan and picture of the Taigenkyū, see Scheid, *Der Einer und Einzige Weg*, 45, 46.

10. *Engishiki* (Bock) 1: 53.

11. KDJ 6: 146, "Saigū ato"; and Saigū rekishi hakubutsukan, ed., *Saigū ato hakkutsu*, maps following p. 33.

12. KDJ 6: 144–145, "Saigū."

13. KDJ 6: 144–145, "Saigū." For the *saiō's* yearly calendar of duties, see Tokoro Kyōko, "Kami no Mikado no mitsueshiro," 64–65.

14. Similarly, sacrificial offerings were also presented to China's mythic first five emperors at the Mingtang (Gt 240; Cd 390–391).

15. Tanaka Kimio, "Saiō gunkō to hokushin-sai," 107–120. *Engishiki* (Torao) 1: 303, 850 note "miakashi." Felicia Bock (*Engishiki* 1: 167) erroneously translates the text as stating that lanterns are lighted for the North Star, whereas it was prohibited to light them in the capital, the inner provinces, Ise, and Ōmi. The first evidence of this prohibition is dated 799/9; see *Nihon kōki*, 187.

16. For example, "blood" is called "sweat," "death" is "getting well," "meat" is "vegetables," "illness" is "slumber" (*Engishiki* [Bock] 2: 10, 33).

17. SNG 4: 505, "Ise ōkami no tera"; *Shinto jiten*, 108, "*jingūji*." The Ōkasedera had probably been built following a promise by Emperor Shōmu after the suppression of Fujiwara Hirotsugu's rebellion in 740.

18. The narrative and analysis of this event follows Takatori, *Shinto*, 37–63; the text can be found in the *Shoku Nihongi*, under the date 765/11/23. On Kōken-Shōtoku's reign, see Piggott, "The Last Classical Female Sovereign."

19. Shōtoku's association with Dōkyō started when she was cured by his healing powers. This was between her reign as Kōken (749–758) and as Shōtoku (764–770).

20. *Ritsuryō*, NST 3: 158 (*Shiki'in-ryō*, art. 2).

21. SNG 4: 507 n41.

22. Piggott, *Emergence*, 264, figure 15.

23. Yokota, *Dōkyō*, 156; SNG 4: 507n41.

24. Takatori, *Shinto*, 98–104.

25. KDJ 1: 875, "*ingaikan*."

26. SNG 4: 225, 527n50.

27. Yokota, *Dōkyō*, 160; for a full discussion of Dōkyō's promotion of his clan, see 116–117; for his attempts to control militarily important positions, see 118, 122. During his tenure of eight years, Dōkyō granted ten relatives ranks five or above (119). Dōkyō created the Office of the Pages (Naijushō), which was directly under the emperor's control. Since several of the staff of eleven who ran the office held joint appointments in the guard units, there was an important political and military side to this otherwise innocuous-sounding office (SNG 4: 515–16n28).

28. I have culled the information on the *Dazai sochi* from Bender, "Political Meaning," 14, 24–25. In 732, Muchimaro, one of the Fujiwara Four, was appointed to that position, which he held concurrently with that of Dainagon. In 750 Nakamaro's brother Otomaro was appointed to the post "according to instructions of Hachiman" (24). Head Priest (*kanzukasa*) Ōmiwa Tamaro interpreted words of the medium Ōmiwa Morime. They were both escorted to Nara with Hachiman in 749, but stripped of their court rank a few years later and exiled, accused of having been involved in a conspiracy with a Nara priest and having practiced sorcery (754/11/24, 27) (25). Tamaro was restored to his court rank in 766 and received office in the provincial government of Bungo; in 767 construction started on a temple at the Hachiman shrine (39); in 768, Kiyohito and Asomaro were appointed (39–40).

29. SNG 4: 514n12; on 767/4/21, 155 shrine slaves (*shinsen*) were set free.

30. SNG 4: 471–472n16.

31. Yokota, *Dōkyō*, 176.

32. *Heian ibun* 1, doc. 233, p. 343; cited in Takatori, *Shinto*, 47.

33. After Fujiwara Nagate, minister of the left, died the same year, his position was left open during the decade of Kiyomaro's tenure; Kiyomaro resigned in 781, shortly after Kanmu succeeded Kōnin.

34. Takatori, *Shinto*, 58–63.

35. Piggott, *Emergence*, 264, fig. 15.

36. Watanabe Akihiro, *Heijō-kyō*, 259–261.

37. Bender, "Political Meaning," 29.

38. Naoki, "Nara State," 256; Matsumae, "Early Kami Worship," 356–357; Sonoda Kōyū, "Early Buddha Worship," 412–413.

39. Bender, "Political Meaning," 21; SNG 3: 93, 95 (749/11/19, 24, and 12/24, 27).

40. "So lange es japanisches Wesen gibt, wird man in Japan Wake Ason no Kiyomaro's in einer im Tiefsten gleichen Weise Dank opfernd gedenken" (Bohner, "Wake-no-Kiyomaro-den," 240).

41. Toby, "Why leave Nara?" 345–346.

42. Bourdieu, *Masculine Domination*, 93.

43. SNG 4:87 (765/8/1).

44. SNG 3: 507n26.

45. SNG 4: 181, 345, 451.

46. Hayashi, *Jōdai seiji shakai*, 127.

47. See Piggott, *Emergence*, 248, fig. 13.

48. On the likelihood that Prince Nagaya was in the line of succession, see Joan Piggott, "Mokkan: Wooden Documents from the Nara Period," MN 45 (1990): 460–461; but also Terasaki, *Nagaya-ō*, 54–56, 137–140.

49. For the information of this paragraph, see Katsuura, *Kōken to Bukkyō*, 98–104; idem, *Nihon kodai no sōni to shakai*, 223–232.

50. Watanabe Akihiro, *Heijō-kyō*, 284, 287–288; SNG 3: 15n22 (plotting since 745); 247 (sake prohibition).

51. *Nihon kōki*, 157.

52. On partial and full tonsure for nuns, see Katsuura Noriko, "Tonsure Forms for Nuns: Classification of Nuns according to Hairstyle," chap. 5 in *Engendering Faith: Women and Buddhism in Premodern Japan*, edited by Barbara Rush (Ann Arbor: Center for Japanese Studies, University of Michigan Press, 2002).

53. Hayashi, *Jodai seiji shakai*, 166–172; Abe Takeshi, *Heian seijishi*, 17–28.

54. SNG 5: 225 (782/i1/19).

55. *Nihon kōki*, 339.

56. KDJ 6: 144, "*saigū*."

57. For a fine reconstruction and analysis of the relationship between Ōku and Prince Ōtsu around Tenmu's death and Ōtsu's plot, see Ebersole, *Ritual Poetry*, 241–244, 248–254.

58. Ōta, *Seishi kakei daijiten* 1: 57–61.

59. SNG, 2: 207 (729/2/18); 4: 373 (772/3/2).

60. SNG 2: 239.

61. Hayashi, *Jōdai seiji shakai*, 135.

62. SNG 5: 165.

63. Shinkawa, *Dōkyō*, 109–120.

64. On Ōtsu and Arima's footprint in the *Manyōshū*, see Kondō, "*Manyōshū* to goryō," 41–44.

65. NSK, 2: 486 (686/10/2, 3, 29). The careers are described in Shinkawa, *Dōkyō*, 105–108.

66. Hon'iden, "Kakumeikan," 208: 32–33.

Chapter 9: Spirits

Epigraphs: SNG 2: 205; KST 10: 266.

1. See *Nihon kōki*, 792/7/10 and 17, as extant in *Nihon kiryaku* (KST 10), 1: 266.

2. Walls and fences were believed to contain pollution; neither does pollution spread to a neighboring field if it belongs to a different proprietor (Yamamoto, *Kegare to ōharae*, 48–51).

3. *Nihon kiryaku* (KST 10), 1: 271.

4. *Nihon kōki*, 155.

5. *Nihon kiryaku* (KST 10), 1: 275.

6. *Nihon kōki*, 299.

7. *Sandai jitsuroku*, 182–183.

8. *Ruiju kokushi* (KST 6), 2: 88–90, or (same text) *Nihon isshi* (KST 8: 17); Lewin, *Regierungsannalen*, 308–310; Sakamoto, *Six National Histories*, 90–91.

9. *Nihon kōki*, 517; Sakaue, *Ritsuryō kokka*, 80; Sakamoto, *Six National Histories*, 116–117.

10. Sakaue, *Ritsuryō kokka*, 40; McCullough, "Heian Court," 33–34.

11. Sakaue, *Ritsuryō kokka*, 122–124; *Nihon kōki*, KST 3: 127–128, extortion (842/1/10), and 164, plot (843/12). For a French translation of the first passage, see von Verschuer, *Relations*, 358–360.

12. Sakaue, *Ritsuryō kokka*, 124.

13. Bouchy, "Du bon usage de la malemort," 207n6; see also Kuroda, "World of Spirit Pacification," 231–251; McMullin, "On Placating the Gods," 288–290.

14. "The *kami* of Tamatsushima, the *mitama* of Akanoura..." (724/10/16); "The *mitama* of the *kami* of Heaven and Earth" (769/10/1). They respond to prayers (741/3/24). In the three armed rebellions of the Nara period, *shinrei* and *rei* are assumed to have played a role. On 740/11/5, Fujiwara Hirotsugu wondered during his failed rebellion in Kyushu: "Will the *shinrei* abandon me? I fear that relying on *shinryoku* (*kami* power) . . ." On 757/8/18, "in the thick of the action" (*hansoku no aida*) during Tachibana Naramaro's rebellion, "the character *rei* appeared by itself," which was later interpreted as an omen predicting that, with the help of Heaven, Kōken would crush the rebellion. The *shinrei* are said on 764/1/7 to have protected the realm against Fujiwara Nakamaro's rebellion.

15. *Reibutsu*: 770/5/11; *reiken*: 799/5/13, 805/12/20.

16. The *Nihon ryōiki* (K. Nakamura, *Miraculous Stories*) was written by the monk Kyōkai, probably during Kanmu's reign, the end of the eighth–beginning of the ninth century. On 780/12/22, it is recorded that some free people were lured into becoming shrine serfs (*shinsen*, "*kami* base people") under the pretext of *ryōi*. On 743/10/15, Buddhism's supreme supernatural power is called *iryō*.

17. *Kami*: 672/6/27. References to the emperor's *mitama* can be found among others in entries of 727/11/1, 749/4/1, 757/7/12, 767/1/8, and 769/3/5. *Mikage* (honorable shadow) seems to be an older, rarely used reading for the spirit of rulers: Bidatsu (581/12), Tenmu (672/6/27).

18. K. Nakamura, *Miraculous Stories*, Part 2, Tale 1, pp. 158–159.

19. On Nagaya's spirit, see Murayama, "Goryō shinkō to wa;" Kondō, "*Manyōshū* to goryō." For the *Fudoki*, see Ikoma, " 'Fudoki' ni miru tatarigami."

20. SNG 3: 31. David Bialock drew my attention to the case of Mononobe Moriya. In 587, after his suicide and when his corpse was about to be dismembered, "thunder pealed, and a great rain fell" (Aston 2: 116).

21. Katsuura, *Sōni to shakai*, 147.

22. Suinin (Aston 2: 167); other entries with *urami* date from 64 CE /2, 540/9/5, 562/6. For Nagaya, see SNG 2: 179; for Kōken, SNG 3: 201.

23. For *ifu*, see *Ruijū kokushi* (KST 6), 2: 335, 337 (800/3/1 and 813/11/21); Prince Wake, SNG 4: 87; Kanmu, SNG 5: 203–205.

24. *Nihon kōki* (Kuroita and Morita), 157–158.

25. *Nihon kōki* (Kuroita and Morita), 289.

26. *Nihon kōki* (Kuroita and Morita), 299.

27. *Sandai jitsuroku*, 182–183. This work, compiled in 901, was the final volume of the *Rikkokushi* (Six National Histories). A shorter version is copied in the *Nihon*

kiryaku (KST 10), 2: 420. The *Nihon kiryaku* dates from the late eleventh century, and consists of a selected anthology from the national histories, including sections of the *Nihon kōki* that are now lost and some other sources, covering Japanese history from the beginning until 1036.

28. We know that others were held in 994, 1001, 1004, 1015, and 1052 (Nakai, "Goryō-e to matsuri," 167).

29. These epidemics are listed chronologically in *Ruijū kokushi*, vol. 2, Book 173. The edict in question can be found under that date (194); see also Itō Yuishin, "Shinsen'en to goryō-e," 103–111.

30. The Shinsen'en, approximately 500 meters north-south by 250 meters east-west, was situated at the southeast corner of the palace grounds; at a pond in its center, said to house a dragon, Kūkai performed a rainmaking ceremony in 825.

31. *Engishiki*, Book 12 (KST 26), 355.

32. Nakai, "Goryō-e to matsuri," 160–161; Bouchy, "Du bon usage de la male-mort," 219; Kuroda, "Spirit Pacification," 327–330.

33. The prohibited, nonextant works on imperial genealogies were the *Wakan sōrekitei fuzu* and the *Teiō keizu* (Brownlee, "Ideological Control," 131–132). See *Nihon kōki*, 469 (809/2/5); *Kōnin shiki* 7.

34. Sonoda, "Early Buddha Worship," 375.

35. I arrived at these (approximate) figures in three ways. I first relied on table B in the Appendix of Farris, *Population*, 158–161. The source for this Table of Epidemics in Japan, 698–898, is Fujikawa, *Nihon shippei shi*, 12–25. In addition, I found fifteen more entries for eleven more years recorded under *shippeki* in the *Ruijū kokushi* (KST 6), 2: 189–200. I included as outbreaks of epidemics any mention of offerings made to "epidemic spirits." This work, completed in 892 by Sugawara Michizane, collated information from the *Six National Histories* by category, arranged chronologically; only 61 of its 205 fascicles survive. I also searched key terms related to epidemics (outbreaks or apotropaic rituals) in the database of the Rikkokushi (http://kodaishi-db.hp.infoseek.co.jp). Charlotte von Verschuer reports twenty-four bad crops for the first half of the eighth century in the Kinai and sixty-six natural disasters hitting one or several provinces between 784 and 805, resulting in thirty-seven distributions of rice, eleven cancellations of tribute, and six prayer sessions, the others cases being unknown (*Le riz*, 267, 296n21).

36. Farris, "Trade," 316.

37. For a detailed study of the 735–737 epidemic, see Farris, *Population*, chap. 2.

38. See *Engishiki* (Bock) 2: 90–92; see also *Ritsuryō*, NST 3: 212 (Jingi-ryō, art. 5).

39. Ware, *Alchemy*, 104–105, 282.

40. For a quick survey of the texts and dates, see *Ruijū kokushi* (KST 6), 2: 192–193.

41. The text of 774/4/11 in part repeats, this time in the context of a real epidemic, an entry from 758/8/18 that praises the efficacy of the *Makahannya haramitta* (Great Wisdom Sutra) to protect the realm and all households against epidemics.

42. SNG 3: 580–582.

43. The eighth-century *koku* is less than half the early modern (Tokugawa)

koku, which measures 180 liters (KDJ 10: 481, "*doryōkō*"). On the complicated matter of conversions, see Dettmer, "Die Maßeinheite," 10–12.

44. The original lineages of these *fudai* had been "vassals" with hereditary positions since the time when districts, *gun*, were formed under Great King Kōtoku during the Taika Reforms around 650. These positions went to chieftains of *kōri* (*miyatsuko*), the subprovincial administrative units preceding the *gun*. A hundred years later, branch families started to engage in fights to share the privileges of the stem families. Steps were taken to appoint talent from among applicants nominated at the provincial level (limited to documented *fudai* families who had held positions for at least two generations). The nominated candidates went to the capital to take a written and oral examination, a practice most likely introduced by the Kiyomihara Code of 689. (The exams for posts in the central administration were abandoned, however, very soon after the promulgation of the Taihō Code.) Japan counted 555 districts by the early eighth century. On these developments, see SNG 2: 567–568n18; Hayakawa, *Kodai kanryōsei*, 260–262, 271, 284–287. On the complicated system of local government in early Heian, see Kiley, "Provincial Administration and Land Tenure in Early Heian," esp. 239–264.

45. SNG 2: 205. That the accusation was false was at least an opinion some people felt strong about to the point of killing one of the accusers ten years later (738/7/10).

46. That year Nagaya, at age twenty-one (Japanese reckoning), was the first one to receive so-called grace rank (*on'i*; literally "shadow rank"), the system whereby children and grandchildren of male members of the royal family or of rank holders one to three, or children of rank holders five and four, received a rank calibrated lower than their father's or grandfather's. Nagaya, son of Daijōdaijin Takechi, received senior fourth rank upper, three steps above what he was entitled to, possibly to assuage friction between Fujiwara Fuhito and the royals (KDJ 10: 666, "*Nagaya-ō*").

47. Hon'iden, "Kakumeikan," 209: 26.

48. Shinkawa, *Dōkyō*, 175–180. The sutra had been brought over by a Silla delegation in 703.

49. For the natural disasters under Nagaya's tenure, see Hon'iden, "Kakumeikan," 209: 23.

50. Shinkawa, *Dōkyō*, 196–199.

51. Kawasaki, *Kiki manyō no sekai*, 138.

52. Shinkawa, *Dōkyō*, 200. The three time periods were the Kōnin (810–823), Jōgan (859–876), and Engi years (901–922). *Ruiju sandaikyaku*, 589.

53. SNG 2: 211.

54. *Ritsuryō*, NST 3: 216.

55. *Ryō no shūge*, KST 23: 214.

56. *Ritsuryō*, NST 3: 97.

57. On this question and the discussion that follows, see Shinkawa, "Nihon kodai ni okeru bukkyō to dōkyō," 51–83; see also Bialock, *Eccentric Spaces*, 93, 348–349n105.

58. K. Nakamura, *Miraculous Stories*, Part 1, Tale 28, pp. 140–141.

59. See Shinkawa, "Nihon kodai ni okeru bukkyō to dōkyō," 54; *Dōkyō*, 209–210; Wada, "Nanzan no kyūtōryū." The *Baopuzi neipian* (Book 5) states that "man is [engulfed] in the breath [Ch. *qi*; Jp. *ki*] and the breath is [engulfed] in him . . . [H]e who knows charms and spells can venture in the midst of epidemics and not get infected . . . [T]he breath allows him to charm ghosts and spirits . . . tigers, leopards, and venomous snakes" (Ware, *Alchemy*, 104–105; Ge, *La voie*, 103). Book 17 notes that "one should hang amulets from one's belt when entering the mountains . . . they should be placed above the door, at the four sides of the house, at the four corners . . . distributed over the beams and pillars within the house" (Ware, *Alchemy*, 282, 296).

60. *Nihon shoki* (NKBT 68), 2: 512n13.

61. K. Nakamura, *Miraculous Stories*, Part 1, Tale 18, p. 141.

62. Strickmann, *Chinese Medicine*, 108–109. Strickmann explains that "[i]n India, peacocks have long been associated with sorcery and exorcism" (109).

63. Shinkawa, "Nihon kodai ni okeru bukkyō to dōkyō," 63–68.

64. Shinkawa, "Nihon kodai ni okeru bukkyō to dōkyō," 73–75.

65. Von Verschuer, *Relations*, 102–103, 371.

66. Shinkawa, *Dōkyō*, 208; see also Barrett, *Taoism*, 33.

67. See Wada, "Nanzan no kyūtōryū," esp. 307, 317. The tablet in question is number 467-83-7-032. The original, published in 652 (*Qinjing fang*), has been translated by Catherine Despeux, *Prescriptions d'acuponcture valant mille onces d'or: traité d'acuponcture de Sun Simiao du VIIe siècle* (Paris: Trédaniel, 1987). The supplement has been translated by Ling Fang in her Ph.D. dissertation, "La tradition sacrée de la médecine chinoise ancienne: étude sur le livre des exorcismes de Sun Simiao (581–682)" at the École Pratique des Hautes Études" (Forthcoming).

68. Shinkawa, *Dōkyō*, 211.

69. When Emperor Gaozong died in 683, his wife, Empress Wu, took over the court, forced his successor, Zhongzong, into exile six weeks after ascending the throne, and did the same with his brother successor, Ruizong, six years later. She got rid of other crown princes, relied on a "magician-sorcerer," Ming Chongyan, who was also murdered. Zhongzong was restored in 705, but eventually poisoned five years later. See Twitchett, "Kao-tsung," 270–271; Guisso, "Reigns," 290–291, 295, 321; Shinkawa, *Dōkyō*, 212.

70. Shinkawa, *Dōkyō*, 215–217.

71. The edict issued that day is concerned with improving the appearance of temples and shrines as dignified sites for worship ("reverence the *kami* and venerate the buddhas by valuing purity foremost") and coordinating the reading of the *Konkōmyō-kyo* and, in case that sutra is not available, the *Saishōō-kyo*. The former was distributed to all the provinces three years later (Shinkawa, "Nihon kodai ni okeru bukkyō to dōkyō," 68).

72. Sutra expounding or chanting against sickness or death took place in 621/2 for the death of a prince, and six times during Tenmu's final sickness to extend his life (685/9/24–686/8/2); rain, flood, or drought-related recitations occurred four times; once a massive chanting took place for the inauguration of a new palace (651/12/31); seven times no specific reason was given for the event.

73. We know the details of Ganjin's trip to Japan mainly through a narrative (*Tō daiwajō tōsei den*), written in 779 by Genkai, one of his disciples. See Andō, *Ganjin*, 147–171; Takusu, "Le voyage de Kanshin." William Bodiford has translated part of Genkai's biography of Ganjin into English, unfortunately not the part about Ganjin's sixth and final crossing: "Taking the Vinaya across the Sea," in *Buddhist Scriptures*, edited by Donald S. Lopez, Jr. (New York: Penguin Books, 2004), 306–317.

74. Yōei and Fūshō were the two monks dispatched in 733. Yōei lost his life in the shipwreck of 748, one of Ganjin's five failed attempts to reach Japan; it was during this voyage that he lost his eyesight. Fūshō returned with Ganjin in 754; they were on one of the three ships, out of four, that made the crossing.

75. SNG 3: 431–433 (763/5/6), the entry on the occasion of Ganjin's death; von Verschuer, *Relations*, 106–107.

76. The ambassador of the mission, Fujiwara Kiyokawa (Kōmyō's nephew and Kōken's cousin), and Abe Nakamaro were on the ship that drifted off course to Annam, where almost all were killed by natives. Kiyokawa and Nakamaro, however, escaped and made their way to China. Nakamaro had a successful career at the Chinese court and even returned to Annam as governor of the protectorate. In 776, Kiyokawa's daughter joined an embassy to search for her father, who had been in China for twenty-four years. After various difficulties, they arrived at Changan two years later, only to learn that Kiyokawa had died eight years earlier. The return ship that carried the daughter broke into two in the open sea. Fifty-three passengers were lost. The daughter was among forty-one who drifted on the prow of the ship for nine days before reaching Amakusa. On the careers of many prominent members, clerical and other, associated with Ganjin, and on relations with China around that time, see Takusu, "Le voyage de Kanshin." For Nakamaro and Kiyokawa, see 8–16.

77. Shinkawa, *Dōkyō*, 244.

78. Barrett, *Taoism*, 53.

79. Barrett, *Taoism*, 55–56.

80. 736/8/23 and 10/2; von Verschuer, *Relations*, 104, 267, 399, 410–411.

81. Shinkawa, *Dōkyō*, 238–243.

82. Shinkawa, *Dōkyō*, 240.

83. Ōtsuka, "Sadaijin Mononobe Maro," 57–65

84. Bentley, *Authenticity*, 117. The Mononobe also claimed, in the same work, to have provided twenty-five protectors to Ninigi when he descended to earth (161).

85. The episode that follows can be found in *Nihon kōki*, 259 (804/2/5), 289–293 (805/2/10); Lewin, *Regierungsannalen*, 461, 488–491.

86. Lewin, *Regierungsannalen*, 488n210.

87. I came across this entry of 1010/8/24 in Fujiwara Michinaga's diary: see Hérail, *Notes journalières de Fujiwara no Michinaga*, 421; for the original text, see Fujiwara Michinaga, *Midō kanpakuki* (Tokyo: Nihon koten zenshū kankōkai, 1921) 1: 219.

Chapter 10: Purity

Epigraphs: Aston, 368 (NSK 2: 468); SNG 2: 161; SNG 4: 103.

1. As is well known, the *Nihon shoki* and *Kojiki* record several famous mythical episodes related to ritual pollution and purification, such as Izanagi's visit to Yomi, the Land of Death.

2. According to my colleague William Bodiford, "*jōgyō* is a standard Chinese translation of the Sanskrit *brahma-carya*, which simply means sexual abstinence" (personal communication, November 20, 2001).

3. When Soga Umako fell ill on 614/8/8, a thousand people, men and women, were ordered to retire from the world (without purity being mentioned).

4. Maspero, "Le mot *ming*," 261–262; Couvreur, *Mémoires*, 327–328.

5. Maspero, "Le mot *ming*," 276.

6. Maspero, "Le mot *ming*," 252ff.

7. Maspero, "Le mot *ming*," 261–262.

8. "Des objects exclus de l'usage profane pour être réservés soit aux morts, soit à ceux des vivants que des tabous temporaires (jeûne, deuil) ou perpétuels (fonction royale) séparent de la communauté" (Maspero, "Le mot *ming*," 278–279, 283).

9. Maspero, "Le mot *ming*," 278–280, 283.

10. Maspero, "Le mot *ming*," 280, 282.

11. Maspero, "Le mot *ming*," 270.

12. Maspero, "Le mot *ming*," 283–284. Maspero thus prefers to render Ming-tang, the imperial ceremonial hall, not as Halls of Light, but as Sacred Hall.

13. Quoted in Puett, *Become a God*, 172.

14. Ōwa, *Tenmu tennō ron* 2: 18–19. The poem was titled "Master of the Way" (Daoshi/Dōshi). Ōwa places the work in the fifth century. Fukunaga maintains that purity was a particularly prominent value in South Chinese Daoism (Mori and Kadowaki, *Jinshin no ran*, 39).

15. *Shenming* means "gods"; the *ming* is read *myō* or *akarui* in Japanese, and *akitsu* in *akitsukami* (manifest *kami*). Other examples are Shangqing, Highest Clarity; Taiqing, Great Clarity or Purity, the realm of the heavenly immortals; *Qingjing xinjing*, the eighth-century *Heart Scripture of Purity and Tranquility*; the Jingming, School of Pure Brightness. Beyond the shell of the sky, the Daoists constructed a hierarchy of three celestial realms, called the Three Clarities (Sanqing) — the Jade, the Highest, and the Great Clarity (Robinet, "Shangqing, 215; Schafer has three other names for them in *Pacing the Void*, 37–38). Anna Seidel ("Neue Testament des Tao," 168) writes of the Three Pure Ones that were venerated since the fourth century: The Heavenly Highest Venerable Ur-Beginning manifestation of the Ur-Pneuma, the Lord of the Tao, and the Lord Lao.

16. Hosokawa ("'Shōjō' to iu go," 168) points out that *seijō* is not used in Daoist titles, but *shōsei* is.

17. Gt 236b; Cd 356. See note 35 of chapter 7.

18. Seidel, "Neue Testament des Tao," 168; Benn, "Daoist Ordinations," 319, 332.

19. Tsuchiya, "Confession of Sins," 45.

20. Schipper, "Purity and Strangers," 67; Malek, *Das* Chai-chieh lu, 16.

21. Mather, "The Bonze's Begging Bowl," 419 (quoted in Malek, *Das* Chai-chieh lu, 16–17).

22. Ware, *Alchemy*, 93; Pregadio, "Elixirs," 187.

23. Malek, *Das* Chai-chieh lu, 44; Benn, "Daoist Ordinations," 312; Asano, "Offerings in Daoist Ritual," 284–285.

24. On horse sacrifices, see the *Nihon shoki* entry of 642/7/25, and also chapter 4, note 18. Inbe Hironari writes in 807 that offerings of "a white wild boar, a white wild horse, and white domestic fowls" were made in his day to the Mitoshi no kami shrine; see *Kogoshūi* (Katō), 52; *(Gunsho)*, 5. On the absence of a meat-eating taboo in Tang, see Okada Shigekiyo, *Kodai no imi*, 106.

25. For the Taihō Code, see art. 10, 11, and 12 of Jingi-ryō, and art. 8 and 9 of the *Shikisei-ritsu* (Penal Law for Officials) (*Ritsuryō*, NST 3: 64–65, 113–114); for the Tang Code, see art. 8 and 9 of chap. 9, Administrative Regulations, *Zhizhi* (Johnson, *T'ang Code* 2: 67–70 [art. 98, 99]); Mitsuhashi, "Ōharae kenkyū josetsu," 292–297.

26. For instance, failure to prepare certain paraphernalia for great festivals according to the prescriptions is punished in China by seventy blows of the heavy stick, sixty in Japan; the correct number of ritual items, one hundred blows of the heavy stick versus eighty.

27. *Jingi-ryō*, art. 10; *Engishiki* (Bock) 1: 59 (Book 1); 2: 33 (Book 7).

28. Two centuries later, the *Engishiki* lists a number of additional taboos for this festival: *Engishiki* (Bock) 2: 33 (Book 7); and in general *Engishiki* (Bock) 1: 116–117 (Book 3).

29. Examples of irregularly held purification ceremonies in eighth-century Japan can be found in the entry of 702/3/12 (held at the Daianden at the capital), and later ones during the last three decades of the Nara period, one in 761 under Junnin, six under Kōnin, 770–781, and three under Kanmu prior to his moving out of Nara to Nagaoka in 784 (Mitsuhashi, "Ōharae kenkyū josetsu," 298–300). Okada Shigekiyo (*Kodai no imi*, 185–187) has listed the thirty-six great purification ceremonies between 707 and 886 for which the reasons were recorded; they were about evenly divided between death pollution (prevalent in Heian) and natural disasters or anomalies. For the most comprehensive lists of occasions, places, and dates for great purifications during the Heian period, see the tables in Yamamoto, *Kegare*, 263–298.

30. Jinno, "Tenmu jūnen-ki," 54.

31. Mitsuhashi, "*Engishiki* kegare," 53; Niunoya, *Kebiishi*, 50.

32. Quoted in Itō Kiyoshi, *Chūsei ōken*, 139–140.

33. Quoted in Mitsuhashi, "*Engishiki* kegare," 46.

34. See my *Tokugawa Village Practice*, chap. 5.

35. The term appears for the first time in Monmu's enthronement edict of 697/8/16, but probably goes back to Tenmu's reign.

36. Jinno, *Ritsuryō senmin*, 42, 55–56. Scholars now believe that the purpose for drawing up population registers in the late seventh century may have been military, as a preparation for conscription in possible armed confrontations with Tang

China or Silla (Farris, *Heavenly Warriors*, 78); for an argument pointing to the early influence of the Wei on late-sixth-century Yamato in this area, see Shinkawa, "Rettō Nihon," 104.

37. According to Jinno (*Ritsuryō senmin*, 52, 62, 68, 73), the edict of 697 implies that lower functionaries (*zōshiki*), the prebend households of temples and shrines (*fuko*), and the *zakko* (manual laborers and skilled craftsmen) were not unfree then, and thus not like the slaves.

38. Jinno, *Ritsuryō senmin*, 20–26.

39. Jinno, *Ritsuryō senmin*, 27–38.

40. This is the interpretation scholars have given to the first color, white, in the dress color ranking as stipulated in article 7 of the Dress Code (Ebuku-ryō). See Jinno, *Ritsuryō senmin*, 14–15. In late Nara when, coincidentally, the *ryōmin/senmin* legal categories were abolished, the color for the emperor's ceremonial attire, as mentioned, was changed to red.

41. Jinno, *Ritsuryō senmin*, 185–195.

42. Jinno, *Ritsuryō senmin*, 105, 112, 117, 119.

43. Jinno, *Ritsuryō senmin*, 137–139.

44. Jinno, *Ritsuryō senmin*, 127, 146.

45. Jinno, *Ritsuryō senmin*, 146–149, 152–155.

46. Takatori, *Shinto*, 47.

47. Bourdieu, *Masculine Domination*, 7–8.

48. *Manyōshū*, Book XVI, poem 3828; Cranston, 281.

49. Bourdieu, *Masculine Domination*, 14.

Note: Place of publication is Tokyo, unless otherwise noted.

Abé, Ryūichi. *The Weaving of the Mantra: Kūkai and the Construction of Esoteric Buddhist Discourse*. New York: Columbia University Press, 1999.

Abe Takeshi. "Fukai jōten." In *Nihon kodaishi kenkyū jiten*, 60–61. Tokyodō, 1995.

———. *Heian zenki seijishi no kenkyū*. Ōhara shinseisha, 1974.

———. "Jinshin no ran." In *Nihon kodaishi kenkyū jiten*, 37–39. Tokyodō, 1995.

Aboshi Yoshinori. "Hakkaku hōfun to sono igi." *Kashihara kōkogaku kenkyūjo ronshū* 5 (1979): 181–226.

Andersen, Poul. "The Practice of *bugang*." CdEA 5 (1989–1990): 15–53.

Andō Kōsei. *Ganjin*. Jimbutsu sōsho. Yoshikawa kōbunkan, 1967.

Aoki, Michiko. *Records of Wind and Earth: A Translation of Fudoki with Introduction and Commentaries*. Association for Asian Studies Monograph. Ann Arbor: University of Michigan, 1997.

Asano, Haruji. "Offerings in Daoist Ritual." In *Daoist Identity: History, Lineage, and Ritual*, edited by Livia Kohn and Harold Roth, 274–294. Honolulu: University of Hawai'i Press, 2002.

Aston, W. G., trans. *Nihongi: Chronicles of Japan from the Earliest Times to A.D. 697*. 2 vols. in 1; separate pagination. Rutland, Vt.: Charles Tuttle, 1972.

Barnes, Gina. *State Formation in Japan: Emergence of a Fourth-century Ruling Elite*. London and New York: Routledge, 2007.

———. *State Formation in Korea: Historical and Archeological Perspectives*. Richmond, Surrey: Curzon Press, 2001.

Barrett, T. H. *Taoism under the T'ang: Religion and Empire during the Golden Age of Chinese History*. London: Wellsweep, 1996.

Batten, Bruce L. "Foreign Threat and Domestic Reform: The Emergence of the *Ritsuryō* State." MN 41, no. 2 (1986): 199–219.

———. *To the Ends of Japan: Premodern Frontiers, Boundaries, and Interactions*. Honolulu: University of Hawai'i Press, 2003.

Bender, Ross Lynn. "The Political Meaning of the Hachiman Cult in Ancient and Early Medieval Japan." Ph.D. dissertation. Columbia University, 1980.

Benn, Charles. "Daoist Ordinations and *zhai* Rituals in Medieval China." In DH, 309–339.

Bentley, John. *The Authenticity of Sendai Kuji Hongi: A New Examination of Texts, with a Translation and Commentary*. Leiden: Brill, 2006.

———. *Historiographical Trends in Early Japan*. Lewiston, N.Y.: Edwin Mellon Press, 2002.

Bialock, David. *Eccentric Spaces, Hidden Histories: Narrative, Ritual, and Royal*

Authority from The Chronicles of Japan *to* The Tale of the Heike. Stanford, Calif.: Stanford University Press, 2007.

Bock, Felicia, trans. *Engi-shiki: Procedures of the Engi Era*. 2 vols. Tokyo: Sophia University Press, 1970, 1972.

————. "The Enthronement Rites: The Text of *Engishiki*, 927." MN 45, no. 3 (1990): 307–337.

Bohner, Hermann. "Wake-no-Kiyomaro-den." MN 3 (1940): 240–273.

Bokenkamp, Stephen. "Time after Time: Taoist Apocalyptic History and the Founding of the T'ang Dynasty." *Asia Major*, ser. 3, 7 (1994): 59–88.

Bouchy, Anne. "Du bon usage de la malemort: Traitement des "âmes rancuneuses" et rituels oraculaires dans la société japonaise." In *De la malemort en quelques pays d'Asie*, edited by Brigitte Baptandier, 201–234. Paris: Kathala, 2001.

————. "Du légitime et de l'illégitime dans le Shugendō, ou 'sang du buddha', 'sang des êtres des montagnes'?" In LL, 111–173.

Bourdieu, Pierre. *The Logic of Practice*. Stanford, Calif.: Stanford University Press, 1990.

————. *Masculine Domination*. Cambridge: Polity Press, 2001.

Brown, Delmer. "Introduction." In CHJ 1:1–47.

————. "The Yamato Kingdom." In CHJ 1:108–162.

Brownlee, John. "Ideological Control in Ancient Japan." *Historical Reflections/Reflexions Historiques* 14, no. 1 (1987): 113–133.

Bujard, Marianne. *Le sacrifice au ciel dans la Chine ancienne: Théorie et pratique sous les Han Occidentaux*. Paris: École française d'Extrême-Orient, 2000.

Cammann, Schuyler. "The Magic Square of Three in Old Chinese Philosophy and Religion." *History of Religions* 1 (1961): 37–80.

Chan, Alan. "The *Daode jing* and Its Tradition." In DH, 1–29.

Chavannes, Édouard, trans. *Les mémoires historiques de Se-ma Ts'ien*. 5 vols. in 6. Paris: E. Leroux, 1895–1905.

————. *Le T'ai chan: Essai de monographie d'un culte chinois*. Paris: Ernest Leroux, éditeur, 1910.

Ch'en, Kenneth. *Buddhism in China: A Historical Survey*. Princeton, N.J.: Princeton University Press, 1964.

Como, Michael. "Ethnicity, Sagehood, and the Politics of Literacy in Asuka Japan." JJRS 30, no. 1–2 (2003): 61–84.

Couvreur, Seraphin. *Li chi ou mémoires sur les bienséances et les cérémonies*. 2 vols. Paris: Cathasia, 1950.

Cranston, Edwin. *A Waka Anthology*. Vol. 1: *The Gem-Glistening Cup*. Stanford, Calif.: Stanford University Press, 1993.

Csikszentmihàlyi, Mark. "Han Cosmology and Mantic Practices." In DH, 53–73.

Dagron, Gilbert. *Empereur et prêtre: Étude sur le "césaropapisme" byzantin*. Paris: Gallimard, 1996.

de Bary, Theodore, et al., eds. *Sources of Japanese Tradition*. 2 vols. 2nd ed. New York: Columbia University Press, 2002–2006.

De Visser, Marinus. *Ancient Buddhism in Japan*. 2 vols. Leiden: Brill, 1935.

Denecke, Wiebke. "Chinese Antiquity and Court Spectacle in Early *Kanshi*." JJS 30 (2004): 97–122.

Dettmer, Hans Adalbert. "Die Maßeinheiten der Nara-Zeit." *Japonica Humbold-tiana* 9 (2005): 5–16.

Doe, Paula. *A Warbler's Song in the Dusk: The Life and Work of Ōtomo Yakamochi (718–785)*. Berkeley: University of California Press, 1982.

Dull, Jack. "A Historical Introduction to the Apocryphal (ch'an-wei) Texts of the Han Dynasty." Ph.D. dissertation. University of Washington, 1966. University Microfilms.

Ebersole, Gary. *Ritual Poetry and the Politics of Death in Early Japan*. Princeton, N.J.: Princeton University Press, 1989.

Edwards, Walter. "Contested Access: The Imperial Tombs in the Postwar Period." JJS 26 (2000): 371–392.

———. "Forging Tradition for a Holy War: The *Hakkō ichiu* Tower in Miyazaki and Japanese Wartime Ideology." JJS 29 (2003): 289–324.

Ellwood, Robert. *The Feast of Kingship: Accession Ceremonies in Ancient Japan*. Tokyo: Sophia University, 1973.

———. "The Saigū: Princess and Priestess." *History of Religions* 7 (1967): 35–60.

———. "The Spring Prayer (Toshigoi) Ceremony of the Heian Court." *Asian Folklore Studies* 30 (1971): 1–30.

Engishiki. Translated by Felicia Bock. See Bock.

Engishiki. Vol 1. Edited by Torao Toshiya. Shūeisha, 2000.

Farris, William. *Heavenly Warriors: The Evolution of Japan's Military, 500–1300*. Cambridge: Harvard University Press, 1992.

———. *Population, Disease, and Land in Early Japan, 645–900*. Harvard-Yenching Institute Monograph. Cambridge: Harvard University Press, 1985.

———. *Sacred Texts and Buried Treasures: Issues in the Historical Archaeology of Ancient Japan*. Honolulu: University of Hawai'i Press, 1998.

———. "Trade, Money and Merchants in Nara Japan." MN 53 (1998): 303–334.

Forte, Antonio. *Mingtang and Buddhist Utopias in the History of the Astronomical Clock*. Roma: Istituto Italiano per il Medio ed Estremo Oriente; Paris: École française d'Extrême-Orient, 1988.

———. *Political Propaganda and Ideology in China at the End of the Seventh Century*. Napoli: Istituto Universitario Orientale Seminario di Studi Asiatici, 1976.

Fracasso, Riccardo. "The Nine Tripods of Empress Wu." In *Tang China and Beyond*, edited by Antonino Forte, 85–96. Kyoto: Istituto Italiano di Cultura, Scuola de Studi sull' Asia Orientale, 1988.

Frank, Bernard. *Kata-imi et Kata-tagae: Étude sur les interdits de direction à l'époque Heian*. Paris: Collège de France, Institut des Hautes Études Japonaises [Tokyo: Maison Franco-Japonaise, 1958], 1998.

Fujidō Kahoru. "Ritsuryō kokka no koki to haimu: hasseiki no sentei ishiki to Tenji no ichizuke." *Nihonshi kenkyū* 430 (1998): 1–24.

————. "Tenji misasagi no keizō to ritsuryō kokka no sentei ishiki: Yamashina misasagi no ichi to Mommu sannen no shūryō o megutte." *Nihon rekishi* 602 (1998): 1–15.

Fujikawa Yū. *Nihon shippei shi*. New ed. by Matsuda Michio. Heibonsha, 1969.

Fujiwara Michinaga. *Midō kanpakuki*. 2 vols. Nihon koten zenshū kankōkai, 1921.

Fujiwara Nakamaro. *Tōshi kaden*. Parts 1, 2. In Gunsho ruijū 78: *Kaden 4*. Separate pagination. Keizai zasshisha, 1893. Part 2. In *Kodai seiji shakai shisō*, 26–38. NST 8.

Fukunaga Mitsuji. "Dōkyō ni okeru kagami to ken: sono shisō no genryū." *Tōhō gakuhō* (Kyoto) 45 (1973): 59–120.

————. *Dōkyō to Nihon bunka*. Kyoto: Jinbun shoin, 1982.

————. *Dōkyō to kodai Nihon*. Kyoto: Jinbun shoin, 1987.

————. "Kōten jōtei to tennō taitei to genshi tenson: Jukyō no saikōshin to dōkyō no saikōshin." *Chūtetsubun gakkaihō* 2 (1976): 1–34.

————. "Taoizumu kara mita Jinshin no ran." In *Jinshin no ran: Ōama no ōji kara Tenmu tennō e*, edited by Mori Kōichi and Kadowaki Teiji, 5–46. Kasugai Shinpojumu 3. Taikosha, 1996.

————. "Tennō to shikyū to mahito: Chūgoku kodai no shintō." *Shisō* 637 (1977): 955–973.

————. *Uma no bunka to fune no bunka: Kodai Nihon to Chūgoku bunka*. Kyoto: Jinbun shoin, 1996.

Fung, Yu-lan. *A History of Chinese Philosophy*. 2 vols. Princeton, N.J.: Princeton University Press, 1952–1953.

Ge Hong. *La voie des divins immortels: Les chapitres discursifs du Baopuzi neipian*. Translated by Philippe Che. Paris: Gallimard, 1999.

Goodman, Howard. *Ts'ao P'i Transcendent: The Political Culture of Dynasty-founding in China at the End of the Han*. Seattle, Wash.: Scripta Serica; Richmond, Surrey: Distributed by Curzon Press, 1998.

Goodrich, Carrington, ed. *Japan in the Chinese Dynastic Histories: Later Han through Ming Dynasties*. South Pasadena, Calif.: P. D. and Ione Perkins, 1951.

Grapard, Allan. "The Economics of Ritual Power." In *Shinto in History: Ways of the Kami*, edited by John Breen and Mark Teeuwen, 68–94. Richmond, Surrey: Curzon Press, 2000.

————. "Shrines Registered in Ancient Japanese Law." JJRS 29, no. 3–4 (2002): 209–232.

Grayson, James. *Myths and Legends from Korea: An Annotated Compendium of Ancient and Modern Materials*. Richmond, Surrey: Curzon Press, 2001.

Guisso, Richard. "The Reigns of the Empress Wu, Chung-tsung and Jui-tsung (684–712)." In CHC 3, part 1, 290–332.

Harper, Donald. "Warring States, Ch'in and Han Periods." In "Chinese Religions: The State of the Field, Part I," edited by Daniel Overmeyer et al. *JAS* 51 (1995): 152–160.

Hashimoto Yoshihiko. *Nihon kodai no girei to tenseki*. Seishi shuppan, 1999.

Hayakawa Shōhachi. *Nihon kodai kanryōsei no kenkyū*. Iwanami shoten, 1986.

Hayami Tasuku. "Ritsuryō kokka to bukkyō." In *Ronshū Nihon bukkyō-shi 2: Nara jidai*, edited by Hayami Tasuku, 2–30. Yūzankyaku, 1986.

Hayashi Rokurō. *Jōdai seiji shakai no kenkyū*. Yoshikawa kōbunkan, 1969.

———. "Jōdai shinshoku seido no ichi kōsatsu." *Shintogaku* 29 (1961): 1–26.

Heian ibun. 13 vols. Kaiteiban. Tokyodō, 1963–1969.

Heine-Geldern, Robert. "Conceptions of State and Kingship in Southeast Asia." *Far Eastern Quarterly* 2 (1942): 15–30.

Hendrichke, Barbara. "Early Daoist Movements." In DH, 34–64.

Hérail, Francine, trans. *Notes journalières de Fujiwara no Michinaga, ministre à la cour de Heian (995–1018): Traduction du Midō kanpakuki*. Genève-Paris: Librairie Droz, 1988.

Hereto Nobuo. *Rekishi no naka no kome to niku: shokubutsu to tennō, sabetsu*. Heibonsha, 1993.

Hesselink, Reinier. "The Introduction of the Art of Mounted Archery into Japan." TASJ ser. 4, 6 (1991): 28–47.

Hirohata Sukeo. *Bansei ikkei ōchō shiso: Jimmu tennō no densetsu*. Kazama shobō, 1993.

Hon'iden Kikushi. "Kakumeikan to sai'i shisō: Ritsuryō kokka seiritsuki ni okeru henran no tokushitsu (1) (2)." *Seijikeizai shigaku* 208 (1983): 24–38; 209 (1983): 21–34.

Hosokawa Kazutoshi. "'Seijō' to iu go ni tsuite no ichi kōsatsu." In *Dōkyō to shūkyō bunka*, edited by Azuki Kan'ei, 154–169. Hirakawa shuppan, 1987.

Hsiao, Kung-chuan. *A History of Chinese Political Thought*. Complete in 1 vol. Princeton, N.J.: Princeton University Pres, 1979.

Hudson, Mark. "Ethnicity in East Asian Archaeology: Approaches to the Wa." *Archeology Review from Cambridge* 8, no. 1 (1989): 46–63.

Ikoma Nagayuki. "'Fudoki' ni miru tatarigami shinkō." In KBKK 802: *Kodai ni miru goryō to shinbutsu shūgō* (1998): 33–40.

Inbe Hironari. *Kogoshūi: Gleanings from Ancient Stories*. Translated by Genchi Katō and Hoshino Hikoshiro. London: Curzon Press, 1926.

———. *Kogoshūi*. Gunsho ruijū, 16: 1–13. Keizai zasshisha, 1893.

Inoue, Mitsusada. "The Century of Reform." In CHJ 1:163–220.

Inoue Wataru. *Nihon kodai no tennō to saigi*. Yoshikawa kōbunkan, 1998.

Ishi Ryōsuke. *Nihon sozoku hōshi*. Sōbunsha, 1979.

Ishigami Ei'ichi. "Ritsuryō kokka to tennō." In *Tennō kenryoku no kōzō to tenkai*, edited by Ishigami Ei'ichi et al., 39–65. Kōza zenkindai no tennō, vol. 1. Aoki shobō, 1992.

——— et al., eds. *Tennō kenryoku no kōzō to tenkai*. Kōza zenkindai no tennō, vol. 1. Aoki shobō, 1992.

Itō Kiyoshi. *Chūsei ōken no seiritsu*. Aoki Library Nihon no rekishi. Chūsei: Aoki shoten, 1995.

Itō Yuishin. "Shinsen'en to goryō-e." KBKK 802: *Kodai ni miru goryō to shinbutsu shūgō* (1998): 103–111.

Iwanami shoten Nihonshi jiten. Iwanami shoten, 1999. DVD.

Janousch, Andreas. "The Emperor as Bodhisattva: The Bodhisattva Ordination and Ritual Assemblies of Emperor Wu of the Liang Dynasty." In *State and Court Ritual in China*, edited by Joseph McDermott, 112–149. Cambridge: Cambridge University Press, 1999.

Jinno Kiyokazu. *Ritsuryō kokka to senmin*. Yoshikawa kōbunkan, 1986.

———. "Tenmu jūnen-ki no tenka daikaijo to haraetsumono yatsuko ni tsuite." *Rekishi hyōron* 366 (1980): 53–62.

Johnson, Wallace, trans. *The T'ang Code*. 2 vols. Princeton, N.J.: Princeton University Press, 1979.

Jung, Jaeseo. "Daoism in Korea." In DH, 792–820.

———. "Kankoku dōkyō no kigen." In *Ajia shochiiki to dōkyō*, edited by Yuki Noboru, Nozaki Mitsuhiko, and Masuo Shin'ichirō, 206–222. Kōza dōkyō, vol. 6. Yuzankyaku, 2001.

Kaifūsō, Bunka shūreishū, Honchō monzui. NKBT 69.

Kakubayashi, Fumio. "Reconstruction of the History of Fourth Century Japan." *Journal of Oriental Studies* (University of Hong Kong), 221 (1983): 1–18.

Kalinowski, Marc. *Cosmologie et divination dans la Chine ancienne: Le compendium des cinq agents* (Wuxing dayi, VIe siècle). Paris: École française d'Extrême-Orient, 1991.

Kamikawa Michio. "Chūsei no sokui girei to bukkyō." In *Tennō daigawari gishiki no rekishiteki tenkai: Sokuigi to daijōsai*, edited by Iwai Tadakuma and Okada Seishi, 105–141. Kashiwa shobō, 1989.

———. "L'ondoiement d'intronisation' impériale au moyen âge: réalités et questionnements." In LL, 179–181.

Kan'yaku chūshaku Shoku Nihongi. Annotated by Hayashi Rokurō. 7 vols. Koten bunkō. Gendai shichosha, 1985.

Kanō Hisashi. *Nihon kodai no kokka to tojō*. Tokyo Daigaku Shuppankai, 1990.

Kasahara Hidehiko. "Kōi keichō to kanryōsei: Fujiwara Fuhito." In *Taika no kaishin to Jinshin no ran: Kodai tennōsei no seiritsu*, edited by Hirano Kunio, 217–237. Shiwa Nihon kodai, vol. 6. Sakuhinsha, 2003.

Katsuura Noriko. "Kōken/Shōtoku tennō to Bukkyō." KBKK 69, no. 6 (2004): 98–104.

———. *Nihon kodai no sōni to shakai*. Yoshikawa kōbunkan, 2000.

Kawamura Kunimitsu. "Miwa no kami to saishi no denshō." In *Yamato ōken no seiritsu: Miwasan o meguru kodai Nihon*, 122–152. Tenri daigaku no kodaishi kyōshitsu. Gakuseisha, 1992.

Kawasaki Tsuneyuki. *Kiki manyō no sekai*. Tokyo daigaku shuppankai, 1982.

Kidder, Edward. "The Newly Discovered Takamatsuzuka Tomb." MN 27 (1972): 245–251.

Kiley, Cornelius. "A Note on the Surnames of Immigrant Officials in Japan." *Harvard Journal of Asiatic Studies* 29 (1969): 177–189.

———. "Provincial Administration and Land Tenure in Early Heian." In CHJ 2:236–340.

———. "State and Dynasty in Archaic Yamato." JAS 33 (1973): 25–47.

Kimoto Yoshinobu. *Nara-chō seiji to kōi keishō*. Takashina shoten, 1995.

Kleeman, Terry. "Ethnic Identity and Daoist Identity in Traditional China." In

Daoist Identity: History, Lineage and Ritual, edited by Livia Kohn and Harold Roth, 23–38. Honolulu: University of Hawai'i Press, 2002.

Kluge, Inge-Lore. *Miyoshi Kiyoyuki: sein Leben und seine Zeit.* Deutsche Akademie der Wissenschaften zu Berlin Institut für Orientforschung. Berlin: Academie-Verlag, 1958.

Kodai seiji shakai shisō. NST 8.

Kohn, Livia, ed. *Daoism Handbook.* Leiden: Brill, 2000.

———. "Taoism in Japan: Positions and Evaluations." CdEA 8 (1995): 389–412.

———, and Russell Kirkland. "Daoism in the Tang (618–907)." In DH, 339–383.

Kojiki. Edited by Nishimiya Kazutami. Shincho Nihon koten shūsei. Shincho-sha, 1979.

———. Edited by Yamaguchi Yoshinoru and Kōnoshi Takamitsu. Shinsen Nihon koten bungaku zenshū, vol. 1. Shogakkan, 1997.

———. Translated by Donald Philippi. See Philippi.

———. NST 1. Iwanami shoten, 1982.

Kondō Nobuyoshi. "'Manyōshū' to goryō." In KBKK 802: *Kodai ni miru goryō to shinbutsu shūgō* (1998): 41–47.

Kōnin shiki. In *Nihon shoki shiki,* Part 1. KST 8.

Kōnoshi, Takamitsu. "Constructing Imperial Mythology: *Kojiki* and *Nihon shoki.*" In *Inventing the Classics: Modernity, National Identity, and Japanese Literature,* edited by Haruo Shirane and Tomi Suzuki, 51–67. Stanford, Calif.: Stanford University Press, 2000.

———. *Kakinomototo Hitomaro kenkyū: kodai waka bungaku no seiritsu.* Hanawa shobō, 1992.

———. "Kodai shinwa no porifonii." *Gendai shisō: Tokushū: Datsushinwa suru Kojiki,* no. 4 (1994): 46–57.

———. *Kojiki no sekaikan.* Yoshikawa kōbunkan, 1986.

———. *"Nihon" to wa nanika: Kokugō no imi to rekishi.* Kodansha gendai shincho, 2005.

———, and Mizubayashi Takeshi. "Tairon: Kojiki no honshitsu o dō toraeru ka." In *Kojiki no genzai,* edited by Kōnoshi Takamitsu, 101–151. Kasama shoin, 1999.

Kouchi Shōsuke. *Kodai seijishi ni okeru tennōsei no ronri.* Yoshikawa kōbunkan, 1986.

———. "Ōi keishōhō shikiron." In *Nihon kodaishi ronkō,* edited by Saeki Ari-kiyo, 63–90. Yoshikawa kōbunkan, 1980.

Kujihongi. KST 7.

Kumagai Kimio. *Ōkimi kara tennō e.* Nihon no rekishi, vol. 3. Kodansha, 2001.

Kuramoto Kazuhiro. "'Jinshin-nen kōshin' tachi no sono ato." HAKB 118 (2004): 11–19.

Kuroda, Toshio. "Shinto in the History of Japanese Religion." JJS 7, no. 1 (1981): 1–21.

———. "The World of Spirit Pacification: Issues of State and Religion." JJRS 23, no. 3–4 (1996): 231–251.

Kyoto bunka hakubutsukan. *Abe no Seimei to onmyōdō ten.* Osaka: Yomiuri shinbun, 2003.

Kyōkai. *Miraculous Stories from the Japanese Buddhist Tradition: The* Nihon ryōiki *of the Monk Kyōkai.* Translated by Kyoko Motomochi Nakamura. Cambridge: Harvard University Press, 1973.

Lamotte, Étienne. *Le traité de la Grande Vertu de Sagesse de Nāgārjuna (Mahāprajñāpāramitāśāstra),* vol. 1. Louvain-la-neuve: Institut orientaliste, 1981.

Larre, Claude; Isabelle Robinet; and Elisabeth Rochat de la Vallée, trans. *Les grands traités du Huainanzi.* Paris: Les Éditions du Cerf, 1993.

Le Blanc, Charles. *Huai-nan Tzu: Philosophical Synthesis in Early Han Thought — The Idea of Resonance. With a Translation and Analysis of Chapter Six.* Hong Kong: Hong Kong University Press, 1985.

Lee, Ki-baik. *A New History of Korea.* Translated by Edward Wagner. Seoul: Ilchokak Publishers, 1984.

Lee, Sungsi. "Koguryŏ no taiwa gaikō: sono gaikōsenro to higashi ajia jōsei — Koguryŏ's Foreign Policy toward the Wa: Their Diplomatic Strategy and the Situation in East Asia." In *A Conference on Ancient Korean History: Koguryŏ and Its Neighbors; International Relations in Early Northeast Asia,* 29 pp., discontinuous pagination. UCLA Center for Korean Studies, February 24, 2007.

Legge, James, trans. *The Ch'un Ts'ew with the Tso Chuen.* Vol. 5 of *The Chinese Classics.* Oxford: Clarendon Press, 1895.

———. *The Shoo King, or, The Book of Historical Documents.* 2nd ed., rev. Vol. 3 of *The Chinese Classics.* Oxford: Clarendon Press, 1939.

Lewin, Bruno. *Aya und Hata: Bevölkerungsgruppen Altjapans koninentaler Herkunft.* Wiesbaden: Otto Harrassowitz, 1962.

———, trans. *Die Regierungsannalen des Kammu-tennō: Shoku-Nihongi 36–40 und Nihon-kōki 1–13.* Vol. 1 of *Rikkokushi, Die amtlichen Reichsannalen Japans: Die Regierungsannalen des Kammu-tennō,* edited by Horst Hammitzsch. Tokyo: Deutsche Gesellschaft für Natur- und Völkerkunde Ostasiens, 1962.

Ling, Li. "An Archeological Study of Taiyi (Grand One) Worship." *Early Medieval China* 2 (1995–1996): 1–39.

Little, Stephen, with Shawn Eichman, eds. *Taoism and the Arts of China.* Chicago: Art Institute of Chicago, 2000.

Loewe, Michael. *Chinese Ideas of Life and Death: Faith, Myth, and Reason in the Han Period (202 BC–AD 220).* London: George Allen and Unwin, 1982.

———. *Divination, Mythology and Monarchy in Han China.* Cambridge: Cambridge University Press, 1994.

———. *Ways to Paradise: The Chinese Quest for Immortality.* London: George Allen and Unwin, 1979.

———, and Edward Shaughnessy, eds. *CHC 1: The Cambridge History of Ancient China.* Cambridge: Cambridge University Press, 1999.

Macé, François. "Notes et commentaires sur les *Hayato.*" *Éloge des sources: Re-*

flets du Japon ancien et moderne, edited by Joseph Kyburz, François Macé, and Charlotte von Verschuer, 43–73. Arles: Éditions Philippe Picquier, 2004.

Mair, Victor. "The *Zhuangzi* and Its Impact." In DH, 30–52.

Major, John S. *Heaven and Earth in Early Han Thought: Chapters Three, Four, and Five of the* Huainanzi. Albany: State University of New York Press, 1993.

Malek, Roman. *Das* Chai-chieh lu: *Materialen zur Liturgie im Taoismus.* Würzburger Sino-Japonica. Frankfurt am Main: Verlag Peter Lang, 1985.

Maruyama Yumiko. "Sai'in niiname-sai to shosha ainamesai: Ritsuryō ainamesai no kōzō to tenkai." *Aichi kenritsu daigaku bungakubu ronshū* 1999:71–94.

Maruyama, Masao. "The Structure of *Matsurigoto*: The *basso ostinato* of Japanese Political Life." In *Themes and Theories in Modern Japanese History: Essays in Memory of Richard Storry*, edited by Sue Henny and Jean-Pierre Lehman, 27–43. London: Athlone Press, 1988.

Maspero, Henri. "Le Ming-t'ang et la crise religieuse chinoise avant les Han." *Mélanges chinois et bouddhiques* 9 (1951): 1–71.

————. "Le mot *ming*." *Journal Asiatique* 223 (1933): 249–296.

Masuo, Shin'ichirō. "Daoism in Japan." In DH, 821–842.

————. *Manyō kajin to chūgoku shisō*. Yoshikawa kōbunkan, 1997.

————. "Nihon kodai no dōkyō juyō to gigi kyōten." In *Dōkyō to rekishi to bunka*, edited by Yamada Toshiaki and Tanaka Fumio, 297–320. Yūzankyaku, 1998.

————. "Nihon kodai no shūkyō bunka to dōkyō." In *Ajia shochiiki to dōkyō*, edited by Yuki Noboru, Nozaki Mitsuhiko, and Masuo Shin'ichirō, 256–284. Kōza dōkyō, vol. 6. Yūzankyaku, 2001.

Mather, Richard. "The Bonze's Begging Bowl: Eating Practices in Buddhist Monasteries of Medieval India and China." *Journal of the American Oriental Society* 101, no. 4 (1981): 417–424.

————. "K'ou Ch'ien-chih and the Taoist Theocracy at the Northern Wei Court, 425–451." In *Facets of Taoism: Essays in Chinese Culture*, edited by Holmes Welch and Anna Seidel, 103–122. New Haven, Conn.: Yale University Press, 1979.

Matsumae, Takeshi. "Early Kami worship." In CHJ 1:317–358.

————. "The Heavenly Rock-Grotto Myth and the Chinkon Ceremony." *Asian Folklore Studies* 39, no. 2 (1980): 9–22.

————. *Matsumae Takeshi chosakushū*. 13 vols. Ōfū, 1997–1998.

Matsumoto Takuya. "Ritsuryō kokka ni okeru sai-i shisō: sono seiji hihan no yōso no bunseki." In *Kodai ōken to saigi*, edited by Mayuzumi Hiromichi, 145–164. Yoshikawa kōbunkan, 1990.

Mauclaire, Simone. "La construction du rôle du père à l'apogée de l'aristocratie de la cour de Heian (Xe–XIe siècle)." *L'Homme* 140 (1996): 25–61.

————. "Histoire et événement rituel: le cas du Ten-no-kami-matsuri à Makiyama-gō, Tosa, Japon." *Journal Asiatique* 290, no. 1 (2002): 53–99.

————. "Que transmettre par l'adoption? La construction du rapport parent / enfant dans le Japon ancien." In *Adoption et fosterage*, edited by Mireille Corbier, 157–181. Paris: De Brocard, 1999.

Mayuzumi Hiromichi. *Kodai ōken to saigi.* Yoshikawa kōbunkan, 1990.

———. *Ritsuryō kokka seiritsu-shi no kenkyū.* Yoshikawa kōbunkan, 1982.

McCullough, William. "The Capital and Its Society." In CHJ 2:97–182.

———. "The Heian Court." In CHJ 2:20–96.

McMullin, Neil. "On Placating the Gods and Pacifying the Populace: The Case of the Gion 'Goryō' Cult." *History of Religions* 27 (1988): 270–293.

Mitsuhashi Takeshi. "*Engishiki* kegare kitei to kegare ishiki." *Engishiki kenkyū* 2 (1989): 40–75.

———. "Ōharae kenkyū josetsu: Yōrō no 'Shingiryō' o tsūro to shite." In *Shinto-shi ronsō: Takigawa Seijirō sensei beiju kinen ronbun-shū,* 289–323. Kokusho kankōkai, 1984.

Miyake Hitoshi. *En no Gyōja to shugendō no rekishi.* Rekishi bunka no raiburari. Yoshikawa kōbunkan, 2000.

Miyoshi Kiyoyuki. *Iken jūnikajō.* In *Gunsho ruijū,* 27:117–130. Gunsho ruijū kanseikai, 1931.

Mizubayashi Takeshi. "Heijō-gū dokukai: zenki Heijō-gū chūku, tōku nigenteki chitsujo no imi." In *Nihon kodai ōken no seiritsu,* edited by Hirose Kazuo and Kojita Yasunao, 105–188. Aoki shoten, 2002.

———. "Heijō-gū-*Kojiki* shinwa sekai no keisei." In *Kodai ōken no kūkan shihai,* edited by Hirose Kazuo and Kojita Yasunao, 119–194. Aoki shoten, 2003.

———. *Kiki shinwa to ōken no matsuri.* Iwanami shoten, [1991] 2001.

———. "Ritsuryō tennōsei no kōtō ishiki to shinwa: seitō (*Kojiki*) to itan (*Nihon shoki*) (1) (2)." *Shisō* 966 (2004): 142–160; 967 (2004): 93–112.

———. "Ritsuryō tennōsei no shinwateki kosumoroji: shoki senmyō oyobi *Kojiki* no tennōzō." In *Ōken no kosumoroji,* edited by Mizubayashi Takeshi et al., 17–47. Hikaku rekishigaku taikei, vol. 1. Kōbundō, 1998.

Moerman, Max. *Localizing Paradise: Kumano Pilgrimage and the Religious Landscape of Premodern Japan.* Harvard East Asia Monographs. Cambridge: Harvard University Press, 2005.

Mori Kōichi and Kadowaki Teiji. *Jinshin no ran: Ōama no ōji kara Tenmu tennō e.* Taikōsha, 1996.

Morohashi Tetsuji. *Dai kanwa jiten.* 13 vols. Tashūkan, 1955–1960.

Muchimaro-den. In *Kodai seiji shakai shisō.* NST 8:25–38.

Murayama Shūichi. "Goryō shinkō to wa." In KBKK 802: *Kodai ni miru goryō to shinbutsu shūgō* (1998): 10–16.

———. "Kodai Nihon no Onmyōdō." In OMS 1:17–31.

———, ed. *Nihon onmyōdō-shi sōsetsu.* Hanawa shobō, 1981.

Nakagawa, Masako. "The *Shan-hai ching* and *Wo*: A Japanese Connection." *Sino-Japanese Studies* 15 (2003): 45–55.

Nakai Shinkō. "Goryō-e to matsuri: reikon e no shinkō to matsuri no hajimari." In *Chingo kokka to jujutsu,* edited by Uehara Shōichi et al., 158–175. Zusetsu Nihon bukkyō no sekai, vol. 2. Shūeisha, 1989.

Nakamura Ikuo. "'Osukuni' no shisō: tennō no saishi to 'kōmin' (ōmitakara) tōgō." In *Ōken to jingi,* edited by Imatani Akira, 315–337. Shibunkyaku, 2002.

Nakamura, Kyoko Motomochi, trans. *Miraculous Stories from the Japanese Buddhist Tradition: The* Nihon ryōiki *of the Monk Kyōkai.* Cambridge: Harvard University Press, 1973.

Nakamura Shohachi. *Gogyō taigi.* Chūgoku koten shinsho. Meitoku Shuppan-sha, 1973.

Naoki, Kōjirō. "The Nara State." In CHJ 1: 221–267.

———, and Kuroiwa Jūgo. "Tenmu-Jitō-chō no jidai: Tenmu tennō no kōshitachi o chūshin ni." HAKB 40 (1984): 2–26.

Nara bunkazai kenkyūjo. *Kitora kofun hekiga.* Kyoto: Kansai prosesu, 2002.

Nara bunkazai kenkyūjo sōritsu gojū shūnen kinen. *Asuka, Fujiwara-kyō ten.* Asahi shinbunsha, 2002.

Nara kokuritsu hakubutsukan. *Dai gojikkai Shōsōin ten.* 1998.

Naumann, Nelly. *Die Einheimlische Religion Japans.* 2 vols. Leiden: Brill, 1988, 1994.

———. "Einige Bemerkungen zum sogenannten Ur-Shintō." *Nachrichten der Gesellschaft für Natur- und Völkerkunde Ostasiens* (Hamburg) 107–108 (1970): 5–13.

———. "The State Cult of Nara and Early Heian Periods." In *Shinto in History: Ways of the Kami,* edited by John Breen and Mark Teeuwen, 47–67. Richmond, Surrey: Curzon Press, 2000.

———. "Taoist Thought, Political Speculation, and the Three Creational Deities of the *Kojiki*." *Nachrichten der Gesellschaft für Natur- und Vökerkunde Ostasiens* 157–158 (1995): 165–174.

———. "Der Tiger in chinesischen Märchen, Sagen und frühen religiösen Vorstellungen." *Fabula* 38, no. 1–2 (1997): 112–121.

Nihon kiryaku. KST 10.

Nihon kōki. Edited by Kuroita Nobuo and Morita Tei. Shūeisha, 2003.

Nihon shoki. 2 vols. NKBT, 67, 68.

Nishimiya Hideki. *Ritsuryō kokka to jingi saishi seido no kenkyū.* Hanawa shobō, 2004.

Nishimura, Key. "The Prince and the Pauper: The Dynamics of a Shōtoku Legend." MN 40 (1985): 299–310.

Niunoya Tetsuichi. *Kebiishi: chūsei no kegare to kenryoku.* Heibonsha, 1986.

Noda Kōsaburō. "Onmyōdō no seiritsu." In OMS, 61–82.

Nylan, Michael. "Afterword: The Legacies of the Chengdu Plain." In *Ancient Sichuan: Treasures from a Lost Civilization,* edited by Robert Bragley, 309–325. Seattle, Wash.: Seattle Art Museum; Princeton, N.J.: Princeton University Press, 2001.

———. *The Canon of Supreme Mystery by Yang Hsiung.* Albany: State University of New York Press, 1993.

Ōi Takeshi. "Les nom d'ères (*nengō*): Indices d'autonomie et de dépendance." In *Identités, marges, médiations: Regards croisés sur la société japonaise,* edited by Jean-Pierre Berthon, Anne Bouchy, and Pierre F. Souyri, 39–50. Paris: École française d'Extrême-Orient, 2001.

Okada Seishi. "Ōkimi jūnin gishiki no genkei to sono tenkai." In *Tennō daigawari gishiki no rekishiteki tenkai: sokuigi to daijōsai*, edited by Iwai Tadakuma and Okada Seishi, 7–50. Kashiwa Shobo, 1989.

Okada Shigekiyo. *Kodai no imi: Nihonjin no kisō shinkō*. Kokusho kankōkai, 1982.

Ooms, Herman. *Tokugawa Ideology: Early Constructs, 1570–1680*. Princeton, N.J.: Princeton University Press, 1985.

———. *Tokugawa Village Practice: Class, Status, Power, Law*. Berkeley: University of California Press, 1996.

Orzech, Charles D. "A Buddhist Image of (Im)Perfect Rule in Fifth-century China." CdEA 8 (1995): 139–153.

Ōta Akira. *Seishi kakei daijiten*. Kadokawa shoten, 1963.

Ōtsu Tōru. *Kodai no tennōsei*. Iwanami shoten, 1999.

———. *Ritsuryō kokka shihai kōzō no kenkyū*. Iwanami shoten, 1993.

Ōtsuka Yasujirō. "Sadaijin Mononobe Maro to Jinshin no ran." HAKB 41 (1984): 57–65.

Ōwa Iwao. "Himiko no kidō to shinsen shisō." HAKB 116 (2003): 84–108.

———. *Tenmu tennō ron*. 2 vols. Daiwa shobō, 1987.

Ozawa Tsuyoshi. *Nihon kodai kyūto kōzō no kenkyū*. Aoki shoten, 2003.

Palmer, Edwina. "Land of the Rising Sun. The Predominant East-West Axis among the Early Japanese." MN 46 (1991): 69–90.

Pearce, Scott. "Form and Matter: Archaizing Reform in Sixth-Century China." In *Culture and Power in the Reconstruction of the Chinese Realm, 200–600*, edited by Scott Pearce, Audrey Spiro, and Patricia Ebrey, 149–180. Cambridge: Harvard University Asia Center; Harvard University Press, 2001.

Penny, Benjamin. "Immortality and Transcendence." In DH, 109–133.

Philippi, Donald, trans. *Kojiki*. Princeton, N.J.: Princeton University Press, 1969.

———, trans. *Norito: A Translation of the Ancient Japanese Rituals*. Princeton, N.J.: Princeton University Press, 1990.

Piggott, Joan. "Chieftain Pairs and Co-rulers: Female Sovereignty in Early Japan." In *Women and Class in Japanese History*, edited by Hitomi Tonomura et. al., 17–52. Ann Arbor: Center for Japanese Studies, University of Michigan, 1999.

———. *The Emergence of Japanese Kingship*. Stanford, Calif.: Stanford University Press, 1997.

———. "The Last Classical Female Sovereign: Kōken-Shōtoku Tennō." In *Women and Confucian Cultures in Premodern China, Korea, and Japan*, edited by Dorothy Ko et al., chap. 2. Berkeley: University of California Press, 2003.

Portal, Jane. *Korea: Art and Archaeology*. London: British Museum, 2000.

Pouillon, Jean. *Le cru et le su*. Paris: Éditions du Seuil, 1993.

Pradel, Chari. "The Tenjukoku Shūchō Mandara: Reconstruction of the Iconography and Ritual Context." In *Images in Asian Religions: Texts and Contexts*, edited by Phyllis Granoff and Koichi Shinohara, 257–289. Asian Religions and Society series. Vancouver: University of British Columbia Press, 2004.

Pregadio, Fabrizio. "Elixirs and Alchemy." In DH, 165–195.

Puett, Michael. *To Become a God: Cosmology, Sacrifice, and Self-divinization in Early China*. Cambridge: Harvard University Press, 2002.

Rekishigaku jiten. 13 vols. Kōbundō, 1994–2006.

Rikkokushi. http://kodaishi-db.hp.infoseek.co.jp.

Ritsuryō. NST 3.

Robinet, Isabelle. "Shangqing — Highest Clarity." In DH, 196–224.

———. *Taoism: Growth of a Religion*. Stanford, Calif.: Stanford University Press, 1997.

Roger, Alain. *Mythe et souveraineté au Japon*. Paris: Presses Universitaires de France, 1997.

Ruijū kokushi. 2 vols. KST 5, 6.

Ruijū sandaikyaku. KST 25.

Ryō no gige. KST 22.

Ryō no shūge. 2 vols. KST 23, 24.

Saeki Arikiyo. *Nihon kodai no seiji to shakai*. Yoshikawa kōbunkan, 1970.

———. *Nihon kodaishi ronkō*. Yoshikawa kōbunkan, 1980.

———. *Shinsen shōjiroku no kenkyū*. Honbun-hen. Yoshikawa kōbunkan, 1962.

Saigō Nobutsuna. *Jinshinki o yomu: rekishi to bunka to gengo*. Heibonsha sensho. Heibonsha, 1993.

Saigū rekishi hakubutsukan, ed. *Saigū ato hakkutsu shiryōsen*. Mie-ken Taki-gun Meiwa-chō: Saigū rekishi hakubutsukan, 1989.

Sakade, Yoshinobu. "Divination as Daoist Practice." In DH, 541–566.

Sakaehara Towao. "Heijō-kyō jūmin no seikatsu-shi." In Nihon kodai. Vol. 9: *Tojō no seitai*, edited by Kishi Toshio, 187–266. Chūōkōronsha, 1987.

Sakamoto, Tarō. *The Six National Histories of Japan*. Translated by John Brownlee. Vancouver: University of British Columbia Press; Tokyo: University of Tokyo Press, 1991.

Sakaue Yasutoshi. *Ritsuryō kokka no tenkan to "Nihon."* Nihon no rekishi, vol. 5. Kodansha, 2001.

Sandai jitsuroku. Rikkokushi, vol. 9. Asahi shinbun, 1940.

Sansom, G. B. "The Imperial Edicts in the Shoku-Nihongi (700–790 A.D.)." TASJ, ser. 2, 1 (1923, 1924): 1–39.

Sasada Yū. "Kenkyū nōto: Ritsuryōsei saishi no keisei katei: Tenmu-chō no igi no saikentō." *Shigaku zasshi* 111, no. 12 (2002): 37–62.

———. "Ritsuryō kokka no chihō saishi kōzō." *Nihonshi kenkyū* 516 (2005): 1–26.

Schafer, Edward. *Pacing the Void: T'ang Approaches to the Stars*. Berkeley: University of California Press, 1977.

Scheid, Bernard. *Der Eine und Einzige Weg der Götter: Yoshida Kanetomo und die Erfindung des Shinto*. Wien: Verlag der Österreichischen Akademie der Wissenschaften, 2001.

Schipper, Kristofer. "Purity and Strangers: Shifting Boundaries in Medieval Taoism." *T'oung Pao* 80 (1994): 61–80.

———. "Taoism: The Story of the Way." In *Taoism and the Arts of China*, edited by Stephen Little, with Shawn Eichman, 33–56. Berkeley: University of California Press; Art Institute of Chicago, 2000.

———, and Wang Hsiu-huei. "Progressive and Regressive Time Cycles in Taoist

Ritual." In *Time, Science, and Society in China and the West*, edited by J. T. Frazer et al., 185–205. The Study of Time 5. Amherst: University of Massachusetts Press, 1986.

Schlegel, Gustave. *Uranographie chinoise*. Leiden: Brill, 1875.

Seidel, Anna. "Chronicle of Taoist Studies in the West, 1950–1990." CdEA 5 (1989–1990): 223–348.

———. "The Image of the Perfect Ruler in Early Taoist Messianism: Lao-tzu and Li Hung." *History of Religions* 9 (1970): 216–247.

———. "Imperial Treasures and Taoist Sacraments: Taoist Roots in the Apocrypha." In *Tantric and Taoist Studies*, vol. 2, edited by Michel Strickmann, 291–371. Mélanges chinois et bouddhiques. Bruxelles: Institut Belge des Hautes Études Chinoises, 1983.

———. "Das neue Testament des Tao: Lao tzu und die Entstehung des taoistischen Religion am Ende des Han-Zeit." *Saeculum* 29, no. 2 (1978): 147–172.

———. "Post-mortem Immortality: The Taoist Resurrection of the Body." In *Gilgul: Essays in Transformation, Revolution and Permanence in the History of Religions*, edited by S. Shaked et al., 223–237. Leiden: Brill, 1987.

———. "Taoist Messianism." *Numen* 31 (1984): 161–174.

———. "Tokens of Immortality in Han graves." *Numen* 29 (1982): 79–112.

Seki Akira. *Kodai no kikajin*. Yoshikawa kōbunkan, 1996.

Senda Minoru. "Tokoyo to shinsenkyō." HAKB 116 (2003): 40–47.

Shinkawa Tokio. *Dōkyō o meguru kōbō: Nihon no kunnō, dōshi no hō o agamezu*. Taishūkan shoten, 1999.

———. "Nihon kodai ni okeru bukkyō to dōkyō." In *Kodai bunka no tenkai to dōkyō*, edited by Noguchi Tetsuro and Nakamura Shōhachi, 51–83. Senshū dōkyō to Nihon, vol. 2. Yūzankyaku, 2001.

———. *Nihon kodai no girei to hyōgen*. Yoshikawa kōbunkan, 1999.

———. "Rettō Nihon no shakai hensei to tairiku-hantō ajia sekai." In *Ajia chiiki bunkagaku no hatten: 21 seiki CEO puroguramu kenkyū hensei*, edited by Waseda daigaku Ajia chiiki bunka enhanshingu kenkyū senta, 88–124. Ajia chiiki bunkagaku sōsho, vol. 2. Yūzankyaku, 2006.

Shinto jiten. Shukusatsuban. Edited by Kokugakuin daigaku Nihon bunka kenkyūjo. Kōbundō, 1999.

Shiraishi Ta'ichirō. "Kinai ni okeru kofun no shūmatsu." *Kokuritsu rekishi minzoku hakubutsukan kenkyū hōkoku* 1 (1982): 79–120.

Shoku Nihon kōki. In KST 3 (1934).

Shoku Nihongi. 6 vols. SNKBT (1989–2000).

Sima Qian. *Records of the Grand Historian: Han Dynasty*. 2 vols. Translated by Burton Watson. Rev. ed. Hong Kong: Research Centre for Translation, Chinese University of Hong Kong; New York: *Renditions*-Columbia University Press, 1993.

———. *Records of the Grand Historian: Qin Dynasty*. Translated by Burton Watson. Hong Kong: Research Centre for Translation, Chinese University of Hong Kong; New York: *Renditions*-Columbia University Press, 1993.

Smith, Kidder. "Sima Tan and the Invention of Daoism, 'Legalism,' 'et cetera.'" JAS 62 (2003): 129–156.

Snellen, J. B. "*Shoku Nihongi*: Chronicles of Japan." TASJ 11 (1934): 151–239; 14 (1937): 209–278.

Sonoda Kōyū. "Early Buddha Worship." In CHJ 1:359–414.

Soothill, William. *The Hall of Light: A Study of Early Chinese Kingship*. London: Lutterworth Press, 1952.

South, Mary. "Po Chü-i's 'The Observation Tower.'" *Journal of the Oriental Society of Australia* 9, no. 1–2 (1972): 3–13.

Spae, Joseph John. *Itō Jinsai: A Philosopher, Educator and Sinologist of the Tokugawa Period* [1948]. New York: Paragon Book Reprint, 1967.

Steinhardt, Nancy Shatzman. *Chinese Imperial City Planning*. Honolulu: University of Hawai'i Press, 1990.

———. "Taoist Architecture." In *Taoism and the Arts of China*, edited by Stephen Little, with Shawn Eichman, 57–76. Chicago: Art Institute of Chicago, 2000.

Stephenson, Richard. "Chinese and Korean Star Maps and Catalogs." In *History of Cartography*. Vol. 2, Bk. 2: *Cartography in the Traditional East and Southeast Asian Societies*, edited by J. B. Harvey and David Woodward, 511–578. Chicago: University of Chicago Press, 1994.

Strickmann, Michel. *Chinese Magical Medicine*. Stanford, Calif.: Stanford University Press, 2002.

———. "On the Alchemy of T'ao Hung-ching." In *Facets of Taoism: Essays in Chinese Culture*, edited by Holmes Welch and Anna Seidel, 123–192. New Haven, Conn.: Yale University Press, 1979.

Sun, Xiaochun, and Jacob Kistemaker. *The Chinese Sky during the Han: Constellating Stars and Society*. Leiden: Brill, 1997.

Suzuki Yasutami. *Kodai taigai kankeishi no kenkyū*. Yoshikawa kōbunkan, 1985.

Taira Masayuki. "La légitimation de la violence dans le bouddhisme au moyen âge." In LL, 79–104.

Takagi Ichinosuke. *Yoshino no ayu: Kiki Manyō zakkō*. Iwanami shoten, 1941.

Takatori Masao. *Shinto no seiritsu*. Heibonsha, 1979.

Takeda Sachiko. "Kodai tennō no kan to ifuku: chūgoku ifukusei no keiju o megutte." In Tennō to ōken o kangaeru. Vol. 9: *Seikatsu sekai to fōkuroa*, edited by Amino Yoshihiko et al., 75–104. Iwanami shoten, 2003.

Takeda Yukio. *Kōkuri shi to Higashi Ajia: "Kōkaido-ō hi" kenkyū josetsu*. Iwanami shoten, 1989.

Takusu J. "Le voyage de Kanshin en Orient (742–754) par Aomi-no Mabito Genkai (779)." *Bulletin de l'École Française d'Extrême-Orient* 28 (1928): 1–41, 441–472; 29 (1929): 47–62.

Tambiah, Stanley. *The Buddhist Conception of Universal King and Its Manifestations in Southeast Asia*. Kuala Lumpur: University of Malaya, 1987.

Tamaki Taeko. "Jinshin no ran: Ōama kōshi kyohei e no michi." HAKB 118 (2004): 20–30.

Tamura Enchō. "Onmyōryō seiritsu izen." In OMS 1:35–60.

Tanaka Kimio. "Saiō gunkō to hokushin-sai ni tsuite." In *Hoshi no shinkō: Myōken, Kokuzō*, edited by Sano Kenji, 107–120. Tansuisha, Hokushindō, 1994.

Tanaka Takashi. *Shinsen shōjiroku no kenkyū*. Tanaka Takashi chosakushū, vol. 9. Kokusho kankōkai, 1996.

Tanaka, Tan. "The Appearance and Background of the *Lou*: Multi-storied Timberwork Towers in Ancient China." In *East Asian Science: Tradition and Beyond*, edited by Hashimoto Keizō et al., 281–289. Osaka: Kansai University Press, 1995.

Tateno Kazumi. *Kodai toshi Heijō-kyō no sekai*. Yamakawa shuppansha, 2001.

Tatsumi Masayuki. "Hyūga to Hitachi: Taiyō saishisen to Nihon shinwa (2)." HAKB 29 (1980): 104–115.

———. "Yama to kyoseki to taiyō saishi: Taiyō saishisen to Nihon shinwa (1)." HAKB 28 (1980): 57–71.

Teeuwen, Mark. "From *Jindō* to Shinto." JJRS 29, no. 3–4 (2002): 233–263.

———, and Bernhard Scheid. "Tracing Shinto in the History of Kami Worship." JJRS 29, no. 3–4 (2002): 195–207.

Terasaki Yasuhiro. *Nagaya-ō*. Jinbutsu sōsho shinsoban. Yoshikawa kōbunkan, 1999.

Toby, Ronald. "Why leave Nara? Kammu and the Transfer of the Capital." MN 40 (1985): 331–347.

Tokoro Isao. *Nengō no rekishi*. Zōhohan. Yūzankyaku, 1989.

Tokoro Kyōko. "Kami no Mikado no mitsueshiro: Ise Saiō no yakuwari." HAKB 119 (2004): 55–67.

Tokyo Daigaku Shiryōhensanjo. *Dai Nihon komonjo*. 25 vols. Tokyo Teikoku Daigaku: Yoshikawa Hanshichi hatsubai, 1901–1940.

Tsuchiya, Masaaki. "Confession of Sins and Awareness of Self in the *Taiping jing*." In *Daoist Identity: History, Lineage, and Ritual*, edited by Livia Kohn and Harold Roth, 39–75. Honolulu: University of Hawai'i Press, 2002.

Twitchett, Denis, ed. CHC 3: *Sui and T'ang China, 589–906*, part 1.

———. "Hsüan-tsung (Reign 712–756)." In CHC 3, part 1, 333–463.

———. "Kao-tsung (Reign 649–683) and the Empress Wu: The Inheritor and the Usurper." In CHC 3, part 1, 242–289.

Ueda Masa'aki. "Dōkyō no ryūden to *Nihon shoki*." HAKB 116 (2003): 2–16.

———, ed. *Kamigami no saishi to denshō: Matsumae Takeshi kyōju koki kinen ronbunshū*. Dōhōha, 1993.

Umezawa Isezō. *Kiki hihan: Kojiki oyobi Nihon shoki no seiritsu ni kansuru kenkyū*. Sōbunsha, 1962.

Unschuld, Paul. *Medicine in China: A History of Ideas*. Berkeley: University of California Press, 1985.

von Verschuer, Charlotte. "Le Japon, contrée du Penglai? — Note sur le mercure —." CdEA 8 (1995): 439–452.

———. *Les relations officielles du Japon avec la Chine aux VIIIe et IXe siècles*. Genève: Librairie Droz, 1985.

———. *Le riz dans la culture de Heian, mythe et réalité.* Collège de France, Institut des Hautes Études Japonaises. Paris: De Boccard, 2003.

Wada Atsumu. *"Kusakari to Honzōshūchū: Nihon kodai no minkan dōkyō no jissai."* In *Senshū dōkyō to Nihon 2: Kodai bunka no tenkai to dōkyō,* 3–50. Yūzankyaku, 1998.

———. "Nanzan no kyūtōryū." In *Nagayaō-ke, nijō dairo mokkan o yomu,* 303–319. Nara kokuritsu bunkazai kenkyūjo gakuhō, 61: Kenkyū ronshū XII, 2001.

———. *Nihon kodai no girei to saishi, shinkō.* 3 vols. Hanawa shobō, 1995.

———. "Shinpinron: Arasou ō, tōji suru ō." In *Tōji to kenryoku.* Iwanami shoten kōza Tennō to ōken o kangaeru, 2:61–82. Iwanami shoten, 2002.

Wang, Aihe. *Cosmology and Political Culture in Early China.* Cambridge: Cambridge University Press, 2000.

Wang, Zhenping. *Ambassadors from the Islands of Immortals: China-Japan Relations in the Han-Tang Period.* Honolulu: University of Hawai'i Press, 2005.

———. "Chinese Titles as a Means of Diplomatic Communication between China and Japan during the Han-Tang Period." *Studies in Chinese History* 1 (1991): 7–34.

———. "Manuscript Copies of Chinese Books in Ancient Japan." *Gest Library Journal* 4, no. 2 (1991): 35–67.

———. "Speaking with a Forked Tongue: Diplomatic Correspondence between China and Japan, 238–608 A.D." *Journal of the American Oriental Society* 114 (1994): 23–32.

Ware, James, trans. *Alchemy, Medicine, Religion in the China of A.D. 320: The Nei P'ien of Ko Hung (Pao-pu tzu).* Cambridge: M.I.T. Press, 1966.

Watanabe Akihiro. *Heijō-kyō to mokkan no seiki.* Nihon no rekishi, vol. 4. Kodansha, 2001.

Watanabe Hiroshi. *Higashi Ajia no ōken to shisō.* Tokyo Daigaku shuppankai, 1997.

Watanabe Katsuyoshi. *Chinkon-sai no kenkyū.* Meicho shuppan, 1994.

Weber, Max. *Economy and Society.* 2 vols. Edited by Guenther Roth and Claus Wittich. Berkeley: University of California Press, 1978.

Wechsler, Howard. "The Founding of the T'ang dynasty: Kao-tsu (Reign 618–626)." In CHC 3, part 1, 150–187.

———. "T'ai-tsung (Reign 626–649) the Consolidator." In CHC 3, part 1, 188–241.

Wheatley, Paul. *The Pivot of the Four Quarters: A Preliminary Enquiry into the Origins and Character of the Ancient Chinese City.* Chicago: Aldine, 1971.

Wilhelm, Hellmut. *Change: Eight Lectures on the I Ching.* Translated from the German by Cary F. Baynes. New York: Harper and Row, 1960.

Wilhelm, Richard, trans. *Frühling und Herbst des Lü Bu We.* Jena: Eugen Diederichs, 1928.

———, and Carey Baynes. *The I Ching or Book of Changes.* Bollingen Series 19. Princeton, N.J.: Princeton University Press, 1950.

Williams, Yoko. *Tsumi — Offence and Retribution in Early Japan*. London: Routledge Curzon, 2003.

Wright, Arthur. "The Formation of Sui Ideology, 581–604." In *Chinese Thought and Institutions*, edited by John Fairbank, 71–104. Phoenix Books. Chicago: University of Chicago Press, 1957.

———. "The Sui Dynasty (581–617)." In CHC 3, part 1, 48–149.

Xiong Lihui. *Xin yi Huainan zi*. Taipei: San shu ju, 1997.

Xiong, Victor Cunrui. *Sui-Tang Chang'an: A Study in the Urban History of Medieval China*. Ann Arbor: Center for Chinese Studies, University of Michigan, 2000.

Yamada Toshiaki. "The Lingbao School." DH 225–255.

Yamada Yasuhiko. *Kodai no hōi shinkō to chiiki keikaku*. Kokon shoin, 1986.

Yamamoto Kōji. *Kegare to ōharae*. Heibonsha, 1992.

Yokota Ken'ichi. *Dōkyō*. Jinbutsu sōsho, vol. 18. Yoshikawa kōbunkan, 1964.

Yoshie, Akiko. "Gender in Early Classical Japan: Marriage, Leadership, and Political Status in Village and Palace." MN 60 (2005): 437–479.

Yoshino Hiroko. *Inyōgogyō shisō kara mita Nihon no matsuri: Ise jingū saishi, daijōsai o chūshin to shite*. Kōbundō, 1978.

———. *Inyōgogyō to Nihon no tennō*. Kyoto: Jinbun shoin, 1998.

———. *Jitō Tennō: Nihon kodai teiō no jujutsu*. Kyoto: Jinbun shoin, 1987.

Yu, David. *History of Chinese Daoism*. Vol. 1. Lanham, Md.: University Press of America, 2000–.

Yü, Ying-Shih. "'Oh Soul, Come Back!' A Study in the Changing Conceptions of the Soul and Afterlife in Pre-Buddhist China." *Harvard Journal of Asiatic Studies* 47, no. 1 (1987): 363–395.

Zachert, Herbert. *Semmyō: Die kaiserlichen Erlasse des Shoku-Nihongi*. Deutsche Akademie der Wissenschaften zu Berlin Institut für Orientforschung, Veröffentlichung nr. 4. Berlin: Akademie Verlag, 1950.

ABOUT THE AUTHOR

Herman Ooms holds degrees from universities in Belgium, Japan, and the United States and is professor of Japanese history at the University of California, Los Angeles. He is the author of *Charismatic Bureaucrat: A Political Biography of Matsudaira Sadanobu (1758–1829)*; *Tokugawa Ideology: Early Constructs (1570–1680)*; and *Tokugawa Village Practice: Class, Status, Power, Law.*

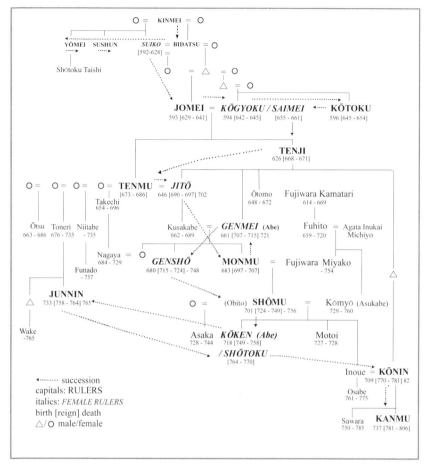

RULER LINEAGES IN THE 7TH AND 8TH CENTURIES.

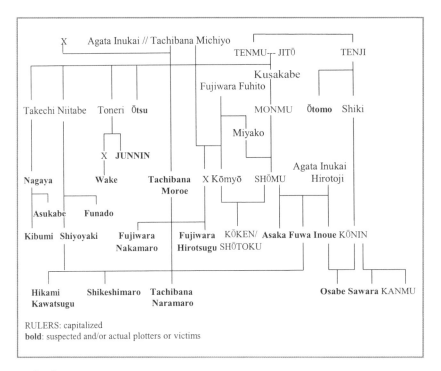

RULERS: capitalized
bold: suspected and/or actual plotters or victims

PLOTS